THE FOUR
CHINESE CLASSICS

OTHER BOOKS BY DAVID HINTON

Writing

FOSSIL SKY

HUNGER MOUNTAIN: A FIELD GUIDE TO MIND AND
LANDSCAPE

Translation

I CHING

THE MOUNTAIN POEMS OF WANG AN-SHIH

CLASSICAL CHINESE POETRY: AN ANTHOLOGY

THE SELECTED POEMS OF WANG WEI

THE MOUNTAIN POEMS OF MENG HAO-JAN

MOUNTAIN HOME: THE WILDERNESS POETRY OF
ANCIENT CHINA

THE MOUNTAIN POEMS OF HSIEH LING-YÜN

TAO TE CHING

THE SELECTED POEMS OF PO CHÜ-I

ANALECTS

MENCIUS

CHUANG TZU: THE INNER CHAPTERS

THE LATE POEMS OF MENG CHIAO

THE SELECTED POEMS OF LI PO

THE SELECTED POEMS OF T'AO CH'IEN

THE SELECTED POEMS OF TU FU

THE FOUR CHINESE CLASSICS

TAO TE CHING

CHUANG TZU

ANALECTS

MENCIUS

TRANSLATED BY
DAVID HINTON

COUNTERPOINT
BERKELEY

Library of Congress Cataloging-in-Publication is available.
ISBN 978-1-61902-834-0

Image of Lao Tzu traveling out of China into the West: Chang Lu (ca. 1490-1563).
Courtesy of the National Palace Museum, Taipei, Taiwan, Republic of China.
Image of Northern Darkness: Chou Ch'en (ca. 1455-after 1536). Courtesy of
The Nelson-Atkins Museum of Art, Kansas City, Missouri. Confucus' Encounter
with the Taoist Hermit Jung Ch'i-ch'i: Anonymous (late 12th c.). Courtesy of
The Museum of Fine Arts, Boston. Auspicious Grain: Anonymous (late 12th c.).
Courtesy of The National Palace Museum, Taipei, Taiwan, Republic of China.
Nine Dragons: Ch'en Jung. Courtesy of The Museum of Fine Arts, Boston. Li-ch'i
Stele at Confucius' Tomb: Anonymous (c. 156 C.E.).

Cover design by Gopa & Ted2, Inc.
Interior design by David Bullen

COUNTERPOINT
2560 Ninth St, Suite 318
Berkeley, CA 94710
www.counterpointpress.com

Printed in the United States of America

10 9 8 7 6 5

CONTENTS

I
TAOIST CLASSICS

Tao Te Ching

Chuang Tzu

II
CONFUCIAN CLASSICS

Analects

Mencius

ILLUSTRATIONS

Cover

Left: Lao Tzu Riding an Ox
Image of Lao Tzu traveling out of China into the West. See *Tao Te Ching*, Introduction, p. 29-30.
Chang Lu (ca. 1490–1563). Courtesy of the National Palace Museum, Taipei, Taiwan, Republic of China

Upper Center: Northern Darkness (detail)
Image of Northern Darkness, from the opening tale in the *Chuang Tzu* about the vast Two-Moon bird who emerges from Northern Darkness. See *Chuang Tzu*: Introduction p. 138 and Chapter 1, sections 1-3, 7-8.
Chou Ch'en (ca. 1455-after 1536). Courtesy of The Nelson-Atkins Museum of Art, Kansas City, Missouri

Lower Center: Confucius' Encounter with the Taoist Hermit Jung Ch'i-ch'i
Jung Ch'i-ch'i was playing a *ch'in* and chanting because, as he explained when Confucius inquired, he was infused with the wonder of existence itself.
Anonymous (late 12th c.). Courtesy of The Museum of Fine Arts, Boston.

Right: Auspicious Grain
Image representing the people's prosperity under a ruler who is fulfilling the Mandate of Heaven. See *Mencius*, Introduction p. 394.
Anonymous (late 12th c.). Courtesy of The National Palace Museum, Taipei, Taiwan, Republic of China.

Tao Te Ching: Nine Dragons (detail)
Image of ancient dragon (on the left) instructing a young dragon (on the right). See *Tao Te Ching*, Introduction p. 15-16.
Ch'en Jung (active first half of the 13th century). Courtesy of The Museum of Fine Arts, Boston.

Chuang Tzu: Northern Darkness (detail)
Image of Northern Darkness, from the opening tale in the *Chuang Tzu* about the vast Two-Moon bird who emerges from Northern Darkness. See *Chuang Tzu*, Introduction p. 138 and Chapter 1, sections 1-3, 7-8.
Chou Ch'en (ca. 1455–after 1536). Courtesy of The Nelson-Atkins Museum of Art, Kansas City, Missouri.

Analects: Li-ch'i Stele at Confucius' Tomb
Celebrated calligraphy from the memorial stone at Confucius' tomb. Anonymous (c. 156 C.E.). Ink Rubbing.

Mencius: Auspicious Grain
Image representing the people's prosperity under a ruler who is fulfilling the Mandate of Heaven. See *Mencius*, Introduction p. 394.
Anonymous (late 12th c.). Courtesy of The National Palace Museum, Taipei, Taiwan, Republic of China.

TAO TE CHING

Lao Tzu

Introduction

In the realm of ancient Chinese myth, earth's generative natural process takes the awesome form of dragon. Both feared and revered as the mysterious force of life itself, dragon animates all things in the unending cycle of life and death and rebirth. As it embodies the process of change itself, dragon appears only to disappear again, and so is in constant transformation. Its scales glisten in the bark of rain-swept pines, and it roams seething waters. It descends into deep pools and lakes in autumn, where it hibernates until spring, when its awakening is the awakening of spring and the return of life to earth. It rises from the depths and ascends into the sky, its voice filling the spring winds that scatter autumn leaves. It takes the shape of storm clouds, its claws becoming lightning, and produces the life-bringing spring rains.

Throughout the millennial turning of this seasonal process, spirituality in ancient China was primarily a matter of dwelling at the deepest levels of our belonging to dragon's realm. And this spiritual ecology traces its source back to the origins of Taoist thought: to the sage antics of Chuang Tzu and beyond, to the dark ambiguities and evocative silences of Lao Tzu's mysterious poetry. Indeed, after his legendary encounter with Lao Tzu, an awestruck Confucius exclaimed: "A dragon mounting wind and cloud to soar through the heavens – such things are beyond me. And today, meeting Lao Tzu, it was like facing a dragon."

The question of the historical Lao Tzu is itself a case study in dragon's protean nature. Centuries before the first scraps of Lao Tzu's legend coalesced, he had already vanished into the scattered fragments that eventually evolved into the little book that now bears his name. In the cultural legend, Lao Tzu was an elder contemporary of Confucius (551–479 B.C.E.). But in spite of his stature as a sage, nothing verifiable is known about him, and even the cultural legend is made up of very few facts: he was born in the state of Ch'u and became a court archivist in the Chou capital; he was consulted by Confucius, who emerged from the meeting awestruck; he left the world, heartsick at the ways of people, and as he was going through a mountain pass to vanish into the far west, the gatekeeper there convinced him to leave behind his five-thousand-word scroll of wisdom.

The actual biography of the *Tao Te Ching*'s author, whose name simply means "Old Master," no doubt looks quite different. He was probably constructed out of fragments gleaned from various old sage-masters active between perhaps the sixth and fourth centuries B.C.E., at the historical beginnings of Chinese philosophy. These early texts were worn away, broken up, scattered, assembled, and reassembled: a geologic process lasting several hundred years that apparently included a number of sage editors who wove this material into the single enduring voice that we find in the *Tao Te Ching*. The result of this rather impersonal process was a remarkably personal presence: if we look past the fragmentary text and oracular tone, we find a voice that is consistent and compassionate, unique and rich with the complexities of personality.

It seems likely that a good deal of the material woven into Lao Tzu's voice actually predates the historical beginnings of Chinese philosophy, deriving from an ancient oral tradition. The sayings themselves may predate Lao Tzu by three centuries, but the origins of this oral tradition must go back to the culture's most primal roots, to a level early enough that a distinctively Chinese culture had yet to emerge, for the philosophy of Tao embodies a cosmology rooted in that most primal and wondrous presence: earth's mysterious generative force. This force must have been truly wondrous to those primal people not only because of the unending miracle of new life seemingly appearing from nothing, but also because that miracle was so vital to their well-being, providing them with food, water, clothing, shelter, and of course, a future in their children.

In the Paleolithic, the human experience of the mystery of this generative force gave rise to such early forms of human art as vulvas etched into stone and female figures emphasizing the sense of fecundity. This art was no doubt associated with the development of humankind's earliest spiritual practices: the various forms of obeisance to a Great Mother who continuously gives birth to all creation, and who, like the natural process which she represents, also takes life and regenerates it in an unending cycle of life, death, and rebirth. These phenomena appear to be ubiquitous among later Paleolithic and early Neolithic cultures, where they are integral to gynocentric and egalitarian social structures.

In the *Tao Te Ching,* this venerable generative force appears most explicitly in Lao Tzu's recurring references to the female principle (see Key Terms: *mu,* etc.), such as: "mother of all beneath heaven," "nurturing mother," "valley spirit," "dark female-enigma." But its dark mystery is everywhere in the *Tao Te Ching,* for it is nothing other than Tao itself, the central concept in Lao Tzu's thought. It is a joy to imagine that the earliest of the sages woven into Lao Tzu, those responsible for the core regions of his thought, were in fact women from the culture's proto-Chinese Paleolithic roots.

The primal generative process revered by those earliest of Chinese sages takes on new dimensions in Lao Tzu's Tao, dimensions that carry it into realms we now speak of as ontology and ecology, cosmology, phenomenology, and social philosophy. *Tao* originally meant "way," as in "pathway" or "roadway," and Lao Tzu recast it as a spiritual Way by using it to describe that inexplicable generative force seen as an ongoing process (hence a "Way"). This Way might be provisionally described as a kind of generative ontological process through which all things arise and pass away, and Lao Tzu's way is to dwell as a part of that natural process. In that dwelling, self is but a fleeting form taken on by earth's process of change. Or more absolutely, it is all and none of earth's fleeting forms simultaneously: that is, it is pure dragon.

The story of this dragon has endured for nearly 2500 years now in the voice of Lao Tzu, and as such it has been the defining spiritual way in China. Once your eyes become adjusted to the strange light in the world of this Old Master's teachings, you learn to see yourself inside Ch'en Jung's grand dragon painting (interior illustration). There, a young dragon just appearing from shadowy mist and cloud is being taught by a sage old dragon – its mane thin and white, its teeth half gone, its body fading back into mist and cloud.

Lao Tzu's thought is driven by a sense of exile that derives from a fundamental rupture between human being and natural process. During the Paleolithic, humans began to be aware of themselves as separate from natural process, and the distance that this separation opened allowed the generative-centered worldview to arise. This intermediary stage, where humans were still rooted in natural process and yet separate enough to produce a rich artistic and spiritual tradition, continued into the agrarian cultures of the early Neolithic. But for a number of reasons the separation eventually became a rupture as Neolithic humans in agrarian villages began "controlling nature" in the form of domesticated plants and animals. This process coincides with a shift from the gynocentric worldview to an androcentric worldview. Although he lacked a precise anthropological understanding of human evolution, Lao Tzu often alludes to this historical process, always with disdain. And indeed, at one point he reduces this monumental transformation to a single poetic image: "When all beneath heaven forgets Way, / war horses are bred among the fertility altars" (46.3-4).

In China, this rupture had become a complete separation by the historical beginnings of Chinese civilization in the Shang Dynasty (1766-1040 B.C.E.), which marked the transition from Neolithic to Bronze Age culture and was already fiercely patriarchal. The Shang was preceded by the Neolithic Hsia Dynasty, about which very little is known. But it appears that in the Paleolithic cultures that preceded the Hsia, another spiritual practice developed alongside the reverent celebration of the Great Mother, another reflection of how deeply humans felt their belonging to earth as a whole: nature deities were worshiped as tribal ancestors. Hence a tribe may have traced its lineage back to an originary "High Ancestor River," for instance. This practice apparently survived through the Hsia into the Shang, where evidence of it appears in oracle-bone inscriptions. These nature deities continued to be worshiped in their own right; but within the ideology of

TAO TE CHING

power, religious life focused on the worship of human ancestors, all male.

By forging this new religious system into a powerful form of theocratic government, the Shang was able to dominate Chinese civilization for no less than seven hundred years. The Shang emperors ruled by virtue of their lineage, which was sanctified by Shang Ti ("Celestial Lord"), a supreme deity who functioned as the source of creation, order, ethics, etc. The Shang house may even have traced its lineage directly back to Shang Ti as its originary ancestor. (*Shang* here represents two entirely different words in Chinese.) In any case, Shang Ti provided the Shang rulers with a transcendental source of legitimacy and power: he protected and advanced their interests, and through their spirit-ancestors, they could decisively influence Shang Ti's shaping of events. All aspects of people's lives were thus controlled by the emperor: weather, harvest, politics, economics, religion, etc. Indeed, people didn't experience themselves as substantially different from spirits, for the human realm was simply an extension of the spirit realm.

This represents a complete reversal from the proto-Chinese worldview: feminine to masculine, nurturing to dominating, body to spirit, earthly to heavenly. The Paleolithic unity of human and natural process has become a complete rupture in this worldview, which is very like that of the Judeo-Christian West in its fundamental outlines: a monotheism in which spiritual connections locate the human in a transcendental spirit realm rather than the tangible earthly realm.

Such was the imperial ideology, convenient to the uses of power because it accorded little ethical value to the masses not of select lineages. (Not surprisingly, the rise of Shang Ti seems to coincide with the rise of the Shang Dynasty, and later myth speaks of him as the creator of Shang civilization.) In the cruelest of ironies, it was overwhelming human suffering that brought the Chinese people back into their earthly lives, beginning the transformation of this spiritualistic culture back to a humanistic one. In the cultural legend, the early Shang rulers were paradigms of nobility and benevolence. But by the end of the Shang, the rulers had become cruel and tyrannical, and as there was no ethical system separate from the religious system, there was nothing to shield the people from their depredations. Meanwhile, a small nation was being pushed to the borders of the Shang realm by western tribes. This state of "semi-barbarian" people, known as the Chou, gradually adopted the cultural traits of the Shang. Eventually, under the leadership of the legendary sage-emperors Wen ("cultured") and Wu ("martial"), the Chou overthrew the tyrannical Shang ruler, thus founding the Chou Dynasty (1040-223), which was welcomed wholeheartedly by the Shang people.

The Chou conquerors were faced with an obvious problem: if the Shang lineage had an absolute claim to rule the world, how could the Chou justify replacing it with their own, and how could they legitimize their rule in the eyes of the Shang people? Their solution was to reinvent Shang Ti in the form of heaven, thus ending the Shang's claim to legitimacy by lineage, and then proclaim that the right to rule depended upon the Mandate of Heaven: once a ruler becomes unworthy, heaven withdraws its mandate and bestows it on another. This was a major event in Chinese philosophy: the first investment of power with an ethical imperative. And happily, the early centuries of the Chou appear to have fulfilled that imperative admirably.

But eventually the Chou foundered, both because of its increasing inhumanity and its lack of the Shang's transcendent source of legitimacy: if the Mandate could be transferred to the Chou, it could obviously be transferred again. The rulers of the empire's component states grew increasingly powerful, claiming more and more sovereignty over their lands, until finally they were virtually independent nations. Eventually these rulers (properly entitled "dukes") even began assuming the title of emperor, thus equating themselves with the Chou emperor, who was by now a mere figurehead. The rulers of these autonomous states could at least claim descent from those who were first given the territories by the early Chou rulers. But this last semblance of legitimacy was also crumbling because power was being usurped by a second tier of local lords whenever they had the strength to take it, and even a third tier of high officials serving in the governments of usurping dukes and lords. This history, beginning with the Chou's overthrow of the Shang, represents a geologic split in China's social structure: political power was breaking free of its family/religious context and becoming a separate entity.

The final result of the Chou's "metaphysical" breakdown was, not surprisingly, all too physical: war. In addition to constant pressure from "barbarians" in the north (the first devastating blow to Chou power was a "barbarian" invasion in 770) and the "semi-barbarian" Ch'u realm that dominated south China, there was relentless fighting between the empire's component states and frequent rebellion within them. This internal situation, devastating to the people, continued to deteriorate after Lao Tzu's time, until it finally gave an entire age its name: the Warring States Period (403-221). Meanwhile, rulers caught up in this ruthless competition began looking for the most able men to help them rule their states, and this precipitated the rise of an independent intellectual class – a monumental event, for this class constituted the first open space in the cultural framework from which the imperial ideology could be challenged. The old spiritualist social order had now collapsed entirely, and these intellectuals began struggling to create a new one. Although this was one of the most virulent and chaotic periods in Chinese history, it was the golden age of Chinese philosophy, for there were a "Hundred Schools of Thought" trying to envision what this new social order should be like. These schools were founded by thinkers who wandered the country with their disciples, teaching and trying to convince the various rulers to put their ideas into practice, for the desperate times had given them an urgent sense of political mission.

Confucius was the first great figure in this independent intellectual class, China's first self-conscious philosopher who can be historically verified in any sense, and Lao Tzu may be spoken of as his elder contemporary in terms of both the cultural legend and the development of early Chinese thought. Lao Tzu's appearance at that crucial moment in Chinese history certainly looks very much like the awakening dragon revitalizing a civilization in which the life-force had dwindled to a mere flicker. Formulated in the ruins of a magisterial monotheism that had dominated China for a millennium, a situation not at all unlike that of the modern West, Lao Tzu's Way initiated the transformation of early China's otherworldly spiritualist culture to an earthly humanist culture founded on a spirituality of our immediate empirical experience: our belonging to the realm of dragon.

Although its inexplicable nature is a central motif in the *Tao Te Ching*, we might approach Lao Tzu's Way by speaking of it at its deep ontological level, where the distinction between Presence (Being) and Absence (Nonbeing) arises. Presence (*yu*) can be understood provisionally in a fairly straightforward way as the empirical world, earth's ten thousand living and nonliving things in constant transformation; and Absence (*wu*) as the generative tissue from which Presence arises. This tissue is the ontological substrate infused mysteriously with a generative energy. Although made of the same stuff as Presence, it is "Absence" because it has no particular form. But because of its generative nature, it shapes itself into the individual forms we know, the ten thousand things, then reshapes itself into other forms in the constant process of change. In fact *wu* might more literally be translated as "without form" and *yu* as "within form."

Within this framework, Way can be understood as the process of Absence continuously generating the realm of Presence. But Lao Tzu's descriptions of Way in its more mysterious aspect as Absence tend to the poetic and paradoxical: he speaks of it as "emptiness," "silence," and "dark-enigma." And here we are quickly cast adrift in the realm of unknowing at the heart of Lao Tzu's thought, for in its essential nature as Absence, where it precedes the differentiation of the ten thousand things, Way also precedes the differentiation of language itself. Indeed, *Tao* doesn't necessarily capture what Lao Tzu is describing at all: he says that he doesn't know its name, that he's only calling it *Tao*.

The ontological structure of Way is replicated in the structure of human consciousness, thoughts arising from the same generative emptiness as the ten thousand things. Hence, Way is utterly inexplicable for it quite literally precedes thought. Lao Tzu says that Presence and Absence give birth to one another: they are one and the same, but once they arise, they differ in name. And there before they arise, where they

TAO TE CHING

remain one and the same tissue, is the Way beyond all differentiation.

It is here in the depths of consciousness that Way can be experienced directly through the practice of meditation. You can watch the process of Way as thought burgeons forth from the emptiness and disappears back into it, or you can simply dwell in that undifferentiated emptiness, that generative realm of Absence. With this meditative dwelling in the emptiness of Absence, you are at the heart of Lao Tzu's spiritual ecology, reinhabiting the primal universe in the most profound way. Here where the distinction between subjectivity and objectivity dissolves, conscious-ness and natural process blend into a single tissue. And no doubt a part of what makes meditation so profound an experience is that it frees us from our most fundamental dislocation, for it has only been in the last few thousand years that human consciousness has experienced itself as separate from natural process. So in returning us to the undifferentiated levels of consciousness and ontology, meditative practice returns us to the ancient undifferentiated levels of human culture.

Taoism was eventually supplemented and intensified by Ch'an (Zen) Buddhism, which is a melding of Taoism and Buddhism. Ch'an became widely influential beginning in the T'ang Dynasty (618-907 c.e.) – but Taoism continued as the defining spiritual Way, for its insight remained vital not only in Taoism itself, but also in the essential core of Ch'an practice. And nothing is more essential to Ch'an practice than meditation: indeed, *ch'an* literally means "meditation." The practice of meditation is not discussed extensively in early Taoist literature as it is in Ch'an literature. But it is clear that such meditation was practiced, for the *Tao Te Ching* and *Chuang Tzu* both contain a number of passages that allude to the meditative experience. Not surprisingly, references by Lao Tzu the poet tend to be oblique: in fact, a good deal of the text can be read as describing meditative awareness as the texture defining a sage's every action. Where not oblique or implicit, the references appear in the form of poetry rather than discursive description: "Can you polish the dark-enigma mirror / to a clarity beyond stain?" (10.5-6), "Inhabit the furthest peripheries of emptiness / and abide in the tranquil center" (16.1-2), "sitting still in Way's company" (62.10),

Block the senses
and close the mind,
blunt edges,
loosen tangles,
soften glare,
mingle dust:
this is called *dark-enigma union*.

(56. 3-9)

And perhaps the most impressive aspect of Lao Tzu's power as a poet is how his poetic strategies induce this meditative experience in the reader. Mysterious utterances, misty terminology, fragmentary collage form with open and enigmatic juxtapositions, an abounding ambiguity that exploits the uncertainty inherent to the syntax and semantics of ancient Chinese – these surprisingly modern strategies all keep the poetry as close as possible to the undifferentiated primal mystery of Way, forcing the reader to participate in the generative emptiness at the source of language, mind, and all heaven and earth.

In the context of Lao Tzu's cosmology as a whole, the realm of Presence takes on depths beyond our provisional definition of it as the empirical world around us. In the lexicon of early Taoist texts, *heaven* is a near synonym for *Way* – though it focuses on these depths in the region of Presence, while *Way* tends to focus on the mysterious region of Absence. A term that already had a considerable historical resonance when Lao Tzu and Chuang Tzu adopted it and made it their own, *heaven*'s most primitive meaning is simply "sky." By extension, it also comes to mean "transcendence," for our most primal sense of transcendence may be the simple act of looking up into the sky. By association with the idea of transcendence and that which is beyond us, *heaven* also comes to mean "fate" or "destiny." But this unsurprising complex of ideas is transformed completely when early Taoism adds "nature" or "natural process" to the weave of meaning, for then heaven becomes earth, and earth heaven. Earth's natural process is itself both our fate in life and our transcendence, for self is but a fleeting form taken on by earth's process of change – born out of it, and returned to it in death. Or more

TAO TE CHING

precisely, never *out of it*: totally unborn. Our truest self, being unborn, is all and none of earth's fleeting forms simultaneously.

Not surprisingly, given the apparent antiquity of Lao Tzu's entire cosmology, this unborn perspective seems to have survived from very ancient times in the deep levels of Chinese consciousness, indeed the term *(shen)* meaning "self" meant at the same time "body." However ancient it may be, it is a philosophical statement of a principle central to the modern science of ecology – that the earth's biota is a complex food web and we humans are as much a part of it as any other organism. And in the interim between early China and modern science, this unborn perspective became an enduring source of great solace for the Chinese educated class, not least when confronting their own mortality. They recognized in it a kind of immortality, as Lao Tzu suggests a number of times, and they experienced this unborn perspective routinely in the texture of consciousness. Just as the body dissolves back into the generative process at death, they could watch the movements of self (thought, emotion) dissolve back into the generative source, and there meditatively inhabit that perennial death.

Lao Tzu's heaven represents the endpoint in a millennium-long evolution of mythological thought. He and Chuang Tzu used it to both secularize the sacred and to invest the secular with sacred dimensions. Lao Tzu begins a new tradition free of the dichotomy between secular and sacred in the concept of *tzu-jan,* which is virtually synonymous with heaven but without heaven's transcendental baggage. *Tzu-jan's* literal meaning is "self-so" or "the of-itself," which as a philosophical concept becomes "being such of itself," hence "spontaneous" or "natural." But a more revealing translation of *tzu-jan* might be "occurrence appearing of itself," for it is meant to describe the ten thousand things burgeoning forth spontaneously from the generative source, each according to its own nature, independent and self-sufficient, each dying and returning to the process of change, only to reappear in another self-generating form. Again it is striking how this most primal of worldviews is also utterly modern, for it accords with the science of ecology both in its description of how living systems work as integral wholes and in its attention to the particularity of each individual within the system.

Mythologies are stories about *tzu-jan,* but Lao Tzu returned to occurrence free of myth. This clarity may well derive from the primal oral tradition that persisted outside the mythological power structures of the Shang and Chou, but in any case it represents a return to the same proto-Chinese cultural levels where experience was organized around obeisance to earth's generative force. *Tzu-jan* is nothing other than the earth seen as a boundless generative organism, and this vision gives rise to a very different experience of the world. Rather than the metaphysics of time and space, this experience knows the world as an all-encompassing present, a constant burgeoning forth of something we might now call *spacetime.* Or more precisely, it is a constant transformation in things, for its burgeoning forth stretches out to include what we think of as past and future: like Lao Tzu's Way, it makes no distinction between filling and emptying; hence passing away is as much a part of it as coming to be. In this burgeoning forth, there is also no distinction between subjective and objective, for it includes all that we call mental, all that appears in the mind. And here lies the awesome sense of the sacred in this generative world: each of the ten thousand things, consciousness among them, seems to be miraculously burgeoning forth from a kind of emptiness at its own heart, and at the same time it is always a burgeoing forth from the very heart of the Cosmos itself.

The antiquity of this cosmology may be reflected in the conspicuous absence of a central creation myth in historical China (not surprisingly, it seems such a myth did exist in the Shang), for in such a cosmology there can be no single primordial creation of the world: its creation is an ongoing total event. But in China this cosmology is perhaps most fundamentally alive in the language itself, and its presence there at such deep levels is yet another indication that its origins go back to the earliest cultural levels, levels where culture and language were just emerging, characters just emerging from hieroglyphs. It is alive in the minimal grammar, where meaning is determined simply by the order in which words occur in an open field where much of the ordering human presence is absent, and alive in the immediate physicality of the pictographic nouns and verbs. But it is especially alive in the verbs: rather than embodying a metaphysics of time and space, rather than events in a flow of past, present, and future, the uninflected verbs of ancient Chinese simply register action, that steady burgeoning forth of occurrence appearing of itself. And even in the more articulated grammar of modern Chinese, verbs simply register completed action and action: occurrence and occurrence appearing of itself.

The Taoist Way is to dwell as an organic part of this burgeoning forth by practicing *wu-wei* (see Key Terms), another central term which literally means "not/nothing (*wu*) doing (*wei*)," and so "doing nothing" in the sense of not interfering with the flawless and self-sufficient unfolding of *tzu-jan*. But this must always be conceived together with its mirror image: "nothing doing" or "nothing's own doing," in the sense of being no one separate from *tzu-jan* when acting. *Wu-wei* is the movement of *tzu-jan,* so when we act according to *wu-wei* we act as the generative source. This opens to the deepest level of this philosophical complex, for *wu-wei* can also be read quite literally as "Absence (*wu*) doing." Here, *wu-wei* action is action directly from, or indeed as the ontological source: absence burgeoning forth into presence. This in turn invests the more straightforward reading ("doing nothing") with its fullest dimensions, for "doing nothing" always carries the sense of "enacting nothing/Absence." Thus it might be described as a return to the primal dwelling of the generative worldview.

The principle of *wu-wei* raises the question of Te (Integrity), the other key word in this book's title: *Tao (Way) Te (Integrity) Ching (Classic)*, or *The Classic of the Way and Integrity (to the Way)*. Te involves integrity to the Way in the sense of "abiding by the Way," or "enacting the Way," a concept deepened by *Te's* etymological meaning at the level of pictographic imagery: "heart-sight clarity." For the "nonhuman natural world," Te is not a problem because the ten thousand transformations are wholly *wu-wei*. Only in the human realm is the Integrity of *wu-wei* problematic. Here we encounter the sense of exile that drives much of Lao Tzu's thought, that rupture dividing human being and natural process. While Western civilization set out headlong into the barrens of that exile, China returned and stayed close to its lost homeland, cultivating the rich borderlands.

As humans no longer simply belong to natural process, that belonging was carefully cultivated in the form of *wu-wei* and a more general intimacy with the nonhuman "natural world." Rooted in Lao Tzu's spiritual ecology, these practices became the very terms of self-cultivation throughout the centuries in China. This is most clearly seen in artistic practice, which was a major part of intellectual life for everyone in the educated class, and nothing less than a form of spiritual discipline: calligraphers, poets, and painters aspired to create with the selfless spontaneity of a natural force, and the elements out of which they crafted their artistic visions were primarily aspects of the "natural world:" moon and stars, rivers and mountains, fields and gardens. But it can also be seen, for instance, in the way Chinese intellectuals would sip wine as a way of dissolving the separation between self and "natural world," a practice that usually took place outdoors or in an architectural space that aspired to be a kind of eye-space, its open walls creating an emptiness that contained the world around it. There is a host of other examples, such as the ideal of living as a recluse among the mountains, or meditation which was widely practiced and recognized as perhaps the most fundamental form of *wu-wei* belonging to natural process.

And so it is that Lao Tzu's Way has defined the spiritual Way in China. But like the other Hundred-School philosophers, Lao Tzu felt his primary mission was to rescue the ravaged society of his time, and *wu-wei* Integrity is central to his politics, for it also describes the proper functioning of society as a whole for him. Like human consciousness, the structure of this society echoes the ontological structure of Way. The people (like thoughts) take the place of Presence's ten thousand things burgeoning forth, each according to its own nature. And the ruler/government (like empty mind) takes the place of Absence, simply providing the empty field in which citizens can burgeon forth, each according to their own nature. Hence, he returns society to a state where it functions with the same *wu-wei* Integrity to Way as any other natural process. Lao Tzu's ideal society is essentially an early Neolithic generative-centered culture, though he conceived it as a kind of monarchy, for that was the only political system known or even imaginable in ancient China. But Lao Tzu's is a monarchy in name only, for his ideal monarch is virtually invisible.

Like all Chinese, Lao Tzu believed such a society was once the norm: the cultural legend describes society in the era preceding the Hsia Dynasty in these terms and includes a list of its sage-emperors. Lao Tzu believed that since those early times, society had crumbled as people lost their primal sense of belonging to the generative process of Way. Rather than acting with the simple naturalness of the human animal, they had become driven by self-aggrandizing pursuits: that is, the pursuit of desires beyond "natural" needs such as food, shelter, sex, etc. These "unnatural" desires for wealth and status and power transform an egalitarian society into a virulent web of dominance and submission, where the enhancement of a few comes at great cost to the many. In fact, this is exactly the historical process that began in the Neolithic. And it goes without saying that Lao Tzu's critique represents a fundamental critique of modern capitalism, thriving as it does on fabricating desire.

Lao Tzu's Way to a rich and harmonious society is for people to follow *wu-wei* Integrity, to satisfy needs but forget desires. This political critique of desire echoes the more fundamental critique of desire at the levels where consciousness and ontology merge. Even the least act of desire, saying *yes this* and *no that,* places us outside the spontaneous generative process. Accepting whatever comes of *tzu-jan* is to return to the undifferentiated source in ontology and consciousness. This is the same movement as society's return to *wu-wei* Integrity, and is no doubt its prerequisite. All of these are included when Lao Tzu speaks of "returning to Way." In all three aspects (politics, ontology, consciousness), it is a return to the earliest undifferentiated levels of human culture – levels so early they precede difference altogether, meaning such societies are not only radically egalitarian, but that issues of ethics and social justice hadn't even arisen yet.

Lao Tzu's political philosophy is a logical extension of his ontology – not only replicating its structure, but also replicating its profound subjectivity as a kind of uncompromising individualism. And this is in itself a radical and enduring politics. Still, however accurate and appealing his idealistic vision may be, it had little to offer as a practical prescription for counteracting the ruthless forces that ravage human society, for the simple reason that it fundamentally contradicts the principle of Way. Having associated desire with Presence and said such things as "desire drives change," Lao Tzu knew perfectly well that natural process is itself the boundless form of desire, the ten thousand things pushing beyond themselves through one transformation after another. And humans are a part of those transformations: whatever we do, whatever desires drive us, that too is part of Way. Indeed, as Lao Tzu must have been thinking when he spoke of Way as indifferent and inhumane, even as "the Executioner," the so-called harmony of natural process includes a great deal of waste and destruction. Lao Tzu's prescription for solving social injustice was itself a colossal system of "unnatural" desire, a hopeless attempt to change the most fundamental makeup of not only the human world, but of Way itself.

Chuang Tzu was the more consistent and thoroughgoing Taoist. Realizing that developments in human society, however tragic, were a natural part of Way, he made no attempt to forge Taoist thought into a system of social justice. Indeed, his was a wholesale rejection of the human-centered approach. But although Lao Tzu shared this rejection, he was driven by a profound compassion. Here is the beautiful and compelling humanity of Lao Tzu: his concern for the desperate plight of common people drove him to advocate political principles that contradicted the fundamental terms of his philosophy. And the inevitable failure of these contradictory principles no doubt led to the frustration and hopelessness that drove Lao Tzu over the pass and away into the west. In the end, his is not so much a practical political philosophy as a political poetry, a lament that only grows more and more poignant as stratified societies continue to thrive on social injustice.

While the Way of philosophical Taoism has defined the private spiritual realm for Chinese intellectuals throughout the millennia, the Confucian Way has defined the societal realm. Although Lao Tzu longed to

TAO TE CHING

apply his wisdom to the social problems of his time, this role fell to Confucius, who created a radically new social system, one that was both consistent with the fundamental terms of Lao Tzu's thought and applicable in a practical way to secular society. In his social philosophy, Confucius seems to be drawing out the implications of a cosmology that already existed in the culture. Rather than a newly created replacement for the Shang monotheism, it seems to have survived from the more primal cultures that preceded the Shang, once again revealing Shang monotheism to be a mere ideological overlay convenient to the uses of power. The resilience of this cosmology after a thousand years of neglect is remarkable and especially interesting as it is so consistent with both our immediate experience and the modern scientific account of the cosmos. In any case, it would appear that the earlier levels of Lao Tzu formulated this cosmology for the Hundred-Schools era, and that Confucius relied on that formulation. So the cosmology that shaped Chinese civilization was the resurgence of an ancient cosmology, a return to the culture's most primal roots, though as Marx would expect, even this gynocentric cosmology could not preclude the workaday male tyranny that has dominated Chinese culture throughout its history (hence the sages of ancient China were men, as in this translation). And it is a return not only to the generative worldview, but also to the general sense of *wu-wei* belonging to natural process as a secular extension of the reverence for ancestral nature deities that also typified proto-Chinese cultures.

With the addition of the political dimensions formulated by Confucius, Lao Tzu's majestic vision became the operant possibility for China's secular society, however rarely it was realized in practice: human being nestled in the primal ecology of a spontaneously self-generating and harmonious cosmos. The two regions of this cosmology appear almost schematically in countless Chinese landscape paintings: the pregnant emptiness of Absence, and the landscape of Presence as it burgeons forth from Absence in a perpetual process of transformation. And then, within that cosmology of natural process, there is the human. It was among the vistas of these sparsely peopled landscapes so dramatically burgeoning forth out of vast realms of emptiness that Lao Tzu set out across the mountain pass in Chang Lu's painting (cover illustration, left side): overwhelmed by the intractable grief people were enduring, and yet smiling at a butterfly, Chuang Tzu's famous image for the exquisite and dreamlike transformation of things (II. 24). In leaving through the mountains into dusk-lit mists of the west, Lao Tzu vanished back into that mysterious transformation of things, and the voice that remains is the voice of that mystery herself, the voice of dragon, voice of earth.

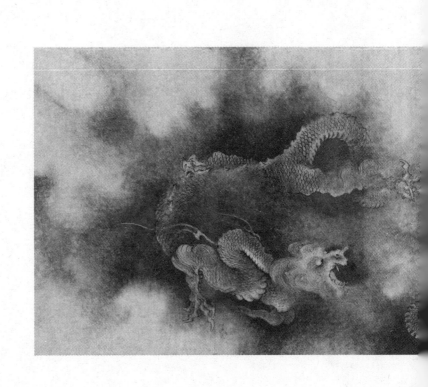

Tao Ching

I

A Way called *Way* isn't the perennial Way.
A name that names isn't the perennial name:

the named is mother to the ten thousand things,
but the unnamed is origin to all heaven and earth.

In perennial Absence you see mystery,
and in perennial Presence you see appearance.
Though the two are one and the same,
once they arise, they differ in name.

One and the same they're called *dark-enigma*,
dark-enigma deep within dark-enigma,

gateway of all mystery.

2

All beneath heaven knows beauty is beauty
only because there's ugliness,
and knows good is good
only because there's evil.

Being and Absence give birth to one another,
difficult and easy complete one another,
long and short measure one another,
high and low fill one another,
music and noise harmonize one another,
before and after follow one another:

that's why a sage abides in the realm of nothing's own doing,
living out that wordless teaching.
The ten thousand things arise without beginnings there,
abide without waiting there,
come to perfection without dwelling there.

Without dwelling there: that's the one way
you'll never lose it.

3

Never bestow honors
and people won't quarrel.
Never prize rare treasures
and people won't steal.
Never flaunt alluring things
and people won't be confused.

This is how a sage governs.
Fill bellies and empty minds,
strengthen bones and weaken ambition,

always keep the people from knowing and wanting,
then those who know are those who never presume to act.

If you're nothing doing what you do
all things will be governed well.

4

Way is empty.
Use it: it never needs filling.
An abyss so deep
it seems ancestor to the ten thousand things,

it blunts edges,
loosens tangles,
softens glare,
mingles dust.

A clarity so clear it only seems real,

whose child could it be? Apparently
it precedes gods and creators.

5

Heaven and earth are Inhumane:
they use the ten thousand things like straw dogs.
And the sage too is Inhumane:
he uses the hundred-fold people like straw dogs.

Is all heaven and earth
really so much like a bellows-chamber?
It's empty but never contracts,
just keeps bringing forth more and more.

Words go on failing and failing,
nothing like abiding in its midst.

6

The valley spirit never dies.

It's called *dark female-enigma*,
and the gateway of dark female-enigma
is called *the root of heaven and earth*,

gossamer so unceasing it seems real.
Use it: it's effortless.

7

Heaven goes on forever.
Earth endures forever.

There's a reason heaven and earth go on enduring forever:
their life isn't their own
so their life goes on forever.

Hence, in putting himself last
the sage puts himself first,
and in giving himself up
he preserves himself.

If you aren't free of yourself
how will you ever become yourself?

8

Lofty nobility is like water.
Water's nobility is to enrich the ten thousand things
and yet never strive:
it just settles through places people everywhere loathe.
Therefore, it's nearly Way.

Dwelling's nobility is earth,
mind's nobility is empty depth,
giving's nobility is Humanity,
word's nobility is sincerity,
government's nobility is accord,
endeavor's nobility is ability,
action's nobility is timing.

When you never strive
you never go wrong.

9

Forcing it fuller and fuller
can't compare to just enough,
and honed sharper and sharper
means it won't keep for long.

Once it's full of jade and gold
your house will never be safe.
Proud of wealth and renown
you bring on your own ruin.

Just do what you do, and then leave:
such is the Way of heaven.

10

Can you let your spirit embrace primal unity
without drifting away?

Can you focus *ch'i* into such softness
you're a newborn again?

Can you polish the dark-enigma mirror
to a clarity beyond stain?

Can you make loving the people and ruling the nation
nothing's own doing?

Can you be female
opening and closing heaven's gate?

Can you fathom earth's four distances with radiant wisdom
and know nothing?

Give birth and nurture.
Give birth without possessing
and foster without dominating:

this is called *dark-enigma Integrity.*

II

Thirty spokes gathered at each hub:
absence makes the cart work.
A storage jar fashioned out of clay:
absence makes the jar work.
Doors and windows cut in a house:
absence makes the house work.

Presence gives things their value,
but absence makes them work.

12

The five colors blind eyes.
The five tones deafen ears.
The five tastes blur tongues.
Fast horses and breathtaking hunts make minds wild and crazy.
Things rare and expensive make people lose their way.

That's why a sage tends to the belly, not the eye,
always ignores *that* and chooses *this*.

13

Honor is a contagion deep as fear,
renown a calamity profound as self.

Why do I call honor a contagion deep as fear?
Honor always dwindles away,
so earning it fills us with fear
and losing it fills us with fear.

And why do I call renown a calamity profound as self?
We only know calamity because we have these selves.
If we didn't have selves
what calamity could touch us?

When all beneath heaven is your self in renown
you trust yourself to all beneath heaven,
and when all beneath heaven is your self in love
you dwell throughout all beneath heaven.

14

Looked at but never seen,
it takes the name *invisible*.
Listened to but never heard,
it takes the name *ethereal*.
Held tight but never felt,
it takes the name *gossamer*.

You can't unravel these three
blurred so utterly they've become one,

rising without radiance
and setting without darkness,
braided together beyond name, woven
back always and forever into nothing:

this is called *formless form*
or *nothing's image*,
called *spectral confusion*,

something you meet without seeing a front
and follow without seeing a back.

Abiding in the ancient Way
to master what has now come to be
and fathom its ancient source:

this is called *thread of the Way*.

TAO TE CHING

15

Ancient masters of Way
all subtle mystery and dark-enigma vision:
they were deep beyond knowing,

so deep beyond knowing
we can only describe their appearance:

perfectly cautious, as if crossing winter streams,
and perfectly watchful, as if neighbors threatened;
perfectly reserved, as if guests,
perfectly expansive, as if ice melting away,
and perfectly simple, as if uncarved wood;
perfectly empty, as if open valleys,
and perfectly shadowy, as if murky water.

Who's murky enough to settle slowly into pure clarity,
and who still enough to awaken slowly into life?

If you nurture this Way, you never crave fullness.
Never crave fullness
and you'll wear away into completion.

16

Inhabit the furthest peripheries of emptiness
and abide in the tranquil center.

There the ten thousand things arise,
and in them I watch the return:
all things on and ever on
each returning to its root.

Returning to the root is called *tranquility*,
tranquility is called *returning to the inevitable unfurling of things*,
returning to the inevitable unfurling of things is called *constancy*,
and to understand constancy is called *enlightenment*.

Without understanding constancy, you stumble deceived.
But understanding constancy, you're all-embracing,

all-embracing and therefore impartial,
impartial and therefore imperial,
imperial and therefore heaven,
heaven and therefore Way,
Way and therefore enduring:

self gone, free of danger.

17

The loftiest ruler is barely known among those below.
Next comes a ruler people love and praise.
After that, one they fear,
and then one they despise.

If you don't stand sincere by your words
how sincere can the people be?
Take great care over words, treasure them,

and when the hundred-fold people see
your work succeed in all they do
they'll say it's just *occurrence appearing of itself.*

18

When the great Way is abandoned
we're faced with Humanity and Duty.

When clever wisdom appears
we're faced with duplicity.

When familial harmony ends
we're faced with obedience and kindness.

And when chaos engulfs the nation
we're faced with trustworthy ministers.

19

If you give up sagehood and abandon wisdom
people will profit a hundred times over.

If you give up Humanity and abandon Duty
people will return to obedience and kindness.

If you give up ingenuity and abandon profit
bandits and thieves will roam no more.

But these three
are mere refinements, nowhere near enough.
They depend on something more:

observe origin's weave, embrace uncarved simplicity,
self nearly forgotten, desires rare.

20

If you give up learning, troubles end.

How much difference is there
beween yes and no?
And is there a difference
between lovely and ugly?

If we can't stop fearing
those things people fear,
it's pure confusion, never-ending confusion.

People all radiate such joy,
happily offering a sacrificial ox
or climbing a tower in spring.
But I go nowhere and reveal nothing,
like a newborn child who has yet to smile,
aimless and worn out
as if the way home were lost.

People all have enough and more.
But I'm abandoned and destitute,
an absolute simpleton, this mind of mine so utterly
muddled and blank.

Others are bright and clear:
I'm dark and murky.
Others are confident and effective:
I'm pensive and withdrawn,
uneasy as boundless seas
or perennial mountain winds.

TAO TE CHING

People all have a purpose in life,
but I'm inept, thoroughly useless and backward.
I'll never be like other people:
I keep to the nurturing mother.

21

The nature of great Integrity
is to follow Way absolutely.

Becoming things, Way appears
vague and hazy.
All hazy and impossibly vague
it harbors the mind's images.
All vague and impossibly hazy
it harbors the world's things.

All hidden and impossibly dark
it harbors the subtle essence,
and being an essence so real
it harbors the sincerity of facts.

Never, not since the beginning—
its renown has never been far off.
Through it we witness all origins.

And how can we ever know the form of all origins?
Through this.

22

In yielding is completion.
In bent is straight.
In hollow is full.
In exhaustion is renewal.
In little is contentment.
In much is confusion.

This is how a sage embraces primal unity
as the measure of all beneath heaven.

Give up self-reflection
and you're soon enlightened.
Give up self-definition
and you're soon apparent.
Give up self-promotion
and you're soon proverbial.
Give up self-esteem
and you're soon perennial.
Simply give up contention
and soon nothing in all beneath heaven contends with you.

It was hardly empty talk
when the ancients declared *In yielding is completion.*
Once you perfect completion
you've returned home to it all.

23

Keeping words spare: occurrence appearing of itself.

Wild winds never last all morning
and fierce rains never last all day.
Who conjures such things if not heaven and earth,
and if heaven and earth can't make things last,
why should we humans try?

That's why masters devote themselves to Way.
To master Way is to become Way,
to master gain is to become gain,
to master loss is to become loss.
And whatever becomes Way, Way welcomes joyfully,
whatever becomes gain, gain welcomes joyfully,
whatever becomes loss, loss welcomes joyfully.

If you don't stand sincere by your words
how sincere can the people be?

24

Stretch onto tiptoes
and you never stand firm.
Hurry long strides
and you never travel far.

Keep up self-reflection
and you'll never be enlightened.
Keep up self-definition
and you'll never be apparent.
Keep up self-promotion
and you'll never be proverbial.
Keep up self-esteem
and you'll never be perennial.

Travelers of the Way call such striving
too much food and useless baggage.
Things may not all despise such striving,
but a master of the Way stays clear of it.

25

There was something all murky shadow,
born before heaven and earth:

o such utter silence, utter emptiness.

Isolate and changeless,
it moves everywhere without fail:

picture the mother of all beneath heaven.

I don't know its name.
I'll call it *Way,*
and if I must name it, name it *Vast.*

Vast means it's passing beyond,
passing beyond means it's gone far away,
and gone far away means it's come back.

Because Way is vast
heaven is vast,
earth is vast,
and the true emperor too is vast.
In this realm, there are four vast things,
and the true emperor is one of them.

Human abides by earth.
Earth abides by heaven.
Heaven abides by Way.
Way abides by occurrence appearing of itself.

26

Heavy is the root of light,
and tranquil the ruler of reckless.

A sage traveling all day
is never far from the supplies in his cart,
and however spectacular the views
he remains calm and composed.

How can a lord having ten thousand chariots
act lightly in governing all beneath heaven?
Act lightly and you lose your source-root.
Act recklessly and you lose your rule.

27

Perfect travels leave no tracks.
Perfect words leave no doubts.
Perfect accounts need no counting.
Perfect gates close without locks
and so cannot be opened.
Perfect knots bind without rope
and so cannot be loosened.

A sage is always perfect in rescuing people
and so abandons no one,
always perfect in rescuing things
and so abandons nothing.

This is called the *bequest of enlightenment,*

so one who possesses this perfection is a teacher of those who don't,
and those who don't possess it are the resource of one who does.

Without honoring the teacher
and loving the resource,
no amount of wisdom can prevent vast confusion.

This is called *the essential mystery.*

28

Knowing the masculine
and nurturing the feminine
you become the river of all beneath heaven.
River of all beneath heaven
you abide by perennial Integrity
and so return to infancy.

Knowing the white
and nurturing the black
you become the pattern of all beneath heaven.
Pattern of all beneath heaven
you abide by perennial Integrity
and so return to the boundless.

Knowing splendor
and nurturing ruin
you become the valley of all beneath heaven.
Valley of all beneath heaven
you rest content in perennial Integrity
and so return to the simplicity of uncarved wood.

When uncarved wood is split apart
it becomes mere implements.
But when a sage is employed
he becomes a true minister,
for the great governing blade carves nothing.

29

Longing to take hold of all beneath heaven and improve it . . .
I've seen such dreams invariably fail.
All beneath heaven is a sacred vessel,
something beyond all improvement.
Try to improve it and you ruin it.
Try to hold it and you lose it.

For things sometimes lead and sometimes follow,
sometimes sigh and sometimes storm,
sometimes strengthen and sometimes weaken,
sometimes kill and sometimes die.

And so the sage steers clear of extremes,
clear of extravagance,
clear of exhaltation.

TAO TE CHING

30

If you use the Way to help a ruler of people
you never use weapons to coerce all beneath heaven.
Such things always turn against you:

fields where soldiers camp
turn to thorn and bramble,
and vast armies on the march
leave years of misery behind.

The noble prevail if they must, then stop:
they never press on to coerce the world.

Prevail, but never presume.
Prevail, but never boast.
Prevail, but never exult.
Prevail, but never when there's another way.
This is to prevail without coercing.

Things grown strong soon grow old.
This is called *losing the Way:*
Lose the Way and you die young.

31

Auspicious weapons are the tools of misfortune.
Things may not all despise such tools,
but a master of the Way stays clear of them.

The noble-minded treasure the left when home
and the right when taking up weapons of war.

Weapons are tools of misfortune,
not tools of the noble-minded.
When there's no other way,
they take up weapons with tranquil calm,
finding no glory in victory.

To find glory in victory
is to savor killing people,
and if you savor killing people
you'll never guide all beneath heaven.

We honor the left in celebrations
and honor the right in lamentations,
so captains stand on the left
and generals on the right.
But use them both as if conducting a funeral:

when so many people are being killed
it should be done with tears and mourning.
And victory too should be conducted like a funeral.

TAO TE CHING

32

Way is perennially nameless,
an uncarved simplicity. Though small,
it's subject to nothing in all beneath heaven.
But when lords or emperors foster it,
the ten thousand things gladly become their guests,

heaven mingling with earth
sends down sweet dew,
and the people free of mandates
share justice among themselves.

When a governing blade begins carving it up, names arise.
Once names arise,
know that it's time to stop.
Knowing when to stop, you can avoid danger.

Way flowing through all beneath heaven:
it's like valley streams flowing into rivers and seas.

33

To know people is wisdom,
but to know yourself is enlightenment.

To master people takes force,
but to master yourself takes strength.

To know contentment is wealth,
and to live with strength resolve.
To never leave whatever you are
is to abide,
and to die without getting lost—
that is to live on and on.

34

Way is vast, a flood
so utterly vast it's flowing everywhere.

The ten thousand things depend on it:
giving them life and never leaving them
it performs wonders but remains nameless.

Feeding and clothing the ten thousand things
without ruling over them,
perennially that free of desire,
it's small in name.
And being what the ten thousand things return to
without ruling over them,
it's vast in name.

It never makes itself vast
and so becomes utterly vast.

35

Holding to the great image
all beneath heaven sets out:
sets out free of risk,
peace tranquil and vast.

Music and savory food
entice travelers to stop,
but the Way uttered forth
isn't even the thinnest of bland flavors.

Look at it: not enough to see.
Listen to it: not enough to hear.
Use it: not enough to use up.

36

To gather
you must scatter.
To weaken
you must strengthen.
To abandon
you must foster.
To take
you must give.
This is called *dusky enlightenment*.

Soft and weak overcome hard and strong.

Fish should be kept in their watery depths:
a nation's honed instruments of power
should be kept well-hidden from the people.

37

Way is perennially doing nothing
so there's nothing it doesn't do.

When lords and emperors abide by this
the ten thousand things follow change of themselves.

Desire drives change,
but I've stilled it with uncarved nameless simplicity.

Uncarved nameless simplicity
is the perfect absence of desire,
and the absence of desire means repose:
all beneath heaven at rest of itself.

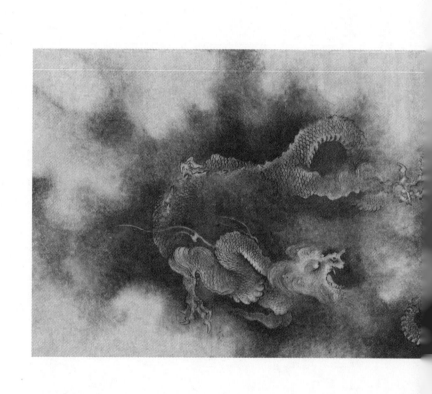

Te Ching

38

High Integrity never has Integrity
and so is indeed Integrity.
Low Integrity never loses Integrity
and so is not at all Integrity.

High Integrity does nothing
and has no motives.
Low Integrity does something
and has sure motives.
High Humanity does something
and has no motives.
High Duty does something
and has sure motives.
High Ritual does something,
and when no one follows along
it rolls up its sleeves
and forces them into line.

Lose Way, and Integrity appears.
Lose Integrity, and Humanity appears.
Lose Humanity, and Duty appears.
Lose Duty, and Ritual apppears.

Ritual is the thinning away of loyalty and sincerity,
the beginning of chaos,
and prophecy is the flowery semblance of Way,
the beginning of folly.

This is why a great elder
inhabits thick rather than thin,
fruitful substance rather than flowery semblance,

always ignores *that* and chooses *this*.

39

Ancients who realized primal unity:

Heaven realized primal unity
and so came to clarity.
Earth realized primal unity
and so came to tranquility.
Gods realized primal unity
and so came to spirit.
Valleys realized primal unity
and so came to fullness.
The ten thousand things realized primal unity
and so came to life.
Lords and emperors realized primal unity
and so came to rectify all beneath heaven.

It's their very existence:
without clarity heaven cracks open,
without tranquility earth bursts forth,
without spirit gods cease,
without fullness valleys run dry,
without life the ten thousand things perish,
without high nobility lords and emperors stumble and fall.

Nobility is rooted in humility,
and high founded on low.
This is why true lords and emperors call themselves
orphaned, destitute, ill-fated.
Isn't this rooted in humility?
Isn't it

counting the world's praise as no praise,
refusing to tinkle like delicate jade bells
or clatter like ponderous stone chimes?

40

Return is the movement of Way,
and yielding the method of Way.

All beneath heaven, the ten thousand things: it's all born of Presence,
and Presence is born of Absence.

41

When the lofty hear of Way
they devote themselves.
When the common hear of Way
they wonder if it's real or not.
And when the lowly hear of Way
they laugh out loud.
Without that laughter, it wouldn't be Way.

Hence the abiding proverbs:

Luminous Way seems dark.
Advancing Way seems retreating.
Formless Way seems manifold.

High Integrity seems low-lying.
Great whiteness seems tarnished.
Abounding Integrity seems lacking.
Abiding Integrity seems missing.
True essence seems protean.

The great square has no corners,
and the great implement completes nothing.
The great voice sounds faint,
and the great image has no shape.

Way remains hidden and nameless,
but it alone nourishes and brings to completion.

42

Way gave birth to one,
and one gave birth to two.
Two gave birth to three,
and three gave birth to the ten thousand things.
Then the ten thousand things shouldered *yin* and embraced *yang*,
blending *ch'i* to establish harmony.

People all hate scraping by
orphaned, destitute, ill-fated,
but true dukes and emperors call themselves just that.

Some things gain by loss,
and some lose by gain.

I only teach
what the people teach:
Tyranny and force never come to a natural end.
I've taken the people as my schoolmaster.

TAO TE CHING

43

The weakest in all beneath heaven gallops through the strongest,
and vacant absence slips inside solid presence.

I know by this the value of nothing's own doing.

The teaching without words,
the value of nothing's own doing:
few indeed master such things.

44

Name or self: which is precious?
Self or wealth: which is treasure?
Gain or loss: which is affliction?

Indulge love and the cost is dear.
Keep treasures and the loss is lavish.

Knowing contentment you avoid tarnish,
and knowing when to stop you avoid danger.

Try it and your life will last and last.

45

Great perfection seems flawed,
but its usefulness never falters.
Great fullness seems empty,
but its usefulness never runs dry.

Great rectitude seems bent low,
great skill seems clumsy,
great eloquence seems quiet.

Bustling around may overcome cold,
but tranquility overcomes heat.
Master lucid tranquility
and you'll govern all beneath heaven.

46

When all beneath heaven abides in Way,
fast horses are kept to work the fields.
When all beneath heaven forgets Way,
war horses are bred among the fertility altars.

What calamity is greater than no contentment,
and what flaw greater than the passion for gain?

The contentment of fathoming contentment—
there lies the contentment that endures.

47

You can know all beneath heaven
though you never step out the door,
and you can see the Way of heaven
though you never look out the window.

The further you explore, the less you know.

So it is that a sage knows by going nowhere,
names by seeing nothing,
perfects by doing nothing.

48

To work at learning brings more each day.
To work at Way brings less each day,

less and still less
until you're nothing's own doing.
And when you're nothing's own doing, there's nothing you don't do.

To grasp all beneath heaven, leave it alone.
Leave it alone, that's all,
and nothing in all beneath heaven will elude you.

49

A sage's mind is never his own:
he makes the hundred-fold people's mind his mind.

I treat the noble with nobility
and the ignoble too:
such is the nobility of Integrity.
I treat the sincere with sincerity
and the insincere too:
such is the sincerity of Integrity.

A sage dwells within all beneath heaven
at ease, mind mingled through it all.
The hundred-fold people devote their eyes and ears,
but a sage inhabits it all like a child.

50

People born into life enter death.
Constant companion in life
and in death,
this body is the kill-site animating their lives.
And isn't that because
they think life is the fullness of life?

I've heard those who encompass the whole of life
could walk on and on without meeting rhinoceros or tiger,
could charge into armies without feeling shield or sword.
A rhinoceros would find nowhere to gore them,
a tiger nowhere to claw them,
a sword nowhere to slice them.

And isn't that because
for them there's no kill-site?

51

Way gives birth to them
and Integrity nurtures them.
Matter shapes them
and conditions complete them.

That's why the ten thousand things always
honor Way and treasure Integrity.

Honoring Way and treasuring Integrity
isn't obedience to command,
it's occurrence perennially appearing of itself.

Way gives birth to them
and Integrity nurtures them:
it fosters and sustains them,
harbors and succors them,
nourishes and shelters them.

Giving birth without possessing,
animating without subjecting,
fostering without dominating:

this is called *dark-enigma Integrity*.

52

There's a source all beneath heaven shares:
call it the mother of all beneath heaven.

Once you fathom the mother
you understand the child,
and once you understand the child
you abide in the mother,

self gone, free of danger.

If you block the senses
and close the mind,
you never struggle.
If you open the senses
and expand your endeavors,
nothing can save you.

Seeing the small is called *enlightenment*,
and abiding in the gentle *strength*.

Wielding radiance
return to enlightenment,
then you're beyond all harm.

This is the cultivation of constancy.

TAO TE CHING

53

Understanding sparse and sparser still
I travel the great Way,
nothing to fear unless I stray.

The great Way is open and smooth,
but people adore twisty paths:
Government in ruins,
fields overgrown
and graineries bare,

they indulge in elegant robes
and sharp swords,
lavish food and drink,
all those trappings of luxury.

It's *vainglorious thievery*—
not the Way, not the Way at all.

54

Something planted so deep it's never rooted up,
something held so tight it's never stolen away:
children and grandchildren will pay it homage always.

Cultivated in yourself
it makes Integrity real.
Cultivated in your family
it makes Integrity plentiful.
Cultivated in your village
it makes Integrity enduring.
Cultivated in your nation
it makes Integrity abundant.
Cultivated in all beneath heaven
it makes Integrity all-encompassing.

So look through self into self,
through family into family,
through village into village,
through nation into nation,
through all beneath heaven into all beneath heaven.

How can I know all beneath heaven as it is?
Through this.

55

Embody Integrity's abundance
and you're like a vibrant child

hornets and vipers can't bite,
savage beasts can't maul
and fierce birds can't claw,

bones supple and muscles tender, but still gripping firmly.

Knowing nothing of male and female mingling
and yet aroused:
this is the utmost essence.
Wailing all day without getting hoarse:
this is the utmost harmony.

To understand harmony is called *constancy,*
and to understand constancy is called *enlightenment.*

To enhance your life is called *tempting fate,*
and to control *ch'i* with the mind is called *violence.*

Things grown strong soon grow old.
This is called *losing the Way:*
Lose the Way and you die young.

56

Those who know don't talk,
and those who talk don't know.

Block the senses
and close the mind,
blunt edges,
loosen tangles,
soften glare,
mingle dust:

this is called *dark-enigma union*.

It can't be embraced
and can't be ignored,
can't be enhanced
and can't be harmed,
can't be treasured
and can't be despised,

for it's the treasure of all beneath heaven.

57

You may govern the nation through principle
and lead armies to victory through craft,
but you win all beneath heaven through indifference.

How can I know this to be so?
Through this.

The more prohibitions rule all beneath heaven
the deeper poverty grows among the people.
The more shrewd leaders there are
the faster dark confusion fills the nation.
The more cleverness people learn
the faster strange things happen.
The faster laws and decrees are issued
the more bandits and thieves appear.

Therefore a sage says:
I do nothing
and the people transform themselves.
I cherish tranquility
and the people rectify themselves.
I cultivate indifference
and the people enrich themselves.
I desire nothing
and the people return of themselves to uncarved simplicity.

58

When government is pensive and withdrawn
people are pure and simple.
When government is confident and effective
people are cunning and secretive.

Prosperity springs from calamity
and calamity lurks in prosperity.
Who knows where it will all end

without leaders of principle?
And principle always reverts to sinister trickery,
virtue to depraved sorcery.

People have been confused for such a long long time.

That's why a sage is sharp but never cuts,
austere but never grates,
forthright but never provokes,
bright but never dazzles.

59

To govern people and serve heaven
there's nothing like thrift.
Thrift means *submitting early,*
and submitting early means *storing up Integrity.*

Store up Integrity and nothing is beyond you.
Once nothing is beyond you,
no one knows where it will all end.
Once no one knows where it will end,
you can nurture a nation.

And nurturing the nation's mother too
you can last and last.
This is called *rooted deep and solid,*
the Way of long life and enduring insight.

60

Govern a great nation as you would cook a small fish.

Use Way to rule all beneath heaven
and spirits never become ghosts.
When spirits don't become ghosts,
ghosts do people no harm.
When ghosts do people no harm,
sages do them no harm.

And once humans and ghosts do each other no harm,
they return together to Integrity.

61

A great nation flows down into
the place where all beneath heaven converges,
the female of all beneath heaven.

In its stillness, female lies perpetually low,
and there perpetually conquers male.

A great nation that puts itself below a small nation
takes over the small nation,
and a small nation that puts itself below a great nation
gives itself over to the great nation.

Some lie low to take over,
and some lie low to give over.

A great nation wanting nothing more
than to unite and nurture the people
and a small nation wanting nothing more
than to join and serve the people:
they both succeed in what they want.

Great things lie low and rest content.

62

Way is the mystery of these ten thousand things.

It's a good person's treasure
and an evil person's refuge.
Its beautiful words are bought and sold
and its noble deeds are gifts enriching people.

It never abandons even the evil among us.

When the Son of Heaven is enthroned
and the three dukes installed,
parades with jade discs and stately horses
can't compare to sitting still in Way's company.

Isn't it said that
the ancients exalted this Way because
in it *whatever we seek we find,*
and whatever seeks us we escape?

No wonder it's exalted throughout all beneath heaven.

63

If you're nothing doing what you do,
you act without acting
and savor without savoring,

you render the small vast and the few many,
use Integrity to repay hatred,
see the complexity in simplicity,
find the vast in the minute.

The complex affairs of all beneath heaven are there in simplicity,
and the vast affairs of all beneath heaven are there in the minute.
That's why a sage never bothers with vastness
and so becomes utterly vast.

Easy promises breed little trust,
and too much simplicity breeds too much complexity.
That's why a sage inhabits the complexity of things
and so avoids all complexity.

64

It's easy to embrace the tranquil
and easy to prevent trouble before omens appear.
It's easy for the trifling to melt away
and easy for the slight to scatter away.

Work at things before they've begun
and establish order before confusion sets in,

for a tree you can barely reach around
grows from the tiniest rootlet,
a nine-tiered tower
starts as a basket of dirt,
a thousand-mile journey
begins with a single step.

Work at things and you ruin them;
cling to things and you lose them.

That's why a sage does nothing
and so ruins nothing,
clings to nothing
and so loses nothing.

When people devote themselves to something
they always ruin it on the verge of success.

TAO TE CHING

Finish with the same care you took in beginning
and you'll avoid ruining things.
This is why a sage desires without desire,
never longing for rare treasures,
learns without learning,
always returning to what people have passed by,

helps the ten thousand things occur of themselves
by never presuming to work at them.

65

Ancient masters of Way
never enlightened people.
They kept people simple-minded.

It's impossible to govern
once you've filled people with knowing.
Use knowing to govern
and you plunder the nation,
but use not-knowing to govern
and you enrich the nation.

Once you understand this, the pattern is clear,
and always understanding the pattern is called *dark-enigma Integrity*.

Dark-enigma Integrity is deep and distant,
is the return of things

back into the vast harmony.

66

Oceans and rivers become emperors of the hundred valleys
because they stay so perfectly below them.
This alone makes them emperors of the hundred valleys.

So, wanting to rule over the people
a sage speaks from below them,
and wanting to lead the people
he follows along behind them,

then he can reign above without weighing the people down
and stay ahead without leading the people to ruin.

All beneath heaven rejoices in its tireless praise of such a sage.
And because he's given up contention,
nothing in all beneath heaven contends with him.

67

People throughout all beneath heaven say
my Tao is so vast it's like nothing at all.
But it's only vast because it's like nothing at all:
if it were like anything else
it would have long since become trifling.

There are three treasures
I hold and nurture:
The first is called *compassion,*
the second *economy,*
and the third *never daring to lead all beneath heaven.*

Courage comes of compassion,
generosity comes of economy,
and commanding leadership comes of never daring to lead all beneath
        heaven.

But these days it's all courage without compassion,
generosity without economy,
and leading without following.
There's nothing but death in that.

To overcome, attack with compassion.
To stand firm, defend with compassion.
Whatever heaven sustains
it shelters with compassion.

68

A noble official is never warlike,
and a noble warrior is never angered.
A noble conqueror never faces an enemy,
and a noble leader stays below the people he wields.

This is called *the Integrity of peacefulness,*
the power of wielding the people,

the fullest extent of our ancient accord with heaven.

69

There was once a saying among those who wielded armies:
I'd much rather be a guest than a host,
much rather retreat a foot than advance an inch.

This is called *marching without marching,*
rolling up sleeves without baring arms,
raising swords without brandishing weapons,
entering battle without facing an enemy.

There's no greater calamity than dishonoring an enemy.
Dishonor an enemy and you'll lose those treasures of mine.

When armies face one another in battle,
it's always the tender-hearted one that prevails.

70

My words are so simple to understand
and so easily put into practice
that no one in all beneath heaven understands them
and no one puts them into practice.

Words have their ancestral origins
and actions their sovereign:

it's only because people don't understand this
that they don't understand me.
And the less people understand me
the more precious I become.

So it is that a sage wears sackcloth,
keeping pure jade harbored deep.

71

Knowing not-knowing is lofty.
Not knowing not-knowing is affliction.

A sage stays free of affliction.
Just recognize it as affliction
and you're free of it.

72

When the people stop fearing the fearsome
something truly fearsome will descend upon them.

Don't hem them in
and choke their lives with oppression.
That's all. Just let them be,
and they'll never tire of you.

A sage sees through himself without revealing himself,
loves himself without exalting himself,

always ignores *that* and chooses *this*.

73

To infuse daring with courage means death.
To infuse caution with courage means life.
The one enriches you, and the other ruins you.

No one knows why heaven
despises what it despises,
that's why a sage inhabits the complexity of things.

The Way of heaven never contends
and so overcomes perfectly,
never speaks
and so answers perfectly,
never summons
and so arrives of itself,
stays calm
and so plans perfectly.

The net of heaven is vast, woven so vast
and wide open nothing slips through.

74

In their misery, the people no longer fear death,
so how can you threaten them even with death?

Let the people fear death always,
then if we seize those who follow sinister ways
and put them to death,
no one will dare live such lives.

The Executioner's killing is perennial, it's true.
But to undertake the killing yourself—
that's like trying to carve lumber for a master carpenter.
Try to carve lumber for a master carpenter
and you'll soon have blood on your hands.

75

The people are starving,
and it's only because you leaders feast on taxes
that they're starving.

The people are impossible to rule,
and it's only because you leaders are masters of extenuation
that they're impossible to rule.

The people take death lightly,
and it's only because you leaders crave life's lavish pleasures
that they take death lightly,

they who act without concern for life:
it's a wisdom far beyond treasuring life.

76

People are soft and weak in life,
hard and strong in death.
The ten thousand plants and trees are soft and frail in life,
withered and brittle in death.

Things hard and strong follow death's ways
and things soft and weak follow life's:

so it is that strong armies never overcome
and strong trees always suffer the axe.

Things great and strong dwell below.
Things soft and weak dwell above.

77

The Way of heaven is like a drawn bow
pulling down the high
and raising up the low:

it takes away where there's abundance
and restores where there's want.

The Way of heaven takes away where there's abundance
and restores where there's want,
but the Way of humankind isn't like that:
it takes away where there's want
and gives where there's abundance.

Only a master of the Way
can give abundance to all beneath heaven.
Such a sage acts without presumption
and never dwells on success:

great worth has no need to be seen.

78

Nothing in all beneath heaven is so soft and weak as water.
And yet, for conquering the hard and strong,
nothing succeeds like water.

And nothing can change it:
weak overcoming strong,
soft overcoming hard.
Everything throughout all beneath heaven knows this,
and yet nothing puts it into practice.

That's why the sage said:
*Whoever assumes a nation's disgrace
is called* the sacred leader of a country,
*and whoever assumes a nation's misfortune
is called* the emperor of all beneath heaven.

Words of clarity sound confused.

79

You can resolve great rancor,
but rancor always lingers on.

Understanding the more noble way,
a sage holds the creditor's half of contracts
and yet asks nothing of others.
Those with Integrity tend to such contracts;
those without Integrity tend to the collection of taxes.

The Way of heaven is indifferent,
always abiding with people of nobility.

80

Let nations grow smaller and smaller
and people fewer and fewer,

let weapons become rare
and superfluous,
let people feel death's gravity again
and never wander far from home.
Then boat and carriage will sit unused
and shield and sword lie unnoticed.

Let people knot ropes for notation again
and never need anything more,

let them find pleasure in their food
and beauty in their clothes,
peace in their homes
and joy in their ancestral ways.

Then people in neighboring nations will look across to each other,
their chickens and dogs calling back and forth,

and yet they'll grow old and die
without bothering to exchange visits.

81

Sincere words are never beautiful
and beautiful words never sincere.
The noble are never eloquent
and the eloquent never noble.
The knowing are never learned
and the learned never knowing.

A sage never hoards:

the more you do for others
the more plenty is yours,
and the more you give to others
the more abundance is yours.

The Way of heaven is to profit without causing harm,
and the Way of a sage to act without contending.

Notes

The *Tao Te Ching* is traditionally divided into two parts: *Tao Ching* (*The Classic of Way*) and *Te Ching* (*The Classic of Integrity*).

Notes are keyed to chapter numbers.

1   **way:** See Key Terms: *Tao*.
   heaven and earth: For heaven, see Key Terms: *T'ien*. Given Lao Tzu's cosmology, heaven and earth might be conceived as "creative force and created objects."
   Lines 5-6 are an especially noteworthy instance of the rich linguistic ambiguity in ancient Chinese and how well Lao Tzu exploits that potential, for it is often read:

>   Free of perennial desire, you see mystery,
>   and full of perennial desire, you see appearance.

   Absence: See Key Terms: *Wu*.
   Presence: See Key Terms: *Yu*.
   dark-enigma: See Key Terms: *Hsüan*.

2   **nothing's own doing:** See Key Terms: *Wu-wei*.

4   **gods and creators:** Specifically: Shang Ti, supreme deity of the Shang Dynasty. See Introduction p. 17 f.

5   **Inhumane:** See note to chapter 8 below.
   straw dogs: Offerings used during sacrifices (and then discarded).

8   **Humanity:** Humanity *(jen)* is the touchstone of Confucian virtue. Simply stated, it means to act with a selfless and reverent concern for the well-being of others. See the *Analects*, pp. 231 and 379.

10 **spirit . . . drifting away:** It was generally believed that a person's spirit drifts away after death.
   ch'i: See Key Terms: *Ch'i*.
   mirror: Mind or pure awareness.
   heaven's gate: Gateway through which the ten thousand things come into being and return to nothing.
   Integrity: See Key Terms: *Te*.

17 **stand sincere by your words:** Typically translated as "sincerity" or "trust," *hsin* sometimes appears in this translation as "standing by words" to reflect its full philosophical dimensions and the etymology so apparent visually

in the two elements of its graph, where a person is shown beside words (sounds coming out of a mouth): 信

occurrence appearing of itself: See Key Terms: *Tzu-jan*.

38   **Duty:** In Confucian social philosophy, Duty *(yi)* is the ability to apply the prescriptions of Ritual (see below) in specific situations. See the *Analects*, p. 379.

Ritual: In Confucian social philosophy, Ritual *(li)* is the sacred web of social responsibilities that bind a society together. See the *Analects*, pp. 224 ff. & 379.

60   **Govern . . . fish:** That is: as if it were an insignificant matter, and with the least handling possible.

spirits . . . ghosts: It was generally believed that a person's "spirit" normally thins away shortly after death. But if a person dies an unnatural death, the "spirit" was thought to become an enduring "ghost" which haunts the living world causing trouble.

69   **treasures:** See chapter 67.

74   **the Executioner:** Variously identified as *tzu-jan*, heaven, the Way of heaven, or Way itself.

79   **half of contracts:** Signed contracts were torn in half and each party kept one side as proof of the agreement.

Key Terms
An Outline of Lao Tzu's Thought

Yu: 有 Presence (Being)

The empirical universe, which has its origin in *wu* (Absence: see the following entry). The ancients described Presence as the ten thousand living and nonliving things in constant transformation. It might more literally be translated "within form."

See also: Introduction p. 20 ff.

Ref: 1.6, 2.5, 40.3-4.

Wu: 無 Absence (Nonbeing)

The generative tissue from which the ever-changing realm of Presence perpetually arises. This tissue is the ontological substrate infused mysteriously with a generative energy. Although made of the same stuff as Presence, it is "Absence" because it has no particular form. But because of its generative nature, it shapes itself into the individual forms we know, the ten thousand things, then reshapes itself into other forms in the constant process of change. In fact, a more literal translation of wu might be "without form," in contrast to "within form" for *yu*. Absence is known directly in meditation, widely practiced by ancient Chinese poets and intellectuals, where it is experienced as empty consciousness itself, known in Ch'an (Zen) Buddhist terminology as "empty mind" or "no-mind."

See also: Introduction p. 20 f.

Ref: 1.5, 2.5, 40.4.

Tao: 道 Way

As the generative ontological process through which all things arise and pass away, Tao might provisionally be divided into Presence (the ten thousand things of the empirical world in constant transformation) and Absence, the generative source of Presence and its transformations. See also: Introduction pp. 15 and 20 ff.

Ref: *passim*.

Te: 德 Integrity

Integrity to Tao in the sense of "abiding by the Way," or "enacting the Way." Hence, it is Tao's manifestation in the world, especially in a sage master of Tao. This concept is deepened dramatically by *Te's* etymological meaning at the level of pictographic imagery: "heart-sight clarity." See also: Introduction p. 25.

Ref: *passim.*

Tzu-jan: 自然 Occurrence appearing of itself

The ten thousand things unfolding spontaneously from the generative source, each according to its own nature. Hence, tzu-jan might be described as the mechanism or process of Tao in the empirical world. See also: Introduction pp. 23 ff.

Ref: 17.9, 23.1, 25.22, 51.8, 64.27.

Wu-wei: 無為 Nothing's own doing, etc.

Impossible to translate the same way in every instance, *wu-wei* means acting as a spontaneous part of *tzu-jan* rather than with self-conscious intention. Different contexts emphasize different aspects of this rich philosophical concept as Lao Tzu exploits the term's grammatical ambiguity. Literally meaning "not/nothing *(wu)* doing *(wei)*," *wu-wei's* most straightforward translation is simply "doing nothing" in the sense of not interfering with the flawless and self-sufficient unfolding of *tzu-jan*. But this must always be conceived together with its mirror translation: "nothing doing" or "nothing's own doing," in the sense of being no one separate from *tzu-jan* when acting. As *wu-wei* is the movement of *tzu-jan*, when we act according to *wu-wei* we act as the generative source. This opens to the deepest level of this philosophical complex, for *wu-wei* can also be read quite literally as "Absence (wu) doing." Here, *wu-wei* action is action directly from, or indeed *as* the ontological source: Absence burgeoning forth into Presence. This in turn invests the more straightforward translation ("doing nothing") with its fullest dimensions, for "doing nothing" always carries the sense of "enacting nothing/Absence." See also: Introduction pp. 25 ff.

Ref: 2.11, 3.12, 10.8, 37.1, 38.5, 43.3 & 5, 47.8, 48.4-5, 57.15, 63.1, 64.15.

TAO TE CHING

Ch'i: 氣 Ch'i

The universal breath, vital energy, or cosmic life-force. It is the breath-force that pulses through the Cosmos as both matter and energy simultaneously, giving form and life to the ten thousand things and driving their perpetual transformations. And so it is the tissue of which the Cosmos is made. In its originary form, it is primal-*ch'i* (*yüan-ch'i*), which is present in Absence and is perhaps the aspect that makes the primordial emptiness of Absence pregnant with possibility. Primal-*ch'i* is made up of *yin* and *yang* completely intermingled and indistinguishable. Once primal-*ch'i* separates out into *yin* and *yang*, *yang* rose up to become sky and *yin* sunk down to form earth. As the universal breath, *ch'i* is in constant motion, animating all things, and so is a kind of tissue that connects us always to the empty source. As the universal breath, *ch'i* is in constant motion, animating all things, and so is a kind of tissue that connects us always to the empty source. Ref: 10.3, 42.6, 55.15.

T'ien: 天 Heaven

The Chou Dynasty used the impersonal concept of heaven to replace the Shang Dynasty's monotheistic god. Heaven was eventually secularized by the early Taoists, Lao Tzu and Chuang Tzu, for whom it meant natural process: the constant unfolding of things in the cosmological process. For a somewhat different perspective, consider the recurring entity "heaven and earth," which might be conceived as "creative force and created objects." See also: Introduction pp. 18 and 22 f. Ref: *passim*.

Hsüan   玄 Dark-enigma

Dark-enigma came to have a particular philosophic resonance, for it became the name of a neo-Taoist school of philosophy in the third and fourth centuries C.E.: Dark-Enigma Learning, a school which gave Chinese thought a decidedly ontological turn and became central to the synthesis of Taoism and Buddhism into Ch'an Buddhism. Like Lao Tzu, the thinkers of the Dark-Enigma Learning school equated dark-enigma with Absence, the generative ontological tissue from which the ten thousand things spring. Or more properly, it is Way before it is named, before Absence and Presence give birth to one another—that region where consciousness and ontology share their source.

Ref: 1.9-10, 6.2-3, 10.5-6, 15.2, 51.17, 56.9, 65.11-12.

Mu, etc.　母 Mother, etc.

The philosophy of Tao embodies a cosmology rooted in that most primal and wondrous presence: earth's mysterious generative force. This represents a resurgence of the cosmology of late Paleolithic and early Neolithic cultures, where this force was venerated as the Great Mother. She continuously gives birth to all creation, and like natural process which she represents, she also takes life and regenerates it in an unending cycle of life, death, and rebirth. In the *Tao Te Ching*, this awesome generative force appears most explicitly in Lao Tzu's recurring references to the female principle in a variety of manifestations: mother, female, feminine, yielding, source, origin, etc. But in the end, it is everywhere in the *Tao Te Ching*, for it is nothing other than Tao itself. See also: Introduction pp. 14–15 and *passim*.

Ref: 1.3-4, 4.3-4, 6.1-3, 10.9, 14.20, 19.10, 20.29, 21.15-16, 25.6, 28.2, 42.1f, 51.1&9&14, 52.1-6, 59.10, 61.3-4, 70.5.

CHUANG TZU

The Inner Chapters

Introduction

The Chinese spiritual tradition traces its source back to the two founders of ancient Taoism: Lao Tzu, reputed author of the *Tao Te Ching,* and Chuang Tzu. While Lao Tzu relies on a mysterious poetry of dark ambiguities and evocative silences, Chuang Tzu describes the spiritual ecology of ancient China in a comprehensive way by plundering the full range of linguistic play: humor, parable, irony, caricature, myth, story, philosophical argument, fable, metaphor, paradox, satire. Chuang Tzu was the first to use many of these techniques in China – but his mastery remains unsurpassed, while the collage effect he creates seems thoroughly modern. And the ecology he describes seems if anything more accurate and vital, even urgent, every day.

Tao originally meant "way," as in "pathway" or "roadway." Confucius used *Tao* in the sense of "the proper societal/ethical Way." Then Lao Tzu and Chuang Tzu recast it as a spiritual concept by transforming it into a kind of ontological Way. For them, Tao is the ontological ground or process (hence, a "Way") from which all things arise, and the Taoist Way is to dwell as a part of that natural process. Chinese culture adopted both of these Ways simultaneously: the Confucian Way has defined the societal realm for Chinese intellectuals throughout the millennia, and the Way of philosophical Taoism has defined the spiritual realm. Eventually, Taoism was supplemented and intensified by Ch'an (Zen) Buddhism, which is a melding of Taoism and Buddhism. Ch'an became widely influential beginning in the T'ang Dynasty (618–907 c.e.), but Taoism remained the defining spiritual Way, for its insight remained vital not only in Taoism itself but also in the essential core of Ch'an practice.

Unlike Lao Tzu, Chuang Tzu probably did exist, although historical evidence for his existence is sparse. There are a few biographical details in the definitive history of his times, but that history was not written until 150 years after his death. Virtually all we know about him comes from tales in the *Chuang Tzu* itself, where he is just another in the book's wild menagerie of characters. Still, given his portrait in the *Chuang Tzu,* the claim that he authored at least some of the book that bears his name seems credible enough. But in the end, it is a nebulous Chuang Tzu indeed that has come down to us through the centuries of Chinese culture.

The *Chuang Tzu* text is made up of three sections: Inner Chapters, Outer Chapters, and Miscellaneous Chapters. The Inner Chapters, which make up less than a quarter of the entire text, are generally accepted as the authentic voice of Chuang Tzu himself. The remainder of *Chuang Tzu* is a miscellany: fragmentary work cobbled together from different eras and authors, arranged and rearranged by editors over the course of six centuries – some of it by Chuang Tzu, but much of it clearly not. The Inner Chapters exhibit a virtuosity, coherence, and architecture that set them apart from the rest of the text, and all of Chuang Tzu's major ideas find their most compelling expression there.

Chuang Tzu most likely lived from about 365 to 290 B.C.E., during the Warring States period (403–221 B.C.E.), a time when the Chou Dynasty had splintered into a number of autonomous states that were constantly at war with one another. The old social order had collapsed, and the Chinese were struggling to create a new one. Although this was one of the most virulent and chaotic periods in Chinese history, it was the golden age of Chinese philosophy, for there were a "Hundred Schools of Thought" trying to envision what this new social order should be like. Beginning with Confucianism, these schools were founded by thinkers who wandered the country with their disciples, teaching and trying to convince the various rulers to put their ideas into practice. For centuries, these schools were engaged in a constant debate among themselves, and Chuang Tzu was clearly a part of this ongoing dispute: witness the way Confucius (551–479 B.C.E.) is conveniently transformed in the *Chuang Tzu,* where he appears as a Confucian simpleton at times and a Taoist sage at other times. But virtually all of the philosophers in these "Hundred Schools" were concerned with social philosophy, which made Chuang Tzu very much the odd man out. Not only was he as

CHUANG TZU

much a poet as a philosopher, but his Way represented a wholesale re-jection of the human-centered approach that the others employed.

Mysterious, vast, complex, diverse, slow-moving – Chuang Tzu's spiritual ecology is a difficult idea. But Chuang Tzu is philosopher enough to describe this idea clearly, and poet enough to bring it alive, his virtuosic antics letting us experience it directly. Chuang Tzu's proposi-tions seem to be in constant transformation, for he deploys words and concepts only to free us of words and concepts. Still, it is worthwhile to orient ourselves, however provisionally, and perhaps the best place to begin is the remarkable convergence of meanings that Chuang Tzu employs under the name *heaven (t'ien)*, meanings that thereafter defined the term's range for Chinese culture.

Heaven's most primitive meaning is "sky." By extension, it also comes to mean "transcendence," for our most primal sense of transcen-dence may be the simple act of looking up into the sky. And then, by association with the idea of transcendence and that which is beyond us, *heaven* also comes to mean "fate" or "destiny." But this unsurpris-ing complex of ideas is transformed completely when Chuang Tzu adds "nature" or "natural process" to the weave of meaning, for then heaven becomes earth, and earth heaven. Earth's natural process is itself both our fate in life and our transcendence, for self is but a fleeting form taken on by earth's process of change – born out of it, and returned to it in death. Or more precisely, never *out of it:* totally unborn. Our truest self, being unborn, is all and none of earth's fleeting forms simultane-ously. It is this unborn perspective that resolves all of the apparent con-tradiction and paradox that Chuang Tzu throws at us. Being unborn, "the sage illuminates all in the light of heaven."

Because of the abounding ambiguity of ancient Chinese texts, commentaries are incorporated into the text, and they become the lens through which the text is read. The definitive *Chuang Tzu* commentary was written by Kuo Hsiang (d. 312 c.e.), who also compiled the final form of the text. This commentary became one of the major works in a school of philosophy known as Dark-Enigma Learning, which gave Chinese thought a decidedly ontological turn and became central to the synthesis of Taoism and Buddhism into Ch'an Buddhism. Kuo Hsiang identified heaven with *tzu-jan*, a concept from Lao Tzu and Chuang Tzu that was central to Kuo Hsiang's philosophy and his elucidation of Chuang Tzu's thought. Literally, the term means "self-so" or "the of-itself" or "being such of itself" – hence, "spontaneous" or "natural." But a more descriptive translation of *tzu-jan* might be "occurrence appearing of itself," for it is meant to describe the ten thousand things unfolding spontaneously, each according to its own nature, independent and self-sufficient, each dying and returning to the process of change, only to reappear in another self-generating form. Hence "fate" and "destiny" lose their transcendental reach. To say that one's life is a matter of destiny is not to say that it is somehow predestined, but that it is part of heaven, part of *tzu-jan*'s inevitable unfolding.

These ideas are remarkably consistent with modern ecological science, which describes all forms of life (human included) as fleeting and interpenetrating parts of a single organic system. But the scientific formulations of modern science would be of limited use to Chuang Tzu, for the essence of a sage is the actual life of the unborn self. And, as Kuo Hsiang's commentary stresses, to live this life, to live as an organic part of *tzu-jan*, means practicing *wu-wei* (literally: "nothing doing"), or selfless action:

> the ten thousand things can only take *tzu-jan* as their
> source. It is selfless action *(wu-wei)* that makes *tzu-jan*
> *tzu-jan*. . . . If you act selflessly *(wu-wei)*, you're self-
> reliant, and so act as source.

Chuang Tzu's poetic techniques are thus not only entertaining but essential, as his intent is to startle and amaze us into the immediate experience of that life. Indeed, this strategy remained at the heart of the tradition when Ch'an arose many centuries later, for Chinese spirituality is a matter of direct experience rather than belief or theological speculation. It is also why poetry and the other arts tended to emphasize immediate experience and were considered nothing less than a form of spiritual practice.

Rather than the sustained argument of an imperial mind ordering the world around it, Chuang Tzu's voice is fragmentary and provisional. And those fragments have been worn away, broken up, scattered, and reassembled with other material over the centuries. So to read the Chuang Tzu is to witness Chuang Tzu's selflessness in the book's very form. Meanwhile, in the language itself, selflessness takes the form of a remarkable openness and ambiguity. Ancient Chinese always leaves a great deal unstated, but Chuang Tzu intentionally exploited this characteristic so thoroughly that the process of reading forces the reader to participate in the emptiness of no-mind at the boundaries of its true, speechless form.

To step across that boundary and dwell in the emptiness of no-mind is to plumb *wu-wei* and *tzu-jan,* and the most immediate way to do this is meditation. Such meditation became the primary emphasis of Ch'an practice. Indeed, *Ch'an* literally means "meditation." The practice of meditation is not discussed extensively in the early Taoist literature, as it is in the Ch'an literature. But it is clear that such meditation was practiced, for the *Tao Te Ching* and *Chuang Tzu* both contain a number of passages that allude to the meditative experience. And in this exchange between Confucius and his favorite disciple, Yen Hui, Chuang Tzu offers a step-by-step introduction:

> "May I ask about the mind's fast?"
>
> "Center your attention," began Confucius. "Stop listening with your ears and listen with your mind. Then stop listening with your mind and listen with your primal spirit. Hearing is limited to the ear. Mind is limited to tallying things up. But the primal spirit's empty: it's simply that which awaits things. Way is emptiness merged, and emptiness is the mind's fast."
>
> "Before I begin my practice," said Yen Hui, "I am truly Yen Hui. But once I'm in the midst of my practice, I've never even begun to be Yen Hui. Can this be called emptiness?"
>
> "Yes, that's it exactly," replied Confucius. (IV.1)

Ultimately, the emptiness to which meditation returns us is nothing other than Kuo Hsiang's Dark-Enigma, that generative ontological tissue from which the ten thousand things spring. Dwelling there,

> no-mind inhabits the mystery of things. . . . This is the
> importance of being at the hinge of Way: There you
> can know Dark-Enigma's extent. There your move-
> ments range free.

Amazingly, in the last fragment of the Inner Chapters, Chuang Tzu manages to make even this dark mystery into a character: Primal-Dark. In that fable, a kind of anti–creation myth, Primal-Dark dies when Thunder-Bolt tries to make her human. As this ontological ground precedes the ten thousand things, it therefore precedes all differentiation. While it can be experienced directly as our truest self, this ground exists prior to all human terms and concepts. Hence, the most profound layer of Chuang Tzu's ecology remains beyond words, although it is a tangible presence in the pregnant emptiness filling his language and perhaps all classical Chinese writing. And Chuang Tzu's terminology naturally proliferates when he attempts to describe this ontological ground directly: it transcends heaven; it is where the ten thousand things are one; it is the unknowable, the ancestral source, the Mighty Mudball, the boundless, the Ancestral-Not-Yet-Arising, Tranquil-Turmoil, Primal-Dark, and finally, Way.

Or, returning to the beginning, to the first two words in *Chuang Tzu* – it is Northern Darkness, the sea in which dwells Bright-Posterity, the wondrous fish that rises in a mighty storm, transformed into the vast Two-Moon bird, and flies to Southern Darkness. So it is that Chuang Tzu's world of words begins. If we clear away the words all the way back to the beginning, to the *Bright-Posterity* fish and *Northern Darkness,* we are left looking into whatever it is *Northern Darkness* names, as in Chou Ch'en's great painting *Northern Darkness* (details of which appear on the cover, upper center, and throughout this text). In the Miscellaneous Chapters, Chuang Tzu has a parable about this, too – a kind of invitation:

The point of a fish trap is the fish: once you've got the fish, you can forget the trap. The point of a rabbit snare is the rabbit: once you've got the rabbit, you can forget the snare. And the point of a word is the idea: once you've got the idea, you can forget the word.

How can I find someone who's forgotten words, so we can have a few words together?

I Wandering Boundless and Free

1   In Northern Darkness there lives a fish called Bright-Posterity. This Bright-Posterity is so huge that it stretches who knows how many thousand miles. When it changes into a bird, it's called Two-Moon. This Two-Moon has a back spreading who knows how many thousand miles, and when it thunders up into flight its wings are like clouds hung clear across the sky. It churns up the sea and sets out on its migration to Southern Darkness, which is the Lake of Heaven.[1]

2   Among the strange wonders recorded in *The Book of Laughter and Harmony*, it says: "Setting out for Southern Darkness, Two-Moon beats the water for three thousand miles, whirling up vast gale storms, then climbs ninety thousand miles on the wind. It flies on and on for six months, and then it rests."

Heat waves shimmering, dust and ash and everything alive all buffeted among one another in air – and then it rests.

3   Such azure blue heavens. . . . Are they really blue, or is it that they stretch away without end? Looking down from up there, Two-Moon sees the same thing. It's like piling up water: if the water isn't deep, it can't support large boats. Pour a cup of water into a hollow on the floor, and a mustard seed makes a fine boat. But if you put the cup in, it's stuck fast. The water's shallow, so the boat's large. And piling up wind: if it isn't deep, it can't support huge wings. So it is that Two-Moon needs ninety thousand miles of wind beneath it. That's when it climbs the wind until its back lifts the blue heavens. That's when it turns south and nothing can stop it.

4   The cicada and fledgling dove laugh at it, saying: "If we put our minds to it, we can fly across to the elm or sandalwood. But some-times we don't make it, and we just end up fluttering around on the ground.

What good's all this talk about *ninety thousand miles heading south?*"

5   If you go out into the country for the day, you can carry three meals and your belly's still full when you come home. But if you're going a hundred miles, you need to hull enough grain to stay the night. And if you're going a thousand miles, you'll have to gather enough grain to last three months. So what do those two little creatures know?

6   A little wisdom can't equal great wisdom. A short life can't equal great age. How do I know it's like this? Dawn mushrooms never know the young and old moon. Summer cicadas never know spring and autumn. This is what a short life means. South of Ch'u is a tree named Dark-Spirit. For it, spring lasts five hundred years and autumn lasts another five hundred years. And for the huge *ch'un* tree of ancient times, spring lasts eight thousand years and autumn lasts another eight thousand years. This is what great age means.

But then, these days I keep hearing about Ancestor Drum-Light living seven hundred years. Everyone wants to be like him – and that's pretty sad too, isn't it?

7   Among the questions Emperor T'ang asked of Date-Bramble, it is the same: "Up beyond the barren northlands lies a sea of darkness, which is the Lake of Heaven. In it there lives a fish thousands of miles across and who knows how many miles long. It is called Bright-Posterity. And a bird called Two-Moon also lives there – its back like Exalt Mountain, its wings like clouds hung clear across the sky. Whirling up vast gale storms, it traces ram's-horn spirals ninety thousand miles high, cutting through cloud and mist until its back lifts the blue heavens. Then it turns south and sets out for Southern Darkness."

                                         CHUANG TZU

8   A quail laughs and says: "It's setting out for where? I bound into flight, and before I've soared a dozen yards I'm fluttering around in the brush again. Surely that's the limit of flight. It's setting out for where?"

9   Such is the dispute between large and small.

Men who have wisdom fine enough to take high office, conduct noble enough to inspire the villages, virtue deep enough to govern, and who are therefore called to rule the country – they see themselves the way those little birds see themselves. Master Bright-Beauty just laughed at them. For even if the whole world praised him, he'd be no more heartened; and even if the whole world denounced him, he'd be no more downcast. He was clear about the difference between inner and outer, and he disputed the boundary between splendor and ruin. But that was all. Such men are rare in the world, but even he wasn't rooted deep and perfected.

10   Lieh Tzu[2] rode the wind and set out, boundless and clear, returning after only fifteen days. To be so blessed is rare – and yet however free that wind made him, he still depended on something. But if you mount the source of heaven and earth and the ten thousand changes, if you ride the six seasons of *ch'i*[3] in their endless dispute – then you travel the inexhaustible, depending on nothing at all. Hence the saying: *The realized remain selfless. The sacred remain meritless. The enlightened remain nameless.*

11   Yao[4] was emperor of all beneath heaven. Wanting to leave his world to Pledged-Origin, he said, "Once the sun and moon have risen, candles don't make the light any brighter, so why keep them burning? And once the rains have come, watering doesn't make the fields any

wetter, so why bother? With you here, a master rooted deep, all beneath heaven is in order; and yet I go on ruling things, knowing myself to be useless. Please, this world should be yours."

"A master brings order to the world because the world has long since been in order," replied Pledged-Origin. "If I took over as master, wouldn't it be for a mere name? And since a name is only the guest of reality, wouldn't I be a mere guest? A sparrow nesting in deep forests needs but a single branch. A mole drinking at the river needs but a single bellyful. Go home and rule through idleness. I have no use for the world. At a funeral, even if the cook can't keep the kitchen in order, the kid posing as the corpse won't go bounding over tables of wine and meat to take over."

12   Bearing-Me-Up said to Elders-Gather, "I've listened to the talk pour out of Convergence Crazy-Cart, talk vast and never grounded, setting out and never looking back. It's terrifying: talk that stretches out like the Milky Way and never ends. Distant and unreal as palaces among wild footpaths – there's nothing of people's lives in it."

"So what did he say?" asked Elders-Gather.

"He said: *In the distant Maiden-Arrow Mountains there lives a sage. His skin is like snow and ice, and yet he's as gentle as a young girl. He never eats the five grains, only breathes wind and drinks dew. Ascending cloud and mist, he rides flying dragons and wanders out beyond the four seas. When his spirit is distilled pure as ice, things never get sick and the harvests are plentiful.*[5] It seemed insane to me, and beyond all belief."

"Of course!" replied Elders-Gather. "The blind have no use for the eloquence of beauty and grace, and the deaf have no use for the music of bells and drums. And do you think only the body can be blind and deaf? The mind too suffers from such things. Crazy-Cart's words are like a beautiful girl unnoticed by lovers. A man of such Integrity[6] ranges far and wide through the ten thousand things, mingling with them into one vast embrace of change. So even in a nation on the verge of chaos, why should he wear himself ragged trying to save the world? Nothing can harm such a man. A great flood may reach into heaven, but it cannot drown him. A great heat wave may scorch mountains and valleys, melting rock and metal, but it cannot burn him. Truly, from the chaff and dust of such a man, you could coin the finest of emperors, even a Yao or Shun.⁷ Why should he make the world of things his concern?"

13   Someone in Sung had some marvelous hats to sell, so he took them to Yüeh. But the Yüeh tribes crop their hair short and tattoo their bodies: they had no use for marvelous hats.

14   Emperor Yao brought order to people everywhere under heaven, and peace to government everywhere between the four seas. He went to see the four masters in the distant Maiden-Arrow Mountains, and when he returned north of the Split-Water River deep in thought, he found that he'd given up all beneath heaven in those mountains.

15   "The king of Wei gave me some seeds from a huge gourd," said Hui Tzu⁸ to Chuang Tzu. "I planted them and soon had gourds large enough to hold five bushels. I tried filling one with ricewater, but then it was so heavy I couldn't lift it. I split it in two and tried using it as a ladle, but there's nothing big enough to dip such a gourd into. It isn't that the gourd wasn't utterly huge, but I could see it was useless, so I smashed it to pieces."

"You're awfully stupid about the uses of immensity," replied Chuang Tzu. "A family in Sung possessed a wonderful salve that kept hands from getting chapped. And so, for generation after generation the family had made a business of washing and bleaching fine silk. Eventually a passing traveler heard of this and offered to buy the formula for a hundred in gold. The family gathered to consider the offer, and decided: *We've been bleaching silk for generations, and never made more than a few pieces of gold. But now, in a single morning, we can trade our secret for a hundred in gold. Let's give it to him.*

"The traveler bought the formula and later presented it to the king of Wu. There was trouble with Yüeh, so the pleased king made him a general. That winter, the man gave his salve to the soldiers so they could fight Yüeh's navy on the cold waters. In this way, Wu won a great victory. So the king gave this man land and a noble title. The power to cure chapped hands was the same, but it was used differently: one used it to become a noble, and the other never got beyond bleaching silk.

"Now, you had a five-bushel gourd. Why didn't you make it into a huge tub and go drifting across rivers and lakes? Instead, you mourn that there's nothing big enough to dip your gourd into. No doubt about it – there's still a lot of bramble in that mind of yours."

16   "I have a huge tree," said Hui Tzu to Chuang Tzu, "the kind people call *shu*. Its huge trunk is so gnarled and knotted that no measuring string can gauge it, and its branches are so bent and twisted they defy compass and square. It stands right beside the road, and still carpenters never notice it. These words of yours, so vast and useless – everyone ignores them the same way."

"Haven't you ever seen a wildcat or a weasel?" replied Chuang Tzu. "It crouches low, hiding, waiting. Suddenly it springs up and bounds east and west, uphill and down, centering its trap, and finally it makes the kill there in its net. Then there's the yak: huge as clouds hung clear across the sky. It's mastered immensity, but it can't even catch a mouse. Now you've got this huge tree, and you agonize over how useless it is. Why not plant it in a village where there's nothing at all, a land where emptiness stretches away forever? Then you could be nothing's own doing drifting lazily beside it, roam boundless and free as you doze in its shade. It won't die young from the axe. Nothing will harm it. If you have no use, you have no grief."

II   A Little Talk

About Evening Things Out

1   Leaning on his desk, Adept Piebald sat gazing into the sky, breath shallow and face blank, as if he were lost to himself. Adept Adrift Looking-Realized stood before him, waiting. Finally he said, "How is it possible? How can you make your body withered wood and your heart dead ash? The person leaning on your desk today isn't the person who was leaning on it yesterday."

"That's a fine question, Adrift," replied Adept Piebald. "Just then I'd lost myself completely. Do you understand such things? Perhaps you've heard the music of humans, but you haven't heard the music of earth. Or if you've heard the music of earth, you haven't heard the music of heaven."

"Could I ask you to explain this for me?" asked Adrift.

"This Mighty Mudball of a world spews out breath, and that breath is called wind," began Adept Piebald. "Everything is fine so long as it's still. But when it blows, the ten thousand holes cry and moan. Haven't you heard them wailing on and on? In the awesome beauty of mountain forests, it's all huge trees a hundred feet around, and they're full of wailing hollows and holes – like noses, like mouths, like ears, like posts and beams, like cups and bowls, like empty ditches and puddles: water-splashers, arrow-whistlers, howlers, gaspers, callers, screamers, laughers, warblers – leaders singing out *yuuu!* and followers answering *yeee!* When the wind's light, the harmony's gentle; but when the storm wails, it's a mighty chorus. And then, once the fierce wind has passed through, the holes are all empty again. Haven't you seen felicity and depravity thrashing and flailing together?"

"So the music of earth means all those holes singing together," said Adept Adrift, "and the music of humans means bamboo pipes singing. Could I ask you to explain the music of heaven for me?"

"Sounding the ten thousand things differently, so each becomes itself according to itself alone – who could make such music?"

2   Great understanding is broad and unhurried;
      small understanding is cramped and busy.

      Great words are bright and open;
      small words are chit and chat.

3   When we sleep, our spirits roam. When we wake, we open
to the world again. Day after day, all that we touch entangles us, and the
mind struggles in that net: vast and calm, deep and subtle.

      Small fear is fever and worry;
      great fear is vast and calm.

4   We set out like ingenious machines declaring *yes this* and
no that. Or we hold fast like oath-bound warriors defending victory.
      We can say that to fade away day by day is to die like autumn into
winter. But we're drowning, and nothing we do can bring any of it back.
We can say this drain is backed up in old age, full and content, but a
mind near death cannot recover that autumn blaze.
      Joy and anger, sorrow and delight, hope and regret, doubt and ardor,
diffidence and abandon, candor and reserve: it's all music rising out of
emptiness, mushrooms appearing out of mist. Day and night come and
go, but who knows where it all begins? It is! It just is! If you understand
this day in and day out, you inhabit the very source of it all.

5   No other and no self, no self and no distinctions – that's
almost it. But I don't know what makes it this way. Something true seems
to govern, but I can't find the least trace of it. It acts, nothing could be
more apparent, but we never see its form. It has a nature, but no form.

6   The hundred joints, the nine holes, the six organs – they just came together in this body's life. So which am I closest to? All of them? Or is one more me than the others? But they're all servants, nothing more, and servants cannot govern themselves. And how could they take turns being ruler and servant? There's something true that rules. If we go looking for its nature, there's nothing to find. But that doesn't make its truth any more perfect, or any more ruined.

7   Once we happen into the form of this body, we cannot forget it. And so it is that we wait out the end. Grappling and tangling with things, we rush headlong toward the end, and there's no stopping it. It's sad, isn't it? We slave our lives away and never get anywhere, work ourselves ragged and never find our way home. How could it be anything but sorrow? People can talk about never dying, but what good is that? This form we have soon becomes others, and the mind vanishes with it. How could it be called anything but great sorrow? Life is total confusion. Or is it that I'm the only one who's confused?

8   If you follow the realized mind you've happened into, making it your teacher, how could you be without a teacher? You don't need to understand the realm of change: when mind turns to itself, you've found your teacher. Even a numbskull has mind for a teacher. Not to realize yourself in mind, and to insist on *yes this* and *no that* – it's like leaving for Yüeh when you've already arrived there. It's like believing that what isn't is. What isn't is – even that great sage-emperor Yü[1] couldn't understand such things, so how could someone like me?

9   The spoken isn't just bits of wind. In the spoken, something is spoken. But what it is never stays fixed and constant. So is something spoken, or has nothing ever been spoken? People think

CHUANG TZU

we're different from baby birds cheeping, but are we saying any more than they are?

How could Way be so hidden that there's true and false? How could the spoken be so hidden that there's *yes this* and *no that*? How could Way leave and exist no more? How could the spoken exist and be insufficient? These days, Way is hidden in small realizations and the spoken is hidden in florid extravagance, so we have the philosophies of Confucius and Mo Tzu[3] declaring *yes this* and *no that*. They each affirm what the other denies, deny what the other affirms. If you want to affirm all that they deny and deny all that they affirm, you can't beat illumination.

10   There's nothing anywhere which is not *that*, and nothing which is not *this*. If you rely on *that*, you cannot see. But if you rely on understanding, you can know. And so when I say *"that* arises out of *this,* and *this* exists because of *that,"* I'm describing the way *that* and *this* are born of each other. Life is born of death, and death of life. In sufficiency is insufficiency, in insufficiency sufficiency. There is *no that* because of *yes this,* and *yes this* because of *no that.* But this is not the sage's way: the sage illuminates all in the light of heaven. Such is the sage's *yes this.*

This is *that,* and *that* is *this. That* makes *yes this* and *no that* the same, and *this* makes *yes this* and *no that* the same. So is there a *that* and a *this*? Or is there not a *that* and a *this*? Where *that* and *this* cease to be opposites, you'll find the hinge of Way. Keep that hinge at the center of things, and your movements are inexhaustible. Then *yes this* is whole and inexhaustible, and *no that* is whole and inexhaustible. And so the saying: *You can't beat illumination.*

11   Instead of using a finger to demonstrate how a finger is no-finger, use no-finger to demonstrate how a finger is no-finger. Instead of using a horse to demonstrate how a horse is no-horse, use no-horse

to show how a horse is no-horse. All heaven and earth is one finger, and the ten thousand things are all one horse.

12   Sufficient because *sufficient*. Insufficient because *insufficient*. Traveling the Way makes it Way. Naming things makes them real. Why real? Real because *real*. Why nonreal? Nonreal because *nonreal*. So the real is originally there in things, and the sufficient is originally there in things. There's nothing that is not real, and nothing that is not sufficient.

Hence, the blade of grass and the pillar, the leper and the ravishing West-Ease, the noble, the sniveling, the disingenuous, the strange – in Way they all move as one and the same. In difference is the whole; in wholeness is the broken. Once they are neither whole nor broken, all things move freely as one and the same again.

Only one who has seen through things understands *moving freely as one and the same*. In this way, rather than relying on your own distinctions, you dwell in the ordinary. To be ordinary is to be self-reliant; to be self-reliant is to move freely; and to move freely is to arrive. That's almost it, because to arrive is to be complete. But to be complete without understanding how – that is called Way.

13   To wear yourself out illuminating the unity of all things without realizing that they're the same – this is called *three in the morning*. Why *three in the morning*? There was once a monkey trainer who said at feeding time, "You get three in the morning and four in the evening." The monkeys got very angry, so he said, "Okay, I'll give you four in the morning and three in the evening." At this, the monkeys were happy again. Nothing was lost in either name or reality, but they were angry one way and pleased the other. This is why the sage brings *yes this* and *no that* together and rests in heaven the equalizer. This is called taking two paths at once.

14   The ancients possessed a deep understanding. How deep? A knowing before anything exists – it was that deep, that complete. Such understanding lacks nothing. Later on, there was knowing things before boundaries defined them. Still later, there was knowing boundaries before *yes this* and *no that*. When preferences like *yes this* and *no that* appear, Way is tainted. Way is tainted, and preference perfected as love.

But do taint and perfection really exist, or do they not? Because taint and perfection exist, Patterns-Luminous played the *ch'in*.[4] Because taint and perfection do not exist, Patterns-Luminous let his music fall silent.

Patterns-Luminous playing his *ch'in*, Maestro Wildlands wielding his walking stick, Hui Tzu thinking beside the *wu-tung* tree – the understanding of these three masters was almost perfect. Because it was so rich, it sustained them into old age. It was only in their methods that they differed from one another. Each used his own method to enlighten people – but people aren't what you enlighten, so it all ended up in the darkness of arcane distinctions and foolish quibbling. Patterns-Luminous had a son who carried on his practice, but even his son failed to reach perfection.

If we say they were perfect, then I'm perfect too. If we say they were not perfect, then I'm not either, nor is anything else. This is why a sage steers by the bright light of confusion and doubt. In this way, rather than relying on your own distinctions, you dwell in the ordinary. This is called illumination.

15   Now, I have something to say about these things. I don't know if it's similar to *this,* or if it's dissimilar. But similar and dissimilar are quite similar in the end, so it can't be much different from *that.* But be that as it may, let me try to say it:

Presence all beginning. Presence not yet beginning to be Presence all beginning. Presence not yet beginning to be a not yet beginning to be Presence all beginning. Presence all Presence. Presence all Absence.

Presence not yet beginning to be Presence all Absence. Presence not yet beginning to be Absence not yet beginning to be Presence all Absence. Then suddenly, Presence all Absence. And when it comes to Presence all Absence, I don't know yet what's Presence and what's Absence.

There now: I've spoken. But I still don't know whether it was Presence spoken or Absence spoken.

16 In all beneath heaven there's nothing bigger than the tip of an autumn hair, and Exalt Mountain is tiny. No one lives longer than a child who dies young, and the seven-hundred-year-old Ancestor Drum-Light died an infant.

I was born together with heaven and earth, so the ten thousand things and I are one and the same. Since we're one and the same, how is this Presence spoken? Since I've called it *one and the same,* how is this Absence spoken? The one and the spoken make two, the two and the one make three. . . . If we keep going on this way, even a mathematician will soon be lost – so what happens when we get to everything else? And if we get to three by going from Absence to Presence, what happens when we go from Presence to Presence?

Absence in motion, you rest in *yes this.*

17 When there's Way, boundaries haven't yet become Present. When there's language, the timeless hasn't yet become Present. Yes this happens – and so Presence gets demarcated. Let me tell you about demarcation: There's left and there's right. There's relationship and there's Duty.[5] There's difference and there's division. There's strife and there's struggle. Call them anything – how about the eight virtues?

A sage inquires into realms beyond time and space, but never talks about them. A sage talks about realms within time and space, but never explains. In the *Spring and Autumn Annals,* where it tells about the ancient emperors, it says the sage explains but never divides. Hence, in difference there's no difference, and in division there's no division. You may ask how this can be. The sage embraces it all. Everyone else divides things, and uses one to reveal the other. Therefore I say: "Those who divide things cannot see."

18   The great Way is not named.
      Great division is not spoken.
      Great Humanity⁶ is not Humanity.
      Great purity is not simplicity.
      Great courage is not contentious.

      The evident Way is not Way.
      Spoken division is not sufficient.
      Timeless Humanity is not complete.
      Perfect purity is not trustworthy.
      Contentious courage is not complete.

Five squares: how could you understand them by rounding them off?
Understanding that abides in the unknowable is realization. Who can understand division that is not spoken or Way that is not named? When you can understand such things – that is called *the treasure-house of heaven*. Pour into it, and it never fills up. Pour from it, and it never empties out. And never understanding where it all comes from – that is called *inward radiance*.

19   In ancient times, Emperor Yao asked Shun: "I want to invade Tsung, K'uai, and Hsü-ao. I sit on my throne facing south and just can't stop thinking about it. Why is this?"

"So what if three rulers and their people scratch out a living among brambles and weeds," replied Shun, "why give it a second thought? In ancient times, when ten suns rose together, the ten thousand things were all ablaze equally. And Integrity can burn so much brighter than suns."

20 　　Gap-Tooth asked Horizon-Imperial, "Do you understand how it is that all things are one and the same?"

"How could I understand that?" replied Horizon-Imperial.

"Do you understand what you cannot understand?"

"How could I understand that?"

"So then, is there no understanding things?"

"And how could I understand that?" replied Horizon-Imperial. "But still, there may be something I can tell you. How do I know that what I say I know is not unknowable? And how do I know that what I say I cannot know is not knowable?

"Now maybe there's something *I* can ask *you*," he continued. "If humans sleep on wet ground, their backs ache and they're half paralyzed. But is that true of a mudsucker? If humans live in trees, they tremble and cling in terror. But is that true of a gibbon? So of these three, which knows the truth about dwelling?

"Humans eat meat. Deer eat grass. Centipedes relish snakes. Owls crave mice. So of these four, which knows the truth about flavors?

"Gibbons mate with gibbons. Deer mingle with deer. Mudsuckers carouse with mudsuckers. Humans consider Lady Feather and Deer-Grace the most beautiful of women. But if fish saw them, they'd head for deep water. If birds saw them, they'd scatter into azure depths. If deer saw them, they'd go bounding away. So of these four, which knows the truth about beauty for all beneath heaven?

"Doctrines of Humanity and Duty, paths of *yes this* and *no that* – the way I see it, they're all hopelessly snarled and confused. How could I understand their differences?"

"If you can't understand the beneficial and the harmful," asked Gap-Tooth, "then are such things also beyond the understanding of those who have reached realization?"

"Those who are realized are spiritual beings," replied Horizon-Imperial. "Ponds and lakes could burn, but they'd feel no heat. Streams and rivers could freeze, but they'd feel no cold. Fierce lightning could shatter mountains and gale storms churn up the sea, but they'd feel no fright. Mounting cloud and sky to ride sun and moon, they wander beyond the four seas. Even life and death change nothing for them, so why should doctrines of benefit and harm concern them?"

21 Master Timid-Magpie inquired of Master Noble-Tree: "I have heard from Confucius that a sage pays no attention to the concerns of this world, doesn't chase after profit and doesn't avoid harm, doesn't search for happiness and doesn't follow Way, says something when saying nothing, says nothing when saying something, wanders in realms beyond the tawdry dust of this world. Confucius considers such talk vague and reckless, but I hear the mysterious workings of Way in his description. What do you think of it, master?"

"Even the Yellow Emperor⁷ would be perplexed at hearing such things," began Master Noble-Tree, "so how could Confucius understand? As for you, you're always jumping ahead to grand conclusions. Seeing an egg, you look for a rooster crowing. Seeing a crossbow, you look for an owl roasting over the fire. Listen – I'll try out a few careless and doubtful words, and you listen careless and doubtful. Okay?

"Neighbor to sun and moon through the passing days and nights, the sage embraces time and space, joins it all together into a single whole, letting confusion range free, all its subjects ennobling one another. People struggle and slave – but the sage, being stupid and thoughtless, bundles ten thousand years into a single purity, letting the ten thousand things be what they are, gathering themselves together in that pure whole.

"How do I know that adoring life is not mere delusion? How do I know that we who despise death are not exiled children who don't know their way home?

"Deer-Grace was the beautiful daughter of a guard on the frontier border at Ai. When she was first captured by the Chin army, her dress was bathed in tears. But then she found herself in the king's palace, sharing his fine bed and savoring imperial food, and pretty soon she wondered why she'd ever cried. So how do I know that the dead don't wonder why they'd ever clung to life?

"You might dream that you're drinking fine wine, then the next morning you're weeping and sobbing. You might dream that you're weeping and sobbing, then the next morning you're out on a rollicking hunt. In the midst of a dream, we can't know it's a dream. In the midst of a dream, we might even interpret the dream. After we're awake, we know it was a dream – but only after a great awakening can we understand that all of this is a great dream. Meanwhile, fools everywhere think they're wide awake. They steal around as if they understood things, calling this a king and that a cowherd. It's incredible!

"Confucius is a dream, and you are a dream. And when I say you're both dreams, I too am a dream. People might call such talk a sad and cryptic ruse. But ten thousand generations from now, we'll meet a great sage who understands these things. And when that happens, it will seem like tomorrow."

22 Suppose you and I have an argument. Suppose you win and I lose. Does that mean you're really right and I'm wrong? Suppose I win and you lose. Does that mean I'm really right and you're wrong? Is one of us right and the other wrong? Are we both right and both wrong? If we can't figure it out ourselves, others must be totally in the dark, so who could we get to settle it? We could get someone who agrees with you, but if they agree with you how could they decide who's right and wrong? We could get someone who agrees with me, but if they agree with me how could they decide? We could get someone who disagrees with both of us, but if they disagree with both of us how could they decide? We could get someone who agrees with both of us, but if they

CHUANG TZU

agree with both of us how could they decide? Not I nor you nor anyone else can know who is right and who wrong. So what do we do? Wait for someone else to come along who can decide?

What is meant by *an accord reaching to the very limits of heaven*? I'd say: Right isn't merely right; so isn't merely so. If right is truly right, then not-right is so far from being right that there's no argument. And if so is truly so, not-so is so far from being so that there's no argument. When voices in transformation wait for each other to decide, it's like waiting for nothing. *An accord reaching to the very limits of heaven*: because it's endless, we live clear through all the years. Forget the years, forget Duty: move in the boundless, and the boundless becomes your home.

23 Penumbra inquired of Umbra: "One minute you're walking, and the next you're standing still. One minute you're sitting, and the next you're getting up. Why don't you take control of your life?"

Umbra replied, "Am I waiting for something else to make me thus and so? Is whatever I wait for waiting for something else again to make it thus and so? What am I waiting for, snake skins and cicada wings? How do we recognize what is thus and so, anyway? And how do we recognize what is not thus and not so?"

24 Long ago, a certain Chuang Tzu dreamt he was a butterfly – a butterfly fluttering here and there on a whim, happy and carefree, knowing nothing of Chuang Tzu. Then all of a sudden he woke to find that he was, beyond all doubt, Chuang Tzu. Who knows if it was Chuang Tzu dreaming a butterfly, or a butterfly dreaming Chuang Tzu? Chuang Tzu and butterfly: clearly there's a difference. This is called *the transformation of things*.

III To Care for This Life

1   Life is made of limits, but understanding is limitless. Using the limited to approach the limitless – that's dangerous. To do this and consider it understanding – that's extremely dangerous.

At your best, don't impress anyone. At your worst, don't offend anyone.

Follow the middle way, the constant and essential. Then you can protect yourself and keep life whole; you can care for your family and live out your years.

2   A cook was cutting up an ox for Wen Hui, the king of Wei. Whenever his hand probed or his shoulder heaved, whenever his foot moved or his knee thrust, the flesh whirred and fell away. The blade flashed and hissed, its rhythm centered and ancient and never faltering, like a rainmaker dancing *Mulberry Grove* or an orchestra playing *Origin Constant and Essential*.

"Unbelievable!" said King Wen Hui. "A skill so perfected – it's unbelievable!"

The cook put down his knife and replied: "Way is what I care about, and Way goes beyond mere skill. When I first began cutting up oxen, I could see nothing but the ox. After three years, I could see more than the ox. And now, I meet the ox in spirit. I've stopped looking with my eyes. When perception and understanding cease, the spirit moves freely. Trusting the principles of heaven, I send the blade slicing through huge crevices, lead it through huge hollows. Keeping my skill constant and essential, I just slip the blade through, never touching ligament or tendon, let alone bone.

"An exceptional cook cuts, and so needs a new knife every year. An ordinary cook chops, and so needs a new knife every month. Now, I've had this knife for nineteen years: it's taken apart thousands of oxen but it's still sharp, still fresh from the grindstone. There's space in a joint, and the blade has no thickness. Having no thickness, its slips right through. There's plenty of room – more than enough for a blade to wander. That's why, after nineteen years, it's still fresh from the grindstone.

"Even so, I often come up against a knotty place where I stop and study the difficulties. Growing timid and cautious, I focus my vision, then work slowly, moving the blade with great delicacy – and suddenly *thomp! thomp!* things come apart, like clumps of dirt falling back to earth. Holding the knife, I stand back and look all around me, utterly content and satisfied. Then I wipe the blade clean and put it away."

"How marvelous!" said King Wen Hui. "I listen to the words of a butcher, and suddenly I've learned how to care for life itself!"

3   W hen he saw the Commander on the Right, Duke Parade-Elegance said in astonishment, "What kind of person is this? Was it heaven that made him so strange, or was it something human?"

"It was heaven, not human," another said. "When we're born, heaven makes each of us different. Our appearance is given to us. He understands this and is satisfied with himself: this is how you can tell it must have been heaven, not human."

4   A marsh pheasant has to walk ten paces for a bite to eat and a hundred for a sip of water. But still it wouldn't want to be tamed and put into a cage. Even treated like a king, it could never be happy and content.

5   W hen Lao Tzu died, Modest-Ease went in to mourn for him. He shouted three times, then left.

A disciple asked, "You were the master's friend, weren't you?"

"Yes."

"Then is it acceptable for you to mourn like that?"

"Yes," replied Modest-Ease. "At first I took that to be him in there. But then I saw that it wasn't him at all. When I went in to mourn, there were parents mourning as if they were mourning their own children.

And there were children mourning as if they were mourning their own mothers. All these people gathered around his teachings – and isn't it because they don't speak when they speak, don't mourn when they mourn? This is to hide from heaven, to turn against the actual and forget that it's all given to us. The ancients called this *the crime of hiding from heaven*. The master came in time with his own season and then followed it away. If you're at peace with such seasons, if you're at home following them, then sorrow and joy can never touch you. The ancients called this *getting free of the gods.*"

6   The firewood we can point to is consumed. That's how the flame passes on. And who knows where it all ends?

IV   The Human Realm

1　W anting permission to make a journey, Yen Hui[1] went to see Confucius.

"Where is it you're going?" asked Confucius.

"I'm going to Wei," was the reply.

"What will you do there?"

"I hear that the Wei king is a reckless and self-indulgent young man. He's careless about ruling his kingdom and blind to his own faults. He's even careless about killing his people, so the dead spread like grasses and weeds, turning his kingdom into marshland. The people have nowhere to turn. I've heard you say *Leave a kingdom that's in order and go to a kingdom that's in disorder.* The sick are many at the doctor's gate. If I can put this into practice, perhaps the kingdom of Wei can begin to heal."

"Marvelous," replied Confucius. "As if there weren't a price to pay for danger.

"Way can't be unraveled. With unraveling comes multiplicity. With multiplicity comes trouble. With trouble comes grief. And once you've come to grief, nothing can save you. In ancient times, sages established Way in themselves first. Only then did they establish it among people. If you aren't sure about Way in yourself, you don't have time to worry about the ways of some tyrant.

"Don't you know what makes people ruin Integrity and flaunt understanding? Scrambling for praise and renown – that's what ruins Integrity. And it's argumentation that flaunts understanding. Clutching at praise and renown, people struggle with one another; and understanding is the instrument of argumentation. Both are sinister instruments, not the sort of thing that perfects conduct.

"Your Integrity may be deep and your sincerity true, but you've never fathomed the human spirit. You may impress people without arguing, but you've never fathomed the human mind. To insist on lecturing a tyrant about Humanity and Duty and codes of conduct – that looks like using his sinister ways to show how wonderful you are. This is called *injuring others.* But whoever you injure will soon repay the injury. That's the danger: he'd pay you back in a big way.

"And besides, if he relishes wisdom and detests folly, do you think he still needs people telling him how to change himself? I wouldn't start making grand declarations if I were you. Kings and dukes always lord it over people: they bicker and quarrel just to prove how clever they are. He'd try to dazzle your eyes, to leave you blank-faced and stammering, an empty form, your mind won over completely. So you see, you'd be using fire to rescue fire, water to rescue water – and we call that *piling plenty on plenty*.

"If you followed his lead, you'd never get anywhere. And you might not always be utterly sincere with him. That's the danger: if he suspected that, he'd put you to death right then and there.

"In ancient times, Chieh executed Border Dragon-Met and Chou executed Prince Close-Concern. Border Dragon-Met, Close-Concern – both of these men cultivated themselves diligently in modest positions. There they could reach down to comfort the people and reach up to oppose the folly of emperors. But the tyrants they served only used this determined self-cultivation to trap them – for they were challenging the praise and renown due to emperors.

"Emperor Yao attacked the kingdoms of Ts'ung-chih and Hsü-ao in ancient times, and Emperor Yü attacked the kingdom of Yu-hu. Ts'ung-chih, Hsü-ao, Yu-hu – in their never-ending search for wealth, the rulers of these kingdoms kept armies constantly on the prowl, so they were finally put to death and their kingdoms devastated.

"Those great seekers after wealth and renown – haven't you heard of them? Even a sage cannot overcome wealth and renown, so how could you?

"Nevertheless, I'm sure you have a plan. Come, tell me about it."

"Conduct dignified and thoughts empty, manner diligent and mind focused," offered Yen Hui. "Won't that work?"

"No, never – that'll never work," replied Confucius. "That tyrant contrives a grand and glorious show, and bright displays are fickle: even commoners know better than to oppose his whims. You can try to gauge his feelings and search out his mind, but Integrity in daily doses won't solve anything, let alone Integrity in one grand treatment. He'll cling fast and never change. He may act like he agrees with you, but in fact he won't give it a second thought. So this method of yours – how could it ever work?"

"All right then," responded Yen Hui, "I'll be forthright and direct, but I'll act compliant. I'll be complete in myself, and yet defer to superiors.

"To be forthright and direct," he continued, "is to be heaven's kindred. To be heaven's kindred is to know that both the Son of Heaven and I are born of heaven. In that case, why should I worry whether people approve or disapprove of what I say? People would excuse me, thinking I'm an innocent child. This is what I mean by *heaven's kindred*.

"To act compliant is to be humankind's kindred. Saluting, kneeling, bowing – such are the Rituals[3] of a ruler's subjects. Everyone acts in this way, so how could I dare act otherwise? If I just do what everyone else does, how can anyone object? This is what I mean by *humankind's kindred*.

"To be complete in myself and yet defer to superiors: that is to be antiquity's kindred. Although my words may reproach and instruct, the substance that might offend him belongs to the ancients, not to me. In this way I can be straightforward and direct, and yet not blamed. This is what I mean by *antiquity's kindred*.

"Won't it work if I do it that way?"

"No, never – that'll never work either," replied Confucius. "So many decrees! You lay down laws, but you don't think things through. Yes, it's true that you'd stop his wrath. But that's all you'd stop. How would you get him to change? You're still making the mind a teacher."

"Then I'm all out of ideas," said Yen Hui finally. "May I ask what your strategy would be?"

"Fasting," replied Confucius. "Let me explain something for you. Using your mind to do things – isn't that too easy? And the easy way rarely accords with bright heaven."

"My house is poor," said Yen Hui. "It's been months since I've tasted wine or meat. Isn't that considered fasting?"

"That's the fasting of ceremony and Ritual," replied Confucius, "not the mind's fast."

"May I ask about the mind's fast?"

"Center your attention," began Confucius. "Stop listening with your ears and listen with your mind. Then stop listening with your mind and listen with your primal spirit. Hearing is limited to the ear. Mind is limited to tallying things up. But the primal spirit's empty: it's simply that which awaits things. Way is emptiness merged, and emptiness is the mind's fast."

"Before I begin my practice," said Yen Hui, "I am truly Yen Hui. But once I'm in the midst of my practice, I've never even begun to be Yen Hui. Can this be called emptiness?"

"Yes, that's it exactly," replied Confucius. "I'll explain it to you. You can enter that tyrant's cage and wander there, but don't let praise and renown affect you. If you're invited in, then sing. If you aren't invited, cease. Where there's no door, there's no risk of harm. Be focused in dwelling, and inhabit what remains beyond you. Then you've nearly made it.

"It's easy to cover your tracks. But to walk without touching ground – that's hard. If you serve humankind, it's easy to be false. If you serve heaven, it's hard to be false. You've heard of using wings to fly, but have you heard of using no-wings to fly? You've heard of using knowing to know, but have you heard of using no-knowing to know?

"Gaze into that cloistered calm, that chamber of emptiness where light is born. To rest in stillness is great good fortune. If we don't rest there, we keep racing around even when we're sitting quietly. Follow sight and sound deep inside, and keep the knowing mind outside. Even ghosts and spirits will come to dwell with you there – so how could humans fail to do the same?

"It's what keeps the ten thousand things in constant transformation. Even ancient Yü and Shun were bound by it. Even the ancient emperors Root-Breath and Deergrass-Ease practiced it throughout their lives. So how could rulers far less majestic than they ever manage without it?"

CHUANG TZU

2   When Adept Heights, duke of She, was sent to Ch'i, he went to see Confucius. "The king is sending me to negotiate matters of great importance," he began. "The Ch'i king will treat me with deep respect, but he'll be in no hurry to follow through. You can't force common people to hurry, so how can you force a king? It scares me!

"There's something you've often told me: *In all matters large and small, things rarely turn out well unless you rely on Way. If you don't succeed, you have trouble with people judging you. If you do succeed, you have trouble with* yin *and* yang *thrown out of balance. To be untroubled whether you succeed or not – only a person of great Integrity can manage that.*

"I eat simply, avoiding elaborate meals so I won't get overheated from the stove. But I just received my commission this morning, and tonight I'm already drinking ice water. I'm burning up inside! I hardly know anything about this mission yet, but I'm already having trouble with *yin* and *yang*. And if I don't succeed, I'll surely have trouble with people. Between the two of them, it's just too much for a minister like me. So I've come to ask your advice."

"In all beneath heaven, there are two great precepts," began Confucius. "One is the inevitable unfurling of things[4] and the other is Duty. That a child loves its parents is in the inevitable unfurling of things: you can't wrest such love from the heart. That a minister serves a king is Duty. Wherever you go, he remains your king. There's nowhere in all heaven and earth you can escape this. These are called the *great precepts*. To be at peace serving your parents wherever you may be – that is filial piety perfected. And to be at peace serving your king whatever it may entail – that is loyalty full and complete.

"If you serve your own mind, joy and sorrow rarely appear. If you know what's beyond your control, if you know it follows the inevitable unfurling of things and you live at peace – that is Integrity perfected. Children and ministers inevitably find that much is beyond them. But if you forget about yourself and always do what circumstances require of you, there's no time to cherish life and despise death. Then you do what you can, and whatever happens is fine.

"Shall I tell you something else that I've heard? In all human affairs, proximity makes trust a matter of experience; but with distance, truth becomes a matter of words. And someone has to transmit these words. But to transmit pleasure and anger in words – that's the most difficult thing in the world. If both sides are pleased, things always sound so much better than they are. And if both sides are angry, things always sound so much worse than they are. But any exaggeration is a lie. When there are lies there is no trust; and when there's no trust whoever transmits the words is in peril. Hence the principle: *Transmit the essence of thoughts, not the inflated language.* Do that and you're bound to succeed.

"Games of skill and cleverness begin in a light mood, but they always end up dark and serious. And if things go far enough, it's nothing but guile. Drinking at ceremonies begins orderly enough, but it always ends up wild and chaotic. And if things go far enough, it's nothing but debauchery. All our human affairs seem to work like this. However sincerely they begin, they end in vile deceit. And however simply they begin, they grow enormously complex before they're over.

"Words are all wind and wave, but putting them into practice is all loss and gain. Wind and wave rise up with ease; loss and gain grow treacherous with ease. Hence, anger begins out of nowhere: clever words and shifty talk.

"Facing death, animals don't care what their cries sound like. Panting furiously, their minds grow fierce and wild. And if you push people far enough, they respond in the most dishonorable ways. They don't realize what they're doing. And if they don't realize what they're doing, who knows where it will all end.

"Hence the principle: *Never violate your mandate; never force a settlement.* Going beyond limits is asking too much. To violate your mandate, to force a settlement – these are dangerous things. A good settlement takes a long time, but a bad settlement is something you'll never make good. So how can you be too careful?

"Just let your mind wander along in the drift of things. Trust yourself to what is beyond you – let it be the nurturing center. Then you've made it. In the midst of all this, is there really any response? Nothing can compare to simply living out the inevitable unfurling of your life. And there's nothing more difficult."

3   W hen he was appointed tutor for the eldest son of Ling, duke of Wei, Veiled-Visage went to ask Sudden Elder-Jade for advice. "This man I am to teach," said Veiled-Visage, "in him, heaven's made Integrity[5] a ruthless thing. If I don't try to guide him, I endanger the nation. If I do try to guide him, I endanger myself. He's wise enough to recognize other people's failings, but not wise enough to recognize his own. What am I going to do?"

"A fine, fine question!" replied Sudden Elder-Jade. "Ever watchful, ever cautious – keep yourself honest and firm. There's nothing like an attentive manner, and nothing like a congenial mind. Still, these two things have their dangers. Though attentive, don't get involved. Though congenial, don't get implicated. If your manner is attentive and you're involved, you'll get turned around and ruined, you'll crumble and fall. If your mind is congenial and you're implicated, you'll get denounced and named, called strange and evil.

"If he's childish, be childish with him. If he's unruly, be unruly with him. If he's reckless, be reckless with him. In this way you can awaken him, you can draw him into a flawless existence.

"Don't you know about the mantis, waving its arms furiously against an oncoming cart? It doesn't know that it can't stop the cart, and that's the noble beauty of its nature. Stay watchful, stay cautious: if you flaunt the noble beauty you've cultivated in yourself, you'll be in danger too.

"And don't you know about the tiger trainer? He never feeds live things to his tigers because making a kill whips them into such a fury. And he never feeds whole things to his tigers because tearing flesh apart also whips them into a fury. He gauges the tiger's appetite and knows its fierce mind. Although the tiger is altogether different from the human, it treats you gently if you obey its nature. But if you ignore its nature, it can kill you.

"A lover of horses once collected their shit in fine baskets, their piss in rare clamshells. But when a horsefly landed on his horse and he slapped it at the wrong moment – the startled horse broke its bit, then shattered the man's head and crushed his chest. He was trying to be thorough, but his love killed him in the end. So how can you be too careful?"

4   On his way to Ch'i, a master carpenter named Riprap came to Bent-Shaft Village. At the village shrine, he saw a chestnut oak so huge thousands of oxen could gather in its shade. It measured a hundred spans around, and in height it rivaled mountains. It rose eighty feet before the branches began, and dozens of them were so large you could make them into boats. People came in droves to gaze at this tree. It was like a fair.

The carpenter didn't stop; he just walked past with hardly a glance at the great oak. But his apprentice gazed and gazed. Once he'd caught up with Riprap, he said: "Since I first took up the axe in your service, master, I've never seen timber so marvelous, so full of potential. But you didn't even bother to look at it: you just walked right past without even pausing. Why?"

"No more!" shouted Riprap. "Not another word about that tree! It's worthless wood. If you made a boat from it, the boat would sink. If you made a coffin from it, the coffin would rot in no time. If you made tools from it, the tools would break in no time. If you made doors and gates from it, they'd sweat sticky sap. If you made pillars from it, they'd soon be full of termites. That tree has no potential whatsoever. It's useless: you can't make anything with it. How do you think it's lived so long?"

Eventually, carpenter Riprap returned home. There the shrine oak appeared to him in a dream, saying: "What were you comparing me to? Trees with beautiful, fine-grained wood? Fruit trees – hawthorn, pear, orange, citron? Once their fruit is ripe, they're picked clean, ransacked and plundered. Their large branches are broken down; their small limbs are scattered. It makes their lives miserable. And instead of living out the years heaven gave them, they die halfway along their journey. All that abuse of the world – they bring it upon themselves. It's like this for all things.

"I've been perfecting uselessness for a long time. Now, close to death, I've finally mastered it. And it's of great use to me. If they'd ever found a use for me, would I be this grand? Look – the two of us, we're just things. So how is it things go around denouncing things? And you, a worthless man so close to death – what do you know about *worthless wood*?"

When Riprap awoke and began to interpret his dream, the apprentice asked, "If it's so determined to be useless, why is it the village shrine?"

"Hush! Not a word," replied Riprap. "It's only pretending to be a shrine. If people don't have a way to understand such a great oak, they'll rail against it. So if it weren't a shrine, don't you think someone would have cut it down long ago? Look, it isn't like the rest of us: it's harboring something utterly different. If we praise its practicality, we'll miss the point altogether, won't we?"

5   When Adept Piebald was wandering in the Shang hills, he came across a tree unlike any other. It was so huge it could shelter a thousand teams of horses in its shade.

"What kind of tree is this?" wondered Adept Piebald. "It's timber must be of the rarest and most treasured kind." But looking up, he saw that its spindly branches were too twisted for beams and its massive trunk was too gnarled and mealy for coffins. He tasted a leaf, and it left his mouth burned and blistered. He sniffed, and the smell was bad enough to put someone into a crazed stupor for half a week.

"So this tree's useless after all," he said. "No wonder it's so huge. Yes, yes – that's how it is for the sacred: they too have mastered uselessness."

6   In Sung there's a place called Bramble-Weave that's perfect for catalpa, cypress, and mulberry. But if they're over a hand span around, they're cut by people wanting tether posts for monkeys. If they're three

or four spans, they're cut by people looking for grand roof beams. If they're seven or eight spans, they're cut by families wanting fancy coffins for aristocrats and wealthy merchants. So instead of living out the years heaven gave them, they're hacked down halfway along their journey. Such is the grief of usefulness.

Oxen with white foreheads, pigs with upturned snouts, people with hemorrhoids – in the Chieh sacrifice, they can't be offered to the river. The priests all know this: it's because they think such things bring on bad fortune. But that's exactly why a sacred person knows them to be great good fortune.

7 Scatterment the cripple – chin tucked into belly, shoulders topping skull, nape pointed at sky, vital organs bulging over, thighs become ribs: he can make enough sewing and doing laundry to keep himself fed. And if he shuffles divining straws or winnows grain, he can make enough to feed ten people. When they're out rounding up soldiers for their wars, the cripple rolls up his sleeves for a fight and wanders among them without a care. When they're out rounding up slaves for some grand construction project, the cripple's left behind as a hopeless invalid. But when they're handing out supplies to the sick and needy, he collects three bags of grain and ten bundles of firewood. If a crippled body can earn you a good livelihood and let you live out the years heaven gave you, who knows what crippled Integrity could do?

8 When Confucius went to stay in Ch'u, a local madman named Convergence Crazy-Cart started pacing outside his gate, chanting:

> Phoenix! Hey, sage phoenix,[6]
> how is it Integrity's withered away so?
>
> Holding out for a future is useless,
> and you'll never find the past again.

CHUANG TZU

When Way infuses the world,
sages realize themselves in it,

and when Way leaves the world,
sages find their refuge in it —

but these days you're lucky
just to elude execution in it.

Good fortune's light as a feather,
but who knows how to carry it?

Misfortune's heavy as the earth,
but who knows how to elude it?

Everything is! It just is! Stop
lording Integrity over people:

it's dangerous! It's dangerous
rushing around parsing earth.

Thistle! Hey, sage Thistle-Mouth,
don't scratch my wandering,

my twisty-whimsy wandering.
Don't scratch these carefree feet.

9   Mountain trees plunder themselves. Grease fires broil themselves. Cinnamon's tasty, so the trees are hacked down. Lacquer's useful, so the trees are cut open. Everyone knows that to be useful is useful, but who knows how useful it is to be useless?

v The Talisman of Integrity Replete

1   In Lu there was a man named Tumbledown Imperial who'd committed a crime and so had his foot cut off. As he wandered, he was followed by as many disciples as Confucius.

"Tumbledown Imperial has only one foot," said Constant-Season to Confucius, "and yet Lu is divided evenly between his followers and yours. He never teaches when he stands up and never talks when he sits down. Still, people keep going to him empty and returning home full. Is there really some wordless teaching, some formless way of bringing the mind to realization? What kind of man could this be?"

"A master, a sage," replied Confucius. "If I weren't so backward and slow, I'd be following him too. And if I need such a teacher, is it any wonder that others need him even more? Why just the kingdom of Lu? Let's bring the whole world along, and we'll all go follow him!"

"He's lost his foot," said Constant-Season, "but he's still like a king to you. He's far beyond ordinary people. The way he employs mind, it's like no one else. How does he do it?"

"Birth and death are certainly great events," explained Confucius. "But for him they change nothing. All heaven and earth could be churned over and falling apart, but for him nothing would be lost. He inquires where nothing is false, and he isn't tossed about as things shift back and forth. He knows that the endless transformation of things unfurls according to its own inevitable nature, and he holds fast to the ancestral source."

"Meaning what?" asked Constant-Season.

"If you see the world in terms of difference," replied Confucius, "there are liver and gallbladder, there are Ch'u lands and Yüeh lands. But seen in terms of sameness, the ten thousand things are all one. If you understand this, you forget how eye and ear could love this and hate that. Then the mind wanders the accord of Integrity. And if you see the identity of things, you see there can be no loss. So it is that he saw nothing more in a lost foot than a clump of dirt tossed aside."

"He's utterly self-contained," marveled Constant-Season. "He uses understanding to reach mind. He uses mind to reach timeless mind. So why do things gather around him?"

"People can't see themselves in rushing water," began Confucius. "They see themselves in still water, for only stillness can still stillness.

"Of those who owe their nature to earth, only pines and cedars remain resolute: forever green through summer and winter. Of those who owe their nature to heaven, only emperors Yao and Shun remained resolute: sovereign at the head of all ten thousand things. Because they were able to make their own lives resolute, they were able to make all life resolute.

"Preserving the subtleties of origins: that is an act of fearlessness. A brave warrior seeking praise and renown may attack mighty armies alone. And if a man can do such a thing out of mere ambition, what can you do when all heaven and earth is your palace and the ten thousand things are your treasure-house; when the eyes and ears are empty windows and the body is a mere lodging place; when all that can be known is one and the same, and the mind is deathless? Someone like that just picks a day and rises out of this unreal world. Is it any wonder that followers gather round? But the things of this world never concern such a person."

2   There was once an adept named Empty-Excellence who had only one foot. He and Adept Engenderment, the prime minister of Cheng, were practicing with Elder Twilight-Nobody as their teacher.

"Sometimes I leave first, and you wait humble and still," said Adept Engenderment to Empty-Excellence. "Sometimes you leave first, and I wait humble and still."

They were in the same hall the next day, sitting together on a mat, and again Engenderment said, "Sometimes I leave first, and you wait humble and still. Sometimes you leave first, and I wait humble and still. I'm going away now. Will you wait humble and still until I'm gone, or won't you? When you see a prime minister and don't step aside respectfully – is that because you are the equal of a prime minister?"

"Here within our master's gates, can there be prime ministers?"

replied Empty-Excellence. "You revel in your high position and consider others beneath you. Haven't you heard the saying: *If a mirror is bright, dust never settles on it. If dust can settle on it, the mirror isn't bright?*

"If you spend enough time with someone wise, you may eventually be without trespass. For now you consider our master great, but here you are ready to go away and you still talk like this. Isn't that trespassing?"

"Look at yourself," countered Engenderment, "footless and lame, and you act like your nobility rivals Emperor Yao's. Consider your own Integrity – maybe then you'll see yourself a little differently."

"Many are those who think they should be spared, though they know all about their trespasses," responded Empty-Excellence. "But those who don't expect to be spared, though they know nothing of their trespasses – they are rare.

"To recognize what you cannot change, to be at peace knowing it follows the inevitable unfurling of things – only a person of great Integrity can do that. We wander around, always dead center in the Archer's aim – and dead center means dead center, so if we aren't dead it's because the inevitable unfurling of things simply hasn't come to that yet.

"People all laugh at my missing foot because they have two feet. It makes me furious. But here in the realm of our master, I leave all that behind and return to the timeless. I can't tell if it's his nobility rinsing me clean, or me awakening of myself. I've wandered with him for nineteen years now, and it never occurs to me that I'm a footless cripple. You and I wander outside the body here, but you keep looking for me inside the body. Isn't that pretty serious trespassing?"

Engenderment shifted around uneasily. Suddenly his manner changed, his expression changed, and he said, "Alright, alright – you can skip all the details."

3   In Lu there was a man named No-Toes Elder-Mountain whose foot had been cut off. He went stumping in to see Confucius, and Confucius said to him: "You were careless. You made mistakes long ago,

and you paid with your foot. So why have you come to me now?"

"Not knowing what is essential, I did something foolish with my body and lost my foot," replied No-Toes. "That's all. I came here today because I still possess whatever it is that considers a foot precious, and keeping that whole is essential. There's nothing heaven doesn't shelter, and nothing earth doesn't bear up. I imagined you to be heaven and earth. How was I to know you would be like this?"

"That was awful of me," said Confucius. "I'm sorry. Please, why don't you come in and let me tell you what I've learned about all this?"

No-Toes turned and left.

"Be diligent," said Confucius to his disciples after No-Toes had left. "This No-Toes is a footless cripple, but for him the essential thing was learning and overcoming his failings. So you whose Integrity remains whole – imagine what you can do."

Later on, No-Toes was talking with Lao Tzu and said, "This Confucius – he still hasn't reached realization, has he? He studied humbly with you, and what good did it do him? He's still chasing the shifty deceits, the strange illusions of praise and renown. But once you've reached realization, such things are a tangle of fetters – doesn't he know that?"

"Why don't you just show him that life and death are one and the same strand," asked Lao Tzu, "that sufficient and insufficient are one and the same thread? That should shake those fetters loose and set him free, don't you think?"

"Heaven is punishing him," replied No-Toes. "No one can set him free."

4   Duke Ai of Lu consulted Confucius. "There was an awful-looking man in Wei," he explained. "People called him Hunch Tumbledown. When men stayed with him, they forgot everything else and couldn't bear to leave. And when women saw him, they'd plead with their parents: *I'd rather be his consort than any other man's wife.* It happened over and over and over.

"No one ever heard him say anything interesting; he just agreed with everyone else. He didn't hold high office, so he couldn't help desperate people. He wasn't a man of means, able to fill people's bellies. And he was ugly enough to shock the entire world. He was agreeable and never interesting, understood nothing beyond his everyday world – and still, men and women flocked around him. He was unlike anyone I'd ever heard of, so I summoned him to see what he was like.

"He was indeed ugly enough to shock the entire world. But he'd only been with me a few months when I began to understand him. And before a year was out, I trusted him absolutely. As I had no prime minister, I offered my kingdom to him. After brooding for a while, he answered in vague ways, sounding like he wanted to decline. Though I felt ugly and ashamed, I finally convinced him to take over my kingdom. But before long he left me and went away. I felt crushed – as if I'd suffered a great loss, as if there were no one left to enjoy my kingdom with me. What kind of man could this be?"

"I was once sent to Ch'u," began Confucius, "and on the way I saw some baby pigs suckling at their dead mother. They stayed by her for a little while – then, in the blink of an eye, they all scampered away at once. They didn't see themselves in her anymore, didn't sense anything kindred in her. What they loved in their mother wasn't her form, it was whatever animated her form.

"When a soldier dies in battle, he has no use for the plumes of honor people drape over coffins. And once both feet are cut off, a person stops caring about shoes. In both cases the pretext is gone.

"Consorts for the Son of Heaven never pierce their ears or trim their nails. A newly married man is put on leave and given no more assignments. If it's that important to keep the body's form whole, imagine how important it is to keep Integrity whole.

"Now this Hunch Tumbledown said nothing and did nothing. But you loved and trusted him so much that you gave him your kingdom, worrying only that he might not accept. It must be that he's kept ability whole and Integrity formless."

"What do you mean by *ability whole?*" asked the duke.

"Birth and death, living and dead, failure and success, poverty and wealth, honor and dishonor, slander and praise, hunger and thirst, hot and cold – such are the transformations of this world, this inevitable unfurling of things. They keep vanishing into one another before our very eyes, day in and day out, but we'll never calibrate what drives them. So how can they steal our serenity, how can they plunder the spirit's treasure-house? If you let them move together, at ease and serene, you'll never lose your joy. And if you do this without pause, day in and day out, you'll invest all things with spring. Then, mingling it all together, you'll bring seasons alive in the mind. This is what *ability whole* means."

"And what do you mean by *Integrity formless?*"

"Of all level things, still water is the most perfect," replied Confucius, "and it can be our precept. If we harbor it inside, outside remains calm. *Integrity* means you perfect a lasting serenity. *Integrity formless* means things cannot be separate from it."

Some time later, Duke Ai told Min Tzu-ch'ien about this: "At first I sat on my throne facing south, ruler over all beneath heaven. I governed the people with great care, worried that they might suffer and die. I considered myself the perfect sovereign. But now, having heard one who has reached realization, I realize there isn't much to my character. I never took time to make something of myself, so I was ruining the country. Confucius and I – we aren't ruler and subject, we're friends that Integrity has made true."

5   When No-Lips Lame-Irrelevance advised Duke Ling of Wei, Duke Ling was so pleased with him that everyone else's legs looked fat and puffy. When Jug-Bowl Whopping-Goiter advised Duke Huan of Ch'i, Duke Huan was so pleased with him that everyone else's neck looked thin and spindly.

CHUANG TZU

When Integrity is timeless, the body's form is forgotten. If you don't forget what should be forgotten, and you do forget what should not be forgotten – that is called true forgetting.

So it is that sages have realms to wander. For them, understanding is a curse, convention is a glue, Integrity is something in reserve, and skill is mere merchandise. If you're a sage, you never make plans, so what good is understanding? You never split things apart, so what good is glue? You never know loss, so what good is Integrity? You never peddle your wares, so what good is merchandise?

These four things are heaven's gruel, and the gruel of heaven is the food of heaven. So if you've already tasted food from heaven, what good is the human? You may have human form, but not human nature. Having human form, you live among humans. Not having human nature, you aren't touched by *yes this* and *no that*. Then how small and subtle your share of the human realm becomes! How vast and mighty the heaven you perfect in solitude!

6   "Can a person really have no nature?" asked Hui Tzu of Chuang Tzu.

"Yes," replied Chuang Tzu.

"But if you have no nature, how can you be called human?"

"Way gives you this shape and heaven gives you this form, so why can't you be called human?"

"But if you're called human, how can you have no nature?"

"*Yes this* and *no that* – that's what I call human nature," replied Chuang Tzu. "Not mangling yourself with *good* and *bad* – that's what I call no nature. Instead of struggling to improve on life, you simply abide in occurrence appearing of itself."

"If you don't try to improve on life, how do you stay alive?"

"Way gives you this shape and heaven gives you this form, so why mangle yourself with *good* and *bad*? But you

make an exile of your mind
and wear your spirit away.

You brood, leaning on a tree,
or doze, slumped over a desk.

Heaven made this your form,
and you waste it, twittering

away in a darkness of arcane
distinctions and quibbling."

CHUANG TZU

vi The Great Ancestral Master

1   To understand the human role and the role of heaven – that is to attain realization. If you understand the role of heaven, your life resides in heaven. If you understand the human role, you use understanding to nurture what is beyond understanding. And so, rather than die halfway along your journey, you can live out the years heaven gave you. Such is the fullness of understanding.

Even so, problems remain. Understanding depends on something else for its accuracy. And what it depends on never stays fixed and constant. So how can we know that what we call heaven is not human and what we call human is not heaven?

Only a true sage masters true understanding. What does *true sage* mean? The true sages of old never avoided want, never flaunted perfection, never worked at schemes. If you're like that, you can be wrong without remorse and right without conceit. You can scale the heights without trembling in fear, dive into deep water without getting wet, walk into fire without getting burned. This is how understanding can ascend delusion into the heights of Way.

The true sages of old slept without dreams and woke without worries. Their food was never savory, and their breath was always deep. A true sage breathes from the heels; everyone else breathes from the throat. If you live by acquiescence and compliance, words stick in your throat and to talk is like retching. And if your desires run deep, the impulse of heaven runs shallow in you.

The true sages of old never loved life and never hated death. They never delighted in going forth and never resisted returning to rest. They came on a whim and went on a whim. They never forgot their origin, and they never searched into their extinction. They savored this gift they'd been given and forgot it when they gave it back. This is called *never using the mind to deplete Way, never using the human to assist heaven.* Whoever lives this way is called a *true sage.* If you're like that, your mind is resolved, your face calm, your brow clear. Cool as autumn and warm as spring, your joy and anger stay constant through the four seasons. You're in accord with all things, and so know no limits.

The true sages of old

> *stood towering and alone among people,*
> *seemed wanting but accepted nothing.*
>
> *Content in their precepts and never obstinate,*
> *expansive in emptiness without flaunting it –*
>
> *they were quick to smile, their joy apparent;*
> *mountainous and cragged, as though compelled;*
>
> *impetuous by nature, like flowing water;*
> *blessings that still our Integrity always.*
>
> *Far and wide, and still part of this world –*
> *they were majestic and unrestrained;*
>
> *engaged, though loving life in seclusion;*
> *absorbed and forgetful of what they were saying.*
>
> *So their loves were all one*
> *and their hates were all one.*
>
> *They kept what is all one one*
> *and what is not all one one.*
>
> *They let what is all one follow heaven*
> *and what is not all one follow the human.*

And to keep heaven and human balanced and free of conflict – that is called being a *true sage*.

2   Life and death are inevitable. Heaven gives them the constancy of day and night. And we can't alter any of it – it all belongs to the very nature of things. If we honor heaven as our father and love it

that deeply, imagine honoring something that transcends heaven. If we honor a ruler as our sovereign and offer up our lives for him, imagine honoring something truer than any ruler.

3   If springs dry up, leaving fish stranded together on dry ground, they may keep each other moist with misty breath and frothy spit – but that's nothing like forgetting each other in the depths of rivers and lakes. We can praise Emperor Yao and condemn Chieh the tyrant – but that's nothing like forgetting them both and dwelling in the trans-formations of Way.

4   This Mighty Mudball of a world burdens us with a body, troubles us with life, eases us with old age, and with death gives us rest. We call our life a blessing, so our death must be a blessing too.

5   If you hide your boat in a canyon, and then hide the mountain in a marsh, you may think the boat is safe and secure. But something powerful might come in the dead of night, heave it all onto huge shoul-ders and carry it away. And then in your darkness you'd never know what happened. Something large seems like the perfect place to hide something small, but there's something into which that too can vanish. Only if you hide all beneath heaven inside all beneath heaven, so there's nothing more into which it can vanish – only then have you reached the vast and timeless nature of things.

6   We're cast into this human form, and it's such happiness. This human form knows change, but the ten thousand changes are utterly boundless. Who could calculate the joys they promise?
    And so the sage wanders where nothing is hidden and everything

is preserved. The sage calls dying young a blessing and living long a blessing, calls beginnings a blessing and endings a blessing. We might make such a person our teacher, but there's something the ten thousand things belong to, something all change depends upon – imagine making that your teacher!

7   Way has its own nature and its own reliability: it does nothing and it has no form. It can be passed on, but never received and held. You can master it, but you can't see it. Its own source, its own root – it was there before heaven and earth, firm and constant from ancient times. It makes gods and demons sacred, gives birth to heaven and earth. It's above the absolute pole, but is not high. It's below the six directions, but is not deep. It predates the birth of heaven and earth, but is not ancient. It precedes high antiquity, but is not old.

8   Stray-Paw[1] *mastered it, and so*
holds up all heaven and earth.

Root-Breath[2] mastered it, and so
lives mantled in the ch'i mother.

Polestar mastered it, and so
through all time never wavers.

Sun and Moon mastered it, and so
through all time never rest.

Brick-Maker mastered it, and so
lives mantled in Bright-Prosperity Mountains.

Primal-Chaos mastered it, and so
wanders away majestic rivers.

Shield-Force mastered it, and so
dwells among majestic mountains.

Yellow Emperor mastered it, and so
ascended clouds into heaven.

Watchful-Ease mastered it, and so
dwells in his dark-enigma³ palace.

Fierce-Origins mastered it, and so
inhabits the far end of north.

Queen West-Mother mastered it, and so
mounted her throne in the west:

no one knows her beginning
and no one knows her ending.

Ancestor Drum-Light mastered it, and so
lived out the twenty centuries

from Shun to the Five Tyrants.
Shepherd-Joy mastered it, and so

counseled Emperor Lone-Warrior's
reign over all beneath heaven,

mounted East-Bank Star,
rode Dragon-Tail Star,

and took his place among the constellations.

9   "You're old in years but your complexion is like a child's,"
Adept Sunflower said to Dame Crookback. "How is it you look so
fresh?"

"I have heard Way."

"Is Way something you can learn?"

"No, no, of course not," replied Crookback. "And you aren't cut out for it anyway. Oracle Bridgeworks had the talent of a sage, but not the Way of a sage. But I have the Way of a sage, and not the talent of a sage. So I decided to teach him, thinking he could become a real sage. If nothing else, it should be easy to explain the Way of a sage to someone with the talent of a sage. Still, I had to instruct and guide him carefully. After three days he'd tossed out all beneath heaven. But even though he'd tossed out all beneath heaven, I still had to guide him carefully. After seven days he'd tossed out things themselves. But even though he'd tossed out things, I still had to guide him carefully. After nine days he'd tossed out life itself. And once he'd tossed out life itself, his insight had the clarity of dawn light. Once his insight had the clarity of dawn light, he could see the singular. Once he saw the singular, he could extinguish past and present. And once he'd extinguished past and present, he could enter a place deathless and lifeless. Deathless is the life-killer, and lifeless the life-bringer – so there's nothing that place doesn't send off and nothing it doesn't welcome home, nothing it doesn't bring to ruin and nothing it doesn't bring to perfection. Its name is Tranquil-Turmoil. Tranquil-Turmoil: turmoil brought to perfection."

"Where did you hear about Way?" asked Adept-Sunflower.

"I heard it from Inkstain's child," replied Dame Crookback. "Inkstain's child heard it from Bookworm's grandchild. Bookworm's grandchild heard it from Bright-Eyes. Bright-Eyes heard it from Rumor. Rumor heard it from Indispensable. Indispensable heard it from Singsong, who heard it from Dark Enigma-Midnight. Dark Enigma-Midnight heard it from Ambassador Silence. And Ambassador Silence heard it from Mystery-Arising."

10   Adept Offering, Adept Cart, Adept Plowshare, and Adept Arrival met one day. Talking together, they said: "Who can make

Absence their head, life their spine, and death their butt? Who can understand that birth and death, living and dead are all one body? Such people make true friends."

The four of them looked at each other and laughed. There was no disparity in their minds: they were friends.

Before long, Adept Cart got sick. When Adept Offering came to ask how he was doing, Cart said: "It's amazing! The Maker-of-Things[4] is crumpling me up into such an embrace: a crooked hump sticking out of my back, vital organs bulging over, chin tucked into belly, shoulders topping skull, nape pointed at sky. And my *ch'i* – its *yin* and *yang* seem all out of whack."

Still, his mind remained calm and unconcerned. He hobbled over to a well, looked at himself in the water, and said: "It's incredible! The Maker-of-Things just keeps crumpling me up into this embrace!"

"Do you resent it?" asked Adept Offering.

"No, why should I resent it?" replied Adept Cart. "If my left arm's transformed into a rooster, I'll just go looking for night's end. If my right arm's transformed into a crossbow, I'll just go looking for owls to roast. And if my butt's transformed into a pair of wheels and my spirit's transformed into a horse, I'll just ride away! I'd never need a cart again!

"This life we're given comes in its own season, and then follows its vanishing away. If you're at ease in your season, if you can dwell in its vanishing, joy and sorrow never touch you. This is what the ancients called *getting free*. If you can't get free, you're tangled in things. And things have never overcome heaven. So what is there to resent?"

Before long, Adept Arrival got sick. As he lay gasping and wheezing on the verge of death, his wife and children crowded around, sobbing. When Adept Plowshare came to ask how Arrival was doing, Plowshare shouted: "Out of the way! Shoo! Don't pester change in the making!"

Then, leaning against the door, he said to Adept Arrival: "It's amazing – that Maker-of-Things! What will it make of you next? Where will it send you? Will it make you into a rat's liver? Will it make you into a bug's arm?"

"Our parents are part of us," said Adept Arrival. "East and west, north and south – wherever we go, we follow their wishes. And we obey *yin* and *yang* even more completely. They've brought me here to the brink of death, and to resist their wishes would be such insolence. How could I blame them for this?

"This Mighty Mudball of a world burdens us with a body, troubles us with life, eases us with old age, and with death gives us rest. We call our life a blessing, so our death must be a blessing too.

"Suppose a mighty metalsmith cast a piece of metal and the metal jumped up and said *No, no – I must be one of those legendary Mo-yeh swords!* Wouldn't the metalsmith consider it ominous metal? And suppose, having chanced upon human form, I insist *Human, human, and nothing but human!* Wouldn't the Maker-of-Change⁵ consider me an ominous person? I see heaven and earth as a mighty foundry and the Maker-of-Change as a mighty metalsmith – so wherever they send me, how could I ever complain? I'll sleep soundly – and then suddenly I'll wake."

11   Adept Mulberry-Gate, Adept Elder-Contrary, and Adept Strung-*Ch'in* had become friends. One day they said: "Who can associate in nonassociation and cooperate in noncooperation? Who can ascend heaven, wander mists, and roam the boundless, forgetting their lives together for endless eternities?"

The three of them looked at each other and laughed. There was no disparity in their minds: they were friends.

Things went along quietly for a time. Then Adept Mulberry-Gate passed away. Before he was buried, Confucius heard about his death and sent Adept Kung to pay his respects at the funeral. When he arrived, Elder-Contrary was cooking up tunes, and Strung-*Ch'in* was thrumming a *ch'in*. Suddenly they broke into song together:

> *O Mulberry-Gate, how could you,*
> *O Mulberry-Gate, how could you:*

already back in your true form,
you've left us here in the human!

Adept Kung hurried in and demanded, "Singing to your dead friend's corpse – how can this be in accordance with Ritual?"

Looking at each other, the two friends laughed and said, "What does this guy know about Ritual?"

When he returned home, Adept Kung told Confucius what had happened, and then asked: "What kind of people are they? They're completely uncivil. They cultivate Absence and shuck off their physical form. They sing to their dead friend's corpse, not a trace of grief in their faces. There aren't words to describe them. What kind of people are they?"

"The kind that wander beyond this realm we know," replied Confucius. "And I'm the kind that wanders within it. Beyond and within – they can never meet. So it was clumsy of me, sending you to mourn such a person.

"Companions in their realm to the Maker-of-Things, they're in human form for now, wandering the one *ch'i* that breathes through all heaven and earth. For them, life is a useless appendage, a swollen tumor, and death is like a boil breaking open or pus draining from a festering sore. So how would they choose between life and death, before and after?

"On loan from everything else, they'll soon be entrusted back to the one body. Forgetting liver and gallbladder, abandoning ears and eyes, they'll continue on again, tumbling and twirling through a blur of endings and beginnings. They roam at ease beyond the tawdry dust of this world, nothing's own doing wandering, boundless and free through the selfless unfolding of things. So why would they fuss and stew about the Rituals and customs of this human world? Just to put on a show for the rest of us?"

"And you," asked Adept Kung, "which is your realm?"

"I'm one of those heaven has cursed," replied Confucius. "But there may be something I can tell you anyway."

"Can you explain that other realm for me?" asked Adept Kung.

"Fish flourish in water," said Confucius, "and people flourish in Way. For those who flourish in water – dig a pond and they'll be nurtured. For those who flourish in Way – leave things alone and they'll live secure. Hence the saying: *Fish forget each other in the depths of rivers and lakes; people forget each other in the mysteries of Way.*"

"Can you explain such strange men?"

"They may be strange to people, but they're kindred to heaven. Hence the saying: *A commoner in heaven is a noble among humans, and a noble among humans is a commoner in heaven.*"

12   "When his mother died, Able Elder-Grandchild wept without tears," said Yen Hui to Confucius. "His mind was without grief and his mourning period without sorrow. In spite of these three failings, he was honored for his mourning. In the entire kingdom of Lu, has anyone gained more praise and renown for doing less? This seems utterly bizarre to me."

"Elder-Grandchild has mastered it all," replied Confucius. "He's stepped beyond mere understanding. Even though he couldn't simplify mourning completely, he simplified it a great deal.

"He's lost track of what it is to live and what it is to die. And he's lost track of which comes first, which last. Like any other thing inhabiting change, he simply waits for whatever unfathomed transformation may come over him next. He's changing and yet he knows the changeless. He's changeless and yet he knows change. You and I, on the other hand, we're dreaming: we haven't even begun to awaken. His body may fear for its life but his mind remains unperturbed. His spirit-home may vanish by morning but his true nature never dies. Elder-Grandchild is utterly awake. People weep, so he weeps. And that too is because he's so utterly awake.

"We invest each other with selves. But how can we know that what we call a self is really a self? We dream we're birds soaring through the heavens. We dream we're fish diving into the depths. So when teachers like me speak – how can we know if they're awake or if they're dreaming?

"A pilgrimage can't compare to a good laugh, and a good laugh can't compare to simply letting yourself go. Once you're at peace, letting yourself go and leaving change behind, then you enter the solitary mystery of heaven."

13   **W**hen Master Deliberation came to see him, Pledged-Origin asked, "What riches has Emperor Yao given you?"

"He has told me: *You must devote yourself to Humanity and Duty, and you must speak clearly about right and wrong.*"

"Then why have you come here like this?" asked Pledged-Origin. "Yao's already branded you with Humanity and Duty, and he's lopped off your nose with right and wrong. So how can you wander a path all distance, all free and easy migration?"

"What you say may be true. But still, I might at least wander the borders of that realm."

"Impossible," replied Pledged-Origin. "The blind never know the charms of a beautiful face. And the sightless never see silk lit with the embroidered colors of spring and autumn."

"Never-Adorn losing her beauty, Buttress-Beam losing his strength, Yellow Emperor forgetting his wisdom – it's all part of being forged anew in the foundry of change," countered Master Deliberation. "So how can you know the Maker-of-Things hasn't wiped the brands from my skin, patched my nose back together, and sent me riding my new-found perfection to follow after you?"

"Ah yes, it's true, there's no way of knowing," replied Pledged-Origin. "So I'll give you a summary:

> *O my master,*
> *O my master –*
>
> *mincing the ten thousand things,*
> *you move without serving Duty;*

blessing ten thousand generations,
you move without serving Humanity;

more ancient than high antiquity,
you move without growing old.

You shelter heaven, bear up earth,
and giving form to all things,

you move without a trace of skill.
That's the way of our wandering!"

14   "I'm gaining ground," said Yen Hui.

"What do you mean?" asked Confucius.

"I've forgotten Humanity and Duty completely."

"Not bad! But that's still not it."

A few days later they met again, and Yen Hui said, "I'm gaining ground."

"What do you mean?"

"I've forgotten Ritual and music completely."

"Not bad! But that's still not it."

A few days later they met again, and Yen Hui said, "I'm gaining ground."

"What do you mean?"

"I sit quietly and forget."

Confucius shifted around uneasily. "What do you mean *sit quietly and forget?*" he asked his disciple.

"I let the body fall away and the intellect fade. I throw out form, abandon understanding – and then move freely, blending away into the great transformation. That's what I mean by *sit quietly and forget.*"

"If you blend away like that, you're free of likes and dislikes," said Confucius. "If you're all transformation, you're free of permanence. So in the end, the true sage here is you. So you won't mind if I follow you from now on, will you?"

15   Adept Cart and Adept Mulberry were friends. Once, after ten days of steady rain, Adept Cart said to himself, "Adept Mulberry must be getting desperate by now." So he wrapped up some food and set out to comfort his friend.

When he arrived at Adept Mulberry's gate, he heard a kind of song, or sob – someone thrumming a *ch'in* and chanting:

> *Father?*
> *Mother?*
> *Heaven?*
> *Human?*

It was like a voice that couldn't bear its own sound, and so rushed out into sung words. Adept Cart went inside and asked, "Your song, its words – why are they like this?"

"I was thinking that something must have brought me to such desperation, but can't find what it might be. Father and mother – how could they have wished such poverty on me? Heaven shelters all things and earth bears all things up: they don't pick and choose. So how could heaven and earth have picked me out for such poverty? I keep searching for whatever did all this to me, but can't find anything. It must be that I've come to this desperation of myself, that it's part of the inevitable unfurling of things."

VII   The Way of Emperors and Kings

1   Gap-Tooth inquired of Horizon-Imperial. He asked his question four times, and four times received no answer. Overjoyed, Gap-Tooth leapt up and ran to tell Master Grass-Coat.

"You mean you're only now realizing that there are no answers?" said Master Grass-Coat. "Shun may be a sage emperor, but he's no match for Emperor Inception. Shun never stops treasuring Humanity and using it to lead people. He's mastered the human but never ventured out into the nonhuman.

"Inception, on the other hand, slept in peaceful contentment and woke wide-eyed and blank. He might have been a horse one minute and an ox the next. His understanding was faithful and precise, his Integrity utterly true. He never entered the nonhuman – or the human either."

2   Bearing-Me-Up went to visit Convergence Crazy-Cart, and Crazy-Cart asked him, "What has Noon-Start been telling you?"

"He's been explaining that rulers should serve as examples, establishing canons and standards, precepts and regulations – then the people will follow and be transformed."

"That's the Integrity of oppression," said Convergence Crazy-Cart. "Using it to govern all beneath heaven is like trying to channel a river through an ocean, like asking a mosquito to carry a mountain away. When sages govern, do you think they worry about mere appearance? First they set the terms themselves aright and then they just let it all happen. That way things can simply do what they were meant to do.

"Birds fly high to avoid the hazards of arrows. Mice burrow deep under sacred mounds to avoid the danger of being dug up or smoked out. These two little creatures – even they have better sense than you!"

3   Heaven-Root was wandering at Bright-Abundance Mountain. There, along the banks of Vacant River, he met Person No-Name and said: "Might I ask about bringing order to all beneath heaven?"

"Get lost!" shouted No-Name. "What a slob. How could you ask such trashy questions? I wander with the Maker-of-Things and just now stumbled into this human form. When I get tired of this, I'll mount the Subtle-Confusion Bird and soar out beyond the six horizons. I'll wander in a village where there's nothing at all, dwell in a land where emptiness stretches away forever. So why are you cluttering my mind with your talk about governing all beneath heaven?"

Heaven-Root asked again.

"Let your mind wander the pure and simple," replied No-Name. "Blend your *ch'i* into the boundless, follow occurrence appearing of itself in things, and don't let selfhood get in the way. Then all beneath heaven will be governed well."

4   Adept Light-Dweller went to see Lao Tzu and said: "Imagine someone who's quick as an echo and yet strong and commanding, someone who sees into the actual with a penetrating clarity and yet still pursues Way without pause. Can someone like this be compared to the enlightened emperors of ancient times?"

"Compared to those ancient sages," replied Lao Tzu, "such a person is a scribbling clerk, a toiling craftsman wearing body and mind ragged.

"The beautiful fur of tigers and leopards brings the hunter, and the nimble play of gibbons and monkeys brings the leash. So how can a person like that be compared to the enlightened emperors of ancient times?"

Light-Dweller shifted around uneasily and said: "Might I ask how those enlightened emperors governed?"

Lao Tzu replied:

"When he governs, the sage emperor

fills all beneath heaven with bounty,
and yet he's nowhere to be found.

He transforms the ten thousand things,
and yet no one thinks to rely on him:

people never even mention his name,
for he lets things find their own joy.

He stands firm in the immeasurable
and wanders free in realms
where there's nothing at all."

5   In the kingdom of Cheng there was a holy shaman named Seasons-Alike. By studying people's faces, he could divine everything about them: their birth and death, survival and ruin, good fortune or bad, long life or short. He could predict it all like some god, right down to the year, month, week, and day. Whenever the people of Cheng saw him they turned and ran.

One day Lieh Tzu went to visit him. Drunk with wonder, he returned to his teacher, Master Winepot. "Master," he said, "I always believed yours was the perfect Way. But in him I saw something more perfect still."

"I've shown you the surface," replied Master Winepot, "but I've never shown you the reality. Did you really think you'd mastered this Way of mine?

"If you have a bunch of hens and no rooster, what kind of eggs will you get? You take Way around, lording it over the world, insisting that everyone believe you. It's no wonder such people can know you through and through just by looking at your face. Bring him along next time, and we'll let him take a look at me."

The next day Lieh Tzu brought Seasons-Alike to see Master Winepot. When they left, the shaman said: "I'm so sorry. Your master's all but dead. The life's gone out of him. He won't last more than a week or two. There was something very strange when I looked at him: I could see wet ash."

Lieh Tzu returned to Master Winepot. Sobbing, his robes soaked with tears, he told Master Winepot what the shaman had divined in him.

"This time," replied Master Winepot, "I let him see the earth's veined surface just before spring breaks out: nothing moving, nothing still. But I guess all he saw was the wellspring of my Integrity blocked up. Bring him back for another look sometime."

The next day Lieh Tzu and Seasons-Alike went to see Master Winepot again. When they left, the shaman said: "It's a lucky thing your master consulted me. He's cured! He's full of life now! I can see that his blockage was only temporary."

Lieh Tzu returned to Master Winepot and told him the shaman's good news.

"This time," replied Master Winepot, "I let him see the fertile ground of heaven before appearance and reality emerged, where the very wellsprings themselves arise. But I guess all he saw was the wellspring of my vitality. Bring him back for another look sometime."

The next day Lieh Tzu and Seasons-Alike went to see Master Winepot again. When they left, the shaman said to Lieh Tzu: "Your master is never the same! I studied his face but couldn't divine anything about him. If he'll try to steady himself, I'll come back and take another look."

Lieh Tzu returned to Master Winepot and told him what the shaman had said.

"That time," replied Master Winepot, "I let him see the Mighty Void where nothing wins out. But I guess all he saw was the wellspring of my ch'i in balance.

"Where seething water gathers, it's an abyss. Where still water gathers, it's an abyss. Where flowing water gathers, it's an abyss. The abyss has nine names. Here I have revealed three of them. Bring him back for another look sometime."

The next day Lieh Tzu and Seasons-Alike went to see Master Winepot again. They entered, but before he'd even greeted Master Winepot, the shaman went mad and fled wildly.

"Catch him!" shouted Master Winepot.

Lieh Tzu chased after him but couldn't catch him. "He's disappeared," reported Lieh Tzu when he returned. "Totally vanished. I couldn't catch him."

"That time," said Master Winepot, "I let him see the Ancestral-Not-Yet-Arising: all emptiness perfectly at ease, where you can't tell who's what or what's who. And there he saw the effortless scattering of change, the billows and waves of history flowing away. That's why he took off like that."

At this, Lieh Tzu realized that he hadn't even begun to understand Way, so he returned home and didn't leave for three years. He cooked for his wife, and fed the pigs as though he were feeding people. Human pursuits meant nothing to him. He whittled and polished himself back to utter simplicity: a body standing alone like a clump of earth. Taking this refuge in the midst of all confusion, he kept himself whole to the end.

6   Don't be a carcass of names
       or treasure-house of schemes;

       don't be a servant of pursuits
       or proprietor of fine wisdom.

       Make the inexhaustible your body
       and wander beyond origins.

Make everything heaven gave you treasure enough
and know you have nothing.

Live empty, perfectly empty.

Sage masters always employ mind like a pure mirror:
welcome nothing, refuse nothing,

reflect everything, hold nothing.
And so they triumph over things with never a wound.

7   At the origin of things there was Thunder, ruler of the Southern Ocean, and Bolt, ruler of the Northern Ocean. And in the Middle Realm, Primal-Dark ruled. Thunder and Bolt often met together in the lands of Primal-Dark, and Primal-Dark was always a most gracious host. Eventually, Thunder and Bolt tried to think of a way to repay Primal-Dark's kindness. They said: "People all have seven holes so they can see and hear, eat and breathe. Only Primal-Dark is without them. Why don't we try cutting some for her?"

So Thunder-Bolt began cutting holes, one each day. On the seventh day, Primal-Dark was dead.

Notes

I. Wandering Boundless and Free

1 **heaven:** For the range of meanings informing Chuang Tzu's use of the term *heaven*, see Key Terms *Tien* and the Introduction, page 135 f.

2 **Lieh Tzu:** Reputed author of *Lieh Tzu*, the third classic of ancient Taoism. Some parts of that book may date to Chuang Tzu's time, but most probably were not written until many centuries later. It was apparently attributed to Lieh Tzu in order to give it the authority of an ancient master.

3 *ch'i:* See Key Terms: *Ch'i.*

4 **Yao:** Mythic emperor (regnant 2357–2255 B.C.E.) of great sagacity during the legendary golden age of China.

5 *In the distant Maiden-Arrow Mountains there lives a sage:* There are a number of these fantastical passages in *Chuang Tzu*. To the extent that such passages are authentic, they are read as metaphor by philosophical Taoism, the tradition taken seriously by Chinese intellectual culture. They are read literally by esoteric Taoism, a devolved form that became a popular religion seeking to attain immortality through such techniques as breathing, meditation, and alchemical potions. Chuang Tzu and Lao Tzu would obviously have little patience with such aspirations.

6 **Integrity:** See Key Terms: *Te.*

7 **Shun:** A sage-emperor (regnant 2255–2208 B.C.E.) from China's legendary golden age, Shun was Emperor Yao's successor.

8 **Hui Tzu:** A friend and frequent sparring partner of Chuang Tzu, Hui Tzu (Hui Shih) was the leader of a prominent school of philosophy known as the Sophists or Logicians. The debate between the Hundred Schools of Thought had become more and more rational over the years, reaching its extreme limit in Hui Tzu. Chuang Tzu tipped the scales back, preventing China from following the kind of rationalist path that the ancient Greeks initiated for the West.

II. A Little Talk About Evening Things Out

1 **Yü:** A sage-emperor (regnant 2205–2197 B.C.E.) from China's legendary golden age, Yü was Emperor Shun's successor, and the founder of the Hsia Dynasty.

2   Way: See Key Terms: *Tao.*

3   Mo Tzu: Founder of a major school of social philosophy that competed with Confucius' school.

4   *ch'in*: An ancient stringed instrument played by all literati in ancient China, ancestor to the more familiar Japanese koto.

5   Duty: An important concept in the social philosophy of Confucius, Duty *(Yi)* is the responsibility to care for one another that members of society share. It is the outer manifestation of Humanity, for which see the following note. See the *Analects* Key Terms: *Yi.*

6   time and space: Actually a very different concept of time and space which might better be translated as "breath-seed home." For an explanation of this complex concept, see my *Hunger Mountain*, p. 89 ff. Ref: p. 31.

7   Humanity: One of the central concepts in the social philosophy of Confucius. The character for Humanity *(Jen)* is formed by a combination of the characters for "human being" and "two," and it refers to all of the moral qualities expressed in the behavior of ideal human beings toward one another. It is thus the foundation of human society. See the *Analects* Key Terms: *Jen.*

8   Yellow Emperor: This is Huang Ti, perhaps the most illustrious of China's legendary emperors (regnant 2698–2598 B.C.E.). The diverse legends surrounding this mythic figure go so far as to say that he came into being with the beginning of the world and that he created humankind. In general, legend considers him the creator of civilization, and variously credits him with the invention of writing, agriculture, medicine, music, calendars, silk, and many other instruments of civilization.

IV. The Human Realm

1   Yen Hui: Confucius' favorite and wisest disciple.

2   Ritual: Another central concept in Confucian social philosophy. Ritual is Confucius' way of describing the web of social responsibilities. See the *Analects* Introduction p. 224 f, and Key Terms: *Li.*

3   Root-Breath: The first man and emperor, Root-Breath (Fu Hsi) was half dragon and half human. His wife, Lady Her-Voice (Nü Kua), created people, and he taught them how to hunt and fish, keep livestock, and cook over fire. He also invented the *I Ching* hexagrams.

4   the inevitable unfurling of things: The term that is usually translated "destiny" *("ming")* is translated with variations on the phrase "the inevitable unfurling of things." "Destiny" implies that events are *predestined*

by some outside force, but the sense in Chuang Tzu is that events are inevitable simply because the ten thousand things unfold according to their own nature. See also the discussion in the Introduction, pages 135–36.

5   **Integrity:** When Chuang Tzu is undermining it, Integrity *(Te)* often carries a moralistic Confucian meaning. Paralleling its Taoist meaning, Confucian Integrity is the manifestation of the Confucian Way (Tao) in the human world. Hence, a person of great Integrity is one who has mastered the societal/ethical Way of Confucian political philosophy.

6   **phoenix:** The phoenix appears only in times of peace and sagacious rule. For another version of this story, see the *Analects* XVIII.5.

VI. The Great Ancestral Master

1   The names invoked in this section refer to deities, legendary emperors, and mythic characters, some identifiable and some not.

2   **Stray-Paw:** Mythic figure who gave order to the universe.

3   **Root-breath:** See note IV.3.

4   **dark-enigma:** Lao Tzu adopted this term in an attempt to name Absence, that generative ontological tissue, before it is named. See *Tao Te Ching* Key Terms: *Hsüan.* Ref: p. 191.

5   **Maker-of-Things:** Way or *tzu-jan*, for which see Key Terms.

6   **Maker-of-Change:** Way or *tzu-jan*, for which see Key Terms.

Key Terms
An Outline of Chuang Tzu's Thought

Yu: 有 Presence (Being)

The empirical universe, which has its origin in *wu* (Absence: see the following entry). The ancients described Presence as the ten thousand living and nonliving things in constant transformation. It might more literally be translated as "within form." See also: *Tao Te Ching* Introduction p. 20 ff.

Ref: pp. 153-54.

Wu: 無 Absence (Nonbeing)

The generative tissue from which the ever-changing realm of Presence perpetually arises. This tissue is the ontological substrate infused mysteriously with a generative energy. Although made of the same stuff as Presence, it is "Absence" because it has no particular form. But because of its generative nature, it shapes itself into the individual forms we know, the ten thousand things, then reshapes itself into other forms in the constant process of change. In fact, a more literal translation of *wu* might be "without form," in contrast to "within form" for *yu*. Absence is known directly in meditation, widely practiced by ancient Chinese poets and intellectuals, where it is experienced as empty consciousness itself, known in Ch'an (Zen) Buddhist terminology as "empty mind" or "no-mind."

See also: *Tao Te Ching* Introduction p. 20 ff.

Ref: pp. 153-54, 194.

Tao: 道 Way

As the generative ontological process through which all things arise and pass away, Tao (Way) might provisionally be divided into Presence (the ten thousand things of the empirical world in constant transformation) and Absence, the generative source of being and its transformations. See also: Introduction p. 133 ff.

Ref: *passim*.

Te: 德 Integrity

The *Te* of *Tao Te Ching*, Te means Integrity to Tao (Way) in the sense of "abiding by the Way," or "enacting the Way." Hence, it is Tao manifested in the things of this world, especially in a sage who has mastered the Taoist Way. Such a person could be described as having great Integrity. This concept is deepened dramatically by *Te*'s etymological meaning at the level of pictographic imagery: "heart-sight clarity."

Ref: *passim*.

Tzu-jan: 自然 Occurrence appearing of itself

The ten thousand things unfolding spontaneously from the generative source, each according to its own nature. Hence, *tzu-jan* might be described as the mechanism or process of Tao (Way) in the empirical world. See also: Introduction p. 136 ff.

Ref: 183, 201.

Wu-wei: 無為 Nothing's own doing, etc.

Impossible to translate the same way in every instance, wuwei means acting as a spontaneous part of *tzu-jan* rather than with self-conscious intention. Different contexts emphasize different aspects of this rich philosophical concept as Chuang Tzu exploits the term's grammatical ambiguity. Literally meaning "not/nothing (*wu*) doing (*wei*)," *wu-wei's* most straightforward translation is simply "doing nothing" in the sense of not interfering with the flawless and self-sufficient unfolding of *tzu-jan*. But this must always be conceived together with its mirror translation: "nothing doing" or "nothing's own doing," in the sense of being no one separate from *tzu-jan* when acting. As *wu-wei* is the movement of *tzu-jan*, when we act according to *wu-wei* we act as the generative source. This opens to the deepest level of this philosophical complex, for *wu-wei* can also be read quite literally as "Absence (wu) doing." Here, *wu-wei* action is action directly from, or indeed as the ontological source: Absence burgeoning forth into being. This in turn invests the more straightforward translation ("doing nothing")

CHUANG TZU

with its fullest dimensions, for "doing nothing" always carries the sense of "enacting nothing/Absence." See also: *Tao Te Ching* Introduction p. 20 ff and 25, and *Chuang Tzu* Introduction p. 136 f.

Ref: 146, 189, 194.

Ch'i: 氣 Ch'i

The universal breath, vital energy, or cosmic life-force. It is the breath-force that pulses through the Cosmos as both matter and energy simultaneously, giving form and life to the ten thousand things and driving their perpetual transformations. And so it is the tissue of which the Cosmos is made. In its originary form, it is primal-*ch'i* (*yüan-ch'i*), which is present in Absence and is perhaps the aspect that gives the primordial emptiness of Absence pregnant with possibility. Primal-*ch'i* is made up of *yin* and *yang* completely intermingled and indistinguishable. Once primal-*ch'i* separates out into *yin* and *yang*, *yang* rose up to become sky and *yin* sunk down to form earth. As the universal breath, *ch'i* is in constant motion, animating all things, and so is a kind of tissue that connects us always to the empty source.

Ref: 143, 192, 194, 201, 203.

T'ien: 天 Heaven

The Chou Dynasty used the impersonal concept of heaven to replace the Shang Dynasty's monotheistic god. Heaven was eventually secularized by the early Taoists, Lao Tzu and Chuang Tzu, for whom it meant natural process: the constant unfolding of things in the cosmological process. For a somewhat different perspective, consider the recurring entity "heaven and earth," which might be conceived as "creative force and created objects." See also: Introduction. See also: pp. 135 ff.

Ref: *passim*.

隹月頁鼻造且土
　氏　立扵仁
醫聖心禮玄開
　念器汙君

丰利家真粢以同
青元居虛之往耀
龍　魯世晉水敬
左百親禮禮濟咏
浇王里樂陵海思
斳禾并陵鍾磬禍
霝改官遲瑟　尊

ANALECTS

Confucius

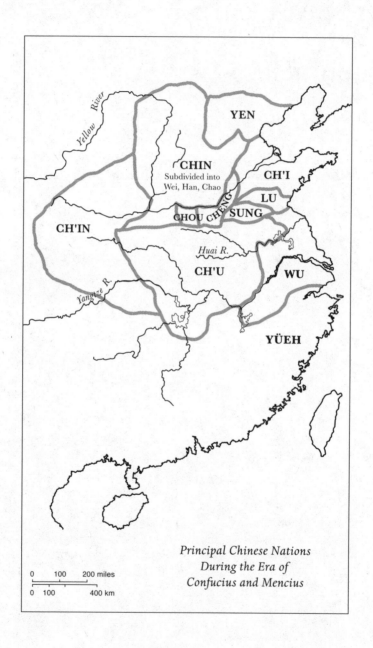

*Principal Chinese Nations
During the Era of
Confucius and Mencius*

Introduction

Asked by a disciple if he should pray for him, a dying Confucius summed up: "My life has been my prayer" (7.35). Although Confucius (551–479 B.C.E.) was to become the most influential sage in human history, his had been a disappointing life indeed, for he had taken as his task the creation of a society in which everyone's life is a prayer. Needless to say, he failed miserably. But he did create the outline of such a society in his social philosophy, and it has survived as China's social ideal ever since, however rarely that ideal has been approached in actual practice. Formulated in the ruins of a magisterial monotheism, a situation not entirely unlike our own, his ideal represents the end of a devastating, millennium-long transformation from a spiritualist to a humanist culture. It recognized society as a structure of human relationships, and spoke of those relationships as a system of "ritual" that people enact in their daily lives, thus infusing the secular with sacred dimensions. The spoken realm of Confucius' teachings is occupied with the practical issues of how society works as a selfless weave of caring relationships; and in the unspoken realm, that ritual weave is extended into the vast primal ecology of a self-generating and harmonious cosmos. This body of thought, still remarkably current and even innovative, survives here in the *Analects*, a collection of aphoristic sayings that has had a deeper impact on more people's lives over a longer period of time than any other book in human history.

The tangible beginnings of Chinese civilization lie in the archaic Shang Dynasty (c. 1766–1040 B.C.E.), which bridged the transition from Neolithic to Bronze Age culture. (For an outline of the early dynasties and rulers that figure prominently in the *Analects*, see Historical Table.) The

Shang was preceded by the Neolithic Hsia Dynasty, about which very little is known. It appears that in the Paleolithic cultures that preceded the Hsia, nature deities were worshiped as tribal ancestors: hence a tribe may have traced its lineage back to an originary "High Ancestor River," for instance. This practice apparently continued through the Hsia into the Shang, where evidence of it appears in oracle-bone inscriptions. Eventually, although these nature deities continued to be worshiped in their own right, religious life focused on the worship of human ancestors. By forging this religious system into a powerful form of theocratic government, the Shang was able to dominate China for no less than seven hundred years.

The Shang Emperors ruled by virtue of their lineage, which was sanctified by Shang Ti ("Celestial Lord"), a supreme deity who functioned as the source of creation, order, ethics, etc. (*Shang* here represents two entirely different words in Chinese.) The Shang lineage may even have led to Shang Ti as its originary ancestor. In any case, Shang Ti provided the Shang rulers with a transcendental source of legitimacy and power: he protected and advanced their interests, and through their spirit-ancestors, they could decisively influence Shang Ti's shaping of events. All aspects of people's lives were thus controlled by the Emperor: weather, harvest, politics, economics, religion, etc. Indeed, people didn't experience themselves as substantially different from spirits, for the human realm was simply an extension of the spirit realm.

Such was the imperial ideology, convenient to the uses of power, as it accorded little ethical value to the masses not of select lineages. (Not surprisingly, the rise of Shang Ti seems to coincide with the rise of the Shang Dynasty, and later myth speaks of him as the creator of Shang civilization.) In the cruelest of ironies, it was overwhelming physical suffering that brought the Chinese people into their earthly lives, beginning the transformation of this spiritualistic culture to a humanistic one. In the cultural legend, the early Shang rulers were paradigms of nobility and benevolence. But by the end of the Shang, the rulers had become cruel and tyrannical, and as there was no ethical system separate from the religious system, there was nothing to shield the people from their depredations. Meanwhile, a small nation was being pushed to the borders of the Shang realm by western tribes. This state of semi-barbarian people, known as the Chou, gradually adopted the cultural traits of the Shang. Eventually, under the leadership of the legendary sage-emperors Wen ("cultured") and Wu ("martial"), the Chou overthrew the tyrannical Shang ruler, thus founding the Chou Dynasty (1122–221), which was welcomed wholeheartedly by the Shang people.

The Chou conquerors were faced with an obvious problem: if the Shang lineage had an absolute claim to rule the world, how could the Chou justify replacing it with their own, and how could they legitimize their rule in the eyes of the Shang people? Their solution was to reinvent Shang Ti as *Heaven,* thus ending the Shang's claim to legitimacy by lineage, and then proclaim that the right to rule depended upon the Mandate of Heaven: once a ruler becomes unworthy, Heaven withdraws its mandate and bestows it on another. This was a major event in Chinese philosophy: the first investment of power with an ethical imperative. And happily, the early centuries of the Chou appear to have fulfilled that imperative admirably.

But eventually, the Chou foundered both because of its increasing inhumanity and its lack of the Shang's transcendent source of legitimacy: if the Mandate could be transferred to the Chou, it could obviously be transferred again. The rulers of the empire's component states (*chu hou:* "august lords") grew increasingly powerful, claiming more and more sovereignty over their lands, until finally they were virtually independent nations. Eventually these rulers (properly entitled "dukes") even began assuming the title of Emperor, thus equating themselves with the Chou Emperor, who was by now a mere figurehead. The rulers of these autonomous states could at least claim descent from those who were first given the territories by the early Chou rulers. But this last semblance of legitimacy was also crumbling because these rulers were frequently at war with one another, which hardly inspired confidence in the claim that they were familial members of the ruling kinship hierarchy that was sanctioned by Heaven. But more importantly, power was being usurped by a second tier of "august lords" whenever they had the strength to take it, and even a third tier of high government officials. In the *Analects,* we see this process primarily in Lu, Confucius' homeland, where the first tier of "august lords" takes the form of the Lu ruling family: Duke Chao (r. 541–509), Duke Ting (r. 509–495), and Duke Ai (r. 494–468). The second tier was the Three Families (Chi, Meng, and Shu), led by the patriarchs of the House of Chi, who had effectively usurped control of the state and set up their own governmental structure. And the rising third tier was made up of the ministers and regents of those Three Families, who had gained control of land and power and begun to challenge the families' dominance. This history, beginning with the Chou's overthrow of the Shang, represents a geologic split in China's social structure: political power was breaking free of its family / religious context and becoming a separate entity.

The final result of the Chou's "metaphysical" breakdown was, not surprisingly, all too physical: war. In addition to constant pressure from barbarians in the north (the first devastating blow to Chou power was a barbarian invasion in 770) and the Ch'u realm that dominated southern China, there was relentless fighting between the empire's component states and frequent rebellion within them. This internal situation, devastating to the people, continued to deteriorate after Confucius' time, until it finally gave an entire age its name: the Warring States Period (403–221). Meanwhile, rulers caught up in this ruthless competition began looking for the most able men to help them govern their states, and this precipitated the rise of an independent intellectual class – a monumental event, for this class constituted the first open space in the cultural framework from which the imperial ideology could be challenged.

The old social order had now collapsed entirely, and these intellectuals began struggling to create a new one. Although this was one of the most virulent and chaotic periods in Chinese history, it was also the golden age of Chinese philosophy, for there were a "Hundred Schools of Thought" trying to envision what this new social order should be like. These schools were founded by thinkers who wandered the country with their disciples, teaching and trying to convince the various rulers to put their ideas into practice, for the desperate times had given them an urgent sense of political mission.

Confucius was the first great figure in this independent intellectual class and China's first self-conscious philosopher who can be historically verified in any sense. As with most intellectual figures in ancient China, very little is known of Confucius' life. But the essential outline of that life took on mythic proportions as the archetypal example of the Confucian Way: Through his devotion to self-cultivation, Confucius made himself into a great sage and devoted himself passionately to the public good in spite of hardships such as hunger, homelessness, unemployment, and life-threatening violence.

Confucius was born in Lu, where the Chou cultural tradition was especially strong, to a family that had once been part of the Shang aristocracy. So he was very conscious of inheriting both Shang and Chou cultures, and he never stopped looking to the golden eras of those dynasties for his models of human society, though his was a selective and idealized version of that past. Confucius' Chinese name was K'ung Ch'iu or K'ung Chung-ni, and he is known as K'ung Tzu or K'ung Fu-tzu, meaning "Master K'ung." It is from the second of these honorary names, K'ung Fu-tzu, that the latinized *Confucius* derives. Although his family technically belonged to the literate aristocracy, it had been reduced to very humble means some generations earlier, after its migration from a neighboring state where it had apparently lost favor with the rulers. So he was born to the literate class, but independent of the usual ties that class had to ruling interests – an unusual family situation which anticipated exactly the situation of the independent intellectual class he did so much to establish.

Confucius devoted himself to studies at a young age and perhaps held a number of menial government positions. But such a brilliant and outspoken character was surely not welcome in government, so Confucius pursued his political mission as a teacher of men (not surprisingly, this was an utterly sexist culture) who aspired to government service.

In this capacity he was widely admired, and his students were eagerly sought as the various rulers knew them to be the best-trained men in the empire – a cruel irony, for this meant that most of the prominent disciples became high officials serving the very families Confucius detested because they were undermining society by usurping power. In his late forties, Confucius took the first of several significant government positions in Lu, the highest of which was Minister of Justice. But at the age of fifty-six, realizing that his Way would always be ignored there, Confucius left Lu and spent thirteen years traveling from state to state advising rulers, hoping his ideas would be put into practice and so lead to a more humane society. Although he was known and respected as a sage by a number of the rulers he visited, none showed any inclination to employ him or enact his ideas. Utterly disappointed at his failure to have any real political impact, he finally returned home in his late sixties and devoted himself to teaching and establishing the classic texts that preserved the ancient cultural tradition.

Our primary surviving source for the teachings of Confucius is the *Lun Yü: The Analects,* or more literally, "The Selected Sayings." The book's defining characteristic is its aphoristic form: it is a collage of brief aphoristic fragments, each appearing with little supporting context. This lack of systematic precision extends to the language as well, for there was little sense of a precise philosophical language prior to Confucius. In the effort to articulate his ideas, Confucius was borrowing older terms and reshaping their meanings. Indeed, the Confucian philosophical world can be outlined by defining a small constellation of such terms (see Key Terms), but in most cases their meanings shift each time they are used and so remain somewhat obscure. So rather than systematically developing a philosophical system, the book attains its sense of coherence through a process of accretion.

The difficulties posed by the text itself are complicated by the question of authenticity. A good share of the book's fragments are assumed to represent the Master's teachings, handed down accurately by his disciples, but a great many clearly do not. Numerous versions of the Master's sayings were edited over the course of centuries, a time when the concept of individual authorship had not been firmly established, and much extraneous material was included by various editors, sometimes with the apparent intent of smuggling their preferred ideas into the canonical text. Although most of these fragments add depth and complexity to the text, some contradict its overall spirit. It is also clear that very little of what the Master said was recorded, and a great deal of what was recorded was not included in the *Analects* we now have: Mencius (4th c. B.C.E.) often cites the Master, for instance, and most of those citations are not included in the *Analects*. But for all the concerns about how authentic the text is and how accurately or thoroughly it portrays the historical Confucius' thought, the *Analects* still possesses an impressive stylistic unity and represents, as a matter of historical fact, the fundamental body of thought that has shaped Chinese civilization for over two thousand years.

Confucius' social philosophy derives from a rational empiricism, a methodology which represents a total break with Shang spiritualism, and this is perhaps why it has proven so enduring. Blatant power politics had made it impossible to believe in Heaven (let alone Shang Ti) as a transcendental source of order and legitimacy, so he tried to rescue the fragmented Chou culture by putting it on a more viable rational and secular basis. Confucius developed a social philosophy from the empirical observation that human society is a structure, a weave of relationships between individuals who each occupy a certain locus in that structure: parent and child, ruler and subject, friend and friend, merchant and customer, and so forth. Confucius invested this anthropological insight with a philosophical dimension by recognizing that a healthy community depends upon an attitude of human caring among its members – most especially its government, which should nurture first, teach second, and only then govern. Always looking to the past as his source of wisdom, Confucius saw that societies flourished when their citizens (their rulers above all) honored this moral principle, and inevitably crumbled when they ignored it: even the powerful transcendental glue of the Shang theocracy couldn't withstand the corrosive influence of the Shang Emperors' depredations.

But Confucius' social philosophy goes well beyond this moral dimension, for he described the web of social responsibilities as a system of "Ritual" (*li:* see Key Terms). *Ritual* is a crucial instance of how Confucius forged a philosophy by reshaping certain key terms, for it had been a religious concept associated with the worship of spirits. The spiritualist regime that had dominated China since the rise of the Shang had crumbled. Although Confucius recognized sacrifices to the spirit-world, he didn't necessarily believe any of the religious claims associated with such worship. For him, the value of such practices lay in the function they served in the Ritual structure of society. (This suggests an explanation for Confucius' oft-noted refusal to speak of the spirit-realm: to affirm the reality of that realm would be duplicitous, and to deny it would undermine the Ritual efficacy of practices associated with it.) It was in this context that Confucius extended the use of Ritual to include all the caring acts by which we fulfill our responsibilities to others in the community – hence the entire weave of everyday social life takes on the numinous aspect of the sacred.

This is a society in which individual identity is defined entirely in terms of the community. There is little sense of the inner self in the *Analects:* the Ritual social fabric is paramount, and individual identity is defined entirely in terms of a person's social roles. All of the Confucian moral virtues (see Key Terms) apply only in the social context: one cannot speak of a person being virtuous in isolation. And there is indeed a kind of spiritual clarity in the selflessness of this Ritual weave, a clarity that became a defining aspect in the structure of Chinese political and spiritual consciousness throughout the ages.

As it has shaped Chinese society for millennia, one must assume this Confucian system has proven useful to those in power. Confucius was struggling to describe this Ritual structure, so he naturally emphasized the individual's social role. This led to the appearance of an undue emphasis on the proper behavior of subordinates, and this is the aspect of Confucian thought that has proven so appealing to the interests of power. The brand of Confucianism wielded throughout the centuries as power's ideology of choice focused on select ideas involving selfless submission to authority: parental, political, masculine, historic, textual. And the "sacred" Ritual dimensions of these hierarchical relationships only made them that much more oppressive. It is this aspect of the Confucian tradition that has become so problematic in modern times, for intellectuals came to recognize it as the force that was preventing China's modernization. But selfless submission plays little part in the thought of Confucius himself, and as his thought was modified over the centuries by thinkers and social forces, this aspect could very well have been replaced. Indeed, not long after Confucius' death, Mencius had already challenged these hierarchies with a fierce insistence on the responsibilities of those in power, even declaring the people more important than the ruler. Nevertheless, China's ruling interests have rarely concerned themselves with the egalitarian ideas so central to Confucius' thought: social justice, political dissent, the role of intellectuals as social critics.

For Confucius, the Ritual community depends upon these egalitarian elements, and they depend ultimately on the education and cultivation of the community members. To call Confucius' contribution in this regard epochal would be an understatement. He was China's first professional teacher, founding the idea of a broad moral education, and in addition, he established the classic texts that defined the essential content of that education. As if that weren't enough, he also established the enduring principle of egalitarian education – that all people should receive some form of education, that this is necessary for the health of a moral community. He focused his attention on the education of intellectuals, which was of necessity much more exhaustive than that of the masses, but he thought even this education should be available to any who seek it, however humble their origins. In fact, not only was the Master himself from a relatively humble background, but nearly all of his disciples were as well.

The purpose of such education and cultivation is to become a *chün-*

tzu, a "noble-minded" one. And here again we find Confucius forging a philosophy by reshaping terminology. *Chün-tzu* had previously referred to those of noble birth, but Confucius redefined the term (and what it is to be noble) to mean those of talent and intellectual accomplishment. Here the application of Confucius' rational methodology to society resulted in a transformation of aristocracy to meritocracy, for government in Confucian society is a government of *chün-tzu,* a government of the high-minded rather than the high-born. To become government officials in China, candidates generally devoted themselves to many years of reflective study in order to pass daunting examinations, thereby proving they possessed formidable learning and moral insight. History thus replaces the spirit-realm as the source of knowledge about government and society, and this knowledge is recorded in books: it is the self-justifying and reasonable discoveries of past sages. Hence the wise man replaced the holy man, whose policy recommendations would have been dictated by oracle-bone divination. As a result of Confucius' legacy, Chinese culture has always had a reverence for learning that is perhaps deeper than in any other culture. And however often their role has been ignored or subverted by ruling interests, China has essentially always been a nation governed by philosophers.

The ideal of such a philosopher, the ideal result of the *chün-tzu's* self-cultivation, is mastery of the *Tao* (Way). Tao originally meant "way," as in "pathway" or "roadway," but Confucius recast it to mean the effortless process of human society functioning according to its natural Ritual structure. This Confucian Tao shows a striking resemblance to the more familiar Tao of the ancient Taoist masters, who recast it as a spiritual concept by transforming it into a kind of ontological Way. For them, Tao is the ontological ground or process (hence, a "Way") from which the ten thousand things arise. In both cases, the term refers to a vast organic process. And in both cases, mastery of the Way involves understanding how to dwell as an integral part of that process. For Confucius, the most exemplary masters of the Way were ancient sage-rulers who led societies in which this Ritual process of *li* functioned effortlessly. Their actions were spontaneous and selfless, for the ruler was simply the ruler: his actions followed directly from his Ritual role in the community, so he himself "did nothing":

> If anyone has managed to rule by doing nothing
> *(wu-wei)*, surely it was Shun. And how did he do so much by
> doing nothing? He just sat reverently facing south, that's all!
>
> (XV.5)

Wu-wei is a central concept in Taoism, where it is associated with *tzu-jan,* the mechanism of the Tao's process. *Tzu-jan*'s literal meaning is "self-so" or "the of-itself" or "being such of itself," hence "spontaneous" or "natural." But a more descriptive translation might be "occurrence appearing of itself," for it is meant to describe the ten thousand things unfolding spontaneously, each according to its own nature. For Taoists, we dwell as an organic part of *tzu-jan* by practicing *wu-wei,* which literally means "nothing doing," or more descriptively, "selfless action": acting as a spontaneous part of *tzu-jan* rather than with self-conscious intention. Here in its sole appearance in the *Analects, wu-wei* functions in much the same way. But rather than making us a part of *tzu-jan,* the Confucian practice of *wu-wei* makes us a part of *tzu-jan*'s Confucian counterpart: *li* (Ritual). Shun has so mastered the Way that he need only sit facing south, the ceremonial position of the Emperor, and the Ritual weave of human community thereby continues its self-generating process, a sacred process inspiring nothing less than reverence.

These structural similarities reflect a deeper unity in the two systems of thought. This unity was explored in a most profound way by the thinkers of a philosophical movement known as Dark-Enigma Learning (Hsüan Hsüeh), which arose in the third and fourth centuries of the current era and explored the dark and enigmatic regions of ontology. There they discovered a fundamental unity in Confucian and Taoist thought when they recognized that Confucius located his human society within a cosmology that the Taoists described eloquently, but which he himself referred to only through silence:

> Adept Kung said: "When the Master talks about

civility and cultivation, you can hear what he says.

But when he talks about the nature of things and the Way of Heaven, you can't hear a word."

(V.12)

"Heaven" is a major component in that shared cosmology, and a particularly significant instance of Confucius developing ideas through terminology. The most primitive meaning of *Heaven (T'ien)* is "sky." By extension, it also comes to mean "transcendence," for our most primal sense of transcendence may be the simple act of looking up into the sky. So it's hardly surprising that when the Chou wanted to reinvent Shang Ti in a more impersonal form, they would choose Heaven. By association with the idea of transcendence and that which is beyond us, it is natural that *Heaven* also comes to mean "fate" or "destiny." And this is precisely what we find in Confucius, where "destiny" has evolved out of the early Chou sense of an impersonal deity. But rather than destiny in the sense of a transcendental force deciding human fate, this is destiny as the inevitable evolution of things according to the principles inherent to them. Although Confucius focuses on its manifestations in human history, there is little real difference between this Confucian Heaven and that of the Taoists, who identified it with the natural process of *tzu-jan*. Confucius even goes so far as to say that the most profound level of his teachings is the silent voice of Heaven's natural process:

> The Master said: "I'd love to just say nothing."
>
> "But if you say nothing," said Adept Kung, "how would we disciples hand down your teachings?"
>
> "What has Heaven ever said?" replied the Master. "The four seasons keep turning and the hundred things keep emerging – but what has Heaven ever said?"

(17.17)

This sounds more like Lao Tzu than Confucius, at least until we realize that the Ritual structure of society is part of a much larger weave, the Ritual structure of natural process, a point made by Hsün Tzu (ca.

313–238 B.C.E.), one of the most important early developers of Confucian philosophy:

> Through Ritual, Heaven and earth join in harmony, sun and moon shine, the four seasons proceed in order, the stars and constellations march, the rivers flow, and all things flourish; men's likes and dislikes are regulated and their joys and hates made appropriate. Those below are obedient and those above are enlightened; all things change but do not become disordered . . . .
>
> *(Hsün Tzu,* trans. Watson, p. 94)

Hence, our initial definition of the Confucian Tao ("the effortless process of human society functioning according to its natural Ritual structure") can be dramatically expanded, making it comparable to the Taoist Tao: "the effortless process of the cosmos functioning according to its natural Ritual structure." This Ritual process of the cosmos never falters, and so it is unproblematic. This is no doubt why Confucius is so unconcerned with it. Instead he focuses his attention on human society, where this Ritual process can so easily fail. So for a society to abide by the Tao means it functions as an organic part of the cosmological process. Here is the probable explanation for why Confucius sometimes speaks of Heaven as if it were a cosmic moral will sustaining the human order: the Ritual structure of the cosmos is a self-generating normative order, so it has the natural urge to restore itself when it is disrupted in the human realm.

It would seem the difference between *li* and *tzu-jan* is a matter of emphasis: while *tzu-jan* emphasizes individual things evolving in a system according to their own nature, *li* emphasizes a system evolving through individuals according to its own nature. But in both cases, it is a dynamic system of complex interrelationships that is being described. The difference in emphasis reflects the overall difference between Confucian and Taoist thought: the Confucian emphasizes community and the Taoist emphasizes individuals. These two Ways are traditionally described as the two poles of Chinese thought, but their shared cosmology affords them a fundamental unity, and that unity is no doubt why

Chinese culture could eventually adopt both of these Ways simultaneously: the Confucian Way has defined the societal realm for Chinese intellectuals throughout the millennia, and the Way of philosophical Taoism has defined the private spiritual realm.

Dark-Enigma Learning traced this fundamental unity to the deepest regions of cosmology: to Absence (see *Tao Te Ching* and *Chuang Tzu* Key Terms: *Wu*), the primal emptiness from which the ten thousand transformations issue forth according to the principles of *tzu-jan* and *li*. Mindful of Lao Tzu's famous dictum "Those who know don't speak, and those who speak don't know," Dark-Enigma Learning held that Lao Tzu and Chuang Tzu hadn't yet fully identified themselves with Absence, so they spoke of it at length because it was something outside themselves, something in which they were still deficient. Confucius, on the other hand, was completely identified with Absence, and so knew how utterly beyond words it is. He therefore spoke only of Presence (see *Tao Te Ching* and *Chuang Tzu* Key Terms: *Wu*), though it is true he does indicate how essential such identification with the emptiness of Absence is for a true sage, as when he speaks of understanding "through dark silence" (VII.2), or in this description of Yen Hui, his favorite and most accomplished disciple: "Yen Hui's nearly made it: He's almost always empty" (XI.19). Indeed, it may well be that this identification with Absence is the epitome of Ritual selflessness.

Given the precision and depth of his subtle references to the cosmology that frames his social philosophy, it seems likely that cosmology played a larger role in Confucius' thought than the surviving record indicates. But even if we had more of his statements in this area, the motif of silence would no doubt remain dominant. Indeed, silence may be the most resounding instance of Confucius crafting a philosophy by crafting a terminology. Whether or not he was in fact identified with Absence, this silence was possible for him because he wasn't struggling to create a cosmology. In his social philosophy, he seems instead to be drawing out the implications of a cosmology that already existed in the culture. Rather than a newly created replacement for the Shang monotheism, it had apparently survived from the more primal cultures that preceded the Shang, thus revealing the Shang monotheism as a mere ideological overlay convenient to the uses of power. The resilience of this cosmology after a thousand years of neglect suggests the possibility that such a cosmology may yet reemerge in the West, especially as it is so consistent with the modern scientific account of the cosmos. We have certainly witnessed the same kind of catastrophic cultural collapse in this last century as China did in Confucius' time, and the insights that emerged so long ago from China's similar experience could well play a significant role in whatever renewal may take place here over the next millennium. For this to happen, it is clear that the hierarchical Ritual relationships of Confucianism must be replaced by egalitarian ones, but there is no structural reason why this cannot happen. In any case, the cosmology that shaped Chinese civilization was a resurgence of an ancient cosmology, a return to the culture's most primal roots – the Paleolithic and beyond. It is a primal realm where the categories of secular and sacred dissolve, where everything and nothing is sacred.

It was Confucius' great achievement to articulate a viable human order that is empirically consistent with the existential verities of that cosmology. In so doing, he combined a rational humanistic conceptual world with a primal organismic cosmos: rationality as a perfectly natural outgrowth of the self-generating cosmos. The Ritual society, a dynamic of relationships, is a kind of human ecology, and it is woven into the vast natural ecology of cosmological process. The spiritual ecology of this shared cosmology might also be seen as a return to the original spirituality of paleolithic China, for the sense of belonging to natural process is a secular version of the worship of nature deities as ancestral spirits.

What distinguishes the human from other manifestations of this cosmos is its particular ecology: people literally make themselves human by fulfilling the responsibilities inherent to their position in the Ritual weave, thereby strengthening the social community. Indeed, the central word that Confucius used to describe a person who masterfully fulfills the responsibilities of Ritual, who dwells as an integral part of the Ritual weave of society, is *jen* (*Humanity:* see Key Terms), a term he broadened to mean a selfless and reverent concern for the well-being of others, but which retained its original meaning as the verbal form of the noun meaning a human. This complex of meanings appears visually in the paired elements in its graph, "human" and "two":仁. Hence the social aspect of being human. So to observe Ritual, to dwell as an integral part of the Ritual weave of society is to be, by definition, human. And conversely, to violate that Ritual weave is to be inhuman, for when that is violated the human ecology threatens to unravel. And this principle might be extended to the full cosmological dimensions of Ritual: to dwell as an integral part of the Ritual weave of the cosmos is to be human in the most elemental sense; and conversely, to violate that Ritual weave is to be inhuman in the most elemental sense, for when that is violated the natural ecology threatens to unravel.

So it is that Confucius established the human community in intimate contact with natural process and its ontological source in Absence, an intimacy that is perhaps the most characteristic and profound aspect in the deep structure of Chinese consciousness: a kind of spiritual ecology that seems to have been there from the beginning in the organic, open-form structure of the language itself, and which eventually became central to Taoist and Ch'an (Zen) Buddhist practices, as well as all the major art forms. The three regions of this cosmology appear almost schematically in countless Chinese landscape paintings, . for instance: the pregnant emptiness of Absence; the natural process of Presence in its constant burgeoning forth from Absence; and finally, within that natural process, the human. And with their sparsely peopled landscapes so dramatically burgeoning forth out of vast realms of emptiness, such paintings do indeed render a majestic vision: human community nestled in the primal ecology of a spontaneously self-generating and harmonious cosmos.

士　直　追　尊　頗　肩　雄

仁　抒　立　尢　氏　　　流

　　聞　玄　禮　心　聖　賣

君　汙　器　念　嬰　　　陂

同　以　沸　真　家　制　年

雇　注　心　盧　宮　元　青

敬　水　昔　世　魯　建　龍

咒　深　待　禮　親　百　在

思　括　鍾　樂　里　主　流

寏　寉　暦　陵　并　亦　勤

嘉　深　遲　官　改　　　霝

I   To Learn, and Then

1   The Master said: "To learn, and then, in its due season, put what you have learned into practice – isn't that still a great pleasure? And to have a friend visit from somewhere far away – isn't that still a great joy? When you're ignored by the world like this, and yet bear no resentment – isn't that great nobility?"

2   Master Yu¹ said: "It's honoring parents and elders that makes people human. Then they rarely turn against authority. And if people don't turn against authority, they never rise up and pitch the country into chaos.

"The noble-minded cultivate roots. When roots are secure, the Way² is born. To honor parents and elders – isn't that the root of Humanity?"³

3   The Master said: "Clever words and sanctimonious looks: in such people, Humanity is rare indeed."

4   Master Tseng⁴ said: "Each day I ask three things of myself: Have I been trustworthy in all that I've done for other people? Have I stood by my words⁵ in dealing with friends? Have I practiced all that I've been taught?"

5   The Master said: "To show the Way for a nation of a thousand war-chariots, a ruler pays reverent attention to the country's affairs and always stands by his words. He maintains economy and simplicity, always loving the people, and so employs the people only in due season."

6   The Master said: "In youth, respect your parents when home and your elders when away. Think carefully before you speak, and stand by your words. Love the whole expanse of things, and make an intimate of Humanity. Then, if you have any energy left, begin cultivating yourself."

7   Adept Hsia[6] said: "Cherishing wisdom as if it were a beautiful woman, devoting their strength to serving parents and their lives to serving a ruler, standing by their words in dealing with friends – such people may say they've never studied, but I would call them learned indeed."

8   The Master said: "If you're grave and thoughtful, people look to you with the veneration due a noble. And if you're learned, too, you're never inflexible.

"Above all else, be loyal and stand by your words. Never befriend those who are not kindred spirits. And when you're wrong, don't be afraid to change."

9   Master Tseng said: "Be thorough in mourning parents, and meticulous in the ancestral sacrifices, then the people's Integrity[7] will return to its original fullness."

10   Adept Ch'in asked of Adept Kung:[8] "Whenever the Master visits a country, he learns all about its government. Does he have to search out this information, or is it just given to him?"

Adept Kung replied: "Congenial, good-natured, reverent, frugal, deferential – that's how he learns so much. It's altogether different from the way others inquire, don't you think?"

11   The Master said: "Consider your plans when your father is alive, then see what you do when he dies. If you leave your father's Way unchanged for all three years of mourning, you are indeed a worthy child."

12   Master Yu said: "The most precious fruit of Ritual is harmony. The Way of the ancient Emperors found its beauty in this, and all matters great and small depend upon it.

"Still, things go wrong. You may understand this harmony and even instill things with it, but if you fail to shape harmony with Ritual, you'll never make things right."

13   Master Yu said:

> *"Make standing by words your Duty,[9]*
> *and your words will last and last,*
>
> *make reverence an everyday Ritual,*
> *and you'll stay clear of all disgrace –*
>
> *then kindred spirits remain kindred,*
> *and you're worthy to be their ancestor."*

14   The Master said: "The noble-minded are content without a full belly or the comforts of home; they're quick in action but cautious in word; they rectify themselves by seeking out a master of the Way. And so they can be called lovers of learning."

15   Adept Kung said: *"When poor, never fawning; when rich, never arrogant.* How does that sound?"

The Master replied: "Not bad. But not so good as *When poor, delighting in the Way; when rich, devoted to Ritual.*"

Adept Kung said: "In *The Book of Songs,* the noble-minded are perfected

> *as if cut, as if polished,*
> *as if carved, as if burnished.*[10]

Is that what you mean?"

The Master replied: "Only with a person like you can I even begin to talk about the *Songs.* When they tell you about the past, you understand the future."

16   The Master said: "Don't grieve when people fail to recognize your ability. Grieve when you fail to recognize theirs."

士　且　廷　□　頎　肩　帽
仁　扵　立　□　氏　□　□
聞　玄　禮　心　里　□　□
君　汙　器　念　□　□　□
同　以　兼　□　家　剌　羊
□　注　之　□　居　元　青
敬　水　昔　世　魯　□　飛
□　沐　衍　禮　親　百　在
思　□　鐘　桼　里　王　漢
□　滕　陵　并　□　□　鄭
□　漢　遅　宮　改　□　霜

II In Government, the Secret

1   The Master said: "In government, the secret is Integrity. Use it, and you'll be like the polestar: always dwelling in its proper place, the other stars turning reverently about it."

2   The Master said: "There are three hundred songs in *The Book of Songs*, but this one phrase tells it all: *thoughts never twisty*."[1]

3   The Master said: "If you use government to show them the Way and punishment to keep them true, the people will grow evasive and lose all remorse. But if you use Integrity to show them the Way and Ritual to keep them true, they'll cultivate remorse and always see deeply into things."

4   The Master said: "At fifteen I devoted myself to learning, and at thirty stood firm. At forty I had no doubts, and at fifty understood the Mandate of Heaven. At sixty I listened in effortless accord. And at seventy I followed the mind's passing fancies without overstepping any bounds."

5   When Lord Meng Yi[2] asked about honoring parents, the Master said: "Never disobey."

Later, when Fan Ch'ih[3] was driving his carriage, the Master said: "Meng asked me about honoring parents, and I said *Never disobey.*"

"What did you mean by that?" asked Fan Ch'ih.

"In life, serve them according to Ritual," replied the Master. "In death, bury them according to Ritual. And then, make offerings to them according to Ritual."

6   When Lord Meng Yi's son, Wu-po, asked about honoring parents, the Master replied: "The only time you should cause your mother and father to worry is when you are sick."

7   When Adept Yu[4] asked about honoring parents, the Master said: "These days, being a worthy child just means keeping parents well-fed. That's what we do for dogs and horses. Everyone can feed their parents – but without reverence, they may as well be feeding animals."

8   When Adept Hsia asked about honoring parents, the Master said: "It's the way you do things that matters. When there's work, children may make it easy for their parents. And when there's wine and food, they may serve their parents first. But isn't there more to honoring parents than this?"

9   The Master said: "I can talk with Yen Hui[5] all day, and he never disagrees. He seems like a fool. But thinking about how he is when alone, I realize that he reveals my most essential principles. Hui is no fool."

10   The Master said: "If you look at their intentions, examine their motives, and scrutinize what brings them contentment – how can people hide who they are? How can they hide who they really are?"

11   The Master said: "If you can revive the ancient and use it to understand the modern, then you're worthy to be a teacher."

12   The Master said: "A noble-minded man is not an implement."

13   Adept Hsia asked about the noble-minded, and the Master said: "Such people act before they speak, then they speak according to their actions."

14   The Master said: "The noble-minded are all-encompassing, not stuck in doctrines. Little people are stuck in doctrines."

15   The Master said: "To learn and never think – that's delusion. But to think and never learn – that is perilous indeed!"

16   The Master said: "Devote yourself to strange doctrines and principles, and there's sure to be pain and suffering."

17   The Master said: "Shall I explain understanding for you, Lu? When you understand something, know that you understand it. When you don't understand something, know that you don't understand it. That's understanding."

18   Adept Chang was studying, hoping for rewards. The Master said: "Listen to all that you can – then, if you forget the deficiencies and speak about the rest cautiously, you'll avoid trouble. See all that you can – then, if you forget the perilous and act upon the rest cautiously, you'll avoid regret. In speech avoid trouble, in action avoid regret – then rewards will come of themselves."

19   Duke Ai[6] asked: "What must I do to make the people willing subjects?"

"If you raise up the straight and cast out the crooked," replied Confucius, "the people will honor you. If you raise up the crooked and cast out the straight, they'll never honor you."

20   Lord Chi K'ang[7] asked how he could persuade the people to be reverent and loyal. The Master said: "Preside over them with solemn dignity, then the people will be reverent. Honor your parents and cherish your children, then the people will be loyal. Promote the worthy and instruct the feckless, then the people will be persuaded."

21   Someone asked Confucius: "Why aren't you in government?"

The Master replied: *"The Book of History says: Honor your parents, simply honor your parents and make your brothers friends – this too is good government.* That's really being in government, so why govern by serving in government?"

22   The Master said: "Unless you stand by your words, you'll never know what you're capable of. A large cart with no yoke-bar for the harness, a small cart with no collar-bar for the harness – what use are they?"

23   Adept Chang asked if we can know what will come ten generations from now. The Master replied: "The first of our dynasties was the Hsia. Although changes were made, the Hsia rituals were continued in the Shang, and so the Shang could be known. Although changes were made, the Shang rituals were continued in the Chou, and so the Chou could be known. Whatever follows our own Chou Dynasty, even if it comes a hundred generations from now, we can know it in the same way."

24   The Master said: "Sacrificing to the spirits of ancestors not your own is mere flattery. And to recognize a Duty without carrying it out is mere cowardice."

雖頑其真遑立士

氏里書元能頑持仁

心念家居魯禮君聞

禮路基昔世以玄君

樂往水持敬種同

水昔世禮親敬

持禮親百左

鍾栗里主洌

陵幷不勤

遲官改露

III Eight Rows of Dancers

1 Speaking of the Chi family patriarch, Confucius said: "Eight rows of dancers at his ancestral temple, as if he were an Emperor: If this can be endured, what can't be?"[1]

2 As they cleared sacrificial vessels from the temple, the Three Families sang the Yung hymn. The Master mimicked its words:

> *the great lords in attendance,*
> *the Emperor august and majestic,*[2]

then asked: "What has this to do with the temple of these Three Families?"

3 The Master said: "If you're human without Humanity, you know nothing of Ritual. If you're human without Humanity, you know nothing of music."

4 Lin Fang[3] asked about the root of Ritual. The Master replied: "What a huge question! In Ritual, simplicity rather than extravagance. In mourning, grief rather than repose."

5   The Master said: "Those wild tribes in the far north and east – they still honor their sovereigns. They're nothing like us: we Chinese have given up such things."

6   The Chi family patriarch went to perform the imperial sacrifice on Exalt Mountain. The master said to Jan Ch'iu:⁴ "That is for Emperors alone to perform. Can't you save us from this?"

"No, I cannot," replied Jan Ch'iu.

"Ohhh," groaned the Master. "And how could the god of Exalt Mountain know even less than Lin Fang about such things?"

7   The Master said: "The noble-minded never contend. It's true that archery is a kind of contention. But even then, they bow and yield to each other when stepping up to the range. And when they step down, they toast each other. Even in contention, they retain their nobility."

8   Adept Hsia asked: "What does it mean when the *Songs* say

Dimpled smile so entrancing,
glancing eyes so full of grace:
purest silk so ready for color?"⁵

"For a painting," replied the Master, "you need a ground of pure silk."

"And for Ritual – what ground do you need?"

"How you've lifted my spirits, Hsia!" exclaimed the Master. "With you, I can truly discuss the *Songs*!"

9 The Master said: "I can speak of the Hsia Dynasty's rituals, though evidence is scarce among the Hsia's descendants in Ch'i. And I can speak of the Shang's rituals, though records and scholars are scarce among the Shang's descendants in Sung. Without such scarcity, I could prove what I say."

10 The Master said: "As for what follows the opening libation at the Imperial Sacrifice, I'd rather not see how they do it these days."

11 Someone asked about the theory of the Imperial Sacrifice. The Master replied: "I've never understood it. If there were someone who understood, he could reveal the workings of all beneath Heaven this easily," and he pointed a finger to the palm of his hand.

12 *Sacrifice as if present* means *Sacrifice to spirits as if the spirits were present*. So the Master said: "If I'm not there at my own ancestral sacrifice, it's as if there were no sacrifice at all."

13 Wang-sun Chia[6] inquired of the Master: "What does it mean to say

As for homage at the household shrine,
homage pays better at the kitchen stove?"

"That's wrong," responded the Master. "Once you've offended Heaven, there's nowhere to turn."

14   The Master said: "The Chou Dynasty looked to its predecessors, the Shang and Hsia. How elegant and majestic Chou culture was – and now, we follow the Chou."

15   When he was in the Grand Temple, the Master asked questions about everything he saw. Someone said: "Who says this son of a Tsou villager understands Ritual? When he was in the Grand Temple, he asked questions about everything he saw."

When he heard this, the Master said: "That questioning is itself Ritual."

16   The Master said: *"People's strength differs. So, in archery, shooting* through *the target-skin isn't the point.* That is the way of the ancients."

17   As the ceremony had fallen into neglect, Adept Kung wanted to do away with sacrificing sheep to announce a new moon to the ancestors. The Master said: "You love sheep, Kung, but I love Ritual."

18   The Master said: "If you make a Ritual of serving your sovereign, people will call it mere flattery."

19   Duke Ting⁷ asked how the sovereign should employ ministers and how ministers should serve the sovereign. Confucius replied: "The sovereign should make employing ministers a matter of Ritual. And ministers should make serving their sovereign a matter of loyalty."

20   The Master said: "In the first of the *Songs*, there's joy without abandon and grief without laceration."

21   Duke Ai asked Tsai Yü[8] about altars to the earth god. Tsai Yü said: "The Hsia Dynasty used a pine grove. The Shang used cedar. And the Chou used chestnut, saying *Then the people will tremble like the chestnut in wind*."

When he heard this, the Master said: "Never speak of what has already happened. Never criticize what has already run its course. Never condemn what is already done and gone."

22   The Master said: "Kuan Chung[9] was truly an implement of little use!"

Someone asked: "But wasn't Kuan Chung terribly frugal?"

"Kuan had three separate homes," replied the Master. "And his officers never did double duty. Is that frugal?"

"But still, Kuan Chung understood Ritual, didn't he?"

"A sovereign screens his gate with trees. But Kuan also built such a screen. After sovereigns meet and toast their friendship, they place the cups on a ceremonial stand. Kuan also had such a stand. If Kuan understood Ritual, who doesn't?"

23   When he was talking about music with the great music-master of Lu, the Master said: "This is what we can know of music: It begins in the sounds of harmony – then, pure and clear and unbroken, it swells into completion."

24   Asking to see the Master, a border-guard at Yi said: "Of all the noble-minded men who've traveled this way, none have declined to see me." So the disciples took him to see the Master.

As he was leaving, the border-guard said: "My friends, why mourn what's been lost? The Way's been unknown everywhere under Heaven for a very long time, and Heaven's about to use your Master like the clapper in a bell."

25   The Master said Emperor Shun's[10] music was perfectly beautiful, and perfectly virtuous, too. He said Emperor Wu's[11] music was perfectly beautiful, but not perfectly virtuous.

26   The Master said: "Governing without generosity, Ritual without reverence, mourning without grief – how could I bear to see such things?"

雍　月　頳　豐　造　宣　王

龍　氏　先　立　　拉　仁

　　聖　入　禮　玄　聞

　　嬰　念　器　汙　君

来　制　家　真　弟　以　同

青　元　宮　廟　之　注　權

龍　　魯　世　音　水　敬

在　百　親　禮　祐　涤　咏

涞　王　里　樂　健　法　思

勤　不　并　陵　廚　庭　遠

霜　改　官　遲　廷

IV   Of Villages, Humanity

1   The Master said: "Of villages, Humanity is the most beautiful. If you choose to dwell anywhere else, how can you be called wise?"

2   The Master said: "Without Humanity, you can't dwell in adversity for long, and you can't dwell in prosperity for long. If you're Humane, Humanity is your repose. And if you're wise, Humanity is your reward."

3   The Master said: "Only the Humane can love people, and only they can despise people."

4   The Master said: "Those who aspire to Humanity – they despise no one."

5   The Master said: "Wealth and position – that's what people want. But if you enjoy wealth and position without following the Way, you'll never dwell at ease. Poverty and obscurity – that's what people despise. And if you endure poverty and obscurity without following the Way, you'll never get free.

   "If you ignore Humanity, how will you gain praise and renown? The noble-minded don't forget Humanity for a single moment, not even in the crush of confusion and desperation."

6   The Master said: "I've never seen a person who really loves Humanity and despises Inhumanity. Those who love Humanity know of nothing more essential. And those who despise Inhumanity act with such Humanity that Inhumanity never touches them.

"Can people devote their full strength to Humanity for even a single day? I've never seen anyone who isn't strong enough. There may be such people, but I've never seen them."

7   The Master said: "A person's various faults are all of a piece. Recognizing your faults is a way of understanding Humanity."

8   The Master said: "If you hear the Way one morning and die that night, you die content."

9   The Master said: "Aspiring to the Way, but ashamed of bad clothes and bad food: such a person knows nothing worth discussing."

10   The Master said: "In their dealings with all beneath Heaven, the noble-minded do not themselves favor some things and oppose others. They form judgments according to Duty."

11   The Master said: "While the noble-minded cherish Integrity, little people cherish territory. And while the noble-minded cherish laws, little people cherish privilege."

12   The Master said: "If profit guides your actions, there will be no end of resentment."

13   The Master said: "If you can found a nation on Ritual and yielding, what more is there? If you cannot found a nation on Ritual and yielding, what's left of Ritual?"

14   The Master said: "Don't worry if you have no position: worry about making yourself worthy of one. Don't worry if you aren't known and admired: devote yourself to a life that deserves admiration."   .

15   The Master said: "Tseng! There's a single thread stringing my Way together."

"There is indeed," replied Master Tseng.

When the Master left, some disciples asked: "What did he mean?"

"Be loyal to the principles of your heart, and treat others with that same loyalty,"[1] answered Master Tseng. "That is the Master's Way. There is nothing more."

16   The Master said: "The noble-minded are clear about Duty. Little people are clear about profit."

17   The Master said: "In the presence of sages, you can see how to perfect your thoughts. In the presence of fools, you must awaken yourself."

18   The Master said: "In serving your mother and father, admonish them gently. If they understand, and yet choose not to follow your advice, deepen your reverence without losing faith. And however exhausting this may be, avoid resentment."

19   The Master said: "While your mother and father are alive, never travel to far-off places. Or if you must, always follow a definite plan."

20   The Master said: "If you leave your father's Way unchanged for all three years of mourning, you are indeed a worthy child."

21   The Master said: "Never forget your parents' age. Though it fills you with dread, it also fills you with joy."

22   The Master said: "The ancients spoke little. They were too ashamed when their actions fell short of their words."

23   The Master said: "To lose by caution is rare indeed."

24   The Master said: "This is what the noble-minded aspire to: slow to speak and quick to act."

25   The Master said: "Integrity's never alone. It always has neighbors."

26   Adept Yu said: "If you scold your sovereign too often, you'll end up disgraced. If you scold your friend too often, you'll end up alone."

月　氏　聖　嬰　牛　青　亂　　　第

顏　元　心　念　家　元　魯　親　主　并　官

真　立　禮　器　真　虛　世　禮　樂　陵　改

起　於　玄　汙　樂　之　晉　衬　鍾　陵　遲

之　仁　聞　君　同　性　敬　永　思

V Kung-yeh Ch'ang

1   The Master said Kung-yeh Ch'ang[1] would make a fine hus-
band, for although he's been in prison, it was through no fault of his
own. And so the Master gave his daughter in marriage to him.

The Master said Nan Jung[2] wouldn't be overlooked in a country that
abides in the Way, and wouldn't be punished in a country that ignores the
Way. And so the Master gave his brother's daughter in marriage to him.

2   Of Adept Chien,[3] the Master said: "Noble-minded indeed!
And if there was no one noble-minded in Lu, how did he get that way?"

3   Adept Kung asked: "And what about me?"
"You're an implement," replied the Master.
"What kind of implement?"
"A sacrificial vessel of jade."

4   Someone said: "Jan Yung[4] is Humane, but he's hardly elo-
quent."

"What good is eloquence?" said the Master. "If you badger people
with clever talk, they usually just end up hating you. I don't know if he's
Humane, but what good is eloquence?"

5   When the Master told him to take a position in government, Ch'i-tiao K'ai⁵ replied: "I still can't trust myself that far."

The Master was delighted.

6   The Master said: "The Way's lost and forgotten in this land. If I found a raft and set out across the sea, I doubt anyone but Lu would follow me."

Hearing this, Adept Lu⁶ was elated.

"Lu's much fonder of courage than I am," said the Master, "but his judgment is poor indeed."

7   Meng Wu-po asked if Adept Lu was Humane, and the Master replied: "I don't know."

When Meng asked again, the Master said: "In a nation of a thousand war-chariots, Lu could be Minister of Defense. But I don't know if he's Humane."

"And Jan Ch'iu – what about Jan Ch'iu?"

"In a city of a thousand families or a territory ruled by a noble house of a hundred war-chariots, Ch'iu could be regent.⁷ But I don't know if he's Humane."

"And Adept Hua?"

"With his sash on at court, Hua could chat with visitors and guests. But I don't know if he's Humane, either."

8   The Master said to Adept Kung: "Who do you think is better, you or Yen Hui?"

"How could I even dare look at Hui?" answered Kung. "When Hui hears one thing, he understands ten. But when I hear one thing, I only understand two."

"Nothing like him!" said the Master. "You and I are nothing like him!"

9   Tsai Yü slept in the daytime. The Master said: "You can't carve much of anything from rotted wood. And you can't whitewash a wall of dung. So why bother scolding a person like Yü?

"In dealing with people," the Master added, "I once listened to their words, and then trusted them to do what they said. Now I listen to their words, and then watch what they do carefully. It was Yü that changed me."

10   The Master said: "I've never met anyone who is truly resolute."
"What about Shen Ch'eng?"
"Ch'eng – that bundle of passions? How resolute can *he* be?"

11   Adept Kung said: "I do nothing to others that I wouldn't want done to me."
"That's something you haven't quite mastered, Kung," the Master replied.

12   Adept Kung said: "When the Master talks about civility and cultivation, you can hear what he says. But when he talks about the nature of things and the Way of Heaven, you can't hear a word."

13   When Adept Lu heard a precept, his one fear was that he might hear another before he could put the first into practice.

14   Adept Kung asked: "If he was so treacherous, why is Lord K'ung Wen called *Wen*?"[8]

"He was diligent in his love of learning," replied the Master, "and he was never ashamed to seek answers from those beneath him. That's why he's called *Wen*."

15   The Master said Prime Minister Ch'an embodied four aspects of the noble-minded Way: humble in living his life and reverent in serving his lord, generous in nurturing the people and responsible in employing them.

16   The Master said: "Yen P'ing-chung[9] was a master of friendship. He still treated old friends with reverence."

17   The Master said: "Tsang Wen-chung[10] kept a sacred divination tortoise among mountain-carved beams and duckweed-carved pillars, as if he were an Emperor. What kind of wisdom is that?"

18   Adept Chang said: "Tzu-wen was appointed Prime Minister three times without ever showing delight. And he resigned three times without ever showing resentment. Instead, he dutifully explained the operation of his government to his successors. What do you think of such a man?"

"He was loyal indeed," replied the Master.

"And was he Humane?"

"I don't know," replied the Master. "Would such things make him Humane?"

Adept Chang began again: "When Ts'ui Tzu killed the Ch'i sovereign, Lord Ch'en Wen was a minister who had ten teams of horses, but he abandoned everything and left. He went to another country – but soon, saying *They're just like our grand Ts'ui Tzu here,* he left. He went to the next country – and soon, saying the same thing, he left there too. What do you think of such a man?"

"He was pure indeed."

"And was he Humane?"

"I don't know," replied the Master. "Would such things make him Humane?"

19   Lord Chi Wen thought three times before taking any action. When the Master heard this, he said: "Twice is plenty enough."

20   The Master said: "People say Lord Ning Wu[11]

> *was a sage when his country followed the Way*
> *and a fool when his country abandoned the Way.*

We may master his wisdom, but never his foolishness."

21   When he was in Ch'en, the Master said: "Back home! Let's go back home! The young in our villages are full of impetuous ambition. They've perfected eloquence and grace, but know nothing about proper measure."

22   The Master said: "Po Yi and Shu Ch'i[12] never harbored old grudges, and so had little use for rancor."

23   The Master said: "How can people say Wei-sheng Kao was

forthright? When someone came to him begging for vinegar, he borrowed some from a neighbor and gave it to them."

24   The Master said: "Clever talk, ingratiating looks, fawning reverence: Tso-ch'iu Ming found that shameful, and so do I. Friendly while harboring resentment: Tso-ch'iu Ming found that shameful, too, and so do I."

25   When Yen Hui and Adept Lu were attending him, the Master said: "Why don't you each tell me what your greatest ambition is?"

"I'd like to share horses and carriages, robes and light furs with friends," said Lu, "to see them well-used, and then rest content."

"I'd like never to promote my virtues," said Yen Hui, "and never to burden others."

Adept Lu then said: "Now Master, we'd like to hear your greatest ambition."

"To comfort the old, to trust my friends, and to cherish the young."

26   The Master said: "It's hopeless! I never see people who can recognize their own faults and then inwardly accuse themselves."

27   The Master said: "In a village of ten homes, you could certainly find someone who stands by words as faithfully as me, but no one who so loves learning."

雖肩頷　尊禮造宣立
　氏聖　心立禮玄扵仁
　寶嬰　念器禮汙　閒
年封家　　樂器以　君
青元宮　世　坒　同
龍　魯　　普水　權
左百親　禮待　　教
洙主里　樂鍾海　思
勤　并　陵齊　
霣改官　官遲

VI Jan Yung Is One Who

1   The Master said: "Jan Yung is one who could take the Emperor's seat and sit facing south."

Jan Yung asked about Tzu-sang Po-tzu, and the Master said: "Yes, with his mastery of simplicity, he too could take the Emperor's seat."

"To act simply because your life is reverent," replied Yung, "isn't that enough to lead the people? But to act simply because your life is simple, isn't that simplicity gone too far?"

"Yes. What you say is quite true."

2   Duke Ai asked which of the disciples had a true love of learning.

"Yen Hui had a true love of learning," replied Confucius. "He never blamed others and never made the same mistake twice. Unfortunately, destiny[1] allowed him but a brief life, and now he's dead. Now, I know of no one who loves learning."

3   When Adept Hua was sent to Ch'i on a mission, his mother was running short of supplies, so Jan Ch'iu asked that she be given grain.

"Give her a basketful," replied the Master.

Jan Ch'iu asked for more.

"Alright, give her a bushel," replied the Master.

Jan gave her twenty-five bushels, whereupon the Master said: "Hua set off for Ch'i riding a sleek horse and wearing light furs. I have heard that the noble-minded give to help the needy, not to subsidize the wealthy."

4   When he was appointed regent, Yüan Szu[2] was offered nine hundred measures of grain, but he refused. The Master said: "Why refuse? Aren't there people in your neighborhoods and villages who need that grain?"

5   Speaking of Jan Yung, the Master said: "If it were born of a common field ox, we may not want to use it in the earth sacrifice, though it have fine horns and sorrel hide – but would mountains and rivers reject it?"

6   The Master said: "Yen Hui can empty his mind of everything but Humanity for three months, and never falter. Others may cling to it for a day or month, but that's all."

7   Lord Chi K'ang asked: "Is Adept Lu worthy of government office?"

"Lu is resolute," replied the Master. "If you appoint him, what could go wrong?"

"And Adept Kung – is he worthy of government office?"

"Kung is wise. If you appoint him, what could go wrong?"

"What about Jan Ch'iu?"

"Ch'iu is skillful. If you appoint him, what could go wrong?"[3]

8   When the House of Chi wanted to appoint him regent in Pi, Min Tzu-ch'ien⁴ said: "Find some diplomatic way of declining for me. If they come after me again, I'll have to cross the Wen River and live in Ch'i."

9   When Jan Po-niu⁵ fell ill, the Master went to visit him. Standing outside the window and holding his hand, the Master said: "He's dying! It's destiny, pure and simple. But how could such a man have such a disease? How could such a man have such a disease?"

10   The Master said: "How noble Yen Hui is! To live in a meager lane with nothing but some rice in a split-bamboo bowl and some water in a gourd cup – no one else could bear such misery. But it doesn't even bother Hui. His joy never wavers. O, how noble Hui is!"

11   Jan Ch'iu said: "It isn't that I'm not happy with your Way, Master, but I'm just not strong enough."

"If someone isn't strong enough," replied the Master, "they give up along the Way. But you'd already set your limits in advance."

12   Speaking to Adept Hsia, the Master said: "Be a noble-minded scholar, not a small-minded one."

13   When Adept Yu was regent in Wu Ch'eng, the Master asked: "Have you come across anyone surprising?"

"There's a certain T'an-t'ai Mieh-ming," replied Yu. "He never takes shortcuts, and he's never come to my office except on official business."

14   The Master said: "Meng Chih-fan⁶ never boasts. When the army fled, he brought up the rear. Then when he was coming in through the gates, he spurred his horse on, saying *It wasn't courage that kept me behind. This horse just won't go any faster.*"

15   The Master said: "These days, without Priest T'o's slick tongue and Chao's good looks, you'll never get away unscathed."

16   The Master said: "Who can set out without using a door? How is it, then, no one uses this Way?"

17   The Master said: "People are too wild when nature dominates culture in them, and too tame when culture dominates nature. But when nature and culture are blended and balanced in them, they're noble-minded."

18   The Master said: "Honesty is our very life. Without it, to elude death is sheer luck."

19   The Master said: "To understand something is nothing like loving it. And to love something is nothing like delighting in it."

20   The Master said: "You can speak of lofty things with those who've made something lofty of themselves, but not with those who haven't."

21   Fan Ch'ih asked about wisdom, and the Master said: "Devotion to perfecting your Duties toward the people, and reverence for gods and spirits while keeping your distance from them – that can be called wisdom."

And when Fan Ch'ih asked about Humanity, the Master said: "The Humane master the difficult parts before expecting any rewards – that can be called Humanity."

22   The Master said: "The wise delight in rivers, and the Humane delight in mountains: the wise are in motion, and the Humane still; the wise are joyful, and the Humane long-lived."

23   The Master said: "A twinkling of change could bring Ch'i to the level of Lu. And a twinkling of change could bring Lu to the Way."

24   The Master said: "A cup not a cup: A cup indeed! A cup indeed!"

25   Tsai Yü asked: "Hearing that Humanity's down in a well, wouldn't a Humane person jump in after it?"

"What makes you think that?" replied the Master. "The noble-minded can perish, but they can't be entrapped. They can be deceived, but they can't be snared in nets."

26   The Master said: "The noble-minded are well-versed in culture and well-grounded in Ritual, so how could they ever go wrong?"

27   The Master went to visit Lady Nan.[7] When he saw how displeased Adept Lu was, the Master declared: "Heaven will renounce me if I've done anything wrong. Heaven will indeed renounce me."

28   The Master said: "The constant commonplace[8] radiates such Integrity – it's boundless! And yet, it's been rare among the people for a very long time."

29   Adept Kung said: "How would you describe a person who sows all the people with blessings and assists everyone in the land? Could such a person be called Humane?"

"What does this have to do with Humanity?" replied the Master. "If you must have a name, call this person a *sage*. For even the enlightened Emperors Yao[9] and Shun would seem lacking by comparison. As for Humanity: if you want to make a stand, help others make a stand, and if you want to reach your goal, help others reach their goal. Consider yourself and treat others accordingly: this is the method of Humanity."

士　亘　遣　遵　頏　肖　雖
仁　扵　立　心　氏　　　流
閒　玄　禮　　　聖　　　
君　汙　器　念　　　
同　以　樂　　　家　刊　年
雅　注　心　盧　宮　元　青
敬　水　曾　世　曾　　　龍
號　泲　苻　禮　親　百　在
思　活　鍾　樂　里　主　法
頌　瀆　陵　　　幷　不　鄴
　　　　遷　　　官　改　霝

VII Transmitting Insight, But

1 The Master said: "Transmitting insight, but never creating insight, standing by my words and devoted to the ancients: perhaps I'm a little like that old sage, P'eng."[1]

2 The Master said: "To understand through dark silence, to study without tiring, to teach without faltering: how could such things still be difficult for me?"

3 The Master said: "These are the kinds of things I find troubling:

> *possessing Integrity without cultivating it*
> *and possessing knowledge without deepening it,*
>
> *knowing Duties without following them*
> *and knowing failings without changing them."*

4 At leisure, the Master was loose and breezy.

5   The Master said: "I've gotten so feeble! It's been forever since I dreamed of the sage Duke Chou."[2]

6   The Master said: "Devote yourself to the Way, depend on Integrity, rely on Humanity, and wander in the arts."

7   The Master said: "I never refuse to teach anyone, not even those so lowly they come offering nothing but a few strips of dried meat."

8   The Master said: "I never instruct those who aren't full of passion, and I never enlighten those who aren't struggling to explain themselves.

  "If I show you one corner and you can't show me the other three, I'll say nothing more."

9   If he was seated next to someone in mourning, the Master never ate his fill.

10   If he'd already wept that day, the Master wouldn't sing.

11   Speaking to Yen Hui, the Master said:

"A leader when appointed to office
and a recluse when sent away.

Only you and I have perfected this."

"If you were leading the Three Armies," asked Adept Lu, "who would you take with you?"

"A man who attacks tigers unarmed and crosses rivers without boats, willing to die without the least regret – that's a man I'd never take with me. The man I'd take always approaches difficulties with due caution and always succeeds by planning carefully."

12　The Master said: "If there were an honorable way to get rich, I'd do it, even if it meant being a stooge standing around with a whip. But there isn't an honorable way, so I just do what I like."

13　The Master treated three things with the greatest care: fasting, war, and sickness.

14　In Ch'i, after hearing the music of Emperor Shun, it was three months before the Master noticed the taste of food again. He just kept saying, "I never dreamed music was capable of such things."

15　Jan Ch'iu said: "Does our Master support the Wei ruler?"[3]

"Yes, I should ask him about that," replied Adept Kung.

So Kung went in to see the Master and asked: "Who were Po Yi and Shu Ch'i?"

"Wise men of ancient times," replied Confucius.

"Did they harbor any resentments?"

"They devoted themselves to Humanity, and so became Humane. How could they harbor any resentments?"

Kung returned to Jan Ch'iu and said: "No, the Master doesn't support him."

16   The Master said: "Poor food and water for dinner, a bent arm for a pillow – that is where joy resides. For me, wealth and renown without honor are nothing but drifting clouds."

17   The Master said: "Grant me a few more years. After studying Change⁴ for fifty years, I'll surely be free of serious flaws."

18   The Master never used Lu dialect⁵ for *The Book of Songs, The Book of History,* or the observance of Ritual. Never.

19   When Duke She⁶ asked Adept Lu about Confucius, Lu ignored him.

Later, the Master said: "Why didn't you just say something like this: *He's a man so full of passion that he forgets to eat, and so full of joy that he forgets to worry. He's never even noticed old age coming over him.*"

20   The Master said: "I am not one who was born with great wisdom. I love the ancients and diligently seek wisdom among them."

21   The Master never spoke of the supernatural, violence, disorder, or gods and spirits.

22   The Master said: "Out walking with two companions, I'm sure to be in my teacher's company. The good in one I adopt in myself; the evil in the other I change in myself."

23   The Master said: "My Integrity is born of Heaven. So what can Huan T'ui's⁷ assassins do to me?"

24   The Master said: "My students, do you think I'm being secretive? But I'm hiding nothing from you. I share my entire life with you, my friends. And that is who I am."

25   The Master taught four things: culture, conduct, loyalty, and standing by your words.

26   The Master said: "I have no hope of meeting a true sage. To meet someone noble-minded would be enough."

The Master said: "I have no hope of meeting a truly virtuous and benevolent person. To meet someone who's mastered constancy would be enough. But constancy is impossible if you imagine yourself having when you have not, full when you're empty, prosperous when you're destitute."

27   The Master fished with hooks, not nets, and he never shot roosting birds.

28   The Master said: "I suppose there are some who don't need wisdom to live wisely. I am not so lucky. I've heard countless things, choosing what is good and adopting it in myself. I've seen countless things and remembered them well. This is a lesser form of wisdom."

29   The people of Hu Village had no interest in the teachings of Confucius. A young boy came to see the Master. When the Master saw that his disciples were perplexed, he said: "Accepting this boy's visit does not mean accepting his entire life. Why be so demanding? If someone purifies himself to come here, we can accept that purification without accepting his entire past."

30   The Master said: "Is Humanity really so far away? We need only want it, and here it is!"

31   The Minister of Justice in Ch'en asked whether Duke Chao of Lu understood Ritual.

"Yes, he does," replied Confucius.

After Confucius left, the minister bowed to Wu-ma Ch'i,[8] inviting him to approach, and said: "I have heard that the noble-minded show no partiality, and yet it seems that some are very partial indeed. The woman Chao married is from the royal house of Wu, and so belongs to his own clan. He just renamed her Lady Wu Meng. If he understands Ritual, who doesn't?"

When Wu-ma Ch'i told him about this, the Master said: "How lucky I am. If I make a mistake, someone is sure to recognize it."

32   When someone sang a song that he liked, the Master always asked them to sing it again before he joined in.

33   The Master said: "No one has been so devoted to learning and culture. But when it comes to the practices of a noble-minded life, I haven't done so well."

34   The Master said: "That I've become a sage and mastered Humanity? How could I say that of myself? I work at it and teach it, never tiring. You could say that much. But no more."

"And that's exactly what we students have failed to learn," said Adept Hua.

35   The Master was terribly sick. Adept Lu asked if he might offer a prayer, and the Master said: "Is there such prayer?"

"There is," replied Lu. *"The Book of Eulogies says: We pray for you to the gods and spirits above and below."*

"My life has been my prayer," responded the Master.

36   The Master said: "The extravagant are soon pompous, and the frugal soon resolute. Better resolute than pompous."

37   The Master said: "The noble-minded are calm and steady. Little people are forever fussing and fretting."

38   The Master was genial and yet austere, awesome and yet not fierce, reverent and yet content.

立　宜　造　尊　頴　肯　雖
仁　拷　立　先　氏　寶　流
聞　玄　禮　心　聖　　　
君　汙　器　念　途　騁　
同　以　樂　真　家　弟　年
耀　注　　　　居　元　青
敬　水　音　世　魯　　龍
　　泳　待　禮　親　百　在
思　悟　建　樂　里　主　流
　　蕎　陵　并　不　龂
　　　　遲　官　改

VIII Surely T'ai Po

1   The Master said: "Surely T'ai Po[1] can be called a master of Integrity. Three times he declined to rule all beneath Heaven, and he did it so discreetly the people never praised him."

2   The Master said: "Reverence becomes tedium without Ritual, and caution becomes timidity. Without Ritual, courage becomes recklessness, and truth becomes intolerance.

"When noble-minded leaders honor their parents, the people feel called to Humanity. And when leaders never forget old friends, the people live open and true."

3   Master Tseng was terribly sick. He summoned his disciples and said: "Look at my feet. Look at my hands. The *Songs* say:

Trembling in watchful terror –
as if facing a deep abyss,
as if walking over thin ice.[2]

Whatever happens, I know now that I am free, my little ones."

4 Master Tseng was terribly sick. When Lord Meng Ching came to ask how he was doing, he said:

> *"When birds are about to die,*
> *their cries are full of sorrow.*
>
> *When humans are about to die,*
> *their words are full of virtue."*

In following the Way, the noble-minded treasure three things: a manner free of violence and arrogance, a countenance full of sincerity and trust, a voice free of vulgarity and impropriety.

"As for sacrificial vessels, that is the business of appointed officers."

5 Master Tseng said: "To be capable, and yet seek advice from the incapable; to be richly endowed, and yet seek advice from the poorly endowed; having as if having not; full as if empty; offended, but never accusing. I had a friend long ago who lived that way."[3]

6 Master Tseng said: "A man who can be entrusted with a small orphan or a large state, who faces a great crisis and remains unshaken – is he not noble-minded? He is indeed noble-minded!"

7 Master Tseng said: "You must be resolute and broad-minded, for the burden is heavy and the Way long. When Humanity is your burden, is it not indeed heavy? And when the Way ends only at death, is it not indeed long?"

8 The Master said: "Be incited by the *Songs*, established by Ritual, and perfected by music."

9   The Master said: "You can make the people follow the Way, but you can't make them understand it."

10   The Master said: "If courageous people suffer from poverty, they'll soon tear the country apart. Unless they've mastered Humanity, anyone whose sufferings are great would tear it apart with abandon."

11   The Master said: "A person may be as nobly endowed as Duke Chou, but all that isn't enough to inspire admiration if they aren't humble and generous."

12   The Master said: "A person who can study for three years and never worry about a salary – that is very difficult to find."

13   The Master said: "Love learning and trust it deeply. Guard the Way of virtue and benevolence unto death. Never enter a dangerous country, and never inhabit a country in turmoil.

"When all beneath Heaven abides in the Way, make yourself known; and when the Way's lost, stay hidden. When the Way rules in your country, there's shame in poverty and obscurity; and when the Way's lost in your country, there's shame in wealth and renown."

14   The Master said: "Unless you've been appointed to office, don't fuss and fret over the business of government."

15   The Master said: "When Music-master Chih begins the climax of 'Ospreys Calling,'⁴ what a swelling sea of sound fills the ears!"

16   The Master said: "Wild and yet dishonest, base and yet insincere, simple-hearted and yet untrustworthy – I'll never understand such people."

17   The Master said: "Study as if you'll never know enough, as if you're afraid of losing it all."

18   The Master said: "How majestic, how exalted and majestic Shun and Yü[5] were: all beneath Heaven was theirs, and yet it was nothing to them!"

19   The Master said: "Great indeed was the rule of Emperor Yao! Heaven alone is truly majestic, exalted and majestic, and only Yao could equal it. He was boundless, so vast and boundless the people couldn't even name him.

"How exalted and majestic his achievements! How bright and glorious the ways of culture he created."[6]

20   Shun had five ministers, and all beneath Heaven was well governed. And Emperor Wu, sage founder of the Chou, once said: "I have ten fine ministers."

Therefore, Confucius said: "*Talent is rare,* as the saying goes, and isn't it true? The time of Yao and Shun was rich in talent. And since one was his mother, Wu really only had nine ministers. Of all beneath Heaven, the Chou held two parts in three, and yet still served the Shang house humbly. Its Integrity was absolute."

21   The Master said: "To me, Yü seems beyond all criticism. He ate the simplest food, but made sumptuous offerings to ancestral gods and spirits. He wore the plainest robes, but wore exquisite regalia for sacrifice and ceremony. He lived in the humblest house, but devoted his energy to irrigation channels and canals. To me, Yü seems beyond all criticism."

雕　首　頴　尊　這　宣　士

氏　心　　　立　於　仁

寶　　　玄　禮　開

嬰　念　器　汙　君

年　耕　家　真　樂　以　同

青　元　居　廬　尼　注　權

前　魯　世　曾　水　敬

左　百　親　禮　荷　泳　思

法　主　里　樂　鍾　活　齊

斷　不　并　陵

霜　改　官　遅

IX The Master Rarely

1   The Master rarely spoke of profit or destiny or Humanity.

2   A villager in Ta Hsiang said: "Great indeed is Confucius! His erudition is truly vast – and still, he's lived without fame and renown."

When the Master heard this, he said to his disciples: "What shall I be – a charioteer or an archer? I'll be a charioteer!"

3   The Master said: "Ritual calls for caps of linen, but now everyone uses black silk. It's more frugal, so I follow the common practice.

"Ritual calls for bowing before ascending the stairs, but now everyone bows only at the top of the stairs. That's too presumptuous, so even though it violates the common practice, I bow before ascending."

4   The Master had freed himself of four things: idle speculation, certainty, inflexibility, and conceit.

5   When he was ambushed in K'uang, the Master said: "Emperor Wen[1] is long since dead, but doesn't culture [wen] still live

here in me? If Heaven wanted this culture to end, it wouldn't survive such deaths. But Heaven's let this culture continue, so what can these K'uang people do to me?"

6   Speaking to Adept Kung, a grand minister asked: "Your master is a great sage, isn't he? And yet, he's learned so many useful skills!"

"It's true Heaven meant him to be a sage," Kung replied, "but he learned many useful skills, too."

When the Master heard this, he said: "That grand minister knows me well! We were humble and poor when I was young: that's why I can do so many practical things. But do the noble-minded need all these skills? No, not so many as this."

7   According to Lao, the Master said: "I was never appointed to office: that's why I'm so handy."

8   The Master said: "Am I a man of great wisdom? Hardly! Even when a simple person brings me a question, my mind goes utterly blank. I just thrash it out until I've exhausted every possibility."

9   The Master said: "The Phoenix hasn't come and the river hasn't revealed its divine chart.[2] This is the end of me."

10   Whenever he met someone in mourning, someone in ceremonial robes, or someone blind – the Master would stand or humbly step aside.

11   Sighing heavily, Yen Hui said: "The more I gaze up into it, the higher it gets, and the more I bore down into it, the harder it gets. In reverence, I see it before me, and suddenly it's behind me.

"The Master is good at luring people on, step by step. He uses culture to broaden us, and Ritual to secure us. Though I often feel like quitting, I can't, because whenever it seems I've reached my limit, something seems to rise before me, lofty and majestic. But however much I long to go there, the path remains a mystery."

12   The Master was terribly sick, so Adept Lu had the disciples dress up as the kind of retainers he had as a minister. The sickness let up for a time, and the Master said to them: "Lu's always been conjuring these deceits. If I pretend to have retainers when I have none, who am I deceiving? Am I deceiving Heaven?

"Don't you think I'd rather face death in your arms than in the arms of strange clerks? I may not have a grand funeral, but I'm hardly dying in some roadside ditch."

13   Adept Kung said: "If I have a beautiful piece of jade, what should I do – lock it away in a case or look for the best price and sell it?"

"Sell it!" was the Master's answer. "Sell it! I'm just waiting to get the right offer for mine!"

14   The Master wanted to go live among the nine wild tribes in the east.

Someone asked: "How could you bear such vulgarity?"

"If someone noble-minded lived there," replied the Master, "how could vulgarity be a problem?"

15   The Master said: "After returning from Wei to Lu, I trued up music and returned the *Songs* to its original form."

16   The Master said: *"Serve family elders when home, serve ruling officials when away, leave nothing undone when mourning, never drink yourself into a stupor* – how could such things still be difficult for me?"

17   Standing beside a river, the Master said: "Everything passes away like this, day and night, never resting."

18   The Master said: "I've never seen anyone for whom loving Integrity is like loving a beautiful woman."

19   The Master said: "It's like building a mountain: even if I don't stop until I'm only short one last basket of dirt – still, I've stopped. It's like leveling ground: even if I'm just starting out with the first basketful – still, I'm forging ahead."

20   The Master said: "If there's anyone who was never careless about what I said, it was Yen Hui."

21   Speaking of Yen Hui, the Master said: "How sad – to watch him forge ahead so resolutely, and never see how far he could go."[3]

22   The Master said: "There are, indeed, sprouts that never come to flower. And there are flowers that never bear fruit."

23   The Master said: "Hold the young in awe. How can we know their generation will not equal our own? Only when they've lived to be forty or fifty without any distinction – only then are they no longer worthy of our awe."

24   The Master said: "Worthy admonitions cannot fail to inspire us, but what matters is changing ourselves. Reverent advice cannot fail to encourage us, but what matters is acting on it. Encouraged without acting, inspired without changing – there's nothing to be done for such people."

25   The Master said: "Above all, be loyal and stand by your words. Befriend only those who are kindred spirits. And when you're wrong, don't be afraid to change."

26   The Master said: "Vast armies can be robbed of their commander, but even the simplest people cannot be robbed of their free will."

27   The Master said: "To wear threadbare hemp robes and stand without shame among those wearing lavish furs of fox and badger – isn't that what Adept Lu is like?

> *He hates nothing and covets nothing.*
> *How could he be anything but good?"*[4]

Adept Lu began chanting these lines to himself over and over. Finally, the Master said: "That isn't enough to make someone all that good, is it?"

28   The Master said: "Only after the seasons turn cold can we truly know the resolve of pine and cypress."

29   The Master said: "The wise never doubt. The Humane never worry. The brave never fear."

30   The Master said: "Some can study with you, but not follow the Way with you. Some can follow the Way with you, but not stand firm with you in its principles. And some can stand firm with you in its principles, but not join you in putting them into practice."

31   *Lavish aspen-plum blossoms*
        tremble and sway alone:

        I haven't stopped loving you,
        but your home is so far away.[5]

The Master said: "If he'd really loved her, he wouldn't have worried about the distance."

雖顏氏聖嬰家封元魯

月氏聖賢嬰家封元魯龍

顏氏聖心念真居魯親里并官

禮立玄禮器樂之世禮親樂陵遲

這禮禮器念真居世禮重樂陵廷

宣扵玄汙以注水晉深待話磬陵建

立仁聞君同以懽敬吮俱禎頹嘉

仁聞君同權敬吮俱禎

x His Native Village

1   In his native village, Confucius was simple and sincere, as if he couldn't speak. But at court or ancestral temple, though always cautious and reverent, he spoke openly and easily.

At court, speaking with lower officials, he was forthright. Speaking with high officials, he was diplomatic. And speaking with the sovereign, he was wary – wary and self-assured.

2   When his sovereign summoned him to receive a guest, his demeanor suddenly changed and his steps grew reverent. When he bowed to his waiting colleagues, his right arm reached out, then his left, but his robes hung straight and true. Then he'd hurry forward, sleeves speading like noble wings. And once the guest had departed, he promptly returned to report: "The guest is no longer looking back."

3   Entering the palace gates, he closed in on himself, as if the gates weren't big enough. Stopping, he never stood in the middle of the gate, and passing through, he never stepped on the threshold.

Passing the royal platform, his demeanor suddenly changed, his steps grew reverent, and words seemed to fail him.

Raising his robe on ascending to the hall, he closed in on himself, focusing his *ch'i*[1] until he scarcely seemed to breathe. And leaving, his expression relaxing on descending the first step, he seemed happy and content. At the bottom of the steps, he'd hurry forward as if borne on noble wings. And then, returning to his station, he grew wary again.

4   Carrying his official scepter, he closed in on himself, as if it were too heavy. He held the top as if bowing, and the bottom as if making an offering. His demeanor turned solemn, and he walked attentively, as if his steps were preordained.

In making Ritual offerings, he looked tranquil. And alone with his sovereign, he was at ease and cheerful.

5   Such a noble-minded man never wore purple or maroon trim. And in his informal robes, he never wore red or chestnut brown.

In summer heat, he chose thin open-weave robes, worn over something light to set them off.

With black silk, he wore lambskin furs. With undyed silk, he wore deerskin furs. And with yellow silk, he wore fox furs.

His informal furs were long, with the right sleeve cut short so his hand was free. And for sleeping, he always wore robes half as long as he himself was.

Because fox and badger furs are so thick, he wore them at home.

Unless in mourning, he wore all his waist-jewels.

Other than ceremonial skirts, his robes were all sewn pieces.

When offering condolences, he never wore lavish lambskin furs or caps of black silk. For the new moon, he went to court in his full court regalia. And during purification for the sacrifice, he wore bright robes of plain linen.

6   During purification for the sacrifice, he changed what he ate and where he sat. Polished rice was fine, and minced meat. He

didn't eat sour rice or rancid fish or spoiled meat. He didn't eat anything that looked or smelled bad. He didn't eat food that wasn't well-cooked and in season, or food that wasn't properly sliced and served with the proper sauce. Even when there was plenty of meat, he only ate enough to balance the *ch'i* of rice. Only in wine did he set no limits, but he never drank himself into confusion. He wouldn't drink wine from a wineshop or eat meat from a market. And though he didn't refuse ginger, he ate it only sparingly.

After the state sacrifice, he never kept the meat overnight. And he never kept meat more than three days after the family sacrifice. After three days, he wouldn't eat it.

He didn't speak at meals, and he didn't talk in bed.

He made an offering of even the simplest rice and vegetable, broth and melon – and he did so with the greatest solemnity.

7   If the mat wasn't laid straight, he wouldn't sit.

When the people of his village were drinking wine, he left only after the elders with walking-sticks had left.

8   When the villagers were out driving evil spirits away, he put on his court robes and stood like a host on the eastern steps.

9   When sending his regards to someone in another country, he bowed twice as the messenger set out.

10   When Lord Chi K'ang sent a certain medicine to him as a gift, Confucius bowed twice, then accepted it, saying: "I'm not familiar with this, so I dare not try it."

11   One day the stables burned down. When he returned from court, the Master asked: "Was anyone hurt?" He didn't ask about the horses.

12   When the sovereign sent a gift of food, he straightened his mat and dined immediately. When the sovereign sent a gift of uncooked food, he cooked it and made an offering. When the sovereign sent a gift of live animals, he always raised them.

When serving at the royal table, he always began with rice once the sovereign had made offerings.

13   When he was sick and his sovereign came to visit, he laid facing east with his court robes draped over him and his sash trailed out across the bed.

14   When summoned by his sovereign, he set out at once, without even waiting for his horses to be harnessed.

15   When he was in the Grand Temple, the Master asked questions about everything he saw.

16   When a friend died and there was no home to which the body could be sent, he said: "Let the funeral be in my home."

17   A friend might send a gift, even something so lavish as a horse and carriage, but he never bowed unless it was sacrificial meat.

18   In bed, he never lay facing north like a corpse.
At home, he moved without formality.

19   Whenever he met someone in mourning garments, even if it was someone he knew well, his expression turned solemn. If his robes were sometimes informal when he met those who were blind or wearing ceremonial caps, his demeanor was always appropriate. For those in mourning and those carrying official documents, he bowed down to the crossbars of his carriage.

When a lavish feast was served, his expression changed and he rose to his feet in reverence for the host.

Startled by a sudden thunderclap or violent wind, his expression always turned solemn.

20   When mounting the carriage, he stood square and gripped the mounting-cord. And while riding in the carriage, he always looked outside but never shouted or pointed.

21   Seeing such an expression, it startled away. It drifted and soared, then settled down again.

He said:

> "A pheasant on the mountain bridge:
> Such omens! Such omens it brings!"

When Adept Lu presented offerings, it sniffed three times and set off.

雍月氏賢丰青龍左涑斯霜改

顏月里嬰封元魯百王并官

豊心聖念家居世親樂陵遲

立禮器樂之昔世符鍾磬廷

逴抒汙以注水昔深居

士仁閒君同權敬咏是瀆

XI Studies Begin

1   The Master said: *"Those whose studies begin with Ritual and music are commoners. Those whose studies end with Ritual and music are noble-minded.*

"If I employed such a saying, I'd say studies begin there."

2   The Master said: "Of my followers in Ch'en and Ts'ai, not one came far enough to enter my gate."

3   For Integrity: Yen Hui, Min Tzu-ch'ien, Jan Po-niu, and Jan Yung.

For eloquence: Tsai Yü and Adept Kung.

For governing: Jan Ch'iu and Adept Lu.

For cultivation: Adept Yu and Adept Hsia.

4   The Master said: "Yen Hui's never helped me much: no matter what I say, he's delighted."

5   The Master said: "What a marvelous child Min Tzu-ch'ien is! In all his family says about him, there isn't a flaw to be found."

6 Nan Jung chanted the lines about a white-jade scepter[1] over and over to himself. Confucius married his brother's daughter to him.

7 Lord Chi K'ang asked which of the disciples had a true love of learning.

"There was a certain Yen Hui who had a true love of learning," replied Confucius. "Unfortunately, destiny allowed him but a brief life, and now he's dead. Now there's no one like him."

8 When Yen Hui died, his father wanted the Master to sell his carriage so they could buy an outer coffin for his son.

The Master said: "Whether they are gifted or not, we all praise our own children. When my son, Po-yü, died, he had a coffin but no outer coffin. I couldn't sell my carriage so he could have an outer coffin. I was in attendance on high ministers: to go on foot would have been improper."

9 When Yen Hui died, the Master cried: "O, Heaven's killing me! It's killing me!"

10 When Yen Hui died, the Master's mourning was extravagant.

"You're being awfully extravagant," said his followers.

"Am I?" replied the Master. "If this man's death doesn't call forth extravagant mourning, whose will?"

11 When Yen Hui died, the disciples wanted to give him a lavish burial. But the Master said: "No, you can't do that."

The disciples went ahead and gave him a lavish burial anyway. Afterward, the Master said to them: "Hui treated me like a father. And now I've failed to treat him like a son. But it wasn't my doing: it was yours."

12   When Adept Lu asked about serving ghosts and spirits, the Master said: "You haven't learned to serve the living, so how could you serve ghosts?"

"Might I ask about death?"

"You don't understand life," the Master replied, "so how could you understand death?"

13   In attendance on the Master – Min Tzu-ch'ien was diplomatic, Adept Lu was dynamic, Jan Ch'iu and Adept Kung were forthright. The Master was pleased. But he said: "People like Adept Lu never live to die of old age."

14   When the officers of Lu were planning to rebuild the treasury building, Min Tzu-ch'ien said: "Just rebuild the old one. Why make it new and different?"

"He's a man who rarely speaks," commented the Master, "but when he does speak, he's always right on target."

15   The Master said: "What is Lu doing, playing his se^2 here inside my gate?"

At this, the disciples' reverence for Lu began to fade. But the Master said: "He may not have entered my grand hall, but Adept Lu has indeed ascended the stairs."

16   When Adept Kung asked who was most worthy, Adept Chang or Adept Hsia, the Master said: "Chang always goes too far, and Hsia always stops short."

"Then hasn't Chang surpassed Hsia?" asked Kung.

"Going too far isn't much different from stopping short," replied the Master.

17   The Chi family patriarch had grown wealthier than Duke Chou himself, and still Jan Ch'iu kept gathering taxes for him, adding greatly to his wealth.

The Master said: "He's no follower of mine. If you sounded the drums and attacked him, my little ones, it wouldn't be such a bad thing."

18   Adept Kao³ is stupid, and Master Tseng dull. Adept Chang is eccentric, and Adept Lu crude.

19   The Master said: "Yen Hui's nearly made it: He's almost always empty.

"Adept Kung, on the other hand, refused his destiny. He went into business instead and grew rich, for his speculations are almost always right on target."

20   When Adept Chang asked about the Way people of virtue and benevolence follow, the Master said: "They never follow in the footsteps of others, and they never enter the inner chambers."

21   The Master said: "Someone's words may be true and sincere – but does that mean they're noble-minded or just full of pretense?"

22   When Adept Lu asked if he should hurry to put sage advice into practice, the Master said: "Your father and elder brother are still alive, so how can you hurry to put sage advice into practice?"

When Jan Ch'iu asked if he should hurry to put sage advice into practice, the Master said: "Of course you should hurry to put sage advice into practice."

At this, Adept Hua said: "When Lu asked if he should hurry to put sage advice into practice, you said *Your father and elder brother are still alive.* But when Ch'iu asked if he should hurry to put sage advice into practice, you said *Of course you should hurry to put sage advice into practice.* I'm confused. Could you please explain this for me?"

"Ch'iu holds back," replied the Master, "so I urge him on. Lu has enough drive for two people, so I hold him back."

23   When the Master was ambushed in K'uang, Yen Hui fell behind.

"I thought you'd been killed!" exclaimed the Master.

"With you still alive, I wouldn't dare get myself killed."

24   Chi Tzu-jan⁴ asked if Adept Lu and Jan Ch'iu could be called great ministers, and the Master said: "I would have asked about some amazing disciple, but here you've just asked about Lu and Ch'iu. What I call a great minister is one who employs the Way in serving his sovereign. If he cannot do that, he resigns. Lu and Ch'iu, on the other hand, could be called makeshift ministers."

"So they just follow any order they're given?" asked Chi Tzu-jan.

"No, not any order," replied the Master. "They'd certainly refuse to kill their fathers or their sovereigns."

25 When Adept Lu arranged to have Adept Kao appointed regent in Pi, the House of Chi's capital, the Master said: "You're ruining someone's son."[5]

"The people are there in Pi," replied Lu, "and the gods of grain. Why must erudition come from books?"

"I can't bear such clever talk," muttered the Master.

26 Adept Lu, Tseng Hsi, Jan Ch'iu, and Adept Hua were all seated in attendance. The Master said: "You think of me as being a little older than you, but I'd like to forget about respect for now. You're always saying *No one recognizes our talents.* Now, tell me openly: if someone did recognize your talents, what would you do?"

Adept Lu took the lead and said: "In a nation of a thousand warchariots hemmed in by powerful neighbors, besieged by invading armies, famine and drought – I could bring courage and direction to the people within three years."

The Master smiled gently.

"What would you do?" he asked Ch'iu.

"In a region of only sixty to seventy square miles, or even fifty to sixty square miles – I could bring satisfaction to the people within three years. As for Ritual and music, I would leave that for someone noble-minded."

"And you?" he asked Hua.

"I don't claim any great ability in such things, but I'm anxious to learn. Then, in court gatherings and ceremonies at the ancestral temple, I might wear the caps and robes of a minor official."

"And what about you?" he asked Hsi.

As the music of his *se* faded away, Tseng Hsi[6] struck a final chord. Then he put the instrument aside, stood, and said: "My aims are quite different from those of my three colleagues."

"What harm is there in that?" asked the Master. "We each have our own ambitions."

"In late spring, when the spring clothes are made, I'd like to go wandering with a few friends and servant boys, bathe in the Yi River, enjoy the wind at Rain-Dance Altar, and then wander back home in song."

The Master sighed deeply, and said: "I'm with Hsi."

When the other three disciples left, Tseng Hsi stayed behind and asked: "What did you think of what the other three said?"

"They each have their own ambitions, that's for sure," replied the Master.

"Why did you smile at Lu?"

"A country is ruled through Ritual," replied the Master, "but there was no deference in his words. That's why I smiled."

"And Ch'iu? He wasn't asking for a country, was he?"

"How could he call a region of sixty to seventy square miles or fifty to sixty square miles anything but a country?"

"And Hua? Surely he wasn't asking for a country, was he?"

"Temple ceremonies and court gatherings – if such things aren't imperial affairs, what is? And if someone like Hua plays only a minor role, who could play a major one?"

士　直　迄　鼻　視　肩　雉
仁　抒　立　先　氏　　
聞　玄　禮　心　聖　醫
君　汙　器　念　嬰　　
尸　以　樂　真　家　利　丰
權　注　之　盧　居　元　青
敬　水　昔　世　魯　　龍
咏　深　狩　禮　親　百　在
具　海　鍾　樂　里　主　洗
薦　庭　橋　陵　并　不　斳
壽　深　遲　遲　宮　改

Yen Hui

1   Yen Hui asked about Humanity, and the Master said: "Giving yourself over to Ritual – that is Humanity. If a ruler gave himself to Ritual for even a single day, all beneath Heaven would return to Humanity. For doesn't the practice of Humanity find its source first in the self, and only then in others?"

"Could you explain how giving yourself to Ritual works?" asked Yen Hui.

"Never look without Ritual. Never listen without Ritual. Never speak without Ritual. Never move without Ritual."

"I'm not terribly clever," said Yen Hui, "but I'll try to serve these words."

2   Jan Yung asked about Humanity, and the Master said: "Go out into the world as if greeting a magnificent guest. Use the people as if offering a magnificent sacrifice. And never impose on others what you would not choose for yourself. Then, there will be no resentment among the people or the great families."

"I'm not terribly clever," said Jan Yung, "but I'll try to serve these words."

3   Szu-ma Niu[1] asked about Humanity, and the Master said: "The Humane speak with slow deliberation."

"So, those who speak with slow deliberation can be called Humane?"

"It's so difficult to put words into action," replied the Master. "How can anyone fail to speak with slow deliberation?"

4 *S*zu-ma Niu asked about the noble-minded, and the Master said: "The noble-minded live free of sorrow and fear."

"So, those who live free of sorrow and fear can be called noble-minded?"

"When you can look within and find no taint," replied the Master, "how can anything bring you sorrow or fear?"

5 *A* sorrowful Szu-ma Niu said: "People all have brothers. I alone have none."

"I have heard," said Adept Hsia, "that life and death are matters of destiny, that wealth and renown are matters of Heaven. If the noble-minded are reverent and leave nothing amiss, if they are humble toward others and observe Ritual – then all within the four seas will be their brothers. So how can you grieve over having no brothers?"

6 *A*dept Chang asked about discrimination, and the Master said: "To hear slander and deception and hollow accusation without acting on them, that is discrimination indeed. To hear slander and deception and hollow accusation without acting on them, that is far-sighted indeed."

7 *A*dept Kung asked about governing, and the Master said: "Plenty of food, plenty of weapons, and the trust of the people."

"If you couldn't have all three," asked Kung, "which would you give up first?"

"I'd give up weapons."

"And if you couldn't have both the others, which would you give up first?"

"I'd give up food," replied the Master. "There's always been death. But without trust, the people are lost."

8   Chi Tzu-ch'eng said: "A person is noble-minded by nature. How could culture make someone noble-minded?"

"To say so is a great pity," replied Adept Kung. "For once the tongue sets out, even a team of horses cannot catch it.

"Culture looks just like nature, and nature like culture. Without fur, the hide of a tiger or leopard looks just like the hide of a dog or sheep."

9   Duke Ai asked Master Yu: "It's a famine year. I don't have enough to run my government. What shall I do?"

"Why not tax people the usual one part in nine?"[2] replied Yu.

"I'm already getting two parts in nine, and I still don't have enough. How could I manage on only one part in nine?"

"When everyone has enough," said Yu, "how could you alone be in need? And when everyone's in need, how could you alone have enough?"

10   Adept Chang asked about *exalting Integrity* and *unraveling delusion*.

The Master said: "Be loyal and stand by your words. Devote yourself to that, above all, and dwell wherever Duty rules – that's exalting Integrity.

"When you love a thing, you wish it life. When you hate a thing, you wish it death. To wish both life and death for a thing – that is delusion.

                                                                       ANALECTS

Maybe it's for her money,
and maybe for the novelty."[3]

11   Duke Ching[4] asked Confucius about governing, and Confucius said: "Ruler a ruler, minister a minister, father a father, son a son."

"How splendid!" exclaimed the Duke. "Truly, if the ruler isn't a ruler, the minister a minister, the father a father, and the son a son – then even if we had grain, how could we survive to eat it?"

12   The Master said: "Someone who can settle a legal dispute having heard only one side of the story? That's Adept Lu."

Adept Lu never slept with a promise left unfulfilled.

13   The Master said: "I can hear a court case as well as anyone. But we need to make a world where there's no reason for a court case."

14   Adept Chang asked about governing, and the Master said: "Contemplate an issue tirelessly at home, then act on it loyally."

15   The Master said: "Well-versed in culture and well-grounded in Ritual – how could you ever go wrong?"

16   The Master said: "The noble-minded encourage what is beautiful in people and discourage what is ugly in them. Little people do just the opposite."

17   Lord Chi K'ang asked Confucius about governing, and Confucius said: "Utter rectitude is utter government. If you let rectitude lead the people, how could anyone fail to be rectified?"

18   Lord Chi K'ang was having trouble with bandits. When he asked Confucius for advice, Confucius said: "If you weren't so full of desire yourself, you couldn't pay people to steal from you."

19   Asking Confucius about governing, Lord Chi K'ang said: "What if I secure those who abide in the Way by killing those who ignore the Way – will that work?"

"How can you govern by killing?" replied Confucius. "Just set your heart on what is virtuous and benevolent, and the people will be virtuous and benevolent. The noble-minded have the Integrity of wind, and little people the Integrity of grass. When the wind sweeps over grass, it bends."

20   Adept Chang asked: "What must a man be like before he is pronounced influential?"

"What on earth do you mean by *influential?*" countered the Master.

"*Influential* means a person who gains renown among the people and the great families," replied Chang.

"But that's only renown," said the Master, "not influence. A person of influence is, by nature, forthright and a lover of Duty. He weighs people's words carefully and studies their faces. He cultivates humility before others. Such a person infuses the people and great families with his influence.

"A person of renown makes a show of Humanity, but acts quite differently. And he never doubts himself. That is the kind of person who gains renown among the people and the great families."

21   Out wandering with the Master near Rain-Dance Altar, Fan Ch'ih said: "May I ask about *exalting Integrity, reforming depravity,* and *unraveling delusion?*"

"A splendid question!" replied the Master. "To serve first, and let the rewards follow as they will – is that not exalting Integrity? To attack evil itself, not the evil person – is that not reforming depravity? To endanger yourself and your family, all in a morning's blind rage – is that not delusion?"

22   Fan Ch'ih asked about Humanity, and the Master said: "Love people."

Then he asked about understanding, and the Master said: "Understand people."

Fan Ch'ih couldn't fathom what he meant, so the Master said: "If you raise up the straight and cast out the crooked, the crooked will be made straight."

After leaving, Fan Ch'ih went to visit Adept Hsia, and said: "I was just visiting the Master. I asked him about understanding, and he said: *If you raise up the straight and cast out the crooked, the crooked will be made straight.* What does he mean by that?"

"O, there's such bounty in those words," replied Hsia. "When Shun possessed all beneath Heaven, he recognized Kao Yao and raised him up, thus leaving those without Humanity far away. And when T'ang⁵ possessed all beneath Heaven, he recognized Yi Yin and raised him up, thus leaving those without Humanity far away."

23   Adept Hsia asked about friends, and the Master said: "Advise them faithfully in perfecting the Way. If that fails, then stop. Don't humiliate yourself."

24   Master Tseng said: "The noble-minded use cultivation to assemble their friends, and friends to sustain their Humanity."

雅頏尊造宣王
氏孔立將仁
里人禮玄閒
器于君
刾家之以同
元居之往
龍魯世晉水敦
在百親禮流
王里樂鍾思
斬弁陵磬
霜改官遲

1   Adept Lu asked about governing, and the Master said: "Put the people first, and reward their efforts well."

When Lu asked further, he said: "Never tire."

2   When he was a regent for the House of Chi, Jan Yung asked about governing, and the Master said: "Depend on the lesser officials. Forgive their minor offenses and raise up worthy talents."

"How will I recognize worthy talents and raise them up?"

"If you raise up those you recognize," replied the Master, "do you think people will let you ignore those you don't recognize?"

3   Adept Lu said: "If the Lord of Wei wanted you to govern his country, what would you put first in importance?"

"The rectification of names," replied the Master. "Without a doubt."

"That's crazy!" countered Lu. ""What does rectification have to do with anything?"

"You're such an uncivil slob," said the Master. "When the noble-minded can't understand something, they remain silent.

"Listen. If names aren't rectified, speech doesn't follow from reality. If speech doesn't follow from reality, endeavors never come to fruition. If endeavors never come to fruition, then Ritual and music cannot flourish. If Ritual and music cannot flourish, punishments don't fit the crime. If punishments don't fit the crime, people can't put their hands and feet anywhere without fear of losing them.[1]

"Naming enables the noble-minded to speak, and speech enables the noble-minded to act. Therefore, the noble-minded are anything but careless in speech."

4   Fan Ch'ih asked to learn about farming, and the Master said: "Any old farmer could teach you that better than me."

Then Fan Ch'ih asked to learn about growing vegetables, and the Master said: "And any old gardener could teach you that better than me."

After Fan Ch'ih left, the Master said: "Fan Ch'ih's such a small-minded person! If leaders love Ritual, the people cannot be anything but reverent. If leaders love Duty, the people cannot be anything but humble. If leaders love standing by their words, the people cannot be anything but sincere. Once this is done, people from all four corners of the earth will come carrying babies wrapped on their backs. So why is he worried about farming?"

5   The Master said: "A man may be able to chant all three hundred *Songs* from memory, and still falter when appointed to office or waver when sent on embassies to the four corners of the earth. What good are all those *Songs* if he can't put them to use?"

6   The Master said: "A ruler who has rectified himself never gives orders, and all goes well. A ruler who has not rectified himself gives orders, and the people never follow them."

7   The Master said: "These two states, Lu and Wei: in politics, they're like brothers."

8   Of Ching, son to the Duke of Wei, the Master said: "He lived in his house nobly. When he moved in, he said: *Quite nice.* When he made it comfortable, he said: *Quite adequate.* And when it was lavishly appointed, he said: *Quite beautiful.*"

9   The Master journeyed to Wei with Jan Ch'iu driving for him. When they arrived, the Master said: "So many people!"

"Once a people has flourished like this," said Jan Ch'iu, "what more could be done for them?"

"Give them prosperity."

"And once they grow prosperous, what then?"

"Educate them."

10   The Master said: "If someone employed me for even a single year, a great deal could be done. And in three years, the work could be complete."

11   The Master said: "They say: *If a country had wise rulers for a hundred years, violence would be conquered and killing vanquished.* And it's so true."

12   The Master said: "Even if a true Emperor arose, it would still take a generation – but then Humanity would rule."

13   The Master said: "Once you've rectified yourself, you can serve in government without difficulty. But if you haven't rectified yourself, how can you rectify the people?"

14   Jan Ch'iu returned from the Chi family's royal court, and the Master said: "Why so late?"

"Urgent government business."

"It must have been family business," replied the Master. "I may not hold any office, but I would have been consulted if it were really government business."

15   Duke Ting asked if there is a precept that could lead a country to prosperity, and the Master said: "Precepts cannot do such things. But they say: *To be a ruler is difficult indeed, and to be a subject is hardly easy.* If a man understands how difficult it is to rule, isn't that close to a single precept leading a country to prosperity?"

"Is there a precept that could destroy a country?" asked the Duke.

"Precepts cannot do such things. But they say: *In ruling, there is but one joy: no one dares defy you.* If a ruler is good and no one dares defy him, isn't that good? But if a ruler is evil and no one dares defy him, isn't that close to a single precept destroying an entire country?"

16   Duke She asked about governing, and the Master said: "When those nearby are pleased, those far away come and gather round."

17   When he was regent in Chü Fu, Adept Hsia asked about governing, and the Master said: "Don't rush things, and don't think about

small gains. If you rush around, your efforts will lead nowhere. If you worry about small gains, your great endeavors will go unrealized."

18   Speaking to Confucius, the Duke She said: "In my village there was a man called Body-Upright. When his father stole a sheep, he testified against him."

"In my village," said Confucius, "to be upright was something else altogether. Fathers harbored sons, and sons harbored fathers – and between them, they were upright."

19   Fan Ch'ih asked about Humanity, and the Master said: "Dwell at home in humility. Conduct your business in reverence. And in your dealings with others, be faithful.

"Even if you go east or north to live among wild tribes, these are things you must never disregard."

20   Adept Kung asked: "To be called a noble official, what must a person be like?"

"Always conducting himself with a sense of shame," replied the Master, "and when sent on embassies to the four corners of the earth, never disgracing his sovereign's commission – such a person can be called a noble official."

"May I ask about those in the next lower rank?"

"Their family elders praise them as filial children," replied the Master, "and their fellow villagers praise them as brothers."

"May I ask about those in the next rank?"

"They always stand by their words and bring their undertakings to completion. They may be stubborn, small-minded people, but still they can be accorded the next rank."

"And those who are running the government now – what do you

think of them?" asked Kung.

"Nothing but utensils!" sighed the Master. "Peck-and-hamper people too small even to measure."

21   The Master said: "I can't find students who steer the middle course, so I turn to the impetuous and the timid. The impetuous forge ahead, and the timid know what to avoid."

22   The Master said: "In the south it is said: *Without constancy, people cannot be shamans or doctors.* That says it well."

Integrity without constancy brings disgrace.[2] "Yes, yes," commented the Master, "you don't need a fortune-teller to see that!"

23   The Master said: "A noble-minded person is different from others, but at peace with them. A small-minded person is the same as others, but never at peace with them."

24   Adept Kung asked: "What do you think of *All the villagers love him?*"

"That is not enough," replied the Master.

"What do you think of *All the villagers hate him?*"

"That isn't enough either. It should be: *All the good villagers love him, and all the evil villagers hate him.*"

25   The Master said: "The noble-minded are easy to serve, but difficult to please. If you ignore the Way in trying to please them, they won't be pleased. But they recognize the limits of those who serve them.

"Little people are difficult to serve, but easy to please. If you ignore the Way in trying to please them, they'll be pleased nonetheless. And they demand perfection from those who serve them."

26 The Master said: "The noble-minded are stately, but never arrogant. Little people are arrogant, but never stately."

27 The Master said: "Enduring, resolute, simple, slow to speak – that's nearly Humanity."

28 Adept Lu asked: "To be called a noble official, what must a person be like?"

"Earnest and exacting, but also genial," replied the Master. "Such a person can be called a noble official. Earnest and exacting with friends, genial with brothers."

29 The Master said: "The people should be broadly educated by a wise teacher for seven years – then they can take up the weapons of war."

30 The Master said: "Sending people to war without educating them first: that is called *throwing the people away.*"

雕月覲豐追士
沈氏立立挹仁
聖心禮玄開
來家念器浮君
青宮昔水同
龍魯世水權
在親禮待深敬
涇百樂禮思號
斬主里鍾活遠
露并陵磬延
官遲遲尋

XIV Yüan Szu Asked About

1   Yüan Szu asked about disgrace, and the Master said: "To enjoy a salary when your country abides in the Way – that is fine. But to enjoy a salary when your country ignores the Way – that is a disgrace."

"Never domineering or arrogant, free of resentment and desire – is that Humanity?" asked Yüan.

"It's certainly difficult," replied the Master. "But I don't know if it's Humanity."

2   The Master said: "A thinker who cherishes the comforts of home isn't much of a thinker."

3   The Master said: "When your country abides in the Way, let your words and actions be daring. When your country ignores the Way, let your actions be daring and your words cautious."

4   The Master said: "Masters of Integrity are sure to be well-spoken, but the well-spoken aren't necessarily masters of Integrity. The Humane are sure to be courageous, but the courageous aren't necessarily Humane."

5   Speaking to Confucius, Nan-kung Kuo asked: "Yi was a mighty archer and Ao could push a boat over dry land, but neither of these legendary warriors lived out their full years. Yü and Chi, on the other hand, devoted themselves to farming and inherited all beneath Heaven in the end."[1]

The Master said nothing.

After Nan-kung Kuo had left, the Master said: "How truly noble-minded he is! And O, how deeply he reveres Integrity!"

6   The Master said: "The noble-minded may not always be Humane. But the small-minded – they never are."

7   The Master said: "How can you love people without encouraging them? And how can you be loyal to people without educating them?"

8   The Master said: "To compose a royal communiqué – P'i Ch'en first drafted the text; Shih Shu reviewed and discussed it; Lord Yü, the minister of foreign embassies, revised and polished it; and finally, Prime Minister Ch'an filled it with beauty."

9   Someone asked about Prime Minister Ch'an, and the Master said: "He was generous."

Asked about Prime Minister Hsi, the Master said: "O, that one! That one!"

Asked about Kuan Chung, the Master said: "In Pien, he seized the Po family's three hundred villages, but even though the family was reduced to eating meager fare, they never uttered a word of resentment. That's what kind of person he was."

CHAPTER XIV

10   The Master said: "To be poor and free of resentment is difficult. To be rich and free of arrogance is easy."

11   The Master said: "Meng Kung-ch'uo[2] would have been fine as senior advisor for some family like Chao or Wei,[3] but not as high minister for an actual country, even a tiny one like T'eng or Hsüeh."

12   Adept Lu asked about the realized person, and the Master said: "One who possesses Tsang Wu-chung's wisdom, Meng Kung-ch'uo's desirelessness, Master Chuang of Pien's courage, and Jan Ch'iu's accomplishments, and who refines these virtues with Ritual and music – that is a realized person.

"But," he added, "perhaps it isn't necessary to ask so much of a realized person these days. If you think of Duty upon seeing profit, risk your life upon seeing danger, and maintain your principles through long hardship – then you, too, are a realized person."

13   Asking Kung-ming Chia about Kung-shu Wen-tzu,[4] the Master said: "Is it really true that your master never spoke, never laughed, and never chose?"

"Whoever told you that was wrong," replied Kung-ming. "The Master spoke only at the proper time, so people never tired of his words. He laughed only when he was happy, so people never tired of his laugh. And he chose only what was right, so people never tired of his choices."

"If that's who he was," responded the Master, "then who was he?"

14   The Master said: "On his way into exile, Tsang Wu-chung[5] occupied his ancestral lands, insisting that the Lu duke leave it in the

hands of his family. People may say this wasn't coercion, but I don't believe it."

15   The Master said: "Duke Wen of Chin was scheming and not at all upright. Duke Huan of Ch'i, on the other hand, was upright and not at all scheming."

16   Adept Lu said: "When Duke Huan⁶ had his brother, Chiu, put to death, Shao Hu died trying to save Chiu, but Kuan Chung did not."

"In this," he added, "Kuan Chung fell short of Humanity, did he not?"

"It was Kuan Chung's strength that allowed Duke Huan to unite the nine lords without force, and so save the empire," replied the Master. "What Humanity! What amazing Humanity!"

17   Adept Kung said: "Kuan Chung was hardly Humane, was he? He didn't die trying to save Chiu when Duke Huan had him put to death – in fact, he became Huan's Prime Minister!"

"As Prime Minister, Kuan Chung enabled Huan to lead the nine lords and unite all beneath Heaven," replied the Master. "Even today, our people still enjoy the blessings he bestowed. If it weren't for him, we'd still let our hair hang loose and button our robes to the left like barbarians.

"Why should such a man commit suicide out in some ditch, with no one the wiser, all in blind obedience to the small fidelities of commoners?"

18   Chuan was a retainer in Kung-shu Wen-tzu's household. Later, he was promoted to a high state office, becoming Kung-shu Wen-tzu's colleague. Hearing of this, the Master said: "Wen:[7] a name well-chosen indeed."

19   The Master was talking about how Duke Ling of Wei had so completely ignored the Way, when Lord Chi K'ang asked: "If that's true, how is it he never came to grief?"

"He trusted foreign affairs to Lord K'ung Wen," replied Confucius, "his ancestral temple to Priest T'o, and his military to Wang-sun Chia. So how could he come to grief?"[8]

20   The Master said: "Immodest words are not easily put into action."

21   When Ch'en Heng[9] assassinated Duke Chien, Confucius bathed according to Ritual and went to court. There, informing Duke Ai, he said: "Ch'en Heng has assassinated his sovereign. I would encourage you to punish him."

"Inform the three family leaders," said the duke.

"I only inform you of such things," replied Confucius, "because I serve under the high ministers, and it is therefore my duty. Now you say *Inform the three family leaders*?"

He thereupon went to inform the three family leaders. When they refused to take action against Ch'en Heng, he said: "I only inform you of such things because I serve under the high ministers, and it is therefore my duty."

22   Adept Lu asked about serving a sovereign, and the Master said: "If you challenge his decisions, do it with honest loyalty."

23   The Master said: "The noble-minded influence those above them. Little people influence those below them."

24   The Master said: "The ancients studied in order to rule themselves. These days, people study in order to rule others."

25   Ch'ü Po-yü[10] sent an emissary to see Confucius. Once they were seated, Confucius asked: "What is your master working on?"

"He's trying to reduce his faults," replied the man, "but he isn't having much luck."

After the emissary left, the Master said: "What an emissary! What an amazing emissary!"

26   The Master said: "Unless you've been appointed to office, don't fuss and fret over the business of government."

And Master Tseng added: "The noble-minded always keep to their place, even in their thoughts."

27   The Master said: "The noble-minded say little and achieve much."

28   The Master said: "The Way of a noble-minded person has three facets, all of which are beyond me: the Humane have no worries; the wise have no doubts; and the courageous have no fear."

"But that," protested Adept Kung, "is precisely the Way you've mastered."

29   Adept Kung was forever comparing and criticizing people. The Master said: "To have time for such things, Kung must have already perfected himself completely! As for me, I am not so lucky."

30   The Master said: "Don't grieve when people fail to recognize your ability. Grieve for your lack of ability instead."

31   The Master said: "One who never anticipates deceit or expects duplicity, and yet is the first to recognize such things – is that not a sage indeed?"

32   Wang-sheng Mu said to Confucius: "Why all this anxious equivocation? It isn't that you're only trying to please people, is it?"

"No, it isn't that," replied Confucius. "It's just that I can't bear stubborn self-righteousness."

33   The Master said: "A legendary horse is praised not for its strength, but for its Integrity."

34   Someone asked: "What do you think of *Answer resentment with Integrity?*"

"Then how do you answer *Integrity?*" responded the Master. "Answer resentment with justice, and use Integrity to answer Integrity."

35 The Master said: "No one's ever understood me."

"Why not?" asked Adept Kung.

"I never resent Heaven or blame people," replied the Master. "In learning the ways of this world, I've fathomed Heaven. So perhaps Heaven, at least, understands me."

36 Speaking to Chi Sun,[11] Kung-po Liao[12] slandered Adept Lu. Telling the Master of this, Tzu-fu Ching-po[13] said: "My master's been taken in by these deceits. But I still have the power to add Kung-po's corpse to the market's display of criminals."

"When the Way abides, it's destiny," said the Master. "And when the Way's cast aside, it's destiny. How could Kung-po Liao alter destiny?"

37 The Master said: "A sage is one who lives beyond his day and age. Next come those who live beyond the place they inhabit. After that, those who live beyond beauty. And after that, those who live beyond words."

The Master said: "There have been only seven."

38 Adept Lu spent a night at Stone Gate, and the gatekeeper asked: "Where are you from?"

"From the House of Confucius," replied Lu.

"Isn't he the one who knows it's hopeless, but keeps trying anyway?"

39 The Master was playing stone chimes at the house where he was staying in Wei. Just then, a passerby carrying a basket stopped at the gate and said: "There's so much passion in that music!"

Then he quickly added: "So much petty urgency in all that stubborn clacking! If no one understands you, then that's that.

When it's deep — you wade through, clothes and all.
When it's shallow — you lift your robes and step across."[14]

"Of course!" said the Master. "Anything else would be difficult indeed!"

40   Adept Chang said: *"The Book of History* says *Kao Tsung*[15] *kept to his mourning hut for three years and never spoke.* What does this mean?"

"Why single out Kao Tsung?" replied the Master. "The ancients were all like that. When a sovereign died, the hundred officers all joined together and for three years trusted government to the Prime Minister."

41   The Master said: "If leaders love Ritual, the people will be easy to rule."

42   Adept Lu asked about the noble-minded, and the Master said: "They cultivate themselves, and so master reverence."

"Is that all it takes?" asked Lu.

"They cultivate themselves, and so bring peace to others."

"Is that all it takes?"

"They cultivate themselves, and so bring peace to the people. If you cultivate yourself, and so bring peace to the people, how could even Yao or Shun criticize you?"

43   Yüan Jang sat waiting on his haunches.

When he arrived, the Master said: "Showing no deference or respect when young, accomplishing nothing worth handing down when grown, and refusing to die when old — such people are nothing but pests."

At that, flicking his walking-stick, the Master cracked Yüan on the shin.

44   A boy from Ch'üeh Village had been hired as the Master's messenger. Asking about him, someone said: "Is he making progress?"

"I've seen him sit and walk among his elders," replied the Master, "as if he were already their equal. He has no interest in making progress. He wants it all right now."

雉　肖　顏　豊　起　是　上
　　氏　於　立　抒　仁
　　聖　心　禮　玄　聞
　　　　念　器　汙　君
丰　　家　馬　乘　以　同
青　元　居　廬　之　注　羅
龍　　魯　世　昔　水　敦
在　百　親　禮　待　涕　嘆
泱　主　里　樂　鍾　者　思
黔　不　并　陵　磬　婷
霜　改　官　遲　瑟

xv Duke Ling of Wei

1   Duke Ling of Wei asked Confucius about tactics, and Confucius said: "I've learned something about the conduct of worship and sacrifice. But as for the conduct of war – that is something I've never studied."

2   Confucius left the next day.
   In Ch'en, when supplies ran out, the disciples grew so weak they couldn't get to their feet. Adept Lu, his anger flaring, asked: "How is it the noble-minded must endure such privation?"
   "If you're noble-minded, you're resolute in privation," the Master replied. "Little people get swept away."

3   The Master said: "Kung, do you think of me as someone who studies widely and remembers what he learns?"
   "Yes," replied Adept Kung. "Aren't you?"
   "No. I've just found a single thread stringing it all together."[1]

4   The Master said: "Those who understand Integrity are rare indeed, Lu."

5   The Master said: "If anyone has managed to rule by doing nothing,[2] surely it was Shun. And how did he do so much by doing nothing? He just sat reverently facing south,[3] that's all!"

6   Adept Chang asked about action, and the Master said: "If you stand by your words, and they're loyal, your actions will be reverent and true. Then you can put your words into action, even in a barbarian country. But if you don't stand by your words, and they aren't loyal, your actions won't be reverent and true. Then how could you ever put your words into action, even in your own neighborhood?

"Keep this precept before you, even when standing or riding, and you'll make your words into actions."

Thereupon Adept Chang wrote it on his sash.

7   The Master said: "How straight and true Shih Yü[4] is! When the country abides in the Way, he's true as an arrow. And when the country ignores the Way, he's still true as an arrow.

"How noble-minded Ch'ü Po-yü is! When the country abides in the Way, he takes office. And when the country ignores the Way, he hides himself away and embraces it alone."

8   The Master said: "When a person is capable of understanding your words, and you refuse to speak, you're wasting a person. When a person isn't capable of understanding your words, and you speak anyway, you're wasting words. The wise waste neither words nor people."

9   The Master said: "As for noble officers of purpose and Humanity – they never wound Humanity to secure life. Indeed, to perfect Humanity, they often endure death."

10   Adept Kung asked about the practice of Humanity, and the Master said: "If a craftsman wants to do good work, he must first sharpen his tools. If you want to settle in a country, you must cultivate its wise ministers and befriend its Humane officials."

11   Yen Hui asked about governing a country, and the Master said: "Follow the Hsia's dynastic calendar, ride the Shang's dynastic carriage, wear the Chou's dynastic cap, and for music, choose the music of Emperors Shun and Wu. Banish the songs of Cheng, and send clever tongues far away. The songs of Cheng are dissolute and clever tongues a peril."

12   The Master said: "If things far away don't concern you, you'll soon mourn things close at hand."

13   The Master said: "It's all over. I've never seen anyone for whom loving Integrity is like loving a beautiful woman."

14   The Master said: "Tsang Wen-chung stole his high position, didn't he? He knew how wise and worthy Liu-hsia Hui⁵ was, and yet didn't offer the position to him."

15   The Master said: "If you expect great things of yourself and demand little of others, you'll keep resentment far away."

16   The Master said: "There's nothing to be done for a person who isn't constantly asking *What should be done? What should be done?*"

17   The Master said: "For people to talk all day, enthralled with their clever chitchat, and never once mention right or wrong – that must be difficult indeed!"

18   The Master said: "The noble-minded make Duty their very nature. They put it into practice through Ritual; they make it shine through humility; and standing by their words, they perfect it. Then they are noble-minded indeed!"

19   The Master said: "The noble-minded worry about their lack of ability, not about people's failure to recognize their ability."

20   The Master said: "Leaving a name that carries no honor through the ages following their death – that is what the noble-minded dread."

21   The Master said: "The noble-minded seek within themselves. Little people seek elsewhere."

22   The Master said: "The noble-minded stand above the fray with dignity. And when they band together with others, they never lose track of themselves."

23   The Master said: "The noble-minded don't honor a person because of something he's said, nor do they dismiss something said because of the person who said it."

24 Adept Kung asked: "Is there any one word that could guide a person throughout life?"

The Master replied: "How about *'shu': never impose on others what you would not choose for yourself*?"

25 The Master said: "Who have I condemned, and who praised? If there are those I have praised, it's easy enough to test them: for it was through the people that the Three Dynasties[6] put this straight Way into practice, and the people are no different today."

26 The Master said: "I can remember when scribes would leave a blank space if they weren't sure of a character, and people would loan their horses to friends. But that's all over now."

27 The Master said: "Clever talk ruins Integrity, and even a little impatience can ruin great plans."

28 The Master said: "When everyone hates a person, you should investigate thoroughly. And when everyone loves a person, you should also investigate thoroughly."

29 The Master said: "People can make the Way great and vast. But the Way isn't what makes people great and vast."

30 The Master said: "To be wrong without trying to change, that is called *wrong* indeed."

31   The Master said: "I've spent days without food and nights without sleep, hoping to purify thought and clarify mind. But it's never done much good. Such practices – they're nothing like devoted study."

32   The Master said: "The noble-minded devote themselves to the Way, not to earning a living. A farmer may go hungry, and a scholar may stumble into a good salary. So it is that the noble-minded worry about the Way, not poverty and hunger."

33   The Master said: "You may understand it, but if you can't sustain it with Humanity, it will slip from your grasp.

"You may understand it and sustain it with Humanity, but if you don't govern with solemn dignity, there'll be no reverence among the people.

"You may understand it, sustain it with Humanity, and govern with solemn dignity, but if you don't put it into practice according to Ritual, no good will come of it."

34   The Master said: "The noble-minded aren't easily known, but they're worthy of great responsibilities. The small-minded aren't worthy of great responsibilities, but they're easily known."

35   The Master said: "Humanity is more essential to the people than fire and water. I've seen people die trying to purify themselves by walking through fire or over water. But I've never seen anyone die because they've walked in Humanity."

36   The Master said: "Abide in Humanity, and you need not defer to any teacher."

37   The Master said: "The noble-minded are principled, but never dogmatic."

38   The Master said: "In serving your sovereign, be reverent about your duties and casual about your salary."

39   The Master said: "In worthy teaching, all things are related."[7]

40   The Master said: "If you don't follow the same Way, don't make plans together."

41   The Master said: "Language is insight itself."

42   Music-master Mien[8] arrived for a visit. When he reached the steps, the Master said: "Here are the steps."

Leading him to the mat, the Master said: "Here's the mat."

Once they were seated, the Master told him: "So-and-so is here. So-and-so is there. . . ."

After Music-master Mien left, Adept Chang asked: "Talking like this to a master musician – is that the Way?"

"Yes," replied the Master. "With a master musician, that is indeed the Way."

仁 抒 立 充 氏 月

閒 玄 禮 心 里 氏

君 汙 器 念 要 盧

以 兼 家 射

往 思 居 元 青

敬 水 曾 世 魯 龍

泳 洛 符 禮 親 百 左

思 洼 鍾 栄 里 王 洗

願 廷 橋 陵 并 不 勤

寒 遲 遲 宦 改 霜

XVI The House of Chi

1   The House of Chi was about to attack Chuan-yü.[1] Jan Ch'iu and Adept Lu went to see Confucius and said: "Our Lord Chi is about to settle things with Chuan-yü."

"Aren't you to blame for this?" responded Confucius. "Long ago, the early Emperors put Chuan-yü in charge of worship and sacrifice at Tung-meng Mountain. And besides, it's part of our own territory: its rulers serve these same gods of earth and grain. How can Chi think of attacking them?"

"It's our master's wish," replied Jan Ch'iu, "not ours."

"Chou Jen had a saying: *The capable join forces; the incapable step aside.* What good are counselors who don't steady him when he's stumbling and support him when he's falling? And besides, what you say is wrong. Isn't someone to blame if tigers and wild bulls escape from their cages, or jewelry of tortoiseshell and jade is crushed in its box?"

"But Chuan-yü has grown very strong," said Jan Ch'iu, "and it's so near the Chi capital. If it isn't dealt with now, it will terrorize the Chi descendants for ages to come."

"The noble-minded can't bear people who hedge around instead of saying what they want," countered Confucius. "This is what I've learned: leaders of countries and noble houses don't worry about having too few people, they worry about equitable rule; and they don't worry about the people living in poverty, they worry about the people living in peace. If rule is equitable, there's no poverty. If there's harmony, there's no lack of people. And if there's peace, there's no rebellion.

"If a ruler's like this, and people in far-off lands still don't turn to him, he cultivates his Integrity to attract them. And after they're attracted, he brings them peace.

"Now you two are this man's high counselors. People in far-off lands haven't turned to him, but you haven't shown him how to attract them. And the country's falling into utter ruins, but you haven't shown him how to preserve it. Instead, you're busy plotting war against your own country! If you want to know what will terrorize the descendants of Chi, don't go looking for it in Chuan-yü: look for it in the palace of Lord Chi himself."

2   Confucius said: "When all beneath Heaven abides in the Way – Ritual, music, and war all emanate from the Son of Heaven.

"When all beneath Heaven ignores the Way – Ritual, music, and war emanate from lords and princes. It's rare for such a nation to outlast ten generations. If they emanate from state ministers, it's rare for a nation to outlast five generations. And once officials start issuing imperial commands, it's rare for a nation to outlast three generations.

"When all beneath Heaven abides in the Way, governing is not left to ministers. And when all beneath Heaven abides in the Way, common people need not discuss politics."

3   Confucius said: "It's been five generations since the Lu rulers lost control of the treasury, and four generations since state ministers took control of the government. No wonder these descendants of the Three Families are in such decline!"

4   Confucius said: "There are three kinds of friends that bring profit, and three kinds that bring ruin. Forthright friends, trustworthy

friends, well-informed friends: these bring profit. Obsequious friends, compliant friends, clever-tongued friends: these bring ruin."

5   Confucius said: "There are three kinds of joy that bring profit, and three kinds that bring ruin. The joy of following Ritual and music, the joy of praising people's virtue and benevolence, the joy of having many wise friends: these bring profit. The joy of extravagant pleasures, the joy of dissolute living, the joy of convivial pleasures: these bring ruin."

6   Confucius said: "In serving a noble-minded leader, there are three common mistakes: speaking without being asked, which is called impetuous; refusing to speak after being asked, which is called aloof; speaking without considering his demeanor, which is called blindness."

7   Confucius said: "The noble-minded guard against three things: in youth, when *ch'i* and blood are unsettled, they guard against beautiful women; in their prime, when *ch'i* and blood are unbending, they guard against belligerence; and in old age, when *ch'i* and blood are withering, they guard against avarice."

8   Confucius said: "The noble-minded stand in awe of three things: the Mandate of Heaven, great men, and the words of a sage. Little people don't understand the Mandate of Heaven, so they aren't awed by it. They scorn great men, and they ridicule the words of a sage."

9   Confucius said: "To be born enlightened: that is highest. To study and so become enlightened: that is next. To feel trapped and so study: that is third. To feel trapped and never study: that is the level of the common people, the lowest level."

10   Confucius said: "The noble-minded have nine states of mind: for eyes, bright; for ears, penetrating; for countenance, cordial; for demeanor, humble; for words, trustworthy; for service, reverent; for doubt, questioning; for anger, circumspect; and for facing a chance to profit, moral."

11   Confucius said: "*I clutch good as if it were eluding me, and touch evil as if testing hot water:* I have seen such people and heard such claims.

"*I live as a recluse to realize my aspirations, and put Duty into practice to extend the Way's influence:* I have heard such claims, but never seen such people."

12   Duke Ching of Ch'i had a thousand teams of horses, but when he died the people couldn't find a single excuse to praise him. But Po Yi and Shu Ch'i starved below Shou-yang Mountain, and the people praise them to this day.

Isn't that what this means?[2]

13   Asking of Po-yü, the son of Confucius, Adept Ch'in said: "You must have learned things we've never been taught."

"No," replied Po-yü. "Once, when my father was standing alone, I was crossing the courtyard. I was hurrying, out of reverence, but he stopped me and asked: *Have you studied the* Songs? When I told him that I hadn't, he said: *Unless you study the* Songs, *you'll have nothing to say.* I withdrew and began studying the *Songs.*

"Another day, he was standing alone again. And again I was hurrying reverently across the courtyard, when he asked: *Have you studied Ritual?* When I told him that I hadn't, he said: *Unless you study Ritual, you'll have nowhere to stand.* I withdrew and began studying Ritual.

"These are the two things I have learned."

Adept Ch'in withdrew in delight, and said: "One question, three answers! I've learned about the *Songs.* I've learned about Ritual. And I've learned that a noble-minded man keeps his son at a distance."

14   The true sovereign calls his wife *lady.* The lady calls herself *little girl.* The people call her *our lord's lady.* But when visiting other countries, they call her *our little lord.* And people in other countries also call her *our lord's lady.*

雕　顏　尊　造　宜　王
氏　　　立　扵　仁
聖　心　禮　玄　聞
啻　念　器　汙　君
家　眞　樂　以　同
宮　盍　之　住　權
魯　世　普　水　敬
親　禮　祐　泳　忝
王　樂　建　活　思
并　陵　齊　　　
官　遲

XVII Yang Huo

1   Yang Huo[1] wanted to visit Confucius, but Confucius refused to see him. So he sent a piglet to Confucius as a gift. Choosing a time Yang would be out, Confucius went to offer the obligatory thanks at Yang's house. But on his way there he met Yang on the street.

"Come," Yang said, "I must speak with you.

"If a man keeps his treasure hidden away while chaos engulfs his country, can he be called Humane? Of course not. And if a man longs for public life but lets the opportunity slip away again and again, can he be called wise? Of course not.

"Days and months are slipping away. The years are not on our side."

"Alright," replied Confucius reluctantly, "I'm ready to take office."

2   The Master said: "We're all the same by nature. It's living that makes us so different."

3   The Master said: "Those of the loftiest wisdom and those of the basest ignorance: they alone never change."

4   The Master went to Wu-ch'eng,[2] and there heard the music of voices and strings. Well-pleased, the Master smiled and said: "What good is a big ox-cleaver when killing chickens?"

"Long ago," replied Adept Yu, "I heard you say: *When the noble-minded study the Way, they love people. When little people study the Way, they're easy to employ.*"

"My disciples," said the Master, "what Yu says is right. What I said before – that was only a joke."

5   When Kung-shan Fu-jao³ rebelled against the House of Chi and took its capital, he summoned the Master. The Master was ready to go, but Adept Lu was very unhappy and said: "You, who never answer such calls – why go to this Kung-shan?"

"He couldn't have summoned me for nothing," replied the Master. "And if he really employs me, I can re-create our glorious Chou in the east."

6   Adept Chang asked about Humanity, and Confucius said: "There are five essentials. If you can put them into practice throughout all beneath Heaven, then you've mastered Humanity."

"What are they?"

"Reverence, broad-mindedness, sincerity, diligence, and generosity. Reverent, and so never scorned; broad-minded, and so winning over the people; sincere, and so trusted; diligent, and so accomplishing much; generous, and so served willingly."

7   Pi Hsi⁴ summoned the Master, and the Master was ready to go. Adept Lu said: "I once heard you say: *The noble-minded never enter the country of a man who chooses evil of his own accord.* This Pi Hsi has rebelled against the House of Chao and taken the city of Chung-mou. How can you think of going to him?"

"Yes, I did say that," replied the Master. "But is it not said: *Hard indeed: a grindstone cannot wear it away*? And is it not said: *White indeed: black mud cannot darken it*?

"Am I to be a bitter gourd, left dangling on a string and never eaten?"

8　　The Master asked: "Have you heard the six precepts and their six deceptions?"

"No," replied Adept Lu.

"Then sit, and I'll tell you," said the Master. "To love Humanity without loving learning: that's the deception of foolishness. To love wisdom without loving learning: that's the deception of dissipation. To love sincerity without loving learning: that's the deception of subterfuge. To love veracity without loving learning: that's the deception of intolerance. To love courage without loving learning: that's the deception of confusion. And to love determination without loving learning: that's the deception of recklessness."

9　　The Master said: "How is it, my little ones, that none of you study the *Songs*? Through the *Songs*, you can inspire people and turn their gaze inward, bring people together and give voice to their grievances. Through them you serve your father when home and your sovereign when away, and you learn the names of countless birds and animals and plants."

Then the Master said to his son, Po-yü: "Have you worked through the *Chou Nan* and the *Shao Nan*?⁵ Until you've worked through at least them, you'll live as if you stood facing a wall."

10　　The Master said: "When I keep saying *Ritual! Ritual!*, do you think I'm just ranting about jade and silk? And when I keep saying *Music! Music!*, do you think I'm just ranting about bells and drums?"

11   The Master said: "Some act fierce and determined, but inside they're cowards. What little people – like petty thieves stealing into courtyards!"

12   The Master said: "A righteous villager is the thief of Integrity."

13   The Master said: "To hear the Way⁶ and speak in muddy alleys – that is to cast away Integrity."

14   The Master said: "How can you take such squalid little people for colleagues and still serve your sovereign? They worry constantly about getting what they want. Once they get it, they worry about losing it. And once they start that, there's nothing they won't do."

15   The Master said: "In ancient times, the people had three weaknesses. Now they rarely even have those. The impetuous were once unrestrained – now they're full of reckless abandon. The proud were once dignified – now they're full of angry indignation. The foolish were once true – now they're full of cunning guile."

16   The Master said: "Clever tongues and fawning looks: such people are rarely Humane."

17   The Master said: "I hate to see purple replacing the purity of vermilion. I hate to see those dissolute songs of Cheng confused with the stately music of Ya.⁷ And I hate to see calculating tongues pitching countries and noble houses into ruin."

18   The Master said: "I'd love to just say nothing."

"But if you say nothing," said Adept Kung, "how would we disciples hand down your teachings?"

"What has Heaven ever said?" replied the Master. "The four seasons keep turning and the hundred things keep emerging – but what has Heaven ever said?"

19   Ju Pei wanted to visit Confucius. Confucius declined, using illness as an excuse. But he picked up his *se* as the messenger was leaving and sang – loud enough that the messenger was sure to hear.

20   Tsai Yü asked about the three-year mourning period: "Surely one year is long enough. If the noble-minded ignore Ritual for three years, Ritual will be in ruins. And if they ignore music for three years, music will be a shambles. Old grain used up, new grain sprouting, and spring's Ritual fires replacing winter's: surely a year is enough."

"So," replied the Master, "by now you're content eating fancy rice and wearing fine brocade?"

"Yes."

"Well, if you're content, then go ahead. For the noble-minded in mourning, there's no savor in food and no joy in music. There's no contentment in their homes, so they don't eat fancy rice or wear fine brocade. But if you're content, you should go ahead and enjoy yourself."

After Tsai Yü left, the Master said: "How Inhumane Yü is! A child spends its first three years in the nurturing arms of its parents. That's why the mourning period lasts three years throughout all beneath Heaven. Didn't Yü also enjoy his parents' loving arms for three years?"

21   The Master said: "All day eating and never thinking: such people are serious trouble. Aren't there games to play, like *go* and chess? Even that is better than nothing."

22   Adept Kung asked: "The noble-minded revere courage, don't they?"

"The noble-minded honor Duty above all," replied the Master. "In the noble-minded, courage without Duty leads to turmoil. In little people, courage without Duty leads to theft and robbery."

23   Adept Kung asked: "Aren't there things the noble-minded hate?"

"Yes, there are," replied the Master. "They hate those who denounce what is hateful in others. They hate those who live poor and revile the privileged. They hate those who honor courage and neglect Ritual. And they hate those who are impetuous and yet frustrated."

Then Kung asked: "And aren't there things you hate?"

"I hate those who mistake secondhand knowledge for wisdom," offered Kung. "I hate those who mistake audacity for courage. And I hate those who mistake gossip for honest candor."

24   The Master said: "It's women and small-minded men that are impossible to nurture. If you're close and familiar with them, they lose all humility. If you keep your distance, they're full of resentment."

25   The Master said: "If you reach forty and find it all hateful, you'll be that way to the death."

觀禮心聖氏流精

立抒玄聖心念

君汙器念睽賓

同以弟其家帝

權注之歷居元圭

敬水昔世魯魯青龍

呪涼待禮親百在

思海鍾樂里主涼

演逞磬陵並不艱

涉遲官改霜

XVIII   The Lord of Wei

1   The Lord of Wei fled the Tyrant Chou.[1] The Lord of Chi became his slave. Pi Kan tried to advise him and was put to death.

Confucius said: "In them, the Shang had three men of great Humanity."

2   When Liu-hsia Hui was Chief Judge, he was dismissed three times. People said: "Why haven't you gone somewhere else, master?"

"If I follow the straight Way in serving people," replied Hui, "where could I go that I wouldn't be dismissed three times? If I follow a twisty Way in serving people, why should I leave this land of my parents?"

3   Waiting for Confucius to arrive, Duke Ching of Ch'i said: "I certainly can't honor him like a patriarch from the House of Chi. I'll receive him like a patriarch from a house greater than Meng but not so great as Chi.

Then he said: "I'm so old now, I can't see how to use his ideas."

Confucius thereupon left Ch'i.

4   Ch'i sent a gift of singing courtesans to Lu. Lord Chi Huan[2] accepted them and held no court for three days. Confucius thereupon left Lu.

5   A madman of Ch'u named Convergence Crazy-Cart passed by Confucius singing:

> *"Phoenix!³ Hey, sage phoenix,*
> *how's Integrity withered away so?*
>
> *What's happened can't be changed,*
> *but the future's there to be made.*
>
> *Give it up! Give it all up!*
> *High office – these days, that's the gravest of dangers."*

Confucius stepped down from his carriage, wanting to speak with this man. But Crazy-Cart ignored him and hurried away, so Confucius never spoke with him.⁴

6   As Confucius passed by, Settled-Constant and Brave-Seclusion were in the field plowing together. He sent Adept Lu to ask them about the river crossing.⁵

"Who's that you're driving for?" asked Settled-Constant.

"Confucius," replied Adept Lu.

"You mean Confucius of Lu?"

"Yes."

"Then he must know the river crossing well."

Adept Lu then asked Brave-Seclusion, but Brave-Seclusion replied, "So who are you?"

"I am Chung Yu," replied Adept Lu.

"You mean Chung Yu who follows Confucius of Lu?"

"Yes."

"It's all surging and swelling," continued Brave-Seclusion. "All beneath Heaven's foundering deep, and who's going to change it? To follow a man who stays clear of one person or another – how could that ever compare with following one who stays clear of the world?"

And folding earth back over seed, he went on working without pause.

Adept Lu went back and told Confucius what had happened. The Master seemed lost in troubled thought, then said: "Flocks of birds, herds of animals – we can't go roaming with them. So who can I live with, if not these humans? It's all beneath Heaven that ignores the Way: if it didn't, I wouldn't be trying so hard to change things."

7   Adept Lu was traveling with Confucius and fell behind. Meeting an old man with a basket slung from a walking-stick over his shoulder, he asked: "Have you seen the Master pass by here?"

"Your four limbs have never known work," the old man replied, "and you can't even tell the five grains apart. Who could be your Master?"

At this, he planted his walking-stick and began pulling weeds.

Adept Lu bowed and stood by reverently. So the old man invited him to stay the night. He killed a chicken and cooked up some millet. He served dinner and introduced his two sons.

The next day, Lu caught up with the Master and told him what had happened.

"Such is the recluse," responded the Master.

Then he sent Lu back to see the man again. But when Lu got there, the old man had vanished.

"To refuse office is to ignore Duty," pronounced Adept Lu. "The obligations of youth and age cannot be abandoned. And the Duty of rulers and officials – what would happen if that were abandoned? In such devotion to self-purification, the great bonds of human community are thrown into confusion. The noble-minded put Duty into practice: they serve in office, though they know full well this world will never put the Way into practice."

8   Po Yi, Shu Ch'i, Yü Chung, Yi Yi, Chu Chang, Liu-hsia Hui, Shao Lien: of these recluse scholars, the Master said: "Perhaps it's true

that Po Yi and Shu Ch'i remained free of compromise and disgrace. It's said that Liu-hsia Hui and Shao Lien were compromised and disgraced, though their words were at least true to the bonds of human community and their actions true to their principles. And it's said that Yü Chung and Yi Yi lived in seclusion and gave up speech altogether, keeping themselves pure and turning exile into a position of authority.

"But I'm not like them. I have no use for the strictures of *You must. You must not.*"

9   Chih, Grand Music-master for banquet music, left for Ch'i. Kan, Music-master for the second course, left for Ch'u. Liao, Music-master for the third course, left for Ts'ai. And Ch'üeh, Music-master for the fourth course, left for Ch'in.

Fang Shu, master of the drum, went to live north of the Yellow River. Wu, master of the hand-drum, went to live beyond the Han River. Yang, the Grand Music-master's deputy, and Hsiang, master of the stone chimes – they went to live beyond the sea.

10   Speaking to Duke Lu, Duke Chou said: "The noble-minded never neglect their own family, and they never give their ministers cause for resentment. Unless the crimes are huge, they never abandon those they've long trusted, and they never expect perfection from anyone."

11   The great Chou had its eight noble ones:[6] elder brothers Ta and Kua, middle brothers T'u and Hu, young brothers Yeh and Hsia, younger brothers Sui and Kua.

土　宣　造　尊　顏　？　雖
仁　挓　立　尤　氏　心　？
聞　玄　禮　心　聖　質　？
君　汙　器　念　？　？　其
同　以　粟　真　家　杓　青
權　注　之　盧　居　元　飛
敬　水　普　世　魯　？　？
？　濟　待　禮　親　百　在
思　安　建　樂　里　主　決
頹　？　馨　陵　并　不　斷
壽　泰　瑟　遲　進　官　改

Adept Chang

1   Adept Chang said: "Willing to give up life when seeing danger, and thinking first of Duty when seeing a chance to profit; full of reverence during sacrifices, and full of grief during mourning: Fine enough! Fine enough!"

2   Adept Chang said: "Halfhearted in embracing Integrity and capricious in trusting the Way: how can they even *have it* or *have it not?*"

3   Adept Hsia's disciples asked Adept Chang about fellowship.
     "What does Adept Hsia say about it?" said Chang.
     "He says *Join with those who are capable and avoid those who are not.*"
     "That isn't what I've heard," replied Chang. "I've heard that the noble-minded honor the wise, but make room for everyone; that they admire the virtuous and benevolent, but pity those who fall short. If I am a person of great wisdom, how can I fail to make room for everyone? And if I am less than wise, people will avoid me, so how could I think of avoiding them?"

4   Adept Hsia said: "There are lesser Ways, and there's much to be said for them. But if you follow them very far, there's sure to be mud and mire – so the noble-minded stay clear of them."

5   Adept Hsia said: "All day knowing what is beyond you, and all month never forgetting what you've mastered – then you can indeed be called a lover of learning."

6   Adept Hsia said: "Broad learning with resolute purpose, earnest inquiry with attentive reflection on things at hand – therein lies Humanity."

7   Adept Hsia said: "To perfect the hundred crafts, artisans live in their shops. To perfect the Way, the noble-minded work tirelessly at learning."

8   Adept Hsia said: "Little people always disguise their faults with pretense."

9   Adept Hsia said: "The noble-minded have three different aspects: Seen from a distance, they're majestic. Face to face, they're genial. And when they speak, they're incisive."

10   Adept Hsia said: "When the noble-minded stand by their words, they can put the people to work. When they don't stand by their words, the people call work grinding oppression.

"When the noble-minded stand by their words, they can advise the sovereign. When they don't stand by their words, the sovereign calls their advice slander."

11   Adept Hsia said: "Keep within the bounds of great Integrity. Then, in matters of small Integrity, you needn't worry about a little coming and going."

12   Adept Yu said: "Adept Hsia's disciples are so small-minded! They're fine when it comes to dusting and sweeping, replies and rejoinders, greetings and farewells. But these are frivolous things. When it comes to the deep essentials, they don't have a clue. How can this be?"

When Adept Hsia heard this, he said: "That's crazy! Yu doesn't know what he's talking about. If you start teaching the noble-minded Way too soon, people are sick of it before they're ready to learn. It's like plants and trees: you need to gauge differences. The noble-minded Way never disappoints anyone – but still, only a great sage can embrace it right through from beginning to end."

13   Adept Hsia said: "When you're an official with free time, study. When you're a student with free time, take office."

14   Adept Yu said: "In mourning – grieve fully, and then stop."

15   Adept Yu said: "My friend Adept Chang can master the most difficult things, but he still hasn't mastered Humanity."

16   Master Tseng said: "Chang is great and venerable indeed: it's impossible to work beside him cultivating Humanity."

17   Master Tseng said: "I once heard the Master say *If you haven't yet faced yourself, you will when the time comes to mourn your parents.*"

18   Master Tseng said: "I once heard the Master say *Lord Meng Chuang's filial piety might be equaled in many ways. But leaving his father's policies and advisors unchanged – that seems beyond compare.*"

19   When Yang Fu was appointed judge by the House of Meng, he went to Master Tseng for advice. Master Tseng said: "Our leaders lost the Way long ago, abandoning the people to ruin. So don't feel happy when you manage to untangle the facts of a case; grieve in sympathy for everyone involved."

20   Adept Kung said: "Even Tyrant Chou wasn't as depraved as he's made out to be. So it is that the noble-minded keep to the high ground: everything hateful on earth flows back down to low places."

21   Adept Kung said: "Mistakes of the noble-minded are like eclipses of sun and moon: they make a mistake, and it's there for everyone to see; they make it right, and everyone looks up in awe."

22   Kung-sun Ch'ao of Wei asked Adept Kung: "Where did Confucius acquire such learning?"

"The Way of Emperors Wen and Wu never fell into ruins," replied Kung. "It abides in the people. The sage sees that greatness; others see only smallness. Something of the Way is there in everyone, so where could Confucius go without learning of it? And why would he spend years studying with some master teacher?"

23   Speaking with the ministers at court, Shu-sun Wu-shu[1] said: "Adept Kung is a greater sage than Confucius."

When Tzu-fu Ching-po reported this to him, Adept Kung said: "It's like courtyard walls. Mine stand shoulder-height, so people can look over and see how lovely the house is. But the Master's wall is fifteen or twenty feet high. Unless they're admitted through the gate, people never see the beauty of his temple and the splendor of his hundred rooms. And those who are admitted are very few indeed. So it makes perfect sense for your master to say that, doesn't it?"

24   Shu-sun Wu-shu was speaking ill of Confucius. Adept Kung said: "It's no use. There's nothing bad to say about Confucius. Others are certainly wise, but they're like mounds and hillocks, easy to scale. Confucius is like the sun and moon. How could anyone scale such heights?

"People may choose to live in darkness, but sun and moon suffer no harm. And the folly of it all is apparent to everyone."

25   Adept Ch'in said to Adept Kung: "It's just your reverent humility. How can Confucius be a greater sage than you?"

"The noble-minded reveal their wisdom in a single word," replied Kung, "and in a single word they reveal their ignorance. So you can't afford to speak carelessly.

"Now, we can't reach Confucius any more than we can reach Heaven: you can't just climb a set of stairs into the sky. If Confucius were in charge of a country or noble house, it would be like the saying: *He raised them up and they stood; he showed them the Way and they set out; he offered them peace and they came; he roused them and they carried through in harmony.* He was exalted in life and mourned deeply in death. So how could we ever reach him?"

雎　肎　頫　豊　迋　　士
氏　光　立　扜　仁
里　心　禮　玄　閒
念　器　汙　君
家　其　兼　以　同
官　　往　䨥
魯　世　晉　水　敬
親　禮　符　涂
里　柋　建　浩　思
幷　陵　盤
官　改　遲　悲

xx Emperor Yao Said

1 Emperor Yao said:

> *"O Shun—*
> *Heaven has passed its throne on to you now.*
>
> *Hold fast to the middle way:*
> *If you let this land of the four seas*
> *fall into poverty and desperation,*
> *the gift of Heaven is lost forever."*

And in passing the throne on to Yü, Shun administered this same charge.

Emperor T'ang said: "I, your little child, dare to offer a dusky bull and call out to you, O most august and majestic Lord. You dare not pardon those who commit offense, and we servants can hide nothing from you: we are revealed in your heart. But if I commit offense, blame not the people of my ten thousand districts. And if the ten thousand districts commit offense, the blame is mine alone."

Emperor Wu knew great bounty, and so virtuous people flourished. He said:

> *Though I have my own family,*
> *the Humane are beyond compare.*

If the people ever transgress,
let the fault be mine alone.[1]

Pay close attention to weights and measures, re-examine laws and statutes, restore neglected offices and ministries – then the four regions will be well-governed.

Renew ravaged states, re-establish lines of succession, raise up all those who have gone into hiding – then, throughout all beneath Heaven, the people will cherish you once again in their hearts.

Matters of great weight and importance: the people, food, mourning, sacrifice.

Broad-minded, and so winning over the people; sincere, and so trusted; diligent, and so accomplishing much; fair, and so fostering joy.

2   Adept Chang asked Confucius: "What makes a person fit to govern?"

"Honoring the five graces and despising the four deformities," replied the Master, "that's what makes a person fit to govern."

"What are the five graces?" asked Adept Chang.

"The noble-minded are generous without expense, hardworking without resentment, wishful without greed, stately without arrogance, stern without cruelty."

"What is *generous without expense*?" asked Chang.

"To reward people with the rewards due them," said the Master, "is that not *generous without expense*?

"If you work people hard, but always according to their ability, how can anyone resent you? If you wish for Humanity and Humanity is realized, how is that greed? The noble-minded scorn neither the many nor the few, the humble nor the great: is that not *stately without arrogance*? The noble-minded are exacting in their dress and exalted in their gaze, so people look up to their majesty in awe: is that not *stern without cruelty?*"

"And what are the four deformities?" asked Chang.

"Killing instead of teaching, which is called terror. Expecting results without telling people what you want, which is called tyranny. Issuing vague orders and expecting prompt action, which is called plunder. Grudging and miserly when giving people what they deserve, which is called officialdom."

3   The Master said: "If you don't understand destiny, you'll never be noble-minded. If you don't understand Ritual, you'll never stand firm. And if you don't understand words, you'll never understand people."

Notes

I. To Learn, and Then

1 **Master Yu:** Disciple who later became a significant teacher in the Confucian school after Confucius' death.

2 **Way:** See Key Terms: *Tao.*

3 **Humanity:** See Key Terms: *Jen.*

4 **Master Tseng:** Disciple who became a significant teacher in the Confucian school after Confucius' death.

5 **stood by my words:** Typically translated as "sincerity" or "trust," *hsin* generally appears in this translation as "standing by words" to reflect the etymology so apparent visually in the two elements of its graph, where a person is shown beside words (sounds coming out of a mouth): 信

6 **Adept Hsia:** Prominent disciple who also served as a regent for the House of Chi, the most powerful of the Three Families that had usurped governmental power. (See note V.7 for definition of *regent.*)

7 **Integrity:** See Key Terms: *Te.*

8 **Adept Kung:** Prominent disciple who became a regent for the House of Chi and a successful merchant.

9 **Duty:** See Key Terms: *Yi.*

10 **as if burnished:** *The Book of Songs,* 55.

II. In Government, the Secret

1 **thoughts never twisty:** *The Book of Songs,* 297.

2 **Lord Meng Yi:** High minister in Lu and patriarch in the House of Meng, one of the Three Families that had usurped power in Lu.

3 **Fan Ch'ih:** Disciple.

4 **Adept Yu:** Disciple and regent.

5 **Yen Hui:** Perhaps the most able of Confucius' disciples. Confucius admired his wisdom and ability above all others and grieved deeply when he died young.

6 **Duke Ai:** Titular ruler of Lu (494–468), though the Three Families had usurped power. He tried to return power to the royal house and failed.

7 **Lord Chi K'ang:** Patriarch in the House of Chi and high minister who was de facto ruler in Lu from 492 to 468.

III. Eight Rows of Dancers

1   **what can't be?:** The first of many such attacks. The reason for Confucius' outrage is that Ritual is being violated.

2   **august and majestic:** *The Book of Songs,* 282.

3   **Lin Fang:** Nothing is known about this character or just why he appears in section 6 below. Perhaps he was a novice disciple or an influential but incapable official?

4   **Jan Ch'iu:** Disciple and minister for the House of Chi.

5   **ready for color:** *The Book of Songs,* 57 (last line absent).

6   **Wang-sun Chia:** Minister in Wei.

7   **Duke Ting:** Ruler of Lu from 509 to 495, the period during which Confucius was most active in politics.

8   **Tsai Yü:** Disciple.

9   **Kuan Chung:** In the seventh century B.C.E., Duke Huan became sovereign in Ch'i by killing his brother Chiu. Kuan Chung was initially Chiu's advisor, but afterward became a sage Prime Minister under Duke Huan. His talents turned Ch'i into a powerful and rich state, and made Huan first among the august lords.

10   **Emperor Shun:** Mythic ruler (regnant 2255–2208 b.c.e) of great sagacity during the legendary golden age of China. See Historical Table.

11   **Emperor Wu:** Sage founder of the Chou Dynasty. "Wu" means "martial," and although he was a ruler of great virtue, he gained the throne by force. Hence, Confucius' reservation. See Introduction p. 219 and Historical Table.

IV. Of Villages, Humanity

1   **That same loyalty:** See Key Terms: *Shu.*

V. Kung-yeh Ch'ang

1   **Kung-yeh Ch'ang:** Disciple.

2   **Nan Jung:** Disciple.

3   **Adept Chien:** Disciple and regent.

4   **Jan Yung:** Disciple and regent for the House of Chi.

5   **Ch'i-tiao K'ai:** Disciple.

6   **Adept Lu:** Prominent disciple and minister for the House of Chi. He died fighting for Chi.

7   **regent:** Frequently used term *(tsai)* indicating a chief of government

appointed to administer territory controlled by the great families who had usurped power in Lu and the other nations.

8   **Wen:** *Wen* means "cultured and refined."

9   **Yen P'ing-chung:** High minister in Ch'i who survived many changes of government because of his integrity.

10   **Tsang Wen-chung:** Minister in Lu.

11   **Lord Ning Wu:** Lord Ning Wu (seventh century B.C.E.) appeared foolish when he continued serving the Wei ruler after he lost his nation, but in the end Ning Wu saved the nation.

12   **Po Yi and Shu Ch'i:** Brothers (twelfth century B.C.E.) who were heir to the throne, but they felt it would be wrong to accept it, so they refused. As a result, they lived lives of great poverty, finally dying of cold and hunger in the mountains.

VI. Jan Yung Is One Who

1   **destiny:** Destiny in ancient Chinese must be read not in the sense of a transcendental force deciding human fate, but as the inevitable evolution of things according to the principles inherent to them.

2   **Yüan Szu:** Disciple and regent. He reappears in *Chuang Tzu* as a Taoist recluse.

3   **Ch'iu . . . go wrong:** This was a very real request for recommendation, as all three of these disciples were in fact given high positions in the government of the House of Chi.

4   **Min Tzu-ch'ien:** Disciple.

5   **Jan Po-niu:** Disciple.

6   **Meng Chih-fan:** Officer in Lu.

7   **Lady Nan:** Notorious wife of Duke Ling, ruler in Wei. See note VII.3.

8   **the constant commonplace:** *Chung yung:* also the title of the Confucian classic that deals with this principle and is generally known in English as *The Doctrine of the Mean.*

9   **Yao:** Mythic ruler (regnant 2357–2255 B.C.E.) of great sagacity during the legendary golden age of China. Yao was Shun's (note III.9) predecessor. See Historical Table.

VII. Transmitting Insight, But

1   **P'eng:** This character has never been identified with any certainty.

2   **Duke Chou:** A cultural hero much admired by Confucius and Mencius,

Duke Chou helped his brother, Wu, found the Chou Dynasty. He helped set up the institutions of sage government, and is traditionally credited with developing the doctrine of the Mandate of Heaven, which introduced ethics into government (see Historical Table and Introduction pp. 219).

3   **Wei ruler:** This Wei ruler was Ch'u, son of K'uai K'ui, who was the rightful heir to Duke Ling's throne. K'uai K'ui tried to kill Lady Nan (cf. VI.27), Duke Ling's notorious wife, and fled the country when he failed. After Duke Ling's death, Ch'u inherited the throne, whereupon his father raised an army and tried to reclaim the country that was rightfully his.

4   **Change:** There is a rich bit of ambiguity here, for this character *(Yi)* may be translated either as "change" or as *The Book of Change (I Ching).* The latter is the traditional reading.

5   **Lu dialect:** That is, he used the standard literary language that was employed by the intelligentsia throughout the different nations of China. This split between the classical literary language and colloquial language continued into the twentieth century.

6   **Duke She:** Sage governor of She, a territory in the state of Ch'u.

7   **Huan T'ui:** Minister of War in Sung.

8   **Wu-ma Ch'i:** Disciple and regent.

VIII. Surely T'ai Po

1   **T'ai Po:** Eldest son of Emperor T'ai, legendary predecessor of emperors Wen and Wu, the founders of the Chou Dynasty. See Historical Table.

2   **over thin ice:** *The Book of Songs,* 195.

3   **friend:** Tradition identifies this friend as Yen Hui.

4   **"Ospreys Calling":** The first song in *The Book of Songs.*

5   **Yü:** Sage emperor from China's legendary golden age, Yü (regnant 2205–2197) succeeded Shun to the throne and founded the Hsia Dynasty.

6   **Emperor Yao . . . ways of culture:** Yao is credited with teaching humankind the arts of civilization.

IX. The Master Rarely

1   **Emperor Wen:** Father of Wu, the founder of the Chou Dynasty, Wen was considered responsible for the resplendent culture of the Chou Dynasty, hence his name, which means "culture." See Introduction p. 219 and Historical Table.

2   **Phoenix . . . river . . . :** Signs heralding the appearance of a sage ruler who will bring peace and benevolent rule.

3   **Yen Hui:** Confucius' finest disciple, died young.

4   **anything but good:** *The Book of Songs*, 33.

5   **so far away:** Not in the *The Book of Songs* as we know it.

X. His Native Village

1   **Chapter X:** Confucianism was eventually reduced to hollow convention and the details of ritual. There is little justification for such doctrines in the actual teachings of Confucius, so this odd chapter (and no doubt a number of other passages scattered throughout the text) seems to be an attempt by later editors to justify them.

2   ***Ch'i:*** The universal breath, vital energy, or life-force.

XI. Studies Begin

1   **lines about a white-jade scepter:** From *The Book of Songs*, 256:

> *Defects in a white-jade scepter*
> *can still be polished away,*
> *but for defects in your words*
> *there's nothing to be done.*

2   ***se:*** Stringed instrument (similar to the *ch'in*) played by literati in ancient China: predecessor to the more familiar Japanese *koto*.

3   **Adept Kao:** Disciple and regent under the House of Chi.

4   **Chi Tzu-jan:** A leader of the usurping Chi family who employed Adept Lu and Jan Ch'iu as regents.

5   **ruining someone's son:** Both by placing him in the government of the House of Chi, who were usurpers, and by taking him away from his studies.

6   **Tseng Hsi:** Master Tseng's father. See note I.3.

XII. Yen Hui

1   **Szu-ma Niu:** According to tradition, Szu-ma Niu was a disciple of Confucius who had several disreputable brothers, among them Huan T'ui, who tried to assassinate Confucius in VII.23.

2   **one part in nine:** In the traditional well-field system, each parcel of land is divided into nine plots and so looks like the character *ching*, which means

well: 井. The eight outer plots in this configuration are each cultivated by one family. In addition to cultivating their own plot, the eight families cultivate the center plot jointly. This is public land, and its produce is given to the government as a tax.

3   **Maybe . . . novelty:** This passage from *The Book of Songs,* 188 seems to have been placed here through some kind of editorial error.

4   **Duke Ching:** Ruler of Ch'i (regnant 542–490).

5   **T'ang:** Founding emperor of the Shang Dynasty (1766–1122 B.C.E.). See Historical Table.

XIII. Adept Lu

1   **losing them:** Amputation of hands and feet was a common form of punishment.

2   **Integrity . . . disgrace:** *I Ching* 32.3.

XIV. Yüan Szu Asked About

1   **Yi . . . Ao . . . Yü and Chi:** These four figures come from China's legendary prehistory, dating to the third millennium B.C.E. Yü was appointed by Shun to drain away the primal floodwaters that covered the empire, thus making agriculture possible. He later succeeded Shun to the throne and founded the Hsia Dynasty. Chi, serving as Shun's Minister of Agriculture, is credited with the invention of agriculture.

2   **Meng Kung-ch'uo:** As patriarch in the House of Meng, one of the three usurping families in Lu, Meng Kung-ch'uo had great political ambitions. What is more, the state of Lu was far from being a "tiny country."

3   **Chao or Wei:** usurping families in Chin.

4   **Kung-shu Wen-tzu:** High minister in Wei.

5   **Tsang Wu-chung:** Tsang Wu-chung was accused of plotting a revolt, hence his exile. The pretext for his demand would have been that his family needed to keep up their ancestral sacrifices.

6   **Duke Huan:** See note III.8.

7   *Wen:* "cultured and refined."

8   **He trusted . . . grief:** This answer is perhaps meant ironically, for all three figures have already appeared as dubious characters in the *Analects* (V.14, VI.15, and III.13 respectively), and Lord Chi K'ang was asking because he was a usurper who also ignored the Way.

9   **Ch'en Heng:** Patriarch of the House of Ch'en, which had been growing more and more powerul in Ch'i. It was with Ch'en Heng's assassination of

Duke Chien that the usurping Ch'en family took complete control of the state.

10   **Ch'ü Po-yü:** High minister in Wei. He also appears in *Chuang Tzu,* IV.3, where the wordplay in his name is emphasized: Sudden Elder-Jade.

11   **Chi Sun:** Chi family patriarch.

12   **Kung-po Liao:** Perhaps a disciple.

13   **Tzu-fu Ching-po:** High minister of integrity under the Chi family.

14   **"When it's deep . . . step across":** *The Book of Songs,* 34.

15   **Kao Tsung:** After mourning his predecessor thus, Kao Tsung became Wu Ting, a sage Shang Dynasty emperor.

XV. Duke Ling of Wei

1   **single thread . . . :** See Key Terms: *shu.*

2   **doing nothing:** This is *wu-wei* – a concept central to Taoist, and later Ch'an (Zen) Buddhist, thought. See Introduction p. 227.

3   **facing south:** The ceremonial position of the emperor.

4   **Shih Yü:** Like Ch'ü Po-yü below, Shih Yü was a minister in Wei.

5   **Tsang Wen-chung, Liu-hsia Hui:** Ministers in Lu a century or so before Confucius.

6   **Three Dynasties:** Hsia, Shang, and Chou Dynasties.

7   This terse, four-character passage is quite ambiguous. Two other equally important interpretations are possible: "When they're educated, the people are all alike" and "Education is for everyone of every class."

8   **Music-master Mien:** At the time, only the blind entered the musical profession.

XVI. The House of Chi

1   **Chuan-yü:** A small independent state within the borders of Lu.

2   The text for this section is defective. Perhaps Po Yi and Shu Ch'i (see note V.12.) are being given as examples of the model recluse in the previous section, or perhaps there is something missing at the beginning of this section. Also, it seems to be another statement by Confucius, but this is not indicated in the text.

XVII. Yang Huo

1   **Yang Huo:** Although nominally only regent to the House of Chi, Yang Huo wielded the family's power and eventually took control of the entire country of Lu.

2   **Wu-ch'eng:** Place governed by Adept Yu.

3   **Kung-shan Fu-jao:** A regent under the House of Chi and a confederate of Yang Huo. Confucius perhaps imagined that Yang intended to restore power to the rightful ruler of Lu.

4   **Pi Hsi:** Regent under one of the great houses in Chin.

5   ***Chou Nan* and the *Shao Nan:*** The first two chapters in *The Book of Songs.*

6   **Way:** The original meaning of Way *(Tao)* is "road."

7   **songs of Cheng . . . Ya:** Two sections in *The Book of Songs.*

XVIII. The Lord of Wei

1   **Tyrant Chou:** Last emperor of the Shang Dynasty, known for his vicious rule. His overthrow by Emperor Wu marked the beginning of the Chou Dynasty.

2   **Lord Chi Huan:** Patriarch in the House of Chi and high minister who was de facto ruler in Lu from 505 to 492.

3   **Phoenix:** See note IX.2.

4   This begins a group of sections that provide a Taoist counterbalance to Confucian doctrine. They were perhaps included by a later editor with Taoist sympathies.

     For another version of this story, see *Chuang Tzu* IV.8.

5   **river crossing:** The river crossing can be taken literally: the implication then is that Confucius should know where it is because he spends so much time wandering around foolishly trying to save the world. But for later writers who alluded to this passage, T'ao Ch'ien for instance, the river crossing came to represent the Way through this "surging and swelling" world that a sage masters.

6   **eight noble ones:** It was said that when a dynasty truly flourished a woman would give birth to four sets of twins, all of whom would become distinguished men.

XIX. Adept Chang

     Chapter XIX: This chapter seems to involve the disciples after Confucius' death.

1   **Shu-sun Wu-shu:** Minister in Lu.

XX. Emperor Yao Said

1   **Shun . . . Yü . . . T'ang . . . Wu:** The sage-emperor Shun was the last emperor of the legendary pre-dynastic period, and so is a kind of founding

patriarch to the Three Dynasties. Within the Three Dynasties: Yü founded the Hsia Dynasty, T'ang founded the Shang, and Wu founded the Chou. See Historical Table.

Historical Table

Emperors

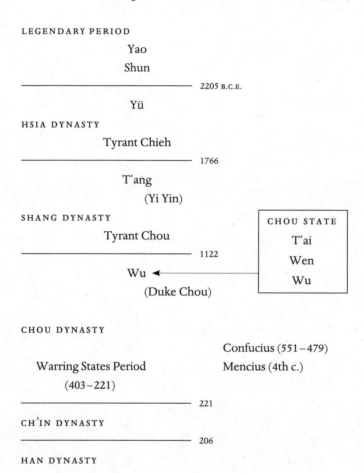

LEGENDARY PERIOD
    Yao
    Shun
———————————————— 2205 B.C.E.
    Yü

HSIA DYNASTY
    Tyrant Chieh
———————————————— 1766
    T'ang
     (Yi Yin)

SHANG DYNASTY
    Tyrant Chou
———————————————— 1122
    Wu ←
     (Duke Chou)

CHOU STATE
  T'ai
  Wen
  Wu

CHOU DYNASTY

         Confucius (551–479)

  Warring States Period   Mencius (4th c.)
    (403–221)
———————————————— 221

CH'IN DYNASTY
———————————————— 206

HAN DYNASTY

378

Key Terms
An Outline of Confucius' Thought

Li: 禮 Ritual

A religious concept associated with the worship of gods and spirits prior to Confucius, Ritual was reconfigured by Confucius to mean the web of social responsibilities that bind a society together. These include the proprieties in virtually all social interactions, and are determined by the individual's position within the structure of society. By calling these secular acts "Ritual," Confucius makes everyday experience itself a sacred realm. This Ritual structure of society is part of a vast cosmological weave: the Ritual structure of natural process as the ten thousand things emerge from the primal emptiness.

Jen: 仁 Humanity (Humane)

The character for *jen* is formed by a combination of the characters for "human being" and "two," and it means all of the moral qualities expressed in the behavior of ideal human beings toward one another. *Jen* is the internalization of *li,* and *li* is the codified external expression of *jen.* So, to be Humane means to master a kind of selflessness by which we dwell as an integral part of the Ritual weave. Or, more simply, practicing *jen* means to act with a selfless and reverent concern for the well-being of others. *Jen* is the touchstone of Confucian sagehood, a kind of enlightenment that Confucius claimed was beyond even him.

Yi: 義 Duty

The prescriptions of Ritual are general in nature. The ability to apply them in specific situations is Duty, and so Duty is the particular ethical expression of Humanity.

Tao: 道 Way

The effortless process of human society functioning according to its natural Ritual structure. It can be expanded to cover Ritual's cosmological dimensions, making it comparable to the Taoist concept of

Tao. Hence: the effortless process of the cosmos functioning according to its natural Ritual structure. The cosmos always abides by the Tao, with the frequent exception of human societies. See also *Tao Te Ching* Key Terms: *Tao*.

Te: 德 Integrity

The ability to act according to the Tao (Way). Or, more precisely, the embodiment of the Tao in the sage, where it becomes a kind of power through which the sage can transform others "by example." This concept is deepened by *Te*'s etymological meaning at the level of pictographic imagery: "heart-sight clarity."

T'ien: 天 Heaven

Natural process. Or, more descriptively, the inevitable unfolding of things in the cosmological process. Hence, Heaven appears as a kind of immanent fate in the human realm – and as Ritual is its organizing principle, it becomes a kind of moral force encouraging societies to abide by Ritual and the Tao.

Shu: 恕

According to Confucius, to "never impose on others what you would not choose for yourself" (XV.24). In a word, it might be defined as "reciprocity," for its etymological meaning is something like: "as if heart," hence "treat others as if their hearts were your own." So the definition of this word is often spoken of as Confucius' "Golden Rule." In any case, when Confucius speaks of the "single thread stringing my Way together," it is identified as *chung shu:* literally "loyalty to *shu*" or "loyalty and *shu*" (IV.15). *Chung*'s etymological meaning is "centered in heart," so this complex little phrase is translated here as "Be loyal to the principles of your heart, and treat others with that same loyalty."

Further Reading

Chan Wing-tsit. *A Source Book of Chinese Philosophy*. New York: Columbia University Press, 1969.

Confucius. *The Analects*. Trans. D. C. Lau. London: Penguin, 1979.

———. *The Analects*, Vol. I The Chinese Classics. Trans. James Legge. 1861–73. Reprint Hong Kong: University of Hong Kong Press, 1960.

———. *The Analects of Confucius*. Trans. Simon Leys. New York: Norton, 1997.

———. *The Analects of Confucius*. Trans. Arthur Waley. London: Allen and Unwin, 1938.

———. *Confucius*. Trans. Ezra Pound. New York: New Directions, 1951.

Confucius, ed. *The Book of Songs*. Trans. Arthur Waley. London: George Allen and Unwin, 1937.

Dawson, Raymond. *Confucius*. New York: Hill and Wang, 1981.

DeBary, William T., Wing-tsit Chan, and Burton Watson, eds. *Sources of Chinese Tradition*. 2 vols. New York: Columbia University Press, 1960.

Eno, Robert. *The Confucian Creation of Heaven*. New York: State University of New York Press, 1990.

Fingarette, Herbert. *Confucius: The Secular as Sacred*. New York: Harper and Row, 1972.

Fung Yu-lan. *A History of Chinese Philosophy*. Trans. Derk Bodde. Princeton: Princeton University Press, 1952–53.

Graham, A. C. *Disputers of the Tao*. LaSalle: Open Court, 1989.

Hall, David, and Roger Ames. *Thinking Through Confucius*. New York: State University of New York Press. 1987.

Hsün Tzu. *Hsün Tzu*. Trans. Burton Watson. New York: Columbia University Press, 1963.

Hughes, E. R. *The Great Learning and the Mean in Action*. London: Dent, 1942.

Mote, Frederick. *Intellectual Foundations of China*. New York: Alfred A. Knopf, 1971.

Ropp, Paul, ed. *Heritage of China*. Berkeley: University of California Press, 1990.

Schwartz, Benjamin. *The World of Thought in Ancient China*. Cambridge: Harvard University Press, 1985.

Tu Wei-ming. *Humanity and Self-Cultivation: Essays in Confucian Thought*. Berkeley: Asian Humanities Press, 1979.

MENCIUS

Introduction

In a culture that makes no distinction between those realms we call the heart and the mind, Mencius was the great thinker of the heart. He was the second originary sage in the Confucian tradition, which has shaped Chinese culture for over two thousand years, and it was he who added the profound inner dimensions of human being to the Confucian vision.

In the ruins of a magisterial monotheism, a situation not entirely unlike our own, Confucius (551–479 B.C.E.) recognized society as a structure of human relationships, and spoke of those relationships as a system of "ritual" that people enact in their daily lives, thus infusing the secular with sacred dimensions. There is little sense of the inner self in Confucius' thought: identity is determined by a person's ritual roles in the social fabric, and this selflessness contributes deeply to the sense of human community as a sacred rite. The explicit realm of Confucius' teachings is occupied with the practical issues of how society works as a selfless weave of caring relationships; and in the implicit realm, that ritual weave is woven into the vast primal ecology of a self-generating and harmonious cosmos.

The Confucian social vision represents the end of a devastating, millennium-long transformation from a spiritualist to a humanist culture, and Mencius (4th C. B.C.E.) invested that humanist vision with its inner dimension by recognizing that the individual too is a part of the primal ecology. He saw all the spiritual depths of that cosmology inside us, and this led to a mystical faith in the inherent nobility of human beings. In his chaotic and war-ravaged times, he was therefore passionate in his defense of the people. Indeed, he advocated a virtual democracy in which a government's legitimacy depended upon the assent of the people. Such is the enduring magic of the Mencian heart – full of compassionate and practical concern for the human condition, and yet so empty that it contains the ten thousand transformations of the entire cosmos.

The tangible beginnings of Chinese civilization lie in the archaic Shang Dynasty (c. 1766–1040 B.C.E.), which bridged the transition from Neolithic to Bronze Age culture. (For an outline of the early dynasties and rulers that figure prominently in Mencius' writings, see Historical Table.) The Shang was preceded by the Neolithic Hsia Dynasty, about which very little is known. It appears that in the Paleolithic cultures that preceded the Hsia, nature deities were worshiped as tribal ancestors: hence a tribe may have traced its lineage back to an originary "High Ancestor River," for instance. This practice apparently continued through the Hsia into the Shang, where evidence of it appears in oracle-bone inscriptions. Eventually, although these nature deities continued to be worshiped in their own right, religious life focused on the worship of human ancestors. By forging this religious system into a powerful form of theocratic government, the Shang was able to dominate China for no less than seven hundred years.

The Shang emperors ruled by virtue of their lineage, which was sanctified by Shang Ti ("Celestial Lord"), a supreme deity who functioned as the source of creation, order, ethics, etc. (*Shang* here represents two entirely different words in Chinese.) The Shang lineage may even have led to Shang Ti as its originary ancestor. In any case, Shang Ti provided the Shang rulers with a transcendental source of legitimacy and power: he protected and advanced their interests, and through their spirit-ancestors, they could decisively influence Shang Ti's shaping of events. All aspects of people's lives were thus controlled by the emperor: weather, harvest, politics, economics, religion, etc. Indeed, people didn't experience themselves as substantially different from spirits, for the human realm was simply an extension of the spirit realm.

Such was the imperial ideology, so convenient to the uses of power as it accorded little ethical value to the masses, who were not of select lineages. (Not surprisingly, the rise of Shang Ti seems to coincide with the rise of the Shang Dynasty, and later myth speaks of him as the creator of Shang civilization.) In the cruelest of ironies, it was overwhelming human suffering that brought the Chinese people into their earthly lives, beginning the transformation of this spiritualistic culture to a humanistic one. In the cultural legend, the early Shang rulers were paradigms of nobility and benevolence. But by the end of the Shang, the rulers had become cruel and tyrannical, and as there was no ethical system separate from the religious system, there was nothing to shield the people from their depredations. Meanwhile, a small nation was being pushed to the borders of the Shang realm by western tribes. This state of semi-barbarian people known as the Chou gradually adopted the cultural traits of the Shang. Eventually, under the leadership of the legendary sage-emperors Wen ("cultured") and Wu ("martial"), the Chou overthrew the tyrannical Shang ruler, thus founding the Chou Dynasty (1040–223 B.C.E.), which was welcomed wholeheartedly by the Shang people.

The Chou conquerors were faced with an obvious problem: if the Shang lineage had an absolute claim to rule the world, how could the Chou justify replacing it with their own, and how could they legitimize their rule in the eyes of the Shang people? Their solution was to redefine Shang Ti as *Heaven*, thus ending the Shang's claim to legitimacy by lineage, and then proclaim that the right to rule depended upon the Mandate of Heaven: once a ruler becomes unworthy, Heaven withdraws its mandate and bestows it on another. This was a major event in Chinese philosophy: the first investment of power with an ethical imperative. And happily, the early centuries of the Chou appear to have fulfilled that imperative admirably.

But eventually the Chou foundered because of its increasing inhumanity and its lack of the Shang's transcendent source of legitimacy: if the Mandate could be transferred to the Chou, it could obviously be transferred again. The rulers of the empire's component states (*chu hou:* "august lords") grew increasingly powerful, claiming more and more sovereignty over their lands, until finally they had established virtually independent nations. Eventually these rulers (properly called "dukes") even began assuming the title of emperor, thus equating themselves with the Chou emperor, who was by now a mere figurehead. The rulers of these autonomous states could at least claim descent from those who were first given the territories by the early Chou rulers. But this last semblance of legitimacy was also crumbling because these rulers were frequently at war with one another, which hardly inspired confidence in the claim that they were familial members of the ruling kinship hierarchy that was sanctioned by Heaven. More importantly, power was being usurped by a second tier of "august lords" whenever they had the strength to take it, and even by a third tier of high government officials. This history, beginning with the Chou's overthrow of the Shang, represents a geologic split in China's social structure: political power was breaking free of its family/religious context and becoming a separate entity.

The final result of the Chou's "metaphysical" breakdown was, not surprisingly, all too physical: war. In addition to constant pressure from barbarians in the north (the first devastating blow to Chou power was a barbarian invasion in 770 B.C.E.) and the Ch'u realm that dominated south China, there was relentless fighting between the empire's component states and frequent rebellion within them. This internal situation, so devastating to the people, continued to deteriorate after Confucius' time, until it finally gave an entire age its name: the Warring States Period (403–221 B.C.E.). Meanwhile, rulers caught up in this ruthless competition began looking for the most able men to help them rule their states, and this precipitated the rise of an independent intellectual class – a monumental event, for this class constituted the first open space in the cultural framework from which the imperial ideology could be challenged.

The old social order had now collapsed entirely, and these intellectuals began struggling to create a new one. Although this was one of the most virulent and chaotic periods in Chinese history, it was the golden age of Chinese philosophy, for there were a "Hundred Schools of Thought" trying to envision what this new social order should be like. These schools were founded by thinkers who wandered the country with their disciples, teaching and trying to convince the various rulers to put their ideas into practice, for the desperate times had given them an urgent sense of political mission.

The first great figure of this intellectual class was Confucius, whose thought survives in a collection of aphoristic sayings entitled the *Analects*. Confucius' social philosophy derives from a rational empiricism, a methodology which Mencius shared and which represents a total break with Shang spiritualism. Blatant power-politics had made it impossible to believe in Heaven (let alone Shang Ti) as a transcendental source of order and legitimacy, so Confucius tried to rescue the fragmented Chou culture by putting it on a more viable rational and secular basis. He began from the empirical observation that human society is a structure, a weave of relationships between individuals who each occupy a certain locus in that structure: parent and child, ruler and subject, friend and friend, merchant and customer, and so forth. Confucius invested this anthropological observation with a philosophical dimension by recognizing that a vital community depends upon its members' fulfilling their communal responsibilities with an attitude of human caring. Always looking to the past as his source of wisdom, Confucius saw that societies flourished when their citizens (most especially their rulers) honored this moral principle, and inevitably crumbled when they ignored it: even the powerful transcendental glue of the Shang theocracy couldn't withstand the corrosive influence of the Shang emperors' depredations.

But Confucius' social philosophy goes well beyond this moral dimension, for he described the web of social responsibilities as a system of "Ritual" (*li:* see Key Terms). *Ritual* had been a religious concept associated with the worship of spirits, but Confucius extended its use to include all the caring acts by which we fulfill our responsibilities to others in the community. Hence, the entire weave of everyday social life takes on the numinous aspect of the sacred. There is little sense of the inner self in the *Analects:* the Ritual social fabric is paramount, and individual identity is defined entirely in terms of a person's social roles. All of the Confucian moral virtues (see Key Terms) apply only in the social context: one cannot speak of a person being virtuous in isolation. And there is indeed a kind of spiritual clarity in the selflessness of this Ritual weave, a clarity which became a defining aspect in the structure of Chinese political and spiritual consciousness throughout the ages.

Confucius located his human society within a cosmology that the Taoists described eloquently, but which he himself referred to only through silence:

> Adept Kung said: "When the Master talks about civility and cultivation, you can hear what he says. But when he talks about the nature of things and the Way of Heaven, you can't hear a word."
>
> (V.12)

A major component in that cosmology is the evolving concept of "Heaven." The most primitive meaning of *Heaven (t'ien)* is "sky." By extension, it also comes to mean "transcendence," for our most primal sense of transcendence may be the simple act of looking up into the sky. So it's hardly surprising that when the Chou wanted to reinvent Shang Ti in a more impersonal form, they would choose Heaven. By association with the idea of transcendence and that which is beyond us, it is natural that *Heaven* also comes to mean "fate" or "destiny." And this is precisely what we find in Confucius, where "destiny" has evolved out of the early Chou sense of an impersonal deity. But rather than destiny in the sense of a transcendental force deciding human fate, this is destiny as the inevitable evolution of things according to the principles inherent in them. Although Confucius focuses on its manifestations in human history, there is little real difference between this Confucian Heaven and that of the Taoists, who identified it with natural process proceeding according to the principle of *tzu-jan*. *Tzu-jan*'s literal meaning is "self-so" or "the of-itself" or "being such of itself," hence "spontaneous" or "natural." But a more descriptive translation might be "occurrence appearing of itself," for it is meant to describe the ten thousand things unfolding spontaneously, each according to its own nature. The Taoist ideal is to dwell as an organic part of the *tzu-jan* process. For Confucius, the mechanism of Heaven's process would be *tzu-jan*'s Confucian counterpart: *li* (Ritual).

The Ritual structure of society is part of a much larger weave, the Ritual structure of natural process, and the Confucian ideal is for human community to dwell as an organic part of the cosmological weave of *li*.

The Confucian and Taoist Ways are traditionally described as the two poles of Chinese thought, but their shared cosmology affords them a fundamental unity, and that unity is no doubt why Chinese culture could eventually adopt both of these Ways simultaneously: the Confucian Way has defined the societal realm for Chinese intellectuals throughout the millennia, and the Way of philosophical Taoism has defined the private spiritual realm. The spiritual ecology of this shared cosmology might be seen as a return to the original spirituality of paleolithic China, for the sense of belonging to natural process is a secular version of the worship of nature deities as ancestral spirits. And it represents a complete secularization of the spiritualist regime that had dominated China since the rise of the Shang. Although ancestors continued to be attended assiduously, it was now a Confucian ritual of love and respect rather than an appeal to otherworldly powers. And although Confucius and Mencius recognized sacrifices to gods and spirits, they didn't necessarily believe any of the religious claims associated with such worship. For them, the value of such practices lay in the function they served in the Ritual structure of society. Mencius goes so far as to say that if gods and spirits don't fulfill human needs, they should be replaced (XIV.14). At the more fundamental level of the shared cosmology itself, it would appear to represent the resurgence of an ancient cosmology, a return to the culture's most primal roots – the Paleolithic and beyond. "Heaven" had become the current way of referring to its physical processes, and it was by recognizing the vast reach of Heaven within us that Mencius endowed the human with profound inner dimensions:

> *The ten thousand things are all there in me. And there's no joy greater than looking within and finding myself faithful to them.*
>
> (XIII.4)

This inner dimension also takes on ethical and political dimensions in Mencius' thought. Rather than privileged kinship relations as a basis of ethical value, Mencius proposes human belonging to the primal cosmology. Hence, citizens are all of equal value in and of themselves simply because they are all endowed with that vast reach of Heaven.

As with most intellectual figures in ancient China, very little is known of Mencius' life. He was born in Tsou, which was a dependency of Lu, the homeland of Confucius where the Chou cultural tradition was especially strong. His Chinese name was Meng K'o, and he is known as Meng Tzu, meaning "Master Meng," from which the latinized *Mencius* derives. According to tradition, he received his education first under the tutelage of a sagely mother and then under a disciple of Master Szu, who was Confucius' grandson and the reputed author of *The Doctrine of the Mean (Chung Yung)*, a book which came to be associated with the book of Mencius' writings, the *Mencius*. Sharing with most other philosophers of the time a faith in the political mission of the intellectual, he traveled with his disciples to the various states advising their rulers, hoping his ideas would be adopted and so lead to a more humane society. A number of rulers welcomed him, some even becoming benefactors, but his ideas were too radical and threatening. Few, if any, showed much inclination to put them into practice.

The book which bears Mencius' name probably represents the teachings of his mature thought. Unlike the *Analects*, which is largely made up of short aphoristic fragments without any supporting context, the *Mencius* is composed of longer and more developed passages, which makes it a fuller exposition of Confucian thought. It is entirely possible that Mencius wrote part or all of the book himself, though it is perhaps more likely that it was composed by his disciples. But if this is the case, it appears to be a compilation of carefully taken notes that represent pretty exactly the master's actual words. So, unlike the *Analects*, much of which is clearly not written by the historical Confucius, the *Mencius* seems almost entirely authentic. Indeed, it is considered a paragon of literary eloquence and style. The book contains fourteen chapters, arranged in seven pairs. Each pair shares the same title, which is taken from whatever personage happens to appear in the first sentence, a seemingly arbitrary method devised by a later editor. The only exception to this is the final pair: "To Fathom the Mind." This title, also drawn from the first sentence, is expressive of the unique character of these final chapters, for they seem to be an especially late and eloquent distillation of Mencius' ideas, containing many of his most striking and radical statements. An uncanny fact about Mencius is that his most distinctive and fundamental departures are found in only a handful of statements, which suggests that Mencius would appear an even more radical thinker if only more of his teachings had survived.

The inner dimension of human being was a central topic for the early Taoist masters, and they shared Mencius' cosmological view of the inner self; but for Mencius this was part of a political vision, and that is what makes him so important. As the human heart-mind is part of the fabric of Heaven, it is therefore inherently good and moral. Given this central belief in the inherent goodness of human nature, Mencius found the key to a flourishing society in a government that allows our inborn nobility to flourish of itself (here the similarity to Taoist thought is again unmistakable). And spiritual self-cultivation is the key both to that inner flourishing and to a benevolent government. The importance of self-cultivation among intellectuals was paramount in Confucius, who advocated government by a class of highly educated professionals. But in Mencius' cosmological context it takes on a decidedly spiritual dimension, reflecting the unity of self and cosmos:

> To fathom the mind is to understand your nature. And
> when you understand your nature, you understand Heaven.
>
> (XIV.1)

This idea of spiritual self-cultivation as a political act proved very appealing to the Neo-Confucianists of the Sung Dynasty. Although he was certainly influential, Mencius was not considered a preeminent figure until the rise of Neo-Confucianism, about 1,500 years after his death. Hoping to inspire people in the reconstruction of a beleaguered society, the Neo-Confucianists felt a need to give Confucian philosophy something of the spiritual depth that had made Buddhism (especially Ch'an or Zen Buddhism) so compelling in their culture. To do this they redefined the Confucian tradition by supplementing the *Analects* with three lesser-known texts which added a spiritual depth to Confucius' teachings, thus forming the canonical "Four Books": *The Analects, Mencius, The Great Learning,* and *The Doctrine of the Mean.* The Neo-Confucianists expanded Confucian self-cultivation to emphasize Ch'an meditation and the practice of the arts. Indeed, the monumental landscape painting that arose during the Sung was conceived in these Neo-Confucian terms: to look deeply into the ten thousand things is to look deeply into oneself. And, following Mencius, to look deeply into oneself is to look deeply into Heaven.

Given Mencius' faith in the inherent nobility of human beings, it is no surprise that he focuses so resolutely on the responsibility of rulers and intellectuals to create a society in which that nobility can flourish. For Mencius, the Mandate of Heaven is revealed through the will of the people:

> Heaven sees through the eyes of the people. Heaven hears through the
> ears of the people.

(IX.5)

Indeed, the Mencian polity is a virtual democracy, for the emperor only has authority to rule so long as he has the people's approval. Once he loses their approval, he loses the Mandate of Heaven. Then, if they must, the people have every right to overthrow him.

The Mandate of Heaven remained the standard against which rulers were measured throughout the ages, though it was of course a standard they rarely met. Two millennia after Mencius, rulers of dubious repute felt compelled to commission paintings like Auspicious Grain (see cover illustration, right side, and interior illustration), as if they could mask reality by associating themselves with a monumental totemic image representing the people's prosperity under a ruler who is fulfilling the Mandate of Heaven. However rare the society it depicts may be, it is indeed a beautiful image: a sacred human community flourishing in the shimmering weave of Heaven's natural process.

1

Emperor Hui of Liang   Book One

1   Mencius went to see Emperor Hui of Liang, and the emperor said: "Even a thousand miles¹ wasn't too great a journey for you. You must come bringing something of great profit to my nation."

"Don't talk about profit," said Mencius. "It's Humanity² and Duty³ that matter. Emperors say *How can I profit my nation?* Lords say *How can I profit my house?* And everyone else says *How can I profit myself?* Then everyone high and low is scrambling for profit, pitching the nation into grave danger.

"If the ruler in a nation of ten thousand war-chariots is killed, the assassin is no doubt lord to a house of a thousand war-chariots. And if the ruler in a nation of a thousand war-chariots is killed, the assassin is no doubt lord to a house of a hundred war-chariots. A thousand in ten thousand or a hundred in a thousand – this is no small amount. But when people betray Duty and crave profit, they aren't content until they've got it all. If they aren't Humane, they'll abandon their kindred, and if they aren't Dutiful, they'll betray their ruler.

"Just talk about Humanity and Duty, and leave it at that. Don't talk about profit."

2   Mencius went to see Emperor Hui of Liang and found him standing beside a pool. Gazing at the deer and wild geese, the emperor said: "And do the wise also enjoy such things?"

"Only the wise can enjoy them," replied Mencius. "If they aren't wise, even people who have such things can't enjoy them. *The Book of Songs* says:

> *He planned the sacred tower and began.*
> *He planned it well and managed it well,*

and the people worked with devotion,
so it was finished in less than a day.
He planned and began without haste,
and the people were children coming.
With the emperor in the sacred gardens
there, the deer lay in pairs at ease,
paired deer all sleek and glistening,
white birds all bright and shimmering,
and with the emperor at the sacred pool
there, the fish leapt so strong and sure.

Emperor Wen⁴ used the people's labor to build his tower and his pool, and yet the people delighted in them. They called the tower *Sacred Tower* and the pool *Sacred Pool,* and they were delighted that he had deer and fish and turtles. The ancients knew joy because they shared their joy with the people.

"In *The Declaration of T'ang,* the tyrant Chieh's people say: *When will you founder, o sun? We'll die with you gladly.* The people so hated him that they thought dying with him was better than living with him. He had towers and ponds, birds and animals – but how could he enjoy them alone?"

3   Emperor Hui of Liang said: "I've devoted myself entirely to the care of my nation. If there's famine north of the river, I move people east of the river and grain north of the river. And if there's famine east of the river, I do the opposite. I've never seen such devotion in the governments of neighboring countries, but their populations are growing by leaps and bounds while mine hardly grows at all. How can this be?"

"You're fond of war," began Mencius, "so perhaps I could borrow an analogy from war. War drums rumble, armies meet, and just as swords clash, soldiers throw down their armor and flee, dragging their weapons behind them. Some run a hundred feet and stop. Some run fifty feet and stop. Are those who run fifty feet justified in laughing at those who run a hundred feet?"

"No, of course not," replied the emperor. "It's true they didn't run the full hundred feet, but they still ran."

"If you understood this, you wouldn't long to have more people than neighboring countries. Look – when growing seasons aren't ignored, people have more grain than they can eat. When ponds aren't plundered with fine-weave nets, people have more fish and turtles than they can eat. When mountain forests are cut according to their seasons, people have more timber than they can use. When there's more grain and fish than they can eat, and more timber than they can use, people nurture life and mourn death in contentment. People nurturing life and mourning death in contentment – that's where the Way[5] of emperors begins.

"When every five-acre[6] farm has mulberry trees around the farmhouse, people wear silk at fifty. And when the proper seasons of chickens and pigs and dogs are not neglected, people eat meat at seventy. When hundred-acre farms never violate their proper seasons, even large families don't go hungry. Pay close attention to the teaching in village schools, and extend it to the child's family responsibilities – then, when their silver hair glistens, people won't be out on roads and paths hauling heavy loads. Our black-haired people free of hunger and cold, wearing silk and eating meat at seventy – there have never been such times without a true emperor.

"But you don't think about tomorrow when people are feeding surplus grain to pigs and dogs. So when people are starving to death in the streets, you don't think about emptying storehouses to feed them. People die, and you say *It's not my fault, it's the harvest.* How is this any different from stabbing someone to death and saying *It's not me, it's the sword*? Stop blaming harvests, and people everywhere under Heaven will come flocking to you."

4   Emperor Hui of Liang said: "I'm ready to be taught without resenting it."

"Is there any difference between killing someone with a stick or killing them with a sword?" began Mencius.

"No, there's no difference."

"And killing with a sword or a government – any difference?"

"No difference."

"There's plenty of juicy meat in your kitchen and plenty of well-fed horses in your stable," continued Mencius, "but the people here look hungry, and in the countryside they're starving to death. You're feeding humans to animals. Everyone hates to see animals eat each other, and an emperor is the people's father and mother – but if his government feeds humans to animals, how can he claim to be the people's father and mother?

"When Confucius said *Whoever invented burial figures deserved no descendants,* he was condemning the way people make human figures only to bury them with the dead. But that's nothing compared to the way you're pitching your people into starvation."

5   Emperor Hui of Liang said: "As you know, this country was once the strongest anywhere under Heaven. But here I am: defeated by Ch'i in the east, my eldest son dead in the battle; seven hundred square miles[7] lost to Ch'in in the west; and humiliated by Ch'u in the south. Now, out of respect for the dead, I long to wash all this shame away. How can I do that?"

"To be a true emperor, even a hundred square miles can be land enough," replied Mencius. "If an emperor's rule is Humane – punishment and taxation are light, people plow deep and hoe often, and strong men use their leisure time to cultivate themselves as sons and brothers, loyal subjects and trustworthy friends. They serve father and brother when home, and when away they serve elders and superiors. So even with nothing but sticks for weapons, they can overcome the fierce swords and armor of nations like Ch'in or Ch'u.

"In such countries, emperors violate the proper seasons of their people. They don't let them plow or weed or tend to their parents. Parents are cold and hungry, brothers and wives and children are scattered far apart. Those emperors are dragging their people down into ruin. So if a true emperor invaded their countries, who would oppose him? Therefore it is said: *No one can oppose the Humane.* If only you would believe this."

6   Mencius went to see Emperor Hsiang of Liang.[8] Talking with someone after he'd left, he said: "At first sight, he didn't seem like much of a sovereign, and after meeting him I saw nothing to command respect. But suddenly he began asking questions.

"What could bring stability to all beneath Heaven? he asked.

"In unity is stability, I replied.

"Who can unify all beneath Heaven?

"One who has no lust for killing.

"But who would give it all to him?

"Is there anyone who wouldn't give it to him? Don't you know about rice shoots? If there's a drought in the sixth or seventh month, rice shoots wither. But if the Heavens then fill with clouds, and rain falls in sheets, the shoots burst into life again. When this happens, who can resist it? Today, all of the world's great shepherds share a lust for killing. If there were someone free of that lust, people everywhere under Heaven would crane their necks watching for him to come. And if such a man really appeared, the people going home to him would be like a flood of water pouring down. Who could resist it?"

7   Emperor Hsüan of Ch'i said: "I'd like to hear about Duke Huan[9] of Ch'i and Duke Wen of Chin."

"The disciples of Confucius never spoke of Huan or Wen," replied Mencius, "so their histories weren't passed down through the generations, and I've heard nothing of them. You won't learn much about the true emperor from them."

"Tell me then – this Integrity[10] that makes a true emperor, what is it?" asked Emperor Hsüan.

"If you watch over the people, you're a true emperor and nothing can resist you."

"Can someone like me watch over the people?"

"Yes."

"How do you know this?"

"I heard a story about you from Hu He: *Sitting in the palace one day, the emperor saw some people leading an ox past outside.*

"*'Where's that ox being taken?' he asked.*

"*'We're going to consecrate the new bell with its blood.'*

"*'Let it go. I can't bear to see it shivering with fear like an innocent person being hauled off to the executioner.'*

"*'Then shall we leave the bell unconsecrated?'*

"*'No, no – that would never do. Use a sheep instead.'* Did that really happen?"

"Yes," replied the emperor.

"You have the heart of a true emperor. The people all thought you were being miserly. But I know you just couldn't bear the suffering."

"Are the people really like that? Ch'i may be a small country, but how could I begrudge a single ox? I just couldn't bear to see it shivering with fear like an innocent person being hauled off to the executioner. So I told them to use a sheep instead."

"It isn't so strange that the people thought you miserly," said Mencius. "You wanted to use a small animal instead of a large one, so how were they to know? If you were so grieved by something innocent going to the executioner, then what's the difference between an ox and a sheep?"

The emperor laughed and said: "What was going on in this heart of mine? I certainly didn't begrudge the expense of an ox, but I wanted to use a sheep instead. No wonder the people called me a miser."

"No harm done," said Mencius. "That's how Humanity works. You'd seen the ox, but not the sheep. And when noble-minded people see birds and animals alive, they can't bear to see them die. Hearing them cry out, they can't bear to eat their meat. That's why the noble-minded stay clear of their kitchens."

After a moment, the emperor spoke: "The *Songs* say

> *It's another person's heart,*
> *but mine has fathomed it.*

This describes you perfectly. It was I who did these things, but when I turned inward in search of motives, I couldn't fathom my own heart. It was you who explained it, and only then did I come to this realization. So how can this heart of mine be that of a true emperor?"

"What if someone said this to you: *I'm strong enough to lift a thousand pounds, but I can't lift a feather?* Or: *My sight's so good I can see the tip of an autumn hair, but I can't see a cartload of firewood?* Would you believe it?"

"No, of course not."

"You have compassion enough for birds and animals, but you do nothing for your people. And why is that? When feathers can't be lifted, someone isn't using their strength. When a cartload of firewood can't be seen, someone isn't using their sight. And when the people aren't watched over, someone isn't using their compassion. So if you aren't a true emperor, it's only because you're unwilling, not because you're incapable."

"The unwilling and the incapable – is there any difference in form?" asked the emperor.

"You can say that you're incapable of bounding over the North Sea with T'ai Mountain tucked under your arm, and in fact you are incapable. You can also say that you're incapable of breaking up a little kindling for an old woman, but in fact you're unwilling, not incapable. Your failure to be a true emperor isn't like failing to bound over the North Sea with T'ai Mountain tucked under your arm. It's like failing to break up a little kindling for an old woman.

"Honor your own elders as befits elders, and extend this honor to all elders. Honor your own children as befits children, and extend this honor to all children. Then you can turn all beneath Heaven in the palm of your hand.

"The *Songs* say:

> *Setting an example for his wife*
> *and extending it to his brothers,*
> *he ruled both home and country,*

which describes how this heart here can be applied elsewhere. Just do that and your compassion will be expansive enough to watch over all within the four seas. If your compassion isn't expansive, you can't even watch over your own wife and child. This is precisely why the ancients so completely surpassed the rest of us: they made whatever they did expansive. That's all. You have compassion enough for birds and animals, but you do nothing for your people. And why is that?

"To know whether something is light or heavy, you must weigh it. To know whether something is long or short, you must measure it. It's like this for all things, and especially for the heart. If only you would measure yours.

"Or perhaps you want to keep sending out your armies with their armor and swords, endangering your subjects and stirring up hatred among the other rulers. Is that what fills your heart with delight?"

"No," replied the emperor. "How could I delight in that? I only do it for the sake of a great dream."

"And this great dream – may I hear what it is?"

The emperor just smiled and said nothing.

"Is your grand cuisine not enough for your tongue? Are your summer and winter robes not enough for your body? Perhaps all the beautiful sights here aren't enough for your eyes, and the beautiful music isn't enough for your ears? Or is it that your attendants aren't fine enough to serve you? But you have many assistants and advisors: whatever you find wanting, they can supply. So this can't be the kind of dream you harbor."

"No," replied the emperor, "it isn't."

"Then it isn't hard to guess what your great dream is. You dream of more land. You dream of Ch'in and Ch'u paying court to you, of ruling over the entire Middle Kingdom[11] and pacifying the barbarian nations on all four borders. Doing the kinds of things you do in search of such a dream – that's like climbing a tree in search of a fish."

"Is it really so bad?" asked the emperor.

"Yes, and it's much more dangerous," replied Mencius. "Climb a tree in search of a fish, and though you won't find a fish, you also won't find disaster. But do the kinds of things you do in search of your dream, and though you wear body and mind ragged, you'll find disaster for sure."

"Please – can you tell me more about this?"

"If Chou and Ch'u went to war, who do you think would win?"

"Ch'u would win."

"So the small is clearly no match for the large," continued Mencius, "the few is clearly no match for the many, and the weak is clearly no match for the strong. Here within the vast seas, there are nine regions, each spreading a thousand square miles, and your Ch'i is but one of them. To conquer eight with one, how is that any different from Chou declaring war on Ch'u?

"You must return to fundamentals. If you were renowned for Humane government, every scholar under Heaven would long to stand in your court, every farmer would long to plow in your countryside, every merchant would long to trade in your markets, every traveler would long to travel your roads, and everyone beneath Heaven who despised their rulers would long to rush here and confide in you. If you made this happen, who could resist it?"

"I'm not all that bright," said the emperor. "I still can't see my way through this. But I'm determined and want your help. If you'll explain clearly, perhaps I can learn, and even though I'm not terribly clever, I'll try to act on your counsel."

"To keep the mind constant without a constant livelihood – only the wisest among us can do that. Unless they have a constant livelihood, the common people will never have constant minds. And without constant minds, they'll wander loose and wild. They'll stop at nothing, and soon cross the law. Then, if you punish them accordingly, you've done nothing but snare the people in your own trap. And if they're Humane, how can those in high position snare their people in traps? Therefore, in securing the people's livelihood, an enlightened ruler ensures that they have enough to serve their parents and nurture their wives and children, that everyone has plenty to eat in good years and no one starves in bad years. If you do that, you'll be leading the people toward virtue and benevolence, so it will be easy for them to follow you.

"But now, with you securing their livelihood, the people never have enough to serve their parents or nurture their wives and children. In good years they live miserable lives, and in bad years they starve to death. All they can do is struggle to stay free of death and worry about failing. Where could they ever find the leisure for Ritual[12] and Duty?

"If you want to put my words into practice, why not return to fundamentals? When every five-acre farm has mulberry trees around the farmhouse, people wear silk at fifty. And when the proper seasons of chickens and pigs and dogs are not neglected, people eat meat at seventy. When hundred-acre farms never violate their proper seasons, even large families don't go hungry. Pay close attention to the teaching in village schools, and extend it to the child's family responsibilities – then, when their silver hair glistens, people won't be out on roads and paths hauling heavy loads. Our black-haired people free of hunger and cold, wearing silk and eating meat in old age – there have never been such times without a true emperor."

11

Emperor Hui of Liang   Book Two

1   Chuang Pao went to see Mencius and said: "I went to see the emperor, and he told me that he loves music. I didn't know what to say. *Loving music* – what do you think of that?"

"If the emperor truly loves music," replied Mencius, "there may be hope for Ch'i."

Some days later, Mencius went to see the emperor and asked: "Is it true you told Chuang that you love music?"

The emperor blushed and said: "I cannot claim to love the music of ancient emperors, only our own trifling music."

"If you truly love music," said Mencius, "there may be hope for Ch'i. And it makes no difference if it's today's music or the music of ancient times."

"Please – can you tell me more about this?" asked the emperor.

"To enjoy music alone or to enjoy it with others," began Mencius, "which is the greater pleasure?"

"With others, of course," replied the emperor.

"And to enjoy music with a few or to enjoy it with many – which is the greater pleasure?"

"With many, of course."

"Can I tell you about enjoyment? Suppose there was a performance of beautiful music here. Suppose the people heard the sound of their emperor's bells and drums, pipes and flutes, and turning faces furrowed with worry toward each other, they said: *Why does our emperor let his love of music make our lives so desperate – father and son, brother and brother, mother and child all separated and scattered apart?* Suppose there was a hunt ranging through the fields here. Suppose the people heard the sound of your carriages and horses, saw the beauty of your banners and streamers, and turning faces furrowed with worry toward each other, they said: *Why does our emperor let his love of hunting make our lives*

so desperate – father and son, brother and brother, mother and child all sepa-
rated and scattered apart?

"There could be only one explanation for all this: never sharing pleasure with the people.

"But suppose there was a performance of beautiful music here. Suppose the people heard the sound of their emperor's bells and drums, pipes and flutes, and turning happy faces full of delight toward each other, they said: *Listen – they're making music, so our emperor must be feeling fine!* And suppose there was a hunt ranging through the fields here. Suppose the people heard the sound of your carriages and horses, saw the beauty of your banners and streamers, and turning happy faces full of delight toward each other, they said: *Look – they're out hunting, so our emperor must be feeling fine!*

"There could be only one explanation for all this: sharing pleasure with the people. Sharing pleasure with the people – that's what makes an emperor an emperor."

2   Emperor Hsüan of Ch'i asked: "Is it true that Emperor Wen's park covered seventy square miles?"

"The *Chronicles* say it did," replied Mencius.

"Was it really so vast?"

"To the people it seemed small."

"My park covers only forty square miles, and yet the people consider it huge," said the emperor. "How can this be?"

"Emperor Wen's park may have covered seventy square miles, but it was open to the people: they gathered dry grasses for their fires there, they hunted pheasants and rabbits there. He shared it with the people, so is it any wonder the people considered it small?

"When I first came to the borders of your nation, I asked about the great prohibitions of this land. Only then did I dare enter. I was told that there is a park covering forty square miles, and that anyone who kills a deer there is punished as if they'd killed a person. So this park is a forty-square-mile trap set in the middle of the country. Is it any wonder the people consider it huge?"

3   Emperor Hsüan of Ch'i asked: "Is there a Way[1] to foster good relations with neighboring countries?"

"There is," replied Mencius. "Only a person of great Humanity can use the large to serve the small. So it is that Emperor T'ang served Ko and Emperor Wen served the K'un tribes. Only a person of great wisdom can use the small to serve the large. So it is that Emperor T'ai[2] served the Hsün-yü tribes and Kou Chien served the nation of Wu.

"Whoever uses the large to serve the small delights in Heaven. Whoever uses the small to serve the large fears Heaven. If you delight in Heaven, you nurture all beneath Heaven. If you fear Heaven, you nurture your own nation. The *Songs* say:

> *Fearing august Heaven's majesty,*
> *we nurture our nation forever."*

"Your words are great indeed," said the emperor. "But I have a weakness: I love valor."

"Then let it not be small valor that you love. That is to clutch your sword and glare angrily, shouting *How dare he oppose me?* It's such coarse valor – at best useful only against a lone opponent. Let it be great valor that you love.

"The *Songs* say:

> *Majestic in his fury and wrath,*
> *the emperor marshalled his forces.*
> *He met the invaders in Chü*
> *and secured Chou's prosperity,*
> *fulfilling all beneath Heaven.*

Such is the valor of Emperor Wen. In a single act of wrath, he brought peace to the people throughout all beneath Heaven.

"The *Book of History* says: *Heaven sent down people. It created a sovereign for them and made him their teacher, saying 'You must help the Celestial Lord[3] show his love for them. To every corner of the land, I will judge those who offend and those who do not. In all beneath Heaven, who will dare cast their ambition against my purpose?'*

"There was only one man causing trouble in all beneath Heaven, but Emperor Wu[4] took it as a personal disgrace. Such is the valor of Emperor Wu. In a single act of wrath, he too brought peace to the people throughout all beneath Heaven.

"Now if you too, in a single act of wrath, bring peace to the people throughout all beneath Heaven, the people's only fear will be that your love of valor may end."

4   Emperor Hsüan of Ch'i received Mencius in the Snow Palace and said: "Does the sage also enjoy such pleasures?"

"Yes," replied Mencius. "Denied such pleasures, there are those who would malign their sovereign. To malign a sovereign because you're denied such pleasures is wrong. But when a sovereign fails to share such pleasures with his people – that too is wrong. If you delight in the people's pleasure, the people will delight in your pleasure. If you worry over the people's troubles, the people will worry over your troubles. Make all beneath Heaven your delight and all beneath Heaven your worry – then how can you fail to be a true emperor?

"Long ago, Duke Ching of Ch'i asked his prime minister, Lord Yen: *I long to visit Chuan-fu Mountain and Ch'ao-wu Mountain, then travel along the coastline south to Lang-yeh Mountain. What can I do to make my travels rival those of the ancient emperors?*

"*What a fine question, replied Lord Yen. When the Son of Heaven visited the august lords, it was called an Inspection Tour because he was inspecting the territories under their care. And when the august lords went to the Son of*

Heaven's court, it was called a Duty Report because they reported on how they had carried out their duties. These things were not done without a purpose. In spring, it was to inspect the planting and provide whatever the farmers lacked. And in autumn, it was to inspect the harvest and help whoever didn't

bring in enough. In the Hsia Dynasty there was a saying:

> If our emperor doesn't journey
> where will we find rest?
> If our emperor doesn't tour,
> where will we find help?
> Each journey, each tour,
> he's a model for august lords.

"It's not like that anymore. Now

> marching armies demand supplies,
> so there's no food for the hungry
> and no rest for the work-weary.
> Looking away, voices full of hate,
> the people turn to shadowy crime.
> Defying the mandate, rulers abuse us.
> They drift, awash in food and drink.
> Adrift, unbridled, wild, wanton:
> among lords this means trouble.

To follow the drift downstream, all thought of return gone: that is called adrift. To follow the drift upstream, all thought of return gone: that is called unbridled. To follow animals, all moderation gone: that is called wild. To wallow in wine, all moderation gone: that is called wanton. The early emperors never indulged in pleasures adrift and unbridled, or actions wild and wanton.

"It is for you to choose your path.

"Duke Ching was overjoyed. He issued great proclamations

throughout the land, then he went to live in a hut outside the city. He opened the granaries to those in need, and summoned his Grand Music-master, saying: *Compose for me the joyous harmony of sovereign and subject.* Hence the *Chih Shao* and *Chüeh Shao,* with lyrics saying: *How can guiding the sovereign be a crime? To guide the sovereign is to love the* sovereign."

5   Emperor Hsüan of Ch'i said: "Since I never use it, people all tell me I should tear down the Palace of Light. Should I tear it down or not?"

"It's the Palace of Light because it's the palace of an emperor," replied Mencius. "If you want to govern as a true emperor, don't tear it down."

"*To govern as a true emperor* – could you explain this for me?"

"In ancient times, when Emperor Wen ruled Ch'i[5] – farmers were taxed one part in nine, descendants of worthy officials were insured a livelihood, there were inspections at border crossings and markets but no taxes, fish traps were not regulated, criminals were punished but not their families.

"Old men without wives we call widowers. Old women without husbands we call widows. Old people without children we call loners. Children without fathers we call orphans. These four kinds of people – they are the forsaken ones of this world. They have no one to turn to. When Emperor Wen's rule spread Humanity throughout the land, he put these four kinds of people above all else. The *Songs* say:

> While the rich manage in fine fashion,
>   the forsaken nurture no hope, no hope.

"Your words are fine indeed," said the emperor.

"You call them fine, but in practice you ignore them. Why is that?"

"I have a weakness," replied the emperor. "I love the bounty of wealth."

"In ancient times, Emperor Kung Liu[6] loved the bounty of wealth," said Mencius. "But the *Songs* say:

> *He filled granaries with stores,*
> *bundled supplies and provisions*
> *into sacks and well-stocked bags.*
> *His splendor spreading repose,*
> *he kept archers in plain sight,*
> *flourished spear, shield, and ax.*
> *Only then did his march begin.*

Hence, those who stayed had granaries full of stores, and those who went had bags well stocked. Only then could he begin his march to settle a homeland. If you love the bounty of wealth, let it be the people's love too – then how will it keep you from being a true emperor?"

"I have another weakness," said the emperor. "I love beauty and passion."

"In ancient times," replied Mencius, "Emperor T'ai also loved beauty and passion. He adored the palace courtesans. But the *Songs* say:

> *Our true old father T'ai*
> *came early on his horse,*
> *skirting a western river*
> *to reach Ch'i Mountain,*
> *and with Lady Chiang*
> *founded our homeland.*

At that time, women never languished without husbands, nor men without wives. If you love beauty and passion – let it be the people's love too, then how will it keep you from being a true emperor?"

6   Mencius said to Emperor Hsüan of Ch'i: "Suppose one of your ministers entrusts his family to the care of a friend and then leaves on a journey to Ch'u. When he returns, he finds that the friend abandoned his family to hunger and cold. What should be done?"

"End the friendship," replied the emperor.

"And if a chief judge can't govern his court – what should be done?"

"Turn him out," pronounced the emperor.

"And if someone can't govern this land stretching out to the four borderlands – what then?"

The emperor suddenly turned to his attendants and spoke of other things.

7   Mencius went to see Emperor Hsüan of Ch'i and said: "If a nation is called ancient, it isn't because the trees there are tall. It's because the ministers there are descended from generations of high officials. But there's no sense of old family bonds between you and your ministers. Those you promote one day are gone the next, and you hardly notice."

"But how can I recognize mediocrity and avoid it?" asked the emperor.

"To advance only the wise," replied Mencius, "a sovereign often promotes the common above the august, the distant above the familial. In deciding who is worthy, always remain cautious. When your attendants all say someone is wise, that doesn't make him worthy. When your high ministers all say someone is wise, that doesn't make him worthy. When everyone in the country says someone is wise, investigate thoroughly. If you find that he is indeed wise and worthy, take him into your government.

"When your attendants all say someone is unworthy, don't listen. When your high ministers all say someone is unworthy, don't listen. When everyone in the country says someone is unworthy, investigate thoroughly. If you find that he is indeed unworthy, turn him out.

"When your attendants all say someone deserves death, don't listen. When your high ministers all say someone deserves death, don't listen. When everyone in the country says someone deserves death, investigate thoroughly. If you find that he does indeed deserve death, put him to death. Then it will be said *The entire country put him to death*.

"If it's like this in your country, you've truly become mother and father to the people."

8   Emperor Hsüan of Ch'i asked: "Is it true that Emperor T'ang banished the tyrant Chieh, and Emperor Wu overthrew the tyrant Chou?"[7]

"Yes, according to the histories," replied Mencius.

"So is the murder of a sovereign acceptable?"

"A thief of Humanity is called a thief," replied Mencius. "A thief of Duty is called a felon. Someone who's both a thief and a felon is called a commoner. I've heard of the commoner Chou's punishment, but I've never heard of a sovereign's murder."

9   Talking with Emperor Hsüan of Ch'i, Mencius said: "To build a grand home, you must send the master carpenter in search of huge trees. If he finds them, you'll be pleased and consider him truly capable. But if the workers then cut them into small pieces, you'll be angry and consider them truly inept.

"When grown, we're anxious to put our youthful learning to use. But what if an emperor says *Put aside what you've learned and obey me*? If you have a piece of jade, even if it's worth ten thousand *yi* in gold, you need to trust a jade-carver to cut and polish it for you. And in governing the nation – if you say *Put aside what you've learned and obey me*, how is that any different from trying to teach the jade-carver how to cut jade?"

10   After Ch'i invaded the nation of Yen and conquered it,[8] Emperor Hsüan said: "Some say I shouldn't annex Yen, and some say I should. For a nation of ten thousand war-chariots to conquer a nation of ten thousand war-chariots in only fifty days – human strength alone cannot perform such feats. If I don't annex Yen, Heaven will surely be offended and send down calamities. But if I do – what then?"

"If annexation will please the Yen people," replied Mencius, "then do it. There are examples of this among the ancients: Emperor Wu, for instance. And if annexation won't please the Yen people, then don't do it. There are also examples of this among the ancients: Emperor Wen, for instance.

"If a nation of ten thousand war-chariots invades another nation of ten thousand war-chariots, and the invader is welcomed with baskets of food and jars of wine, there can be only one reason: the people are fleeing fire and flood. But if the flood just gets deeper and the fire hotter, they'll no doubt turn again."

11   When Ch'i invaded Yen and annexed it, the other emperors began plotting Yen's rescue.

Emperor Hsüan said: "The other emperors are planning to invade. What shall I do?"

"I've heard of having seventy square miles and ruling all beneath Heaven," replied Mencius. "Emperor T'ang is an example. But I've never heard of ruling a thousand square miles and cowering in fear of others.

"The *Book of History* says: *Emperor T'ang's expeditions began in Ko.* There he gained the trust of all beneath Heaven – so when he marched east, the western tribes complained. And when he marched south, the northern tribes complained: *Why does he leave us for last?* People watched for him the way they watched for rain in the midst of a great drought. When he came, they went to market unhindered again and tended their fields without interference. He punished the rulers and comforted the people, like rain falling in its season. And so, a great joy rose among the people. The *Book of History* also says: *We're waiting for our lord: his coming will bring us back to life.*

"Now the Yen emperor tyrannized his people, so you attacked him. The people thought they were being rescued from fire and flood, so they welcomed you with baskets of food and jars of wine. How can you justify killing elders and taking the young captive, tearing down temples and stealing sacred vessels? The power of Ch'i was already feared throughout all beneath Heaven, and now you've doubled your territory without making your government Humane. No wonder all beneath Heaven is up in arms.

"Hurry! Send out orders to release old and young, to leave the sacred vessels where they are. Consult the people of Yen, appoint a new ruler, and then leave. There's still time to prevent this invasion."

12   There was a battle on the border between Chou and Lu.

"I lost thirty-three officials," complained Duke Mu of Chou, "but not one of my people died. There are too many to punish. But if I don't punish them, I'll be condoning what they did: watching their leaders die without lifting a finger to help. What can I do?"

"In years of calamity and failed harvests," replied Mencius, "how many thousands of your people suffered – young and old alike abandoned to gutters and ditches, the strong scattered to every corner of the land? Meanwhile, your granaries were full and your storehouses well stocked. Your officers kept all this from you, thus disparaging their lord and ravaging their people.

"Master Tseng[9] said: *Beware! Beware! Whatever you give out is given back.* It was only now that the people had a chance to give back what you'd given them. You mustn't blame them. If you governed with Humanity, the people would love your officers and die willingly to protect them."

13   Duke Wen of T'eng said: "T'eng is a small nation wedged in between two powerful neighbors. Should I pay court to Ch'i or Ch'u?"

"This kind of thing is beyond me," replied Mencius. "But if you need an answer, I have one suggestion: make your moats deeper and your city walls stronger, then stand beside your people to defend your land. If they would rather die than desert you, your country will be safe."

14   Duke Wen of T'eng said: "The Ch'i army is fortifying Hsüeh. I'm terribly worried. What shall I do?"

"In ancient times," replied Mencius, "Emperor T'ai lived in Pin. But the Ti tribes kept attacking, so he went to settle below Ch'i Mountain.[10] It wasn't something he wanted: he had no choice. If your actions are noble, true emperors will rise again among the children and grandchildren of future generations. Your own success depends upon Heaven alone, but whatever you make and hand down – that will continue.

"What can you possibly do about Ch'i? Just devote yourself to noble actions, and let come what will."

15   Duke Wen of T'eng said: "T'eng is a small nation. We'll run ourselves into the ground paying these great neighbors homage, and still never escape them. What shall I do?"

"In ancient times," replied Mencius, "Emperor T'ai lived in Pin. But the Ti tribes kept attacking. He paid them homage with furs and silks but didn't escape them. He paid them homage with horses and hounds but didn't escape them. He paid them homage with pearls and jade but still didn't escape them. Finally, he called the elders together and said: *What the Ti want is my land. I have heard that the noble-minded will not use what nurtures the people to harm the people. Living without a ruler seems innocuous enough, my friends, so I've decided to leave you. Setting* out from Pin, he crossed the Liang Mountains, founded a new capital below Ch'i Mountain, and there he settled.

"*What Humanity!* cried out the people of Pin. *We can't lose him!*

"Some people followed him like crowds flocking to market. Others said: *This is the land our ancestors watched over. It isn't a question of what we want. We may die defending it, but we can't abandon this land.*

"Choose between these two ways, and you will choose well."

16   Duke P'ing of Lu was about to leave the palace when a trusted advisor named Tsang Ts'ang said: "When you leave you always tell your officials where you're going, my Lord. But now your horses are harnessed and your carriage ready, and you haven't told anyone where you're going. May I ask?"

"I'm going to see Mencius."

"Incredible!" exclaimed Tsang. "How could you debase yourself by going to visit such a commoner, my Lord? Is it because you think he's a sage? A sage is the source of Ritual and Duty. But this Mencius gave his mother a more lavish funeral than his father. You mustn't go see him."

"Yes, perhaps you're right."

Later, Adept Yüeh Cheng entered and said: "Why haven't you gone to see Mencius, my Lord?"

"Because someone told me that Mencius gave his mother a more lavish funeral than his father," replied the duke.

"Incredible! Why do you say it was more lavish? Is it because he mourned his father as a scholar should and mourned his mother as a state minister should? Is it because he made offerings in three vessels for his father and in five for his mother?"

"No, I was thinking about the beauty of his mother's coffin and shroud."

"But it isn't that one was more lavish than the other," said Yüeh Cheng. "He just had more money when his mother died."

Later, Yüeh Cheng went to see Mencius and said: "I told Duke P'ing about you, and he was going to come see you. But the duke has a trusted advisor named Tsang Ts'ang, and he talked him out of it."

"If we go, it's because something urges us on," commented Mencius. "And if we stay, it's because something holds us back. Going and staying – even these are matters beyond our control. It was Heaven that kept me from meeting the duke. This child of the Tsang family – how could he have done such a thing?"

111

Kung-Sun Ch'ou   Book One

1   Kung-sun Ch'ou[1] said: "If you took charge in Ch'i, could you re-create the successes of Kuan Chung[2] and Lord Yen?"

"You certainly are a man of Ch'i," replied Mencius. "You think of no one but Kuan Chung and Lord Yen.

"Someone once asked Tseng Hsi: *Who is the wiser, you or Adept Lu?*

"Tseng Hsi shifted around uneasily and replied: *My father was Master Tseng, and even he was in awe of Lu.*

"*Well then, who is the wiser, you or Kuan Chung?*

"Tseng's face flushed with anger, and he said: *How could you compare me with Kuan Chung? His sovereign trusted him so utterly, and he ran the government for so long – but his achievements were still utterly meager. How could you compare me with him?*

"If even Tseng Hsi bridled at the idea of being another Kuan Chung, how could you suggest that I would want such a thing?"

"But Kuan Chung made his sovereign the finest of august lords," said Kung-sun, "and Lord Yen led his to such splendor. Are such achievements not worthy of your aspirations?"

"To be a true emperor in Ch'i," replied Mencius, "that would be a simple matter – no harder than turning your hand over."

"Then I'm more confused than ever," said Kung-sun. "Emperor Wen's Integrity was unsurpassed, and he lived to be a hundred, but he still couldn't spread his tranquil rule to all beneath Heaven. His practices were carried on by Emperor Wu and Duke Chou,[3] and only then did great success come. You act like becoming a true emperor is a simple matter – so is Emperor Wen not a worthy exemplar?"

"How could anyone compare to Emperor Wen?" said Mencius. "In the Shang Dynasty, there were six or seven sage emperors between T'ang and Wu Ting, so all beneath Heaven lived content for a long time. And it's hard to change something that's gone on for so long.

"The august lords all paid court to Wu Ting, and so he commanded all beneath Heaven as if he were turning it in the palm of his hand. Chou was a tyrant, but his rule didn't come that much later than Wu Ting's. The traditions of ancient families had been handed down, the ways of good government had been preserved, and he had counselors of great wisdom: Lord Wei, Wei Chung, Prince Pi Kan, Lord Chi, Chiao Ko. That's why he lasted so long before losing everything to Wen. There wasn't a foot of land that wasn't his territory, or a single person who wasn't his subject. Emperor Wen had such difficulty because he began with only a hundred square miles. The Ch'i people have a saying:

> *Though you may have deep wisdom,*
> *seizing an opportunity works better.*
> *Though you may have a fine hoe,*
> *awaiting the season works better.*

"So in our time, to be a true emperor in Ch'i would be a simple matter. The Hsia, Shang, and Chou never controlled more than a thousand square miles, even at their height – so Ch'i has enough territory. You can hear roosters crowing and dogs barking all the way out to the four borderlands – so Ch'i has enough people. It isn't a question of land or people: to be a true emperor here in Ch'i, all you need is Humane government. Then no one could oppose you.

"But the failures of the emperor have never been greater than they are today, and the sufferings of people under tyranny have never been worse than they are today. It's so easy giving food to the hungry, so easy giving water to the thirsty.

"Confucius said: *Integrity spreads through the land faster than a proclamation sent racing down the line of postal stations.* If a nation of ten thousand war-chariots embraced Humane government today, the people would rejoice as if they'd escaped hanging by their heels. In times like these, you can do half as much as the ancients and get twice the results."

2   Kung-sun Ch'ou said: "Suppose you became prime minis-ter in Ch'i and put the Way into practice, making the Ch'i sovereign an emperor without peer – would you feel moved, or not?"

"My mind[4] has been utterly still since I was forty," replied Mencius.

"Then you must be way beyond Meng Pin."[5]

"That wouldn't be hard. Now Master Kao[6] – he'd stilled his mind even before me."

"Is there a Way to follow in stilling the mind?"

"There is," replied Mencius. "To cultivate great valor, Po-kung Yu never bowed down and never broke off a stare. He knew that the least intimidation was as bad as being slapped in the marketplace. An affront was the same to him whether it came from a peasant or a sovereign who commanded a nation of ten thousand war-chariots, and he'd run his sword through the august lord as easily as the peasant. He knew every insult had to be returned in kind.

"Of cultivating valor, Meng Shih-she said: *I consider defeat victory. To gauge an enemy before attacking, to calculate your chances of success before fighting – that is to live in fear of great armies. How can I ever be certain of victory? All I can do is live without fear.*

"Meng Shih-she was like Master Tseng, and Po-kung Yu was like Adept Hsia. It's impossible to say which of the two had the most profound valor, but Meng Shih-she nurtured his *ch'i*.[7]

"Long ago, Master Tseng said to Adept Hsiang: *Do you love valor? I once heard about great valor from Confucius. If you look within and find yourself less than honorable, you'll fear even a peasant as an enemy. But if you look within and find yourself honorable, you'll face even an army of ten million men.*

"Meng Shih-she nurtured *ch'i*, but that's still nothing like Master Tseng nurturing essentials."

"May I ask about the stillness of your mind, and the stillness of Master Kao's mind?" asked Kung-sun Ch'ou.

"Master Kao says *Don't search the mind for what you can't find in words, and don't search* ch'i *for what you can't find in the mind*," replied Mencius.

"Not searching *ch'i* for what you can't find in the mind – that's fine. But not searching the mind for what you can't find in words – that isn't.

"The will guides *ch'i*, and *ch'i* fills the body. So for us the will comes first, and ch'i second. That's why I say: *Keep a firm grasp on your will, but never tyrannize your ch'i.*"

At this, Kung-sun Ch'ou said: "If you say *For us the will comes first, and ch'i second*, how can you also say *Keep a firm grasp on your will, but never tyrannize your ch'i?*"

"When the will is whole, it moves *ch'i*, and when *ch'i* is whole, it moves the will. When we stumble and hurry, *ch'i* is affected, but that in turn moves the mind."

"May I ask what makes you excel and flourish so?"

"I understand words, and I nurture the *ch'i*-flood."

"May I ask what you mean by *ch'i*-flood?"

"That's hard to explain," replied Mencius. "It's *ch'i* at its limits: vast and relentless. Nourish it with fidelity and allow it no injury – then it fills the space between Heaven and earth. It is the *ch'i* that unifies Duty and the Way. Without it, we starve. And it's born from a lifetime of Duty: a few token acts aren't enough. When the things we do don't satisfy the mind, we starve.

"That's why I say: *Master Kao still doesn't understand Duty. He thinks it's something outside of us.* You must devote yourself to this *ch'i*-flood without forcing it. Don't let it out of your mind, but don't try to help it grow and flourish either.

"If you do, you'll be acting like that man from Sung who worried that his rice shoots weren't growing fast enough, and so went around pulling at them. At the end of the day, he returned home exhausted and said to his family: *I'm worn out. I've been helping the rice grow.* His son ran out to look and found the fields all withered and dying.

"In all beneath Heaven, there are few who can resist helping the rice shoots grow. Some think nothing they do will help, so they ignore them. They are the ones who don't even bother to weed. Some try to help them grow: they are the ones who pull at them. It isn't just that they aren't making things better – they're actually making them worse!"

"What do you mean by *understanding words*?" asked Kung-sun Ch'ou.

"I understand what lies hidden beneath beguiling words. I understand the trap beneath extravagant words. I understand the deceit beneath depraved words. And I understand the weariness beneath evasive words.

"Born of the mind, such things cripple government. And then what is born of government cripples all our endeavors. If ever great sages arise again, they will confirm what I've said.

"Tsai Yü and Adept Kung were masters of eloquence," said Kung-sun Ch'ou. "Jan Po-niu, Min Tzu-ch'ien, and Yen Hui[8] were masters of Integrity's principles. Confucius had mastered both, and still he said: *I'm not much good at eloquence.* So you must already be a great sage, Master."

"What a thing to say!" responded Mencius. "Long ago, Adept Kung asked Confucius: *And are you a great sage, Master?*

"*I couldn't make such a claim,* replied Confucius. *I learn relentlessly and teach relentlessly, that's all.*

"At this, Adept Kung said: *To learn relentlessly is wisdom, and to teach relentlessly is Humanity. To master wisdom and Humanity – isn't that to be a sage?*

"So even Confucius couldn't claim to be a sage. What a thing to say!"

"Of those times," said Kung-sun, "I have heard that Adept Hsia, Adept Yu, and Adept Chang each embodied one aspect of the sage completely. And that Jan Po-niu, Min Tzu-ch'ien, and Yen Hui each embodied all aspects of the sage, but only partially. Which of these is preferable?"

"Let's skip that for now."

"What do you think of Po Yi[9] and Yi Yin[10]?"

"Their Ways were different," replied Mencius. "Po Yi refused to serve a sovereign he disdained or govern a people he disdained. So he took office in times of wise rule and renounced office in times of chaos. Yi Yin, on the other hand, thought any sovereign he served was that much more worthy, and any people he served was that much more worthy. So he took office in times of wise rule, and he took office in times of chaos.

"But Confucius was different. If it was wise to take office, he took office; and if it was wise to stay somewhere, he stayed. If it was wise to linger, he lingered; and if it was wise to hurry away, he hurried away.

"All three were great sages of long ago. I cannot compare to any of them. But Confucius is the one I take for a teacher."

"Did Po Yi and Yi Yin so nearly equal Confucius?"

"No. In all the time since people first came into being, there's never been another like Confucius."

"But were they alike in any way?"

"Yes," replied Mencius. "Given a hundred square miles of territory to rule, they could have inspired the august lords to pay them homage and so made all beneath Heaven their own. But if making all beneath Heaven their own meant violating their Duty even once or killing even a single innocent person, they all would have refused. In this they were alike."

"May I ask how they differed?"

"Tsai Yü, Adept Kung, and Master Yu were all wise enough to understand a sage. And they would never defile themselves by giving someone they admired undue praise. Still, Tsai Yü said: *In my view, the Master was a far greater sage than Yao or Shun.*[11]

"Adept Kung said: *Seeing a state's Ritual, he understood its government. And hearing a state's music, he understood its ruler's Integrity. Looking back, he could gauge all the emperors of a hundred generations. And no one ever proved him wrong. In all the time since people first came into being, there's never been another like him.*

"And Master Yu said: *And why only people? Unicorns are like other animals, phoenixes like other birds, T'ai Mountain like common hills, rivers and* seas like flowing ditches. And the sage is like other people, though he's also different from them: he stands above them. In all the time since people first came into being, there's never been another with the abounding excellence of Confucius."

3   Mencius said: "To pretend force is Humanity – that's the mark of a tyrant, and a tyrant needs a large country. To practice Humanity through Integrity – that's the mark of a true emperor, and a true emperor doesn't need a large country. T'ang began with only seventy square miles, and Emperor Wen began with only a hundred square miles. If you use force to gain the people's submission, it isn't a submission of the heart. It's only a submission of the weak to the strong. But if you use Integrity to gain the people's submission, it's a submission of the sincere and delighted heart. It's like the submission of seventy disciples to Confucius.

"The *Songs* say:

> *From west and from east,*
> *from south and from north –*
> *every thought in submission.*

That says it exactly."

4   Mencius said: "From Humanity comes honor. From Inhumanity comes disgrace. To despise disgrace and yet practice Inhumanity – that's like despising water and living in bottomlands. If you despise disgrace, there's nothing like treasuring Integrity and honoring noble officials. When those of great wisdom are ministers and those of great ability are officials, the nation is untroubled. And if the ruler uses such times of peace to clarify his policies, then even the largest countries will stand in awe of him.

"The *Songs* say:

> *Before the Heavens darkened with rain,*
> *I gathered up mulberry roots,*
> *wove tight window and door.*
> *Now those people down below –*
> *how could they disparage me?*[12]

Whoever wrote this poem certainly understood the Way, commented Confucius. *If a ruler can govern his nation well, how could anyone disparage him?*

"These days, rulers use times of peace to indulge in the pleasures of music and idle amusement. They're bringing ruin down upon themselves. We bring it all upon ourselves: prosperity and ruin alike. The *Songs* say:

> *Always worthy of Heaven's Mandate,*
> *he found great prosperity in himself.*

And the "T'ai Chia"[13] says:

> *Ruin from Heaven*
> *we can weather.*
> *Ruin from ourselves*
> *we never survive.*

That says it exactly."

5 $\quad$ **M**encius said: "Honor the wise, employ the able, and you'll have great worthies for ministers – then every noble official throughout all beneath Heaven will rejoice and long to stand in your court. Collect rent in the markets but no tax, or enforce laws but collect no rent – then every merchant throughout all beneath Heaven

will rejoice and long to trade in your markets. Conduct inspections at the border but collect no tax – then every traveler throughout all beneath Heaven will rejoice and long to travel your roads. Have farmers help with public fields but collect no tax – then every farmer in all beneath Heaven will rejoice and long to work your land. Don't demand tributes in cloth from families and villages – then people throughout all beneath Heaven will rejoice and long to become your subjects.

"If you can do these five things with sincerity, the people in neighboring countries will all revere you as their parent. And not since people first came into being has anyone ever managed to lead children against their own parents. So if you do this, you won't have an enemy anywhere in all beneath Heaven. When you haven't an enemy anywhere in all beneath Heaven, you'll be Heaven's minister. And no one has become that without becoming a true emperor."

6   Mencius said: "Everyone has a heart that can't bear to see others suffer. The ancient emperors had hearts that couldn't bear to see others suffer, and so had governments that couldn't bear to see others suffer. If you lead a government that can't bear to see others suffer, ruling all beneath Heaven is like turning it in the palm of your hand.

"Suddenly seeing a baby about to fall into a well, anyone would be heart-stricken with pity: heart-stricken not because they wanted to curry favor with the baby's parents, not because they wanted the praise of neighbors and friends, and not because they hated the baby's cries. This is why I say everyone has a heart that can't bear to see others suffer.

"And from this we can see that without a heart of compassion we aren't human, without a heart of conscience we aren't human, without a heart of courtesy we aren't human, and without a heart of right and wrong we aren't human. A heart of compassion is the seed of Humanity. A heart of conscience is the seed of Duty. A heart of courtesy is the seed of Ritual. And a heart of right and wrong is the seed of wisdom.

"These four seeds are as much a part of us as our four limbs. To possess them and yet deny their potential – that is to wound yourself. And to deny the sovereign's potential – that is to wound the sovereign. We all possess these four seeds, and if we all understand how to nurture them, it will be like fire blazing forth or springs flooding free. Nurtured, they're enough to watch over all within the four seas. Unnurtured, they aren't enough to serve even our own parents."

7   Mencius said: "How can the arrow-maker be any less Humane than the armor-maker? It's just that the arrow-maker hopes to wound people and the armor-maker hopes to protect them. It's like this for shaman-healers and coffin-makers too. So you can't be too careful in choosing your trade.

"Confucius said: *Of villages, Humanity is the most beautiful. If you choose to dwell anywhere else – how can you be called wise?* Humanity is the noble honor Heaven affirms and the tranquil place humans dwell. Failing to practice Humanity when there's nothing stopping you – that is a failure of wisdom. Without Humanity and wisdom, Ritual and Duty, we're nothing but slaves. A slave ashamed of being a slave – that's like a bow-maker ashamed of making bows or an arrow-maker ashamed of making arrows. If you feel shame, there's nothing like practicing Humanity.

"The Humane are like archers. They square up their stance before shooting. And if they fail to hit the mark, they don't resent the victor who does. Instead, they always look within themselves to find the reason for their failure."

8   Mencius said: "Whenever someone told Adept Lu he'd made a mistake, he was delighted. Whenever Emperor Yü heard someone say something honorable, he bowed. But the great Shun – he went way beyond that. Thinking the honorable was something everyone

shared, he gave up his own ways and followed the people. He was always happy to adopt what the people considered honorable. From his life as a farmer, potter, and fisherman to his life as emperor, there was nothing he didn't learn by adopting it from the people. And to adopt what the people consider honorable is to help them live honorably. So for the noble-minded, nothing is more important than helping the people live honorably."

9   Mencius said: "Po Yi never served a sovereign he disdained, nor did he remain friends with a friend he disdained. He never served in a foul man's court, or even talked with such a man. Serving such a man or even talking with him – for Po Yi, that was like donning fine court robes to sit in mud and ash. He pushed his hatred of the foul impossibly far: if he met a neighbor whose hat wasn't on straight, he would hurry away without looking back, as if it would tarnish him. That's why he refused all offers from august lords, however honorable the offers were. He refused because it was demeaning to attend them.

"Liu-hsia Hui,[14] on the other hand, wasn't shamed by defiled rulers, nor did he consider common positions below him. When in office, he never hid his wisdom and always depended on the Way. When dismissed, he bore no resentment. And suffering adversity, he remained untroubled. He said: *You are who you are, and I am who I am. Even if you stripped naked and stood beside me, how could you ever tarnish me?* Hence he was completely at ease no matter who he was with, and never insisted on leaving. If he was asked to stay, he stayed – for he never felt demeaned and forced to leave.

"Po Yi was too pinched and Liu-hsia Hui too undignified," commented Mencius. "Pinched and undignified: the noble-minded avoid both."

IV

1   Mencius said: "The seasons of Heaven cannot rival the industry of earth. And the industry of earth cannot rival an accord of the people.

"Suppose there were a city with a three-mile inner wall and a seven-mile outer wall. An army surrounds the city and attacks, but fails to conquer it. To surround the city in the first place, this army must have been blessed by the seasons of Heaven. But it failed to conquer the city because the seasons of Heaven cannot rival the industry of earth.

"Now suppose a city's walls are high, its moat deep, its weapons strong and sharp, its supplies plentiful. But this time, the people abandon it and flee. The city falls because the industry of earth cannot rival an accord of the people.

"And so it is said: *Borders and frontiers can't corral the people. Ranges of mountains can't secure a nation. And sharp weapons can't keep all beneath Heaven in awe.*

"Master the Way and your supporters are countless. Lose the Way and your supporters are few. When your supporters are few, even your own family will turn against you. When you supporters are countless, all beneath Heaven will follow you. Hence, the noble-minded ruler never goes to war, or if he does, victory is a simple matter – for he is followed by all beneath Heaven while his enemy's own family is turning against him."

2   Just as Mencius was about to leave for court, a courier arrived with a message from the emperor: "I wanted to come visit you today, but I have a cold and must avoid the wind. I'll hold court again tomorrow, and wonder if I'll have a chance to see you then?"

To this, Mencius replied: "Unfortunately, I too am sick and so cannot attend court."

The next morning, Mencius went to offer the Tung-kuo family his condolences, whereupon Kung-sun Ch'ou said: "Yesterday you declined the emperor's summons, saying you were sick. But today you're out visiting, offering condolences. Should you really be doing this?"

"Yesterday I was sick," replied Mencius, "but today I am well again. So why shouldn't I go out to offer my condolences?"

The emperor sent someone to see how Mencius was feeling, and a doctor came too. Adept Meng Chung told them: "Yesterday, when the emperor's message arrived, Mencius was sick and could not attend court. Today he's feeling a little better, so he hurried off to court. But I don't know if he'll be able to get there or not."

Meng then sent some people to find Mencius and tell him: "You mustn't return home. Go to the emperor's court at once."

But Mencius still didn't go. Instead, he spent the night at Ching Ch'ou's house. There, Lord Ching said: "Inside the home, there is father and son. Outside, there is sovereign and subject. These are the great bonds of human community. Between father and son, affection rules. Between sovereign and subject, reverence rules. I've seen the emperor's reverence for you, but I have yet to see any sign of your reverence for the emperor."

"What a thing to say!" responded Mencius. "In all of Ch'i, there's no one who talks to the emperor about Humanity and Duty. Is that because they don't consider Humanity and Duty to be beautiful things? Or is it because they say to themselves: *Talking to a person like that about Humanity and Duty – what good would it do?* Is anything more irreverent that that? I've never dared offer the emperor anything less than the Way of Yao and Shun. So is there anyone in all of Ch'i with more reverence for the emperor than I?"

"No," said Lord Ching, "that isn't what I meant. The *Book of Ritual* says: *When your father calls, don't pause to answer. When your sovereign summons, don't wait for a carriage.* You were leaving for the emperor's court, but when his summons arrived you refused to go. Isn't this a violation of Ritual?"

"So that's what you meant?" replied Mencius. "Master Tseng said: *Nothing can rival the wealth of Chin and Ch'u. Still – they may have wealth, but I have Humanity; and they may have nobility, but I have Duty. So why should I envy them?* If Master Tseng said this, how could it be wrong? It must be part of the one Way.

"There are three things known throughout all beneath Heaven as exalted: nobility, age, and Integrity. At court, nothing rivals nobility. In the village, nothing rivals age. But for nurturing the people, nothing rivals Integrity. How can you ignore two of these because you possess one of them? If a sovereign is doing great things, he must have advisors he cannot summon. If he wants counsel, he goes to them. If he does not honor Integrity and delight in the Way like this, he is not worthy of their help.

"T'ang first took Yi Yin as a teacher, then as a counselor – and so he became a true emperor with ease. Duke Huan first took Kuan Chung as a teacher, then as a counselor – and so he became the finest of august lords with ease.

"Now all beneath Heaven is full of countries equal in territory and Integrity. None can overcome another for one simple reason: their rulers all want advisors they can teach, rather than advisors they can learn from. T'ang never presumed to summon Yi Yin; Duke Huan never presumed to summon Kuan Chung. And Kuan Chung is scarcely worthy of anyone's aspirations. If he was not to be summoned, am I?"

3   Adept Ch'en said: "The Ch'i emperor once offered you a hundred *yi* in the purest gold, and you refused. But now in Sung you've accepted seventy, and in Hsüeh fifty. If your refusal then was right, your acceptance now is wrong. And if your acceptance now is right, your refusal then was wrong. You can only have it one way."

"Both were right," replied Mencius. "In Sung I was leaving on a long journey, and farewell gifts are always given to departing travelers. So when the emperor said *Please accept this farewell gift,* why should I refuse? In Hsüeh I was worried about my safety. The emperor said *I've heard about your worries. This is to help you buy weapons.* So why should I refuse?

"But in Ch'i there was no reason for the gift. A gift for no reason is a bribe. And when have the noble-minded ever taken bribes?"

4   Mencius went to P'ing Lu and said to the governor there: "If you had a spearman who abandoned his post three times in a single day, would you discharge him or not?"

"I wouldn't wait for three times," replied Governor K'ung Chü-hsin.

"But you have abandoned your own post many times," countered Mencius. "In years of calamity and failed harvests, how many thousands of your people suffered – young and old alike abandoned to gutters and ditches, the strong scattered to every corner of the land?"

"But there was nothing I could do."

"Suppose someone entrusted their cattle and sheep to your care. Surely you would try to find grass and hay for them. And if you couldn't find any, would you return them to their owner or just stand by and watch them die?"

"So, I myself am to blame."

Some time later, Mencius went to see the emperor and said: "I know five provincial governors in your country. The only one who understands how he himself is to blame is K'ung Chü-hsin. Shall I tell you what happened?"

"I myself am to blame," replied the emperor.

5   Mencius said to Ch'ih Wa: "When you resigned as governor of Ling Ch'iu and asked to be appointed chief judge, it seemed a

wise choice because a chief judge advises the emperor. It's been several months since you were appointed – how is it you still haven't counseled the emperor?"

Soon thereafter, Ch'ih Wa offered his counsel to the emperor. When his counsel was ignored, he resigned and went away.

At this, the Ch'i people said: "What Mencius urged Ch'ih Wa to do was fine indeed. As for what Mencius himself does – things aren't so clear."

When Adept Kung-tu told him about this, Mencius said: "I've heard that officials resign if they cannot fulfill their duties, and that counselors resign if they cannot offer their advice. But I'm neither an official nor a counselor, so when it comes to engagement and withdrawal, why shouldn't I just do as I please?"

6   When Mencius was a minister in Ch'i, he went to T'eng on a mission of condolence. The emperor sent as his deputy Wang Huan, the governor of Ko. But even though Mencius saw Wang Huan morning and night on their travels to and from T'eng, he never discussed the purpose of their journey.

"The position of minister in Ch'i is no small thing," commented Kung-sun Ch'ou, "and the road between Ch'i and T'eng is hardly short. How is it you traveled all that way and never discussed the purpose of your journey with him?"

"There were others appointed to arrange things," replied Mencius. "What was there for us to discuss?"

7   Mencius traveled from Ch'i to Lu for the burial of his mother. On his way back to Ch'i, he stopped at Ying. There, Ch'ung Yü said: "You didn't think me unworthy of directing the work of the coffin-makers. The work was urgent, so there was no time for questions. But now there's one I'd like to ask, if you don't mind: *Wasn't that awfully beautiful wood?*"

"In the most ancient times, there weren't rules about how coffins were to be built," replied Mencius. "Later on, there were rules requiring inner and outer coffins to be seven inches thick, whether they were for the Son of Heaven or a common peasant. It isn't a question of beauty, but of expressing all that's in our hearts. If we can't find beautiful wood, we feel uneasy. And if we can't afford it, we feel uneasy. So if they could find it, and they could afford to buy it, the ancients always used the most beautiful wood. How could all this be any different for me?

"And to keep soil from the body of a loved one caught in the midst of such a change – is that not a great joy? I've heard that the noble-minded never scrimp when it comes to parents – not for all beneath Heaven."

8   Acting on his own, Shen T'ung[1] asked: "Is an attack against Yen acceptable?"

"Yes," replied Mencius. "Emperor K'uai had no right to abdicate in favor of Lord Chih. And Lord Chih had no right to accept.

"Suppose there was an official that you especially liked, and you gave him your salary and position without telling the emperor. Suppose that he took it without securing the emperor's approval. Would that be acceptable? And how is that any different from what's happened in Yen?"

Soon Ch'i attacked Yen, and someone asked: "Is it true that you encouraged Ch'i to attack Yen?"

"I did not!" bristled Mencius. "When Shen T'ung asked if an attack against Yen would be acceptable, I said *Yes*. And soon Ch'i attacked. But if he'd asked *For whom is an attack against Yen acceptable?* I would have said: *An attack by someone Heaven appointed is acceptable.*

"Suppose one person killed another, and someone asked: *Is the killing of a person acceptable?* I would answer: Yes. But if the question was: *For whom is the killing of a person acceptable?* I would say: *The killing of a person by a chief judge is acceptable.* Now to attack Yen with another Yen – how could I ever encourage such a thing?"

9   The Yen people had turned to rebellion. The Ch'i emperor said: "I'm too ashamed to face Mencius."

"I wouldn't worry too much," said Ch'en Chia.[2] "Who do you consider the most Humane and wise – you or Duke Chou?"

"What a thing to ask!" said the emperor.

"Duke Chou put Kuan Shu in charge of Shang, and then Kuan Shu used Shang to launch his rebellion. If Chou sent Kuan Shu knowing what would happen, he wasn't Humane. And if he sent Kuan Shu without knowing what would happen, he wasn't wise. So Chou's Humanity and wisdom weren't perfect, and how could yours be anything like his? Shall I go explain this to Mencius?"

Ch'en Chia went to see Mencius and asked: "What kind of man was Duke Chou?"

"An ancient sage," replied Mencius.

"Is it true that he put Kuan Shu in charge of Shang, and then Kuan Shu used Shang to launch his rebellion?"

"It is. "

"Did he send Kuan Shu to Shang knowing he would launch a rebellion?"

"No, he didn't know what Kuan Shu was going to do."

"So even a sage makes mistakes?"

"Duke Chou was the younger brother, and Kuan Shu the elder," replied Mencius. "So it's hardly surprising Chou would make such a mistake. But in ancient times, when the noble-minded made mistakes, they knew how to change. These days, when the noble-minded make mistakes, they persevere to the bitter end. In ancient times, mistakes of the noble-minded were like eclipses of sun and moon: there for all the people to see. And when a mistake was made right, the people all looked up in awe. But these days, the noble-minded just persevere to the bitter end, and then they invent all kinds of explanations."

MENCIUS

10   **M**encius resigned his office and returned home. The emperor went to see him and said: "I wanted to come see you the other day, but could not. When we served together in the same court, I was overjoyed. But now you've left me and returned to your home. I wonder if I can still come here to see you?"

"I wouldn't have dared ask," replied Mencius, "but that is my deepest wish."

Another day, the emperor said to Lord Shih: "I want to give Mencius a house in the center of the capital and ten thousand measures of rice to support his disciples. Then my ministers and people will always have a noble example there before them. Would you talk to him for me?"

Lord Shih passed this message to Mencius through his disciple, Adept Ch'en. When Ch'en gave Shih's message to him, Mencius said: "I see. Yes, how would Lord Shih know such a thing cannot be done? Perhaps he thinks I'm after wealth. But if I were after wealth, why would I give up a hundred thousand so I could have ten thousand?

"Chi Sun once said: *Adept Shu Yi was strange indeed. He arranged an appointment for himself, and when his counsel was ignored, he resigned. But then he used this to arrange lofty appointments for his sons and brothers. People all want wealth and renown, of course. But there in the midst of it, he certainly found his high ground.*

"In the ancient markets, people simply traded what they had for what they had not. The government supervised, nothing more. But then came an uncivil old man who always searched out high ground and climbed up on top. Surveying the situation carefully, he found all the profits to be had, then snared every one. The people all thought him uncivil, so they taxed him. And so it was that the taxing of merchants began."

11   **M**encius left Ch'i and spent the night in Chou. There, on behalf of the Chou emperor, a man wanted to convince Mencius to stay. He sat down and began talking to Mencius, but Mencius said nothing.

Instead, he fell asleep with his head on the table. Quite unhappy, the man said: "I fasted a full day and night before daring to speak with you. But instead of listening, you sleep. I won't disturb you again."

"Please sit," said Mencius. "I'll try to explain this clearly. Long ago, if Duke Mu of Lu didn't have someone always by Master Szu's[3] side, Szu soon lost interest in him. On the other hand – if Hsieh Liu and Shen Hsiang didn't have someone always by Duke Mu's side, Mu soon lost interest in them.

"Now you've gone to all this trouble, but I'm certainly not being treated the way Master Szu was. So am I ignoring you, or are you ignoring me?"

12   Talking with some people after Mencius left Ch'i, Yin Shih said: "If he didn't know the emperor would never be another T'ang or Wu, he isn't very bright. If he knew this and came anyway, he was just trying to get ahead. He came a thousand miles to see the emperor, failed, and left disappointed – but then it took him three days to leave Chou. What made him linger there? It all seems rather suspect to me."

When Adept Kao told him about this, Mencius said: "What does Yin Shih know about me? When I came a thousand miles to see the emperor, that was what I wanted. But to fail and leave disappointed – how could that be what I wanted? It was something I couldn't avoid.

"I waited three days to leave Chou, it's true, but even that felt too soon. The emperor was on the verge of a transformation, and if that had happened he would have called me back. Only when I left Chou and the emperor still didn't send after me – only then did the longing for home well up. But had I abandoned the emperor even then?

"The emperor is capable of noble things. If he'd listened to me, it would have meant peace not just for the people of Ch'i, but for the people throughout all beneath Heaven. The emperor was on the verge of a transformation, and every day I hoped for that. So am I like the little man whose face clouds over with anger and resentment when the sovereign ignores his counsel, who leaves and travels hard all day before stopping?"

When Yin Shih heard this, he said: "It is I who am the little man."

13   **M**encius left Ch'i. As they traveled away, Ch'ung Yü said: "You look so unhappy, Master. But just the other day I heard you say: *The noble-minded never resent Heaven and never blame people.*"

"That was then," replied Mencius. "This is now. A true emperor should arise every five hundred years, and there should also arise others worthy of renown in their time. It's been over seven hundred years since the Chou began: enough time and more. And surely the world is ready. But it seems Heaven still doesn't want to bring peace and order to all beneath Heaven. If it did, who could it choose in our time besides me? So why should I be unhappy?"

14   **M**encius had left Ch'i and was staying in Hsiu. There, Kung-sun Ch'ou asked: "To serve in office but refuse a salary – is that the ancient Way?"

"No," replied Mencius. "I was ready to leave after seeing the Ch'i emperor once. And I wasn't about to change my mind – that's why I refused a salary. But then war broke out, so I couldn't very well ask to leave. I had no intention of staying so long."

V

Duke Wen of T'eng   Book One

1   When he was heir apparent, Duke Wen of T'eng went on a journey to Ch'u. He went by way of Sung, and there stopped to see Mencius. Mencius told him that people are inherently good, and that he must strive to equal Yao and Shun.

When he returned from Ch'u, the duke again stopped to see Mencius, and Mencius said: "Do you doubt what I told you? There is one and only one Way. Ch'eng Chien said to Duke Ching of Ch'i: *Those sage-emperors were men, and I am a man. Why should I be in awe of them?* Yen Hui[1] said: *What kind of man was Shun, and what kind of man am I? If we're devoted, we can be like him.* And Kung-ming Yi said: *Emperor Wen is my teacher. And how could he ever deceive me?*

"Now if you evened out the borders, T'eng would measure fifty square miles: big enough to do great things. The *Book of History* says: *If herbs don't make your head swim, they won't cure your illness.*"

2   Wen was heir apparent when Duke Ting of T'eng passed away, so he said to Jan Yu: "Mencius once counseled me in Sung, and I've never forgotten a word of what he said. The death of a father is a time of great sorrow and responsibility. Before I do anything, I want you to go see Mencius and ask his advice.

Jan Yu went to see Mencius in Chou, and Mencius said: "This is a good thing. Mourning a parent's death – that is when you face yourself utterly. Master Tseng said: *In life, serve parents according to Ritual. In death, bury them according to Ritual. And then make offerings to them according to Ritual. Do this, and you can be called a worthy child.*

"I've never studied the rituals of august lords. Still, I have heard something about such matters. The practice has been the same for three dynasties, and for everyone from the Son of Heaven to simple peasants: a mourning period of three years, clothes of plain cloth cut straight, meals of common porridge."

When Jan Yu returned and reported what Mencius had said, Wen decided to observe a three-year mourning period. But the elders and the hundred officials protested: "This is not the way of the ancestral rulers in Lu, our homeland, nor is it the way of our own ancestral rulers. And to violate their practice – that is not for you to do. The *Annals* say: *In mourning and sacrifice, follow the ways of your ancestors.*"

"My way has also been handed down from the ancients," said Wen.

Later, he said to Jan Yu: "In the past, I spent my time with horses and swords rather than books and teachers. And now the elders and the hundred officials all consider me lacking, so I'm afraid they won't devote themselves to the great issues of our nation. Go for me, and seek the counsel of Mencius."

So Jan Yu returned to Chou and inquired of Mencius.

"I see," replied Mencius. "Why does he look to others for his answers? Confucius said:

> When the sovereign dies – trust government to the prime minister, drink broth, wear a charcoal face dark as ink. Take your place and mourn, then none of the hundred officials will dare be without grief. Show others the way, for the commitments of leaders become the passions of followers. The noble-minded have the Integrity of wind, and little people the Integrity of grass. When the wind sweeps over grass, it bends.

So these things depend upon Wen alone."

When Jan Yu returned and reported what Mencius had said, Wen said: "I see. Yes, these things do depend upon me and me alone."

For five months he stayed in his mourning hut, issuing no proclamations or precepts. Soon both the hundred officials and the family could both say: "How wise!" And when it came time for the burial, people traveled from every corner of the land to watch. The sorrow in his face, the grief in his sobs: it was a great comfort to the other mourners.

3   Duke Wen of T'eng asked about governing his country, and Mencius said: "Never neglect the endeavors of the people. The *Songs* say:

> We gather thatch-reeds by day,
> and braid rope into the night.
> We hurry to build field huts,
> then begin planting the hundred grains.

This is how the people live: it's their Way.

"With a constant livelihood, people's minds are constant. Without a constant livelihood, people's minds are never constant. And without constant minds, they wander loose and wild. They stop at nothing, and soon cross the law. Then, if you punish them accordingly, you've done nothing but snare the people in your own trap. And if they're Humane, how can those in high position snare their people in traps?

"Therefore, the wise ruler practices humility, economy, and reverence toward his subjects. And he takes from the people only what is due him. Yang Hu said: *If you cultivate wealth, you give up Humanity. If you cultivate Humanity, you give up wealth.*

"In the Hsia Dynasty, each family had fifty acres and paid a personal tax. In the Shang, each family had seventy acres and paid a mutual tax. And in the Chou, each family had a hundred acres and paid a communal tax. But in fact, the people always paid one part in ten. *Communal* means *everyone* together, and *mutual* means *mutual assistance.*[2]

"Master Lung said: *In administering the land, nothing is better than the mutual system, and nothing worse than the personal.* The personal tax is based on harvest averages over a number of years. In good years, when there's a wild abundance of rice and a heavy tax would hardly be noticed, little is taken. But in bad years, when the harvest isn't worth the manure it grew from, the tax is exorbitant. When the people's father and mother wears them out with worry, letting them work desperately all year long and then go into debt just to care for their parents, when he abandons young and old alike to gutters and ditches – how can he be called the people's father and mother?

"As for ensuring a livelihood for descendants of worthy officials, that is already the practice in T'eng. But the *Songs* say:

> *When rain falls on our public land,*
> *it also falls on our private land.*

Only in the mutual system is there public land. These lines are about the Chou, so there's no doubt that it too used the mutual system.

"*Hsiang, hsü, hsüeh,* and *hsiao* were established for the education of the people. *Hsiang* for nurturing, *hsiao* for educating, and *hsü* for archery: these are the names used for village schools. In the Hsia Dynasty they were called *hsiao,* in the Shang *hsü,* and in the Chou *hsiang.* For schools of advanced studies, all three dynasties used the name *hsüeh.* But the purpose of all alike was to illuminate the bonds of human community for the people. And when leaders themselves illuminate those bonds, the common people are full of tender affection. If a true emperor arose, he would have to come learn these things from you, and then you would be the teacher of emperors.

"The *Songs* say:

> *Chou may be an ancient country,*
> *but its mandate is renewed again.*

It was Emperor Wen who renewed it. If you devoted yourself, there's no doubt you could renew your own nation in the same way.

Duke Wen sent Pi Chan to ask about the well-field system,[3] and Mencius said: "Your sovereign is anxious to practice Humane government. He chose carefully when he sent you, so you must spare no effort.

"Humane government begins in settled boundaries. Unless settled boundaries are properly fixed, the well-fields won't be divided equally, nor will the yield given for official salaries be fair. This is why tyrants and corrupt officials always avoid settled boundaries. But once settled boundaries are properly fixed, land shares and salary amounts are easily established.

"T'eng has very little territory. Still, you need both noble-minded leaders and peasants in the countryside. Without noble-minded leaders, who will foster order among the peasants? And without peasants, who will nurture the noble-minded leaders?

"In the countryside, tax people one ninth of their produce, according to the well-field system. In the capital, tax people one tenth of their income. From ministers down, officials should all have fifty acres for sacrificial offerings. And among the peasants, each extra man in a family should be given an additional twenty-five acres. People should never leave their village – not when they move their house and not when they die. If villagers sharing well-fields are friends in all things, help each other keep watch, and care for each other in illness – then the people will live in affection and harmony.

"Each square mile of land contains a well-field, and each well-field contains nine hundred acres. The central plot is public land. The eight families each own a hundred acres of private land, and together they cultivate the public land. Once the public land has been tended, they can turn to their own. This is what distinguishes peasants from officials.

"Such are the broad outlines. As for the details of making all this work well, the refinements and elaborations – that's up to you and your sovereign."

4   There was a man named Hsü Hsing who claimed to follow the Way of Shen Nung.[4] He left Ch'u and journeyed to T'eng, where he went to the palace gate and said to Duke Wen: "I lived in a land far away, and there heard that you practice Humane government. I want to live under your rule, so I've come to ask for a piece of land." The

Duke granted Hsü Hsing's request, and Hsü soon had dozens of disciples, all of whom wore sackcloth and earned their living by making sandals and weaving mats.

Ch'en Hsiang and his brother were disciples of Ch'en Liang. Leaving Sung with plows on their backs, they journeyed to T'eng and said: "We have heard that yours is the government of a sage, and we want to live under the rule of a sage."

Ch'en Hsiang went to see Hsü Hsing one day, and was overjoyed. He abandoned his old teacher and took Hsü Hsing as his teacher. He later went to see Mencius and told him what Hsü Hsing had said: "The T'eng sovereign is truly wise and worthy, but he's never learned of the Way. A wise and worthy sovereign earns his living by cultivating the land with his people. It's during breakfast and dinner that he rules. But here, with all his granaries and treasuries, the duke wounds the people while pampering himself. So how can he be wise and worthy?"

"Does Master Hsü eat only the grain he himself has grown?" asked Mencius.

"Yes," replied Ch'en Hsiang.

"And does Master Hsü wear only cloth he himself has woven?"

"No, but he wears only sackcloth."

"Does Master Hsü wear a hat?"

"Yes."

"What kind?"

"Raw silk."

"Did he weave it himself?"

"No, he traded grain for it."

"How is it Master Hsü doesn't weave his own hat?"

"It would interfere with his farm work."

"Does Master Hsü use metal and stoneware for cooking? And for plowing, does he use iron?"

"He does."

"And does he make all these things himself?"

"No, he trades grain for them."

"To trade grain for tools and implements doesn't hurt potters and smithies," said Mencius. "They trade their tools and implements for grain, and does that hurt farmers? Why doesn't Master Hsü become a potter and smithy as well, so he himself can make everything his home needs? The markets of those who practice the hundred crafts are pure bedlam: why does he join in the confusion of barter and trade? How can he bear it?"

"You can't practice a craft and be a farmer too."

"Then how could someone govern all beneath Heaven and also be a farmer? There are the endeavors of great men, and the endeavors of small men. And whatever they need, the hundred crafts provide. If we all had to make things before we could use them, we'd all spend our lives running back and forth on the roads.

"And so it is said:

> Some use their minds to work, and some use their muscles.
> Those who use their minds govern, and those who use their
> muscles are governed. Those who are governed provide for
> those who govern, and those who govern are provided for by
> those who are governed.

People throughout all beneath Heaven know this to be sound practice.

"In the time of Emperor Yao, things were still wild and unsettled in all beneath Heaven. Rivers burst their banks and floods raged across the world. Grasses and trees grew thick with abandon. Birds and animals roamed everywhere in herds and flocks. The five grains never grew tall. Birds and animals crowded people in: even the Middle Kingdom was a tangle of animal trails and bird tracks.

"It was Yao who worried about how to change all this. He fostered Shun so he could bring order to things. Shun assigned Yi to manage fire, and Yi set fire to the mountains and marshes, sending the birds and animals into hiding. Yü carved out the nine rivers. He cleared the Chi and T'a, and sent them flowing into the sea. He opened up the Ju and Han, banked up the Huai and Szu – and sent them all flowing into the Yangtze. Only then were the people of the Middle Kingdom able to grow food. To do this work, Yü spent eight years away from home and passed by his gate three times without entering. Even if he'd wanted to tend fields, how could he have done it?

"Hou Chi taught the ways of agriculture to the people, taught them how to plant the five grains. And when the five grains ripened, the people were well fed. But once people have plenty of food and warm clothes, they lead idle lives. This is their Way. Then, unless they're taught, they're hardly different from the birds and animals. The sage-emperor worried about this. He made Hsieh minister of education so the people would be taught about the bonds of human community: affection between father and son, Duty between sovereign and subject, responsibility between husband and wife, proper station between young and old, sincerity between friend and friend.

"Yao said:

> *Encourage them and reward them.*
> *Help them and perfect them.*
> *Support them and give them wings,*
> *and reveal them to themselves.*
> *Then you will bring Integrity alive in them.*

If a sage ruler worries about his people like this, how could he have time for farming? Yao's great worry was that he might not find a Shun. And Shun's great worry was that he might not find a Yü or Kao Yao.[5] If your great worry is tending your own hundred acres, you're simply a farmer.

"To share your wealth is called generosity. To teach people about living nobly is called loyalty. To be worthy of all beneath Heaven is called Humanity – and so it's easy to give all beneath Heaven away, but to be worthy of it is difficult indeed.

"Confucius said:

> Great indeed was the rule of Yao! Heaven alone is truly majestic, and only Yao could equal it. He was boundless, so vast and boundless the people couldn't even name him. And how majestic, how exalted and majestic a ruler Shun was: possessing all beneath Heaven as if it were nothing to him!

Ruling all beneath Heaven, didn't Yao and Shun have enough to worry about? How could they worry about farm work too? I've heard of our ways converting barbarians into Chinese, but I've never heard of Chinese reverting into barbarians.

"Ch'en Liang is a product of Ch'u. But he admired the Way of Duke Chou and Confucius, so he came north to study in the Middle Kingdom. Among scholars from the north, none could better him. He could only be called a truly great scholar. You and your brother studied under him for dozens of years. Then he dies and you suddenly turn against him.

"After Confucius died and their three years of mourning were over, his disciples packed their things and prepared to return home. They went in and bowed to Adept Kung. They faced each other and wept until they'd all lost their voices. Only then did they leave for home. Adept Kung returned to the burial grounds, built a hut, and lived alone there for another three years before he finally set out for home.

"Eventually, Adept Hsia, Adept Chang and Adept Yu came to think Master Yu was as wise as the sage, and so wanted to study under him as they had under Confucius. They tried to convince Master Tseng to join them, but Tseng said: *I could never do that. Rinsed clean by the Yangtze and Han rivers, bleached by the autumn sun – something shimmering so perfectly white is beyond compare.*

"Now some tribesman with a twittering shrike's tongue comes from the south condemning the Way of the ancient emperors, and you turn against your teacher and go to study with him. You're nothing like Master Tseng. I've heard of leaving dark ravines to live in high trees, but I've never heard of leaving high trees to live in dark ravines.

"In the *Songs,* among the 'Hymns of Lu,' there's a poem that speaks of

> *fighting down the wild tribes*
> *and punishing Ch'u and Shu.*

Duke Chou fought these people to rescue the Middle Kingdom, and now you want to study under them. Yours was a poor conversion indeed.

"In Master Hsü's Way, market prices should all be the same. He claims that would end deceit, that even if children were sent to market, no one would cheat them. Cloth of the same length would bring the same price, whether it was cotton or silk. Bundled fiber of the same weight would bring the same price, whether it was hemp or silk. The five grains would bring the same price for the same measure, and shoes would all bring the same price for the same size.

"But inequality is the very nature of things. One thing may be two or five times as valuable as another, or perhaps ten or a hundred times, or even a thousand or ten thousand times. If you tried to make everything equal in value, confusion would reign in all beneath Heaven. If elegant shoes and workaday shoes brought the same price, who would bother to make elegant shoes? If we follow the Way of Master Hsü, we'll lead each other into utter deceit. How could a nation be governed this way?"

5   A follower of Mo Tzu[6] named Yi Chih wanted to go see Mencius, so he asked Hsü Pi to arrange a visit. Mencius said: "I would like very much to see him, but I'm quite ill. When I'm feeling better, I'll go see him. He needn't come here."

Later, Yi Chih again tried to arrange a visit with Mencius, and Mencius said: "Now I can see him. But first I must straighten him out a little – for if he isn't thinking straight, how can he see the Way?

    MENCIUS

"I have heard Adept Yi is a follower of Mo Tzu. In funerals, Mo Tzu's school follows the Way of simplicity. And Adept Yi apparently thinks such simplicity can transform all beneath Heaven. So how can he himself denounce it instead of treasure it? He gave his parents lavish burials, but the principle of simplicity condemns that as a tawdry way of serving them."

When Master Hsü told Adept Yi what Mencius had said, Adept Yi replied: "According to the Confucian Way, the ancients ruled *as if watching over newborn children.* What can such words mean if not that our love should be the same for everyone, even if it always begins with loving our parents?"

When Master Hsü told Mencius what Adept Yi had said, Mencius replied: "Does Adept Yi really believe we can love a neighbor's newborn child the way we love our own brother's child? The only time that's true is when the newborn is crawling around a well and about to fall in, for the child doesn't know any better. Heaven gives birth to all things: they have a single source. But Adept Yi insists they have two, that's why he believes such things.

"Imagine people long ago who didn't bury their parents. When their parents die, they toss them into gullies. Then one day they pass by and see them there: bodies eaten away by foxes and sucked dry by flies. They break into a sweat and can't bear to look. That sweat on their faces isn't a show for their neighbors: it's a reflection of their deepest feelings. So when they go home and return with baskets and shovels to bury their parents, it's because burying parents truly is the right thing, the Way for all worthy children and Humane people."

When Master Hsü told Adept Yi what Mencius had said, Adept Yi grew pensive. Eventually he said: "I have now been taught."

VI

Duke Wen of T'eng   Book Two

1   Ch'en Tai[1] said: "It seems small of you – refusing to go see the august lords. If you did, you could make whoever you met a true emperor – or at the very least, the finest of august lords. The *Annals* say: *Bend a foot to straighten ten.* It seems worth doing, doesn't it?"

Mencius replied: "Once when he was out hunting, Duke Ching of Ch'i summoned his gamekeeper with a plume-crested flag. The gamekeeper didn't come, so the duke wanted to have him executed, but Confucius said: *A man of great resolve never forgets that he could be abandoned to ditches and gutters, and a man of great valor never forgets that he could lose his head.* What was it Confucius admired in the gamekeeper? The man wasn't entitled to such a lofty summons, so he didn't answer it. And how would it be if people came without waiting for a summons?[2]

"And besides, *bend a foot to straighten ten* is talking about profits. When it's a matter of turning a profit, don't people think it's fine even if they bend ten feet to straighten one?

"Once, because Hsi was a favorite of his, Lord Chien of Chao assigned Wang Liang to drive for him. Hsi didn't catch a single bird all day, so he returned to Lord Chien saying: *He's the worst driver in all beneath Heaven.*

"When someone told him what Hsi had said, Wang Liang said: *Let me try again.* It took no small amount of persuasion, but Hsi finally agreed. This time Hsi caught ten birds in a single morning, and on returning exclaimed: *He's the finest driver in all beneath Heaven!*

"*Then I'll let him drive for you all the time,* said Lord Chien.

"But when he told Wang Liang, Wang Liang refused: *I drove hard for him according to the precepts, and we didn't catch a single bird all day. Then I drove shamelessly for him, and in a single morning we caught ten birds. The Songs say:*

They drove with flawless skill,
shot arrows with fierce precision.

I'm not accustomed to driving for little people. I'll go now, if you please.

"Even though he was a mere driver, Wang was ashamed to compromise for an archer. They could have piled birds and animals up like mountains, but he still wouldn't do it. What kind of person would bend the Way to please others? You've got it all wrong: if you bend yourself, you'll never straighten anyone else."

2   Ching Ch'un[3] said: "How could Kung-sun Yen and Chang Yi[4] be anything less than truly great men? If their anger flashed, the august lords cowered. And if they were content, all beneath Heaven was tranquil."

"Does that make them great men?" replied Mencius. "Haven't you studied Ritual? When a boy comes of age, he receives his father's mandate. When a girl marries, she receives her mother's mandate. Saying farewell at the gate, she cautions her: *Now that you're going to your new home, you must be reverent and cautious, and never disobey your husband.* To make deference the norm – that is the Way of married women.

"As for the man who can be called great: He dwells in the most boundless dwelling-place[5] of all beneath Heaven, places himself at the center of all beneath Heaven, and practices the great Way of all beneath Heaven. If he succeeds in these ambitions, he and the people enjoy the rewards together. If he fails, he follows the Way alone. Wealth and renown never mean much to him, poverty and obscurity never sway him, and imposing force never awes him."

3   Chou Hsiao asked: "In ancient times, did the noble-minded take office?"

"They did," replied Mencius. "The *Chronicles* say: *When Confucius went three months without a position, he got anxious and restless. And when he left one nation for another, he always carried his token of credentials with him.*[6]

"And Kung-ming Yi said: *When the ancients went three months without a position, people began offering condolences.*

"Offering condolences after three months!" responded Chou Hsiao. "Is it really all that urgent?"

"When a man loses his office," replied Mencius, "it's like an august lord losing his nation. The *Book of Ritual* says:

> *An august lord helps plow and plant to provide sacrificial grains. His wife helps spin silk to make sacrificial clothes. If the animals are not fat, the grains not clean, the garments not ready, he dare not perform the sacrifice.*

> *And if an official holds no land, he performs no sacrifice. If the sacrificial animals, ritual vessels, and sacrificial garments are not all ready, he dare not perform the sacrifice or offer a banquet.*

Isn't that reason enough for condolences?"

"Why is it Confucius always carried his token of credentials with him when he left one nation for another?" asked Chou Hsiao.

"An official serving in office is like a farmer working the land. If a farmer left one nation for another, would he leave his plow behind?"

"People serve government here in Chin, too," said Chou Hsiao, "but I've never heard of such urgency. If taking office is such an urgent thing, why is it such a difficult question for the noble-minded?"

"When a son is born, parents hope he will one day have a home and family. When a daughter is born, they hope she will one day find a husband. Parents all feel this way. But if children don't wait for their parents' blessings or the arrangements of a matchmaker, if they drill holes in the wall to peer at each other or climb over it for secret meetings, their parents and everyone else think it's appalling.

"Worthy ancients all wanted to serve in office, but never if it meant violating the Way. To secure a position by violating the Way – is that any different from drilling a hole in a wall?"

4   P'eng Keng[7] said: "Traveling around, preaching to august lords for your rice, scores of carriages and hundreds of followers trailed out behind you – isn't that awfully indulgent?"

"If what you do for someone violates the Way," replied Mencius, "accepting even a basketful of rice from them is too much. But abiding in the Way, Shun accepted all beneath Heaven from Yao and didn't think it indulgent. But perhaps you would call it indulgent?"

"No," replied P'eng Keng. "But still, it's shameful when a man doesn't work to earn his rice."

"If someone like you won't trade what you have for what you need, farmers will be left with useless grain and women with useless cloth. But if you will, carpenters and carriage-makers can earn their rice from you. Now here's a man who is a worthy child at home and humble when away, who learned the Way of ancient emperors, preserving it for future students – and you don't think he's even worth feeding. How can you honor carpenters and carriage-makers, but not a master of Humanity and Duty?"

"When carpenters and carriage-makers work, their motive is rice," replied P'eng Keng. "But when the noble-minded practice the Way – is their motive nothing more than rice?"

"Why are you talking about motives?" countered Mencius. "When someone works for you, he deserves to be fed and should be. And besides, do you feed people for their motives or their work?"

"For their motives."

"So if there's a man flinging mortar around and smashing tiles, and his motive is rice, do you feed him?"

"No."

"Then you don't feed people for their motives; you feed them for their work."

5   Wan Chang[8] said: "Sung is a small nation. If its government became that of a true emperor and it were therefore invaded by Ch'i and Ch'u, what could be done?"

"When T'ang lived in Po," replied Mencius, "Po bordered on Ko, which had a ruler who was dissolute and neglected the sacrifices. When T'ang sent someone to ask why the sacrifices were being neglected, Ko's ruler said: *We don't have enough animals.* T'ang sent him cattle and sheep, but instead of using them for sacrifices, he used them for food.

"Again T'ang sent someone to ask why the sacrifices were being neglected, and the Ko ruler said: *We don't have enough millet.* So T'ang sent Po people to help plow and plant, he sent gifts of food for the old and young. But the Ko ruler ambushed them: he led his people out to steal their wine and food, millet and rice. Anyone who resisted was killed: even a boy bringing millet and meat was killed and his gifts stolen.

"The *Book of History* speaks of this: *For the ruler of Ko, the bearers of gifts were enemies.* And when T'ang sent an army to avenge the murder of this boy, everyone within the four seas said: *It isn't lust for all beneath Heaven: it's revenge for the abuse of common men and women.*

"*Emperor T'ang began his expeditions in Ko,* says the *Book of History.* After eleven expeditions, he hadn't an enemy left anywhere in all beneath Heaven. When he marched east, the western tribes complained. And when he marched south, the northern tribes complained: *Why does he leave us for last?* People watched for him the way they watched for rain in the midst of a great drought. When he came, they went to market unhindered again and weeded their fields without interference. He punished the rulers and comforted the people, like rain falling in its season. And so a great joy rose among the people.

The *Book of History* says: *We're waiting for our lord: his coming will end our suffering.*

"It also says:

> When Yu refused to submit, Emperor Wu marched east and
> soothed its men and women. They filled baskets with azure-
> Heaven silk and yellow-earth silk. They went to Wu saying: 'Let
> us rest here before you. We will cleave to the state of Chou and
> serve it alone.'

The noble-minded of Yu offered baskets of Heaven-and-earth silk to welcome the noble-minded of Chou. The peasants of Yu offered baskets of food and jars of wine to welcome the peasants of Chou. Emperor Wu rescued the people from fire and flood, seizing only their cruel rulers.

"In "The Great Declaration," Wu says:

> Let us brandish weapons and strength.
> Let us strike deep into their homelands,
> and seizing the tyrants ruling there,
> put them to death for everyone to see.
> Then our splendor will outshine T'ang's.

If Sung doesn't have the government of a true emperor, it could fall like that. But if it does have the government of a true emperor, everyone within the four seas will raise their heads and watch for him, wanting him for their sovereign. Then, even though Ch'i and Ch'u are large and powerful nations, what would he have to fear from them?"

6   Mencius said to Tai Pu-sheng: "You wish your emperor were noble and worthy? I'll try to explain this clearly. Suppose a high minister of Ch'u wanted his son to learn the language of Ch'i. Should

he get someone from Ch'i to teach his son, or someone from Ch'u?"

"Someone from Ch'i."

"With only a single teacher from Ch'i and everyone else around the boy yammering in Ch'u, the father could cane him every day and he'd still never speak Ch'i. But if he took his son to some district in Ch'i for a few years, then he could cane the boy every day and he'd never speak Ch'u.

"Now, because you consider Hsüeh Chü-chou a noble and worthy man, you've appointed him to serve among the emperor's closest advisors. If among these advisors old and young, stately and humble, there were only men like Hsüeh Chü-chou – who could help the emperor commit ignoble acts? And if among these advisors old and young, stately and humble, there were none like Hsüeh Chü-chou – who would help him act nobly? One Hsüeh Chü-chou, alone – what can he do for the Sung emperor?"

7   Kung-sun Ch'ou asked: "Never trying to see august lords and advise them: is that a form of Duty?"

"In ancient times, if you didn't hold office you didn't see the sovereign," replied Mencius. "Tuan-kan Mu fled over a wall to avoid his sovereign, and Hsieh Liu bolted the door so his couldn't get in. But they were fanatics. When rulers show such determination, it's all right to see them.

"Yang Hu wanted to see Confucius, and yet wasn't willing to compromise Ritual propriety. But the custom is: if a scholar is not at home to receive a high minister's gift, he goes to the minister's gate and bows in thanks. So Yang Hu waited for Confucius to go out, then sent him a steamed piglet. Confucius likewise waited for Yang Hu to go out, then went to his house and bowed before the gate. If Yang Hu had simply asked to see him, how could Confucius have refused?

"Master Tseng said: *Shrugging shoulders and forcing smiles – it's more grueling than hot summer fieldwork.*

"Adept Lu replied: *To say you agree when you don't, and pretend blushing keeps you honest – I can't understand that at all.*

"From this it's easy to understand what the noble-minded cultivate in themselves."

8   Tai Ying-chih said: "To levy only a ten percent tax on income, to abolish all other taxes, including those at the borders and in the markets – that isn't something we can do this year. What if we reduce these taxes now, and give them up completely next year?"

"Suppose someone stole one of his neighbor's chickens every day," replied Mencius. "Suppose someone said to him *This is not the noble-minded Way,* and he replied *What if I only steal one a month for now, and give it up completely next year?*

"If you recognize something is wrong, you want to see it end quickly. So how can you wait until next year?"

9   Adept Kung-tu said: "Everyone but your own disciples thinks you love to argue, Master. Is it true?"

"It isn't that I love to argue," replied Mencius. "I just can't see how to avoid it. All beneath Heaven has endured for ages and ages – sometimes in peace, sometimes in confusion. In the time of Emperor Yao, floods raged across the Middle Kingdom. Snakes and dragons filled the land, leaving nowhere for the people to settle. Lowland people built nests in the treetops; highland people camped in caves.

"The *Book of History* says: *The flood was a warning to us.* And the flood was nothing less than a vast deluge, so Yao appointed Yü to bring the waters under control. Yü dug furrows in the land and sent the waters flowing into the sea. He drove the snakes and dragons into marshes. Where the water rushed toward the sea, it carved out rivers: the Yangtze and Huai, the Yellow and Han. Obstacles and dangers were rinsed away, and ravaging birds and animals disappeared. Only then could people level farmland and settle down.

"But once Yao and Shun died, the Way of sages began to unravel. One savage ruler followed another. They leveled houses to build their pleasure lakes, leaving the people without a place to rest. They let the fields go wild, turning them into parks and preserves, leaving the people without silk and rice. Twisty words and savage acts became official policy. And with the spread of parks and preserves, ponds and lakes, swarms of birds and animals soon returned. By the time of Tyrant Chou, all beneath Heaven was pure chaos. Duke Chou helped Emperor Wu put an end to Tyrant Chou. He conquered Yen after a three-year war and executed its ruler. He drove Fei Lien to the edge of the sea and there put him to death. He conquered fifty nations, drove away all the tigers and leopards, rhinos and elephants. And so, a great joy rose throughout all beneath Heaven. The *Book of History* says:

> How vast the splendor of Emperor Wen's plans
> and the glory of Emperor Wu fulfilling them:
> preserving and inspiring us who come later,
> they were perfectly true and without flaw.

"But after them, things began to unravel again, and the Way grew weak. Twisty words and savage acts again became official policy. There were ministers killing emperors, and sons killing fathers. Confucius was heartsick, so he wrote *The Spring and Autumn Annals*. It talks about issues the Son of Heaven faces, which is why Confucius said: *If people understand me, it's because of* The Spring and Autumn Annals; *and if they condemn me, it's also because of* The Spring and Autumn Annals.

"But there've been no sage emperors since then, only these august lords indulging themselves with such abandon. Pundits go around talking nonsense, filling all beneath Heaven with the claims of Yang Chu and Mo Tzu: if there's a doctrine that can't be traced back to Yang, it can surely be traced back to Mo. Yang's school preaches *everyone for themselves,* and so denies the sovereign. Mo's school preaches *loving*

everyone equally, and so denies the father. No father and no sovereign –
that's the realm of birds and animals.

"Kung-ming Yi said: *There's plenty of juicy meat in your kitchen and
plenty of well-fed horses in your stable – but the people here look hungry, and
in the countryside they're starving to death. You're feeding humans to animals.*
Unless the Way of Yang and Mo withers and the Way of Confucius
flourishes, twisty words will keep deluding the people and block-
ing the path of Humanity and Duty. When Humanity and Duty are
blocked up, humans are fed to animals. And pretty soon humans will
be feeding on humans. I'm heartsick over it all, and so guard the Way
of ancient sages. If we resist Yang and Mo, driving their reckless ideas
away, those pundits will stop spreading their twisty words. Born of
the mind, such things cripple our endeavors, and then our endeavors
cripple government. If ever great sages arise again, they won't ques-
tion what I've said.

"In ancient times, Yü controlled the floodwaters and brought peace
to all beneath Heaven. Duke Chou subjugated the wild tribes of the
east and north, drove the fierce animals away, and brought peace of
mind to the people. When Confucius finished *The Spring and Autumn
Annals,* rebellious ministers and thieving sons were filled with fear.

"The *Book of Songs* says:

> *fighting down the wild tribes*
> *and punishing Ch'u and Shu.*
> *And so no one dares resist us.*

No father and no sovereign – this is what Duke Chou fought against.
And so, continuing the work of the three sages, I want to rectify peo-
ple's minds and put an end to twisty words, resist dangerous conduct
and drive reckless ideas away. It isn't that I love to argue. I just can't see
how to avoid it, for only those who speak out against Yang and Mo are
true followers of the sages."

10 K'uang Chang⁹ said: "Isn't Master Chung a man of utterly pure principles? A recluse in the wilds of Wu Ling, he once had nothing to eat for three days, which robbed him of hearing and sight. There was a plum tree standing beside his well, dung worms eating at its fruit. He crawled over to it and began eating too. He took three bites, and suddenly he could hear and see again."

"Surely Master Chung is the finest man in the nation of Ch'i," replied Mencius. "But still, how can he be called a man of pure principles? To master his discipline completely, you'd have to be an earthworm – eating leaf rot up above and drinking from the Yellow Springs of graveland down below.

"Was Chung's house built by the great recluse Po Yi or the great bandit Chih? And was his millet grown by Po Yi, or Chih the bandit? How could he know?"

"What difference does it make?" countered K'uang Chang. "He wove sandals with hemp spun by his wife, and they bartered them for the things they needed."

"Master Chung comes from an old and noble family of Ch'i," said Mencius. "His brother's lofty position earned him ten thousand measures of grain. But Chung thought his brother only earned that grain by ignoring Duty, so he refused to eat it. And he thought his brother only paid for his house by ignoring Duty, so he refused to stay in it. Instead, he lived in Wu Ling, far from his brother and mother.

"One day he returned home and found that his brother had been given a live goose by someone wanting favors. He frowned and said: *What good is this cackling creature to you?* A few days later, his mother killed the goose and served it to Chung for dinner. Having been away, his brother returned just then and said: *Isn't this the meat of that cackling goose?* Chung thereupon ran outside and threw it up.

"He never again ate his mother's food, but he ate his wife's. He never again lived in his brother's house, but he lived in his Wu Ling house. So did he perfect that way of life completely? Only an earthworm could master Chung's discipline completely."

VII

Li Lou Book One

1   Mencius said: "Even with the sharp eyes of Li Lou and the skill of Master Kung-shu, you need a compass and square to render circles and squares true. Even with the penetrating ear of Maestro K'uang, you need the six pitch-pipes to tune the five notes true. And even with the Way of emperors Yao and Shun mastered, you need Humane government to govern all beneath Heaven in justice.

"There may be rulers today renowned for their Humanity, but they're neither blessings to the people nor beacons to future generations, for they aren't furthering the Way of ancient emperors. Hence it is said:

> Virtue alone isn't enough for government,
> and law cannot alone put itself into action.

And the *Songs* say:

> Never transgress and never forget:
> always abide in the ancient rules.

Has anyone ever erred by honoring the laws of ancient emperors?

"Having reached the limits of sight trying to render round and square, level and straight, the sage turns to compass and square. You can depend on them always. Having reached the limits of hearing trying to tune the five notes true, the sage turns to the six pitch-pipes. You can depend on them always. And having reached the limits of mind trying to let Humanity shelter all beneath Heaven, the sage turns to government that never oppresses the people. Hence it is said:

> If you want to go high, begin atop hills and mounds.
> If you want to go deep, begin among rivers and marshes.

So if you want to govern and don't begin with the Way of ancient emperors, how can you be called wise?

"That's why only the Humane are fit for high position: if the Inhumane hold high position, evil is sown among the people. When the Way isn't in a leader's thoughts, officials stop fostering the law. When the court doesn't trust the Way, workers don't trust principles. And when a ruler ignores Duty, the people ignore regulations. In such times, a nation survives on luck alone.

"Hence it is said:

> *If city walls are unfinished and weapons scarce, it doesn't spell*
> *disaster for the nation. If people aren't plowing new fields or pil-*
> *ing up wealth, it doesn't spell ruin for the nation. But if a leader*
> *ignores Ritual and officials ignore learning, the people turn to*
> *banditry and rebellion, and the nation crumbles in less than a*
> *day.*

And the *Songs* say:

> *Heaven is dark with menace –*
> *stop this idle drift and chatter.*

Idle drift and chatter means *chitchat doing nothing*. To ignore Duty in serving the ruler, to ignore Ritual in taking office and renouncing office, to deny the Way of ancient emperors in your speech – that is chitchat doing nothing.

"Hence it is said:

> *To expect impossible achievements from a ruler – that is called*
> *honoring him. To open up his virtue and seal up his depravity*
> *– that is called revering him. But to excuse him as incapable of*
> *something – that is called plundering him."*

2   Mencius said: "The final perfection of circle and square is the compass and square. And the final perfection of human community is the sage. If you want to be a ruler, you must enact the Way of a ruler fully. If you want to be a minister, you must enact the Way of a minister fully. In either case, simply take Yao and Shun as your standard and you'll succeed. Unless a minister serves his sovereign the way Shun served Yao, he'll fail to revere his sovereign. And unless a ruler governs his people the way Yao governed his people, he'll do nothing more than plunder them.

"Confucius said:

> There are two Ways: Humanity and Inhumanity. It's that simple. If a ruler tyrannizes his people ruthlessly, he will be killed and his nation destroyed. If he's less than ruthless in his tyranny, his life will be in danger and his nation pared away. Such rulers are given names like The Dark and The Cruel. And such curses are never changed, not even by a hundred generations of the most devoted sons and caring grandsons.

"This is what the *Songs* are talking about when they say:

> A warning to the Shang isn't far off:
> it's the last Hsia tyrant's overthrow."

3   Mencius said: "When the Three Dynasties[1] practiced Humanity, they possessed all beneath Heaven. When they practiced Inhumanity, they lost all beneath Heaven. And when the nations of our time rise and fall, persist and perish – it's no different.

"When the Son of Heaven practices Inhumanity, he cannot preserve all within the four seas. When the august lords practice Inhumanity, they cannot preserve the gods of soil and grain. When high counselors and ministers practice Inhumanity, they cannot preserve the ancestral temples. When officials and common people practice Inhumanity, they cannot preserve their own four limbs.

"To dread death and yet love Inhumanity – that is like dreading drunkenness and yet insisting on wine."

4   Mencius said: "If you try to love people but they keep distant, turn back to your Humanity. If you try to govern people but they resist, turn back to your wisdom. If you try to honor people but they don't reciprocate, turn back to your reverence.

"When you attempt something and fail, always turn back to yourself for the reason. Rectify yourself, and all beneath Heaven will return home to you. The *Songs* say:

> *Always worthy of Heaven's Mandate,*
> *he found great prosperity in himself."*

5   Mencius said: "There is a saying the people keep repeating:

> *All beneath Heaven: nation: family.*

All beneath Heaven is rooted in nation. Nation is rooted in family. And family is rooted in self."

6   Mencius said: "To govern isn't difficult: Just don't offend the great families. Whoever the great families admire, the nation will admire. Whoever the nation admires, all beneath Heaven will admire. And so your Integrity and teaching will flood all within the four seas."

7   Mencius said: "When all beneath Heaven abides in the Way, small Integrity serves great Integrity, and small wisdom serves great wisdom. When all beneath Heaven ignores the Way, small serves large, and weak serves strong. Either way, Heaven issues it forth – and those who abide by Heaven endure, while those who defy Heaven perish.

"Duke Ching of Ch'i said: *We cannot give commands and we refuse to accept them – that is to be cut off from others and doomed.* And so in tears he gave his daughter to Wu as a bride.

"Now, even though small countries take large countries as their teachers in ruthlessness, they're too proud to submit to them. This is like disciples refusing to submit to their teachers. If you're proud, there's nothing like taking Emperor Wen as your teacher. Whoever takes Wen as his teacher will soon govern all beneath Heaven: if he begins with a large country, it will take only five years; and if he begins with a small country, it will take only seven.

"The *Songs* say:

> *The sons and grandsons of Shang*
> *numbered over a hundred thousand.*
> *But the Celestial Lord mandated it,*
> *so they succumbed to Emperor Wen,*
> *to Emperor Wen they succumbed.*
> *Heaven's mandate is not forever:*
> *Shang officials sure and bright*
> *now pour libations in our temples.*

And of this, Confucius said:

> *There's no outnumbering Humanity. If the ruler of a nation loves Humanity, no enemy in all beneath Heaven can stand against him.*

Now, even though they want no enemy in all beneath Heaven to stand against them, rulers refuse to practice Humanity. This is like clutching hot metal without dousing it in water.

> *And who can clutch hot metal*
> *without dousing it in water?*

say the *Songs*."

8   **M**encius said: "You can't talk sense to the Inhumane. They find repose in risk, profit in disaster, and joy in what will destroy them. If you could talk sense to them, would there be ruined countries and ravaged houses?

"A child once sang:

> *When the Ts'ang-lang flows clear*
> *I rinse my hat strings clean.*
> *When the Ts'ang-lang flows muddy*
> *I rinse my feet clean.*[2]

And of this, Confucius said:

> *Listen well, my little ones. When clear it rinses hat strings clean,*
> *and when muddy it rinses feet clean. The choice is its own.*

And so, only after a person has demeaned himself will others demean him. Only after a great family has destroyed itself will others destroy it. And only after a country has torn itself down will others tear it down. The "T'ai Chia" says:

> *Ruin from Heaven*
> *we can weather.*

Ruin from ourselves
we never survive.

That says it exactly."

9   Mencius said: "The tyrants Chieh and Chou lost the people – that's why they lost all beneath Heaven. And it was in losing the people's hearts that they lost the people.

"The way to win over all beneath Heaven is to win over the people. The way to win over the people is to win over the people's hearts. And the way to win over the people's hearts is to surround them with what they want and keep them clear of what they hate.

"The people return to Humanity like water flowing downhill or animals heading into the wilds. Driving fish into them, otters serve deep waters; driving sparrows into them, kestrels serve thickets. And driving the people to them, the tyrants Chieh and Chou likewise served T'ang and Wu. If there were today a single ruler in all beneath Heaven who loved Humanity, the august lords would all serve him by driving the people to him. He may not want to be emperor, but how could he avoid it?

"Those who want to be emperor are like people who start searching for three-year-old moxa, hoping to cure a seven-year-old illness. If they haven't stored it away in advance, they'll have to suffer without it. It's like that with Humanity – if you haven't devoted yourself to it, you'll be hounded by worry and shame until you're finally caught in death's snare. The *Songs* say:

> *You'll never save this world,*
> *just sink into ruin together.*

That says it exactly."

10   Mencius said: "You can't talk sense to the reckless, and you can't help the suicidal. To refuse Ritual and Duty when you speak – that is called reckless. To believe you cannot dwell in Humanity or abide in Duty – that is called suicidal. Humanity is our tranquil home, and Duty our sure path. And how could anyone leave a tranquil home empty or a sure path untraveled?"

11   Mencius said: "The Way is close at hand but sought far off. Essentials are easy but sought in the difficult.

"If people all treated family as family and elders as elders, all beneath Heaven would be at peace."

12   Mencius said: "If a common official cannot inspire a sovereign's trust, he'll never win over the people and govern them. But there's a Way to inspire a sovereign's trust. If you can't inspire trust in your friends, you'll never inspire trust in your sovereign. But there's a Way to inspire trust in your friends. If in serving your family you can't bring them joy, you'll never inspire trust in your friends. There's a Way to bring joy to your family. If you look within and find you aren't faithful to yourself, you'll never please your family. But there's a Way to be faithful to yourself. If you cannot render benevolence clear in the world, you'll never be faithful to yourself.

"Hence, the Way of Heaven is in faithful things, and the Way of humankind is in faithful thought. If you're faithful to yourself, you cannot fail to inspire others. And if you aren't faithful to yourself, you'll never inspire others."

13   Mencius said: "Po Yi fled the tyrant Chou and settled on the shores of the North Sea. On hearing that Emperor Wen had come to power, he said *I hear Wen takes good care of the old, so why not go back*

and serve him? Duke T'ai³ fled the tyrant Chou and settled on the shores of the West Sea. On hearing that Emperor Wen had come to power, he said *I hear Wen takes good care of the old, so why not go back and serve him?*

"These two were the grandest old men in all beneath Heaven. When they returned to him, they were the fathers of all beneath Heaven returning. And when the fathers of all beneath Heaven return to him, where else would the children go? Now if one of our august lords governed the way Emperor Wen did, it wouldn't even be seven years before he governed all beneath Heaven."

14 Mencius said: "When Jan Ch'iu⁴ was governor for the Chi family, he wasn't able to raise their Integrity the least bit. Meanwhile, he managed to double the tax people had to pay. So Confucius said: *He's no follower of mine. If you sounded the drums and attacked him, my little ones, it wouldn't be such a bad thing.*

"It's clear from this that Confucius deplored anyone enriching a ruler who didn't practice Humane government. And he deplored even more those who waged war for such a ruler. In wars for land, the dead crowd the countryside. In wars for cities, the dead fill the cities. This is called helping the land feed on human flesh. Death is not punishment enough for such acts.

"Hence, those who excel at war should receive the highest punishment. Next come those who form the august lords into alliances. And finally those who open up wild land hoping to increase profits."

15 Mencius said: "Nothing reflects the person so well as the eyes. The eyes won't hide the evil in a person. If a person's heart is noble, their eyes are bright and clear. If it is not, their eyes are dark and cloudy. To hear a person's words, look into their eyes – then they can hide nothing."

16   Mencius said: "The dignified never demean others. The thrifty never rob others. A ruler who demeans and robs others can only worry that the people might turn on him – so how can he be dignified or thrifty? Sweet words and smiling faces – how can that make them dignified or thrifty?"

17   Ch'un-yü K'un⁵ said: "When men and women give and receive, is it a violation of Ritual for them to touch?"

"It is," replied Mencius.

"If your sister-in-law was drowning, would you reach out your hand to rescue her?"

"If a sister-in-law was drowning, it would be vicious not to rescue her. When men and women give and receive, it's a violation of Ritual for them to touch. But reaching out your hand to rescue a drowning sister-in-law – it's the only choice you have."

"All beneath Heaven is drowning," continued Ch'un-yü K'un. "Why don't you reach out and rescue it?"

"To rescue all beneath Heaven from drowning, you need the Way. To rescue a sister-in-law, you need only a hand. Do you think a hand is enough to rescue all beneath Heaven?"

18   Kung-sun Ch'ou said: "Why is it the noble-minded never teach their own children?"

"The way people are, it's impossible," replied Mencius. "A teacher's task is to perfect the student, and if the student doesn't improve, the teacher gets angry. When the teacher gets angry, the student in turn feels hurt: *You demand perfection, but you're nowhere near perfect yourself.* So father and son would only hurt each other. And it's a tragedy when fathers and sons hurt each other.

"The ancients taught each other's children. That way father and son never demand perfect virtue of one another. If they demand perfect virtue of one another, they grow distant. And nothing is more ominous than fathers and sons grown distant from one another."

19 Mencius said: "Isn't family the most important thing to serve? And isn't character the most important thing to preserve? I've heard of refusing to squander your character in order to serve your family. But I've never heard of squandering your character in order to serve your family.

"There's no end to what we should serve, but serving family is the basis of all service. And there's no end to what we should preserve, but preserving character is the basis of all preservation.

"When Master Tseng was caring for his father, he always served wine and meat. When he cleared the table, he always asked who the food should be given to. And when his father asked if there were leftovers, he always said there were. His father died, and eventually Master Tseng was cared for by his son, Tseng Yüan. Tseng Yüan also served wine and meat, but when he cleared the table he never asked who the food should be given to. And when his father asked if there were leftovers, he always said there were none so that he could serve the food again. This is called caring for mouth and body alone. But Master Tseng's way is called caring for the essence. In serving family, Master Tseng should be your model."

20 Mencius said: "Admonitions aren't enough for them, and accusations aren't enough for their government. It takes a great man indeed to rectify the depravity in a sovereign's heart.

"When the sovereign is Humane, everyone is Humane. When the sovereign is Dutiful, everyone is Dutiful. And when the sovereign is principled, everyone is principled. Give it a principled sovereign and the nation is secure."

21   Mencius said: "There is the praise of those who demand little, and the derision of those who demand everything."

22   Mencius said: "Talk is easy when you don't have to get the job done."

23   Mencius said: "The trouble with people is that they fancy themselves great teachers."

24   Adept Yüeh-cheng went with Governor Wang Huan to Ch'i, and there he went to visit Mencius.

"So you've come to see me too?" wondered Mencius.

"Why do you ask that, Master?" replied Yüeh-cheng.

"How long have you been here?"

"I arrived yesterday."

"So is it surprising that I ask such a question?"

"But I haven't even found a place to stay yet."

"Is that what you've been taught – that you only visit your elders after finding a place to stay?"

"Yes, it was wrong of me," admitted Yüeh-cheng.

25   Mencius said to Adept Yüeh-cheng: "You've come with Wang Huan just to savor a little food and wine. All your studies of the ancient Way, and for what? A little food and wine?"

26   Mencius said: "There are three ways you can fail to honor your parents, and the worst is to have no heir. Shun married without telling his parents because he was afraid that he might have no heir. For the noble-minded, this is no different than telling them."

27   Mencius said: "The substance of Humanity is nothing other than serving your family, and the substance of Duty nothing other than obeying your elders. The substance of wisdom is to understand these two things and cleave to them always. The substance of Ritual is to shape and embellish these two things. And the substance of music is to infuse these two things with joy. Once joy wells up, how can it be stopped? And if joy can't be stopped, hands and feet soon strike up a dance of their own."

28   Mencius said: "Imagine all beneath Heaven turning to you with great delight. Now imagine seeing that happen and knowing it means nothing more than a wisp of straw: only Shun was capable of that.

"He knew that if you don't realize your parents you aren't a person, and that if you don't lead your parents to share your wisdom you aren't a child. He fulfilled the Way of serving parents completely until Blind Purblind, his depraved father, finally rejoiced in virtue. Once his father rejoiced in virtue, all beneath Heaven was transformed. Once his father rejoiced in virtue, the model for fathers and sons was set for all beneath Heaven. Such is the greatness of honoring parents."

VIII

Li Lou Book Two

1   **M**encius said: "Emperor Shun was a barbarian from the east: he was born in Chu Feng, moved to Fu Hsia, and finally died in Ming T'iao. Emperor Wen was a barbarian from the west: he was born in Ch'i Chou and died in Pi Ying. They lived more than a thousand miles and a thousand years apart – but putting their principles into practice throughout the Middle Kingdom, they were like the matching halves of a jade seal. The first was a sage, and the second was a sage: their thoughts were identical."

2   **E**ven though he was prime minister in Cheng, Lord Ch'an[1] ferried people across the Chen and Wei himself.

"He was certainly kind," said Mencius, "but he didn't know how to govern. If he'd built footbridges every year in the tenth month and cart bridges every year in the eleventh month, the people could have avoided the ordeal of fording rivers. In governing, the noble-minded clear their way of people. How can they help people across rivers one by one? It's impossible to govern by making people happy one at a time: there aren't enough hours in the day."

3   **M**encius said to Emperor Hsüan of Ch'i: "If a sovereign treats the people like his hands and feet, they'll treat him like their stomach and heart. If a sovereign treats the people like his dogs and horses, they'll treat him like a commoner. If a sovereign treats the people like weeds and dirt, they'll treat him like an enemy bandit."

"According to Ritual," said the emperor, "ministers wear mourning clothes when they leave the service of a sovereign. What must an emperor do so that his officials feel that way?"

"Act on their admonitions and listen to their words," replied Mencius, "so blessings rain down on the people. When a minister must travel, send people to escort him across the border and send emissaries ahead wherever he goes to prepare the way. Then give him three years to return before you seize his house and fields. These are called the three Ritual courtesies. If you follow them, your ministers will wear mourning clothes when they leave your service.

"These days a sovereign never acts on a minister's admonitions or listens to his words, and so blessings don't rain down on the people. If a minister must travel, the sovereign arrests him or makes things difficult for him wherever he goes. And the day the minister leaves, the sovereign takes back his house and fields. This is called being an enemy bandit. And why would anyone wear mourning clothes when leaving an enemy bandit?"

4   Mencius said: "When scholars are put to death for no reason, high ministers should resign their office and leave. When the people are slaughtered for no reason, scholars should resign their office and move away."

5   Mencius said: "When the sovereign is Humane, everyone is Humane. When the sovereign is Dutiful, everyone is Dutiful."

6   Mencius said: "Ritual empty of Ritual, Duty empty of Duty – great people never practice such things."

7   Mencius said: "Let the realized nurture the unrealized and the talented nurture the untalented, then people will rejoice in having worthy fathers and elders. If the realized abandon the unrealized and the talented abandon the untalented, there won't be the least difference between the worthy and the debased."

8   *M*encius said: "Once there are things you refuse to do, you have things to do."

9   *M*encius said: "When you speak of the virtues another lacks, think of the trials you may yet endure."

10   *M*encius said: "Confucius was not a man of extremes."

11   *M*encius said: "Great people's words need not be sincere, nor their actions fruitful. They need only abide in Duty."

12   *M*encius said: "Great people never lose their child's heart."

13   *M*encius said: "To nurture the living is not such a great thing. But to nurture them dead and gone – that is a great thing."

14   *M*encius said: "To fathom great depths, the noble-minded realize themselves in the Way. Once they realize themselves in the Way, they dwell at ease in it. Once they dwell at ease in it, they trust themselves to it deeply. And once they trust themselves to it deeply, they find its origins all around them. This is why the noble-minded realize themselves in the Way."

15   *M*encius said: "Make your learning abundant and speak of it with precision, then you will speak of essentials."

16   Mencius said: "If you use virtue to subdue others, you'll never subdue anyone. But if you use virtue to nurture others, you'll soon nurture all beneath Heaven. No one is emperor over all beneath Heaven unless it submits with subdued heart."

17   Mencius said: "Words that defy reality are ominous. And it's ominous reality that confronts those who would obscure the wise and worthy."

18   Master Hsü said: "Confucius often praised water, chanting *O water! O water!* Why was it water that he praised?"

"Springs well up into streams," replied Mencius, "and cascade steadily down night and day, filling every hollow before flowing on to the four seas. Those rooted in a source are like this. That's why Confucius praised water.

"Those not rooted in a source are like water gathering during the autumn rains: ditches and gutters are quickly flooded, but they're always dry again in no time. So it is that renown beyond what they deserve makes the noble-minded uneasy."

19   Mencius said: "The difference between people and animals is slight indeed. Most people blur that difference: it's the noble-minded that preserve it.

"Shun understood the commonplace and looked deeply into human community. He never put Humanity and Duty into action, for Humanity and Duty were always there in his actions."

20   Mencius said: "Yü hated fine wine but loved good advice. T'ang kept to the middle way and didn't need rules when appointing

worthy officials. Emperor Wen cared for the people as if they were invalids and gazed toward the Way as if he'd never seen it. Emperor Wu never slighted intimates and never forgot those far away.

"Duke Chou hoped to combine the methods of these dynastic founders in his rule. When he encountered some difficulty or contradiction, he turned to them and sat through the night deep in thought. If he was lucky enough to resolve the question, he would sit and await the dawn."

21 Mencius said: "When all trace of the sage emperors had vanished, the *Songs* were no longer gathered from the people.[2] After they stopped gathering the *Songs*, the *Spring and Autumn* was written.

"Such chronicles are all the same: for Chin the *Annals*, for Ch'u the *Wooden Tiger* and for Lu there is the *Spring and Autumn Annals*. It tells of such figures as Duke Huan of Ch'i and Duke Wen of Chin, and it's written in the historical style. Of it, Confucius said: *I've stolen all its lofty principles.*"

22 Mencius said: "The influence of someone noble-minded lasts five generations, and the influence of someone small-minded also lasts five generations. I was never a disciple of Confucius: I'm schooled in the clarity he passed on to others."

23 Mencius said: "When you can choose to take or not take, taking offends humility. When you can choose to give or not give, giving offends generosity. When you can choose to die or not die, dying offends courage."

24 P'eng Meng studied archery under Yi. Once he had mastered Yi's Way, he thought Yi was the only archer in all beneath Heaven better than he. So he killed Yi.

"Yi was himself to blame for this," commented Mencius. "Kung-ming Yi said that Yi seemed blameless, but meant only that his blame was slight. How could he be completely blameless?

"Cheng once sent Master Cho Ju to invade Wei, and Wei sent Yü-kung Szu in pursuit. Master Cho Ju said: *I'm too sick: I can't pick up my bow. Today I'll die.* Then he asked his driver: *Who's coming in pursuit?*

"*Yü-kung Szu,* replied the driver.

"*Then today I'll live.*

"*But Yü-kung Szu is Wei's finest archer. Why do you say you'll live?* asked the driver.

"*Yü-kung Szu studied archery under Yin-kung T'o,* replied Master Cho Ju, *and Yin-kung T'o studied under me. Yin-kung T'o is a man of great dignity, and so only chooses friends of great dignity.*

"Yü-kung Szu arrived and said *Why isn't your bow at the ready, Master?*

"*I'm too sick: I can't pick up my bow.*

"*I studied archery under Yin-kung T'o, and Yin-kung T'o studied under you. How could I turn your own Way against you, Master? Still, I am here on my sovereign's business and dare not forsake it.*

"Drawing four arrows, he struck them against the wheel of his chariot, breaking off their tips, then shot them into the air. Whereupon he turned and left."

25   Mencius said: "If the beautiful Lady Hsi wore filthy clothes, people would have held their noses and hurried past her. So it is that a man deformed by his depravity can fast and bathe himself so pure he's fit to perform sacrifices to the Celestial Lord."

26   Mencius said: "It's simple: To say anything about the nature of things, you must attend to the facts, facts in their original form. The trouble with knowledge is that it keeps chiseling things away. If intellectuals were like Yü draining floodwater into the sea, there'd be

nothing wrong with knowing. Yü succeeded by letting water have its way, and if intellectuals just let things have their way, knowing would be great indeed.

"Heaven is high and the stars distant – but if you attend to the facts, you can calculate solstice for a thousand years without ever leaving your seat."

27   Lord Kung-hang's son had died. When Wang Huan arrived to offer his condolences, people hurried over to speak with him. And when he took his place as Counselor on the Right, others hurried over to speak with him. Seeing that Mencius made no attempt to speak with him, Wang Huan felt insulted and said: "Everyone here has had some words for me. Only Mencius has failed to do me that courtesy."

When Mencius heard about this, he said: "According to Ritual, you don't leave your position at court to speak with others, and you don't break ranks to bow to others. I was only observing Ritual. Isn't it strange Wang would consider that an insult?"

28   Mencius said: "What makes the noble-minded different is that they keep their hearts whole. And to do that, they depend on Humanity and Ritual. Those who practice Humanity love people, and those who observe Ritual honor people. If you love people that way, people will always love you faithfully. And if you honor people that way, people will always honor you faithfully.

"Now suppose someone is treating me poorly. If I'm noble-minded I'll turn to myself, thinking *I must be neglecting Humanity. I must be ignoring Ritual. Otherwise, how could such a thing happen?* If I turn to myself and find that I am acting Humane and observing Ritual, but the poor treatment continues, I turn to myself again, thinking *I must be lacking in devotion.* If I turn to myself and find that I am indeed devoted, but the poor treatment still continues, I say: *This person is savage, absolutely savage: no different from an animal! Why should I keep troubling myself over such a creature?*

"This is how the noble-minded worry their whole lives through, and so never know unexpected disaster. They may have worries, but only worries like this: *Shun was a person, and I too am a person. Shun was an exemplar for all beneath Heaven, worthy to guide future generations, but I'm still nothing more than a common villager.* And that's a worthwhile worry, for what can you do about such worries? It's simple: be like Shun.

"The noble-minded never know disaster. If it isn't Humane, they don't do it. If it isn't according to Ritual, they don't do it. Therefore, an unexpected disaster is no disaster for the noble-minded."

29   In times of sage rule, Yü and Hou Chi passed by their own gates three times without entering.[3] Confucius called them wise and worthy. In evil times, Yen Hui lived in a meager lane with nothing but some rice in a split-bamboo bowl and some water in a gourd cup. No one else could bear such misery. But it didn't even bother Hui. His joy never wavered. Confucius also called him wise and worthy.[4]

Mencius said: "Yü, Hou Chi, Yen Hui – they all practiced the same Way. If anyone in all beneath Heaven drowned, Yü felt as if he himself had drowned them. If anyone in all beneath Heaven starved, Hou Chi felt as if he himself had starved them. And so they worked with fierce devotion. If the three of them had traded places, they would each have done as the other did.

"These days, if someone in your house gets in a fight, it's fine to rush out and rescue them with your hair hanging loose and your cap untied. But if it's someone from your village that's fighting, then it's wrong. In fact, it's perfectly fine if you just bolt your door and ignore it."

30   Adept Kung-tu said: "People all through the country talk about how poor a son K'uang Chang was. But you not only befriend him, Master, you treat him with gracious respect. How can that be?"

"It's common now for people to say there are five ways to be unfilial," replied Mencius. "Neglecting the care of parents because you're lazy – that is the first. Neglecting the care of parents because you love wine and *go* – that is the second. Neglecting the care of parents because you love wealth and adore wife and children – that is the third. Disgracing parents because you can't resist beautiful sights and sounds – that is the fourth. Endangering parents because you love valor and conflict – that is the fifth. Does Chang do any of these things?

"Chang and his father had a falling out because they tried to reform each other. Between friends, reform is fine. But between fathers and sons, it's a great destroyer of love. Don't you think Chang longed for the affections of husband and wife, child and mother? Once his father was offended, he wouldn't let Chang come near him. That's why Chang sent his wife away, banished his children, and lived his whole life without their loving care. He was convinced that his offense would be even greater if he didn't do that. That's the kind of man K'uang Chang is."

31   M aster Tseng was living in Wu Ch'eng when some bandits from Yüeh invaded. Someone cried out: "Bandits are coming! Run!"

"Don't let anyone stay in my house or harm the gardens," Tseng commanded his housekeeper. Then, when the bandits left, he sent word: "Get the house ready. I'll be back soon."

Once the bandits had left and Tseng returned, his disciples said: "The Master has been treated with such sincerity and honor here. But when the bandits came, he ran first for all the people to see, and then returned only after the bandits had left. Doesn't that seem wrong?"

"Understanding such things is beyond you," said Shen-yu Hsing. "I once had trouble with people stealing hay, but it didn't involve any of the master's seventy followers."

Master Szu was living in Wei when some bandits from Ch'i invaded. Someone cried out: "Bandits are coming! Run!"

"If I run," replied Master Szu, "who'll help our sovereign defend the country?"

Of these things, Mencius said: "Master Tseng and Master Szu – they both practiced the same Way. Master Tseng was a teacher and elder; Master Szu was a common citizen of no importance. If the two of them had traded places, they would each have done as the other did."

32   Lord Ch'u said: "The emperor sent spies to see if you're really different from other people."

"How would I be different from other people?" exclaimed Mencius. "Even Yao and Shun were just like everyone else."

33   There was a man in Ch'i who lived with his wife and mistress. When he went out, he always came home stuffed with wine and meat. One day his wife asked who his companions were, and he told her they were all men of wealth and renown. So she said to the mistress: "When he goes out, he always comes home stuffed with wine and meat. I ask who his companions are, and he says they're all men of wealth and renown. But we've never had such illustrious guests here in our house. I'm going to follow him and see where he goes."

She rose early the next morning and followed him everywhere he went. But no one in all the city even stopped to talk with him. Finally he went out to the graveyard east of the city, and there begged leftovers from someone performing sacrifices. He didn't get enough, so he went to beg from someone at another grave. That's how he stuffed himself full.

The wife returned home and told the mistress what she'd seen, then said: "A woman looks to her husband for direction and hope throughout life, and *this* is what ours is like." Together they railed against their husband and wept in the courtyard. Later, knowing nothing of this, the husband came swaggering in to impress his women.

In the eyes of the noble-minded, when a man chases after wealth and renown, profit and position, it is rare that his women aren't disgraced and driven to tears.

XI

Wan Chang   Book One

1   **W**an Chang said: "When he was working the fields, Shun wept and cried out to the vast Heavens. Why did he weep and cry out?"

"He was full of resentment and longing," replied Mencius.

"If your parents love you, you rejoice and never forget them," said Wan Chang. "If your parents hate you, you suffer but never resent them. So what is it Shun resented so?"

Mencius said: *"Now I understand Shun working the fields. But weeping and crying out to his parents and the vast Heavens – that I don't understand. When Ch'ang Hsi said this to Kung-ming Kao, Kung-ming Kao replied: Understanding such things is beyond you. So* he certainly didn't believe a worthy child could be indifferent enough to think *I work hard plowing the fields. That's all parents can demand of a child. If they don't love me, how could it be my fault?*

"To help Shun in the fields, Yao sent his nine sons and two daughters, his hundred officials, cattle, sheep, provisions in plenty. Officials throughout all beneath Heaven turned to him. Yao was about to give all beneath Heaven over to his care. But not being in accord with his parents, Shun was like a man so poor he had no home to return to.

"Everyone wants to have officials throughout all beneath Heaven rejoice in them, but that wasn't enough to ease his worry. Everyone wants beautiful women, but even Yao's two daughters weren't enough to ease his worry. Everyone wants wealth, but even the wealth of all beneath Heaven wasn't enough to ease his worry. Everyone wants renown, but even the renown of being the Son of Heaven wasn't enough to ease his worry. People rejoicing in him, beautiful women, wealth, renown – all that wasn't enough to ease his worry. Being in accord with his parents – that was the one thing that could ease his worry.

"When we're young we long for our parents. When we begin thinking of beautiful women, we long for the young and beautiful. When we have a wife and family, we long for wife and family. When we're ready to serve, we long for a sovereign and burn with anxiety if we don't find one. Longing for your parents throughout life – that is the mark of a great child. To see a man who still longed for his parents at the age of fifty, I look to Shun."

2 Wan Chang said: "The *Songs* say:

How do you go about marrying a wife?
You first inform your parents.

No one should be a better example of this than Shun. How is it he married without first informing his parents?"

"If he'd told them, he wouldn't have married," replied Mencius. "A man and woman living together is a great bond of humankind. If he'd told his parents, he would have forsaken that great bond, and that would have been an act of hatred toward his parents. That's why he didn't tell them."

"Now I understand why Shun didn't tell his parents," said Wan Chang, "but how could Yao marry his two daughters to Shun without telling Shun's parents?"

"Yao also understood that if he told them there would be no marriage," replied Mencius.

"Shun's parents sent him to repair the granary," said Wan Chang, "then they pulled down the ladder and his depraved father set the granary on fire. They sent him to dredge the well, then followed him and sealed him in. His brother Hsiang said: *I'm the one who thought of a way to deal with my brother, the city-building sovereign. You can have his granaries, my parents, and his cattle and sheep. But his shield and spear are mine. His ch'in[1] and bow, are mine. And his two wives – they'll offer their comforts in my home now.*

"Later Hsiang went to Shun's house and found him there, sitting on his bed playing the *ch'in*. Blushing, he said: *I was worried and thinking of you, that's all.*

"*And I am thinking of my people,* replied Shun. *Help me govern them.*

"I wonder: didn't Shun realize that Hsiang was trying to kill him?"

"How could he not know?" responded Mencius. "But he was worried when Hsiang was worried, and pleased when Hsiang was pleased."

"So Shun was only pretending to be pleased?" asked Wan Chang.

"No," replied Mencius. "Someone gave a live fish to Lord Ch'an of Cheng. Lord Ch'an told his pond-keeper to put the fish in a pond and take care of it. The pond-keeper cooked the fish, then reported to Ch'an: *When I first let it go, it seemed confused by all that water. Before long it was savoring the vastness. And finally it disappeared into the distance.*

"*It's in its element! It's in its element!* exclaimed Ch'an.

"The pond-keeper left and said: *How can Lord Ch'an be called wise? I cooked his fish and ate it too, and he just says: 'It's in its element! It's in its element!'*

"So, to deceive the noble-minded, you must abide by their principles. It's impossible to trap them unless you use their own Way. Hsiang came in the same loving Way that Shun would have come, so Shun was truly pleased. Is that pretending?"

3    $\mathbf{W}$an Chang said: "Hsiang spent his days trying to kill Shun. So when Shun became the Son of Heaven, why did he only banish him?"

"He gave Hsiang a noble title and land," replied Mencius. "Some called it banishment."

"Shun sent Kung Kung to Yu Chou and banished Huan Tou to Ch'ung Mountain, executed San Miao at San Wei and imprisoned Kun at Yü Mountain," said Wan Chang, "and all beneath Heaven assented, knowing he was rooting out the Inhumane. Hsiang was brutally Inhumane, and yet Shun gave him a title and the lands of Yu Pi. What had the people of Yu Pi done to deserve that? How could a Humane man do such a thing: punishing innocent people so he could give his brother a noble title and land?"

"A Humane man never harbors anger or resentment toward a brother," replied Mencius. "He cherishes and loves him, that's all. Cherishing him, he wants him to enjoy renown; and loving him, he wants him to enjoy wealth. By giving Hsiang a title and the lands of Yu Pi, Shun let him enjoy wealth and renown. To be the Son of Heaven and let your brother live as a mere commoner – how could anyone call that cherishing and loving?"

"What did you mean when you said *Some called it banishment?*" asked Wan Chang.

"Hsiang had no power in his territory," said Mencius. "The Son of Heaven appointed others to govern and collect taxes there. That's why people called it banishment. Do you think Shun would allow him to abuse the people there? Shun still wanted to see him often, so he came to visit often. That's what is meant by:

> He didn't wait for times of tribute:
> he welcomed him as the Lord of Yu Pi."

4   H sien-chiu Meng[2] said: "There is a saying:

> Once rich in Integrity,
> you're subject to no sovereign
> and you're son to no father.

Shun stood facing south at court. Yao, leading the august lords, faced north and paid him homage. Blind Purblind, Shun's depraved father, also faced north in homage. When Shun saw his father there, a troubled look came over his face. Confucius said: *At that moment, all beneath Heaven was in such danger, such utter peril!* I wonder about that – was it really true?"

"No," replied Mencius. "Those are not the words of a noble-minded man. They're the words of a villager from eastern Ch'i. When Yao grew old, Shun helped him govern. The *Record of Yao* says:

> *After twenty-eight years, Yao passed away. The people mourned*
> *three years as if they'd lost their mother and father. And no music*
> *was heard anywhere within the four seas.*

And Confucius said: *The Heavens have not two suns, and the people have not two emperors.* If Shun had become the Son of Heaven and led the august lords of all beneath Heaven in their three years of mourning, there would have been two Sons of Heaven."

"Now I understand that Yao was never Shun's subject," said Hsien-chiu Meng. "But the *Songs* say:

> *Throughout all beneath Heaven*
> *everything is the emperor's land,*
> *and to the borders of this land*
> *everyone is the emperor's subject.*

And yet, after Shun became the Son of Heaven, how is it Blind Purblind wasn't his subject?"

"That isn't what this song is about. It's about people who neglect their parents because they're devoted to the concerns of an emperor's government, people who say: *Everything here is the emperor's concern, and am I alone capable of it?*

"Therefore, in speaking of a song, never let eloquence obscure words, and never let words obscure intent. Instead, let your thoughts inhabit the intention, then you'll understand. In the *Songs*, "The Star River" says:

> *Of those who survived in Chou,*
> *there won't be half a person left.*[3]

If you just look at the words and trust what they say, there wasn't a single person left among all the people of Chou.

"For a worthy child, there's nothing greater than honoring parents; and for honoring parents, there's nothing greater than nurturing them with all beneath Heaven. To be the Son of Heaven's father – that is an honor indeed. And to nurture him with all beneath Heaven – that is nurturing indeed. That's what the *Songs* mean when they say:

> *Devoted always to his parents' care,*
> *great exemplar of the devoted child*

And *The Book of History* says:

> *He went to see Blind Purblind full of respect, veneration, and*
> *awe. And Blind Purblind finally understood.*

That is to be *son to no father*."

5   **W**an Chang said: "Is it true that Yao gave all beneath Heaven to Shun?"

"No," replied Mencius. "The Son of Heaven cannot give all beneath Heaven to another."

"Then who gave all beneath Heaven to Shun?"

"Heaven gave it to him."

"If Heaven gave it to him, did it also school him in the details of its mandate?"

"No. Heaven never speaks: it reveals itself only through actions and events."

"How does it reveal itself through actions and events?"

"The Son of Heaven can recommend someone to Heaven," replied Mencius, "but cannot compel Heaven to give all beneath Heaven over to that person. The august lords can recommend someone to the Son of Heaven, but cannot compel him to give that person a title. Ministers can recommend someone to an august lord, but cannot compel him to appoint that person a minister. In ancient times Yao recommended Shun to Heaven, and Heaven accepted him. Yao presented Shun to the people, and the people accepted him. That's why I say Heaven never speaks: it reveals itself only through actions and events."

"Yao recommended Shun to Heaven, and Heaven accepted him," repeated Wan Chang. "And Yao presented Shun to the people, and the people accepted him. But how did all this take place?"

"When he put Shun in charge of the sacrifices, the spirits welcomed them. This is how Heaven accepted him. When he put Shun in charge of the nation's affairs, they were well ordered and the people were at peace. This is how the people accepted him. So Heaven gave it to him, and the people gave it to him. This is what I mean when I say the Son of Heaven cannot give all beneath Heaven to another.

"Shun assisted Yao for twenty-eight years. People aren't capable of such things: only Heaven could have done it. And after Yao died and the three years of mourning had ended, Shun left for lands south of South River in deference to Yao's son. Even still, when the august lords of all beneath Heaven wanted an audience at court – they went to Shun, not Yao's son. When people had lawsuits to settle – they they went to Shun, not Yao's son. When choruses sang ballads of praise – they sang of Shun, not Yao's son. This is what I mean when I say it was Heaven. For only after all this happened did Shun return to the Middle Kingdom and take his place as the Son of Heaven. If he'd just moved into Yao's palace and driven Yao's son out, it would have been usurping the throne rather than receiving it from Heaven. That's why Emperor Wu says, in "The Great Declaration":

> Heaven sees through the eyes of the people. Heaven hears through the ears of the people.

6   Wan Chang asked: "People say Integrity began crumbling when Yü allowed his son to succeed him rather than choose someone wise and worthy. Is that true?"

"No," replied Mencius. "That isn't how it works. If Heaven wants to give all beneath Heaven to someone wise and worthy, Heaven gives it to someone wise and worthy. If Heaven wants to give it to a son, Heaven gives it to a son.

"In ancient times, Shun recommended Yü to Heaven. He died seventeen years later, and when the three years of mourning ended, Yü left for Yang Ch'eng in deference to Shun's son. The people throughout all beneath Heaven followed him the way they followed Shun after Yao's death, rather than follow Yao's son. Yü recommended Yi to Heaven. He died seven years later, and when the three years of mourning ended, Yi left for the north slope of Ch'i Mountain in deference to Yü's son. But when people wanted an audience at court or they had a lawsuit to settle, they didn't go to Yi, they went to Yü's son Ch'i. And they said: *He's the son of our sovereign.* When choruses sang ballads of praise, they sang of Ch'i, not Yi. And they said: *He's the son of our sovereign.*

"Yao's son was depraved; so was Shun's. Meanwhile Shun was Yao's trusted assistant for many years, and Yü was Shun's, so their blessings had rained down on the people for a long time. Ch'i was wise and worthy, able to carry on Yü's Way and honor it. Meanwhile Yi was Yü's trusted assistant for only a few years, so his blessings hadn't rained down on the people for long. Yi was far from another Shun or Yü, and there was a great difference in how wise and worthy the emperor's sons were. Such circumstances are all acts of Heaven: people aren't capable of such things. When something's done, but no one does it, it's an act of Heaven. When something happens, but no one makes it happen, it's the Mandate of Heaven.

"For a common man to rule all beneath Heaven, he needs the Integrity of a Shun or Yü. But he also needs the Son of Heaven's recommendation. That's why Confucius never ruled all beneath Heaven. But if someone inherits all beneath Heaven, Heaven won't reject him unless he's a tyrant like Chieh or Chou. That's why Yi, Yi Yin and Duke Chou never ruled all beneath Heaven.

"Because Yi Yin was his trusted assistant, T'ang became emperor of all beneath Heaven. When T'ang died, T'ai Ting was no longer alive to succeed him. Wai Ping ruled for two years, and Chung Jen four. Then T'ai Chia⁴ overthrew the laws of T'ang, so Yi Yin banished him to T'ung. After three years, T'ai Chia began to regret his crimes. He reproached himself and changed. There in T'ung, he brought himself into Duty and dwelled in Humanity. After another three years, having taken Yi Yin's admonitions to heart, he returned to Po.

"Duke Chou never ruled all beneath Heaven in the Chou Dynasty, and it was for the same reason that Yi never ruled in the Hsia and Yi Yin never ruled in the Shang. Confucius said: *With Yao and Shun, succession was through abdication to their chosen successors. With the founders of the Hsia, Shang and Chou dynasties, succession was hereditary. But for all, the principle was the same.*"

7   Wan Chang asked: "People say Yi Yin's cooking was marvelous and that he used it to impress T'ang. Is that true?"

"No," replied Mencius. "That isn't what happened. Yi Yin was farming in the countryside at Yu Hsin, delighting in the Way of Yao and Shun. He ignored anything that violated Duty or the Way, even if offered all beneath Heaven. He wouldn't even glance at it for a thousand teams of horses. If something violated Duty or the Way, he wouldn't offer or accept the merest trifle for it.

"T'ang sent lavish gifts, inviting Yi Yin to be his counselor, but Yi Yin was so perfectly content that he said: *What would I do with T'ang's lavish gifts? Why should I stop dwelling in these fields, delighting in the Way of Yao and Shun?* Only after T'ang had sent three invitations did Yi Yin finally agree, saying: *I could go on dwelling in these fields, delighting in the Way of Yao and Shun, but wouldn't it be better to turn this sovereign into another Yao or Shun? Wouldn't it be better to turn our people into another* nation of Yao or Shun, to see this happen with my own eyes? Having brought this people into being, Heaven appointed the wise to awaken those who will be wise, appointed the awakened to awaken those who will be awakened. Of Heaven's people, I am one of the awakened, so I should use this Way to awaken the people. If I don't awaken them, who will?

"If there were any peasants in all beneath Heaven not enjoying the blessings of Yao and Shun, Yi Yin felt as if he himself had thrown them into a ditch. That's how deeply responsible he felt for all beneath Heaven. So he went to T'ang and counseled him to invade Hsia and rescue its people.

"I've never heard of straightening others by bending yourself, let alone straightening all beneath Heaven by disgracing yourself. Sages all have their own methods: some are recluses and some statesmen, some leave and some stay. But these methods all return to the same place: keeping yourself pure.

"I've heard that Yi Yin used the Way of Yao and Shun to earn T'ang's admiration, not that he used his marvelous cooking. In "The Councils of Yi," Yi Yin says:

> Heaven's vengeance sprang from depravity in the Hsia palace.
> Our role sprang from nobility in our Shang palace."

8   Wan Chang asked: "Some people say Confucius stayed with Yung Chü in Wei and the eunuch Chi Huan in Ch'i. Is that true?"

"No," replied Mencius. "That isn't what happened. Some busybody cooked that up. In Wei, Confucius stayed with Yen Ch'ou-yu. In fact, Lord Mi's wife and Adept Lu's wife were sisters, and Lord Mi said to Adept Lu: *If Confucius will stay at my home, I'll make him a minister here in Wei.* When Lu told him about this, Confucius said: *The Mandate of Heaven abides.* Confucius took office according to Ritual and renounced office according to Duty. Through both success and failure, he always said: *The Mandate of Heaven abides.* If he'd stayed with Yung Chü or Chi

Huan, he would have violated both Duty and the Mandate of Heaven.

"Confucius left Lu and Wei in disgust. Huan T'ui, the Minister of War in Sung, wanted to kill him, so he had to travel through Sung in disguise. Then, when he was in such trouble, he stayed with the pure Mayor Chen and advised Chou, Lord of Ch'en.

"I have heard you can judge resident counselors by who stays in their homes, and you can judge visiting counselors by whose home they stay in. If Confucius had stayed with Yung Chü or Chi Huan, how could he be Confucius?"

9   Wan Chang asked: "Some people say Po-li Hsi bartered himself to a Ch'in herdsman for five sheep skins and tended this man's cattle – all to impress Duke Mu of Ch'in. Is it true?"

"No," replied Mencius. "That isn't what happened. Some busybody cooked that up. Po-li Hsi was a native of Yü. Chin offered jade from Ch'ui Chi and horses from Ch'ü, trying to buy safe passage through Yü so its armies could attack Kuo. Kung Ch'i advised against it, and Po-li Hsi said nothing. He knew that giving the Duke of Yü such advice was futile, so he left for Ch'in. He was already seventy when that happened. If he didn't know by then that it was vile to try impressing Duke Mu by tending cattle, how could he be called wise?

"But he knew advice was futile and so didn't offer any – wouldn't you call that wise? He knew the Duke of Yü was about to be destroyed and left before it happened – wouldn't you call that wise? He was appointed to high office in Ch'in, saw Duke Mu was capable of great things and so assisted him – wouldn't you call that wise? And as prime minister, he made Mu a beacon to all beneath Heaven, worthy of guiding future generations – who but a sage is capable of such things? To sell yourself in order to realize your sovereign – no self-respecting villager would do that. So how could a sage do such a thing?"

Wan Chang   Book Two

1   Mencius said: "Po Yi wouldn't look at anything foul, and he wouldn't listen to anything foul. He never served a sovereign he disdained, and never governed a people he disdained. So he took office in times of wise rule, and he renounced office in times of chaos. He couldn't bear to live in a land where perverse government attracted perverse people, where living among villagers was like donning fine court robes to sit in mud and ash. So when the tyrant Chou came to power, Po Yi fled to the shores of the North Sea, where he awaited the return of purity to all beneath Heaven. That's why the greedy are cured of greed when they hear the legend of Po Yi, and the timid grow resolute.

"Yi Yin said:

> Any sovereign I serve is that much more worthy, and any people
> I serve is that much more worthy. So I take office in times of
> wise rule, and I take office in times of chaos. And he also said:
> Having brought this people into being, Heaven appointed the wise
> to awaken those who will be wise, appointed the awakened to
> awaken those who will be awakened. Of Heaven's people, I am one
> of the awakened, so I should use this Way to awaken the people.

If there were peasants anywhere in all beneath Heaven not enjoying the blessings of Yao and Shun, Yi Yin felt as if he himself had thrown them into a ditch. That's how deeply responsible he felt for all beneath Heaven.

"Liu-hsia Hui wasn't shamed by defiled rulers, nor did he consider common positions below him. When in office, he always depended on the Way and never hid his wisdom. When dismissed, he bore no resentment. And suffering adversity, he remained untroubled. Living among villagers, he was so content he couldn't bear to leave. He used to say: *You are you, and I am I. Even if you stripped naked and stood beside me, how could you ever tarnish me?* That's why small minds grow broad when they hear the legend of Liu-hsia Hui, and the niggardly grow generous.

"When Confucius left Ch'i, he simply emptied his rice steamer and set out. But when he left Lu, he said: *There's no hurry, no hurry at all.* That's the Way to leave your parents' country. If it was wise to hurry away, he hurried away; and if it was wise to linger, he lingered. If it was wise to stay somewhere, he stayed; and if it was wise to take office, he took office. That was Confucius."

Then Mencius continued: "Po Yi was a sage of purity, Yi Yin a sage of deep responsibility, Liu-hsia Hui a sage of complaisance – but Confucius was a sage who understood for all things their proper time. You could say he gathered the great perfections into a single orchestra – everything from resounding bells to rustling chimes of jade. Resounding bells begin a performance, and rustling jade ends it. To begin a performance – that is the task of knowledge. And to end a performance – that is the task of a sage's wisdom. A good analogy for knowledge might be skill, and a good analogy for a sage's wisdom might be strength. When you're shooting from beyond a hundred paces and your arrow reaches the target, that is strength. But if it hits the mark, that is something else again."

2   P o-kung Ch'i asked: "How did the system of position and endowment work in the Chou Dynasty?"

"No one knows exactly how it worked," replied Mencius. "The august lords thought the system was hurting them, so they destroyed all the records. Still, I once heard a summary:

"The Son of Heaven held one rank, dukes another, lords another, marquises another, earls and barons together another: that's five grades in all. The sovereign held one rank, ministers another, counselors another, high officials another, middle officials another, low officials another: that's six grades in all. The Son of Heaven controlled a thousand square miles, dukes and lords controlled a hundred square miles, marquises seventy square miles, earls and barons fifty square miles: that's four grades in all. Whoever controlled less than fifty square miles had no relations with the Son of Heaven. They were attached to the august lords and called *dependents*.

"The Son of Heaven's ministers were given the same amount of land as the august lords, his counselors the same as marquises, and his senior officials the same as earls and barons.

"There were a hundred square miles in a large nation, and its sovereign's endowment was ten times that of a minister. A minister's endowment was four times that of a counselor. A counselor's was double that of a high official, a high official's double that of a middle official, a middle official's double that of a low official, and a low official's equaled that of a commoner in government service, which was whatever he could have earned from farming.

"There were seventy square miles in a medium-sized nation, and its sovereign's endowment was ten times that of a minister. A minister's endowment was three times that of a counselor. A counselor's was double that of a high official, a high official's double that of a middle official, a middle official's double that of a low official, and a low official's equaled that of a commoner in government service, which was whatever he could have earned from farming.

"There were fifty square miles in a small nation, and its sovereign's endowment was ten times that of a minister. A minister's endowment was double that of a counselor. A counselor's was double that of a high official, a high official's double that of a middle official, a middle official's double that of a low official, and a low official's equaled that of a commoner in government service, which was whatever he could have earned from farming.

"As for the earnings of farmers: Each man had a hundred acres of land, and with that land an outstanding farmer could feed nine people and a superior farmer could feed eight, an average farmer could feed seven people, a fair farmer could feed six, and a poor farmer could feed five. In government service, the earnings of commoners was likewise calculated according to their different abilities."

3   W an Chang asked: *"May I ask about friendship?"*

"Don't try to intimidate with age or position or powerful relations," replied Mencius. "In making friends, befriend a person's Integrity. Friendship isn't about intimidation. Lord Meng Hsien led a house of a hundred war-chariots, and he had five friends: Yüeh-cheng Ch'iu, Mu Chung, and three others whom I forget. They were only his friends because they weren't of a noble house: if they had been, they wouldn't have been his friends.

"This is true not only for someone who leads a house of a hundred war-chariots, but also for the sovereign of a small nation. Duke Hui of Pi said: *I've made Master Szu my teacher and Yen Pan my friend. But Wang Shun and Ch'ang Hsi – they attend me.* And it's true not only for the sovereign of a small nation, but also for the sovereign of a large nation. Think about Duke P'ing of Chin and the scholar Hai T'ang: Duke P'ing came to visit when Hai T'ang said *come,* sat when he said *sit,* and ate when he said *eat.* Even if it was only vegetables and broth, he ate until he was full. He didn't dare refuse. But nothing more ever came of it: Duke P'ing never shared the position Heaven gave him, never shared the responsibility Heaven gave him to govern, and never shared the endowment Heaven gave him. That's how a scholar should honor the wise and worthy, but not how a duke or emperor should honor the wise and worthy.

"When Shun went to see Emperor Yao, Yao offered him the reserve palace and entertained him lavishly. Sometimes he was Shun's host, and sometimes his guest. This is an instance of the Son of Heaven truly befriending a commoner.

"To revere a superior – that is called exalting the exalted. To revere an inferior – that is called honoring the wise and worthy. Exalting the exalted, honoring the wise and worthy – in principle they are one and the same."

4   **W**an Chang asked: "In exchanging tokens of friendship, what is the proper frame of mind?"

"Reverence," replied Mencius.

"Why is it irreverent to refuse a gift?"

"If a superior presents you with a gift, it's irreverent to accept only after asking yourself *How did he come by this – was it honorable or dishonorable?* So you certainly shouldn't refuse such a gift."

"What if you refuse in thought rather than word – so even though you're thinking *To get this, he did such dishonorable things to the people,* you find some other excuse to decline the gift?"

"If he befriends you according to the Way and presents the gift according to Ritual, then even Confucius would accept the gift."

Wan Chang asked: "Suppose there was a bandit who robbed people outside the city gates. Would you accept his plunder as a gift just because he befriended you according to the Way and offered it to you according to Ritual?"

"No, of course not," replied Mencius. "In the 'Commission of K'ang,' Duke Chou says: *Everyone despises a person who murders and robs without any fear of death.* Such people are fit only for punishment: trying to reform them is pointless. This practice was handed down from the Hsia to the Shang, and from the Shang to the Chou. So by now, there should be no reason to make excuses. No, how can anyone accept a gift of plunder?"

"These days, the august lords extract wealth from the people just like thieving bandits," said Wan Chang. "Suppose they lend their gifts the virtue of Ritual occasion and the noble-minded accept: what would you say of that?"

"Do you imagine that these august lords would be punished if a true emperor appeared?" replied Mencius. "Do you imagine he would try to reform them, and then punish them when they don't change? To call anyone who takes something that isn't theirs a thief – that's pushing righteousness too far. When Confucius took office in Lu, people there fought over the kill after a sacrificial hunt, so Confucius did too. If there's nothing wrong with fighting over the kill, what could be wrong with accepting a gift?"

"He was like that?" said Wan Chang. "So he didn't take office to serve the Way?"

"He served the Way."

"If he served the Way, why did he fight over the kill?"

"Confucius tried to begin by rectifying the proper use of sacrificial vessels, and so put an end to loading them with such exotic foods."

"Why didn't he just leave?"

"He wanted to make a proposal that would indicate his method. His proposal was entirely practical, so when it wasn't put into practice he left. That's why he never served any sovereign for even three years. Confucius served when he thought his proposals would be put into practice, when he was invited earnestly, or when a duke offered to support him. Confucius served Lord Chi Huan because he thought his proposals would be put into practice, served Duke Ling of Wei because he was invited earnestly, and served Duke Hsiao of Wei because the duke offered to support him."

5   Mencius said: "You don't take office just to escape poverty, though there are times that is reason enough. And you don't marry a wife just for the sustenance, though there are times that too is reason enough. When escaping poverty, decline high positions and wealth in favor of common positions and poverty. What positions are fitting for those who would decline high positions and wealth in favor of common positions and poverty? Gatekeeper or night watchman.

"When Confucius was the officer in charge of grain warehouses, he said: *I keep accurate records, that's all.* And when he was in charge of flocks and fields, he said: *I make sure the cattle and sheep grow strong, that's all.* To hold a common position and spout lofty words – that is a crime. And to represent the people in their sovereign's court without putting the Way into practice – that is a disgrace."

6   W̲an Chang said: "Why would a scholar refuse to be under an august lord's protectorate?"

"It would be too presumptuous," replied Mencius. "According to the rites, an august lord lives within another august lord's protectorate only after he has lost his nation. So for a scholar to live within an august lord's protectorate would violate Ritual."

"But if a sovereign presents him with grain, should he accept it?"

"Yes."

"How can it be right to accept?"

"The sovereign always provides for his people."

"If he's providing for you, you accept. But if he's offering you a gift, you refuse. How can that be?"

"It would be too presumptuous."

"Why isn't the other presumptuous?"

"When gatekeepers and night watchmen do their jobs, they're earning a salary. When they don't do their jobs, they're accepting gifts. And that is irreverent."

"Say a sovereign sends provisions and they are accepted," said Wan Chang. "Why shouldn't such gifts continue?"

"Duke Mu asked after Master Szu often, and often presented him with sacrificial meat. But Master Szu was insulted. He hustled the duke's envoy out the gate, made two deep bows facing north, then refused the duke's gifts, saying: *I can see this sovereign wants to tend me the way he tends his dogs and horses.* Perhaps that's when envoys stopped coming with gifts. And how could anyone say that a ruler is pleased with someone wise and worthy if he doesn't appoint him to high office or even support him?"

"What must a nation's sovereign do if he wants to earn a reputation for supporting the noble-minded," asked Wan Chang.

"The sovereign should send something first with his greetings," replied Mencius, "and it should be accepted with two deep bows. But from then on, the granaries and kitchens should send grain and meat without any mention of the sovereign. Being expected to break his back bowing over and over for a little sacrificial meat – that's what bothered Master Szu. He didn't think that was how you supported the noble-minded Way.

"Remember Yao's treatment of Shun? Yao sent his nine sons to serve him, gave his two daughters in marriage to him. He sent his hundred officials, cattle, sheep, provisions in plenty – all to support him as he worked the fields. Then he appointed him to the most exalted position. That's what I'm thinking about when I speak of *how a duke or emperor should honor the wise and worthy*."

7   W an Chang said: "How can it be right to refuse a meeting with an august lord?"

"Scholars in the city are called *ministers of market and well*," replied Mencius, "and scholars in the country are called *ministers of forest and field*. But both are deemed commoners, and according to Ritual a commoner doesn't presume to meet with an august lord until he has presented his token of credentials and been appointed to office."

"When a commoner is summoned to war, he goes to war. So when the sovereign wants to see a scholar and summons him to a meeting, how can he refuse to go?"

"Going to war is proper. Going to such a meeting is not. And why does the sovereign want to see him anyway?"

"Because he's so renowned, so wise and worthy."

"If it's because he's so renowned – the Son of Heaven wouldn't presume to summon his teacher, so how could an august lord? If it's because he's so wise and worthy – I've never heard of summoning someone wise and worthy whenever you want to see him.

"Duke Mu went to see Master Szu often. Once he asked: *In an ancient nation of a thousand war-chariots, how would the sovereign befriend a scholar?* Master Szu was insulted and said: *The ancients had a saying: 'Don't talk about making him your friend, just attend him.'* Being insulted, Szu was blunt: *In terms of position – you are the sovereign and I the subject, so how could I presume to be your friend? In terms of Integrity – you should be attending me, so how could you be my friend?* If that ruler of a thousand war-chariots couldn't even make a scholar his friend, how could he hope to summon such a man?

"Once when he was out hunting, Duke Ching of Ch'i summoned his gamekeeper with a plume-crested flag. The gamekeeper didn't come, so the duke wanted to have him executed, but Confucius said: *A man of great resolve never forgets that he could be abandoned to ditches and gutters, and a man of great valor never forgets that he could lose his head.* The gamekeeper wasn't entitled to such a lofty summons, so he didn't answer it – that's what Confucius admired."

"How should gamekeepers be summoned?" asked Wan Chang.

"With leather caps," replied Mencius. "Commoners should be summoned with plain banners on bent-top staffs, scholars with dragon banners, and high ministers with plume-crested flags. When the gamekeeper was summoned with the summons due a high minister, he preferred death to the presumption of answering. If a commoner is summoned with the summons due a scholar, how could he presume to answer? And that's nothing like a wise and worthy man being summoned with a summons due the unwise and unworthy.

"Wanting to see such a man while not abiding by the Way – that's like inviting someone in while closing the gate. Duty is the road, and Ritual the gate. Only the noble-minded can follow this road, going in and out the gate with ease. The *Songs* say:

> Chou's Way is whetstone smooth,
> and it's straight as an arrow:

the noble-minded travel upon it;
the small-minded gaze upon it."

"When summoned by the sovereign," said Wan Chang, "Confucius didn't wait for a carriage to set out. Does that mean Confucius did wrong?"

"Confucius had taken office and so had responsibilities," replied Mencius. "And he was called with the summons due his position."

8   Speaking to Wan Chang, Mencius said: "Noble scholars in one village befriend noble scholars in another village. Noble scholars in one country befriend noble scholars in another country. Noble scholars throughout all beneath Heaven befriend noble scholars throughout all beneath Heaven. And when the friendship of noble scholars throughout all beneath Heaven isn't enough, we can also rise to converse with the lofty ancients. How can we fail to know them utterly by chanting their poems and reading their words? And we also converse with their age that way. That is lofty friendship."

9   Emperor Hsüan of Ch'i asked about ministers, and Mencius said: "What kind of minister are you asking about?"

"Is there more than one kind?" asked the emperor.

"Yes," replied Mencius. "There are ministers from royal families and there are ministers from common families."

"May I ask about ministers from royal families?"

"If the sovereign is making grave mistakes, they admonish him. If they have to admonish him over and over, and he still refuses to listen – they replace him."

The emperor blanched at this, so Mencius continued: "Why so surprised? You asked, and I wouldn't dare be less than honest and forthright with you."

After he'd recovered his color, the emperor asked about ministers from common families, and Mencius said: "If the sovereign is making mistakes, they admonish him. If they have to admonish him over and over, and he still refuses to listen – they resign and leave his country behind."

XI

Master Kao Book One

1   Master Kao said: "The nature of things is like willow wood, and Duty is like cups and bowls. Shaping human nature into Humanity and Duty is like shaping willow wood into cups and bowls."

"Do you follow the nature of willow wood to shape cups and bowls," replied Mencius, "or do you maul it? If you maul willow wood to make cups and bowls, then I guess you maul human nature to make Humanity and Duty. It's talk like yours that will lead people to ravage Humanity and Duty throughout all beneath Heaven."

2   Master Kao said: "The nature of things is like swirling water: channel it east and it flows east, channel it west and it flows west. And human nature too is like water: it doesn't choose between good and evil any more than water chooses between east and west."

"It's true that water doesn't choose between east and west," replied Mencius, "but doesn't it choose between high and low? Human nature is inherently good, just like water flows inherently downhill. There's no such thing as a person who isn't good, just as there's no water that doesn't flow downhill.

"Think about water: if you slap it, you can make it jump over your head; and if you push and shove, you can make it stay on a mountain. But what does this have to do with the nature of water? It's only responding to the forces around it. It's like that for people too: you can make them evil, but that says nothing about human nature."

3   Master Kao said: *"The nature of things means that which is inborn."*

"The nature of things means *that which is inborn,"* repeated Mencius. "Just like *white* means *that which is white?"*

"Yes."

"So is the whiteness of a white feather the same as the whiteness of white snow? And is the whiteness of white snow the same as the whiteness of white jade?"

"Yes."

"Then is the nature of a dog the same as the nature of an ox? And is the nature of an ox the same as the nature of a human?"

4   Master Kao said: "Hunger for food and sex – that is nature. Then there's Humanity, which is internal not external; and Duty, which is external not internal."

"Why do you say Humanity is internal and Duty is external?" asked Mencius.

"Suppose there was an elder and I treated him with the honor due an elder," replied Master Kao, "it isn't because the honor due elders is somehow within me. It's like seeing something white as white: the whiteness is outside us. That's why I call Duty external."

"The whiteness of a white horse is no different from the whiteness of a white-haired person," said Mencius. "But doesn't the elderliness of an elderly horse mean something quite different to us than the elderliness of an elderly person? And which are you equating with Duty – the elder or the one who treats him with the honor due an elder?"

"I love my own brother, but not the brother of someone in Ch'in," said Master Kao, "so the reason lies within me, which is why I call Humanity internal. But I treat elders as elders, whether they're from Ch'u or my own family: so the reason lies within elderliness, which is why I call Duty external."

"But my enjoyment of roast meat is the same," countered Mencius, "whether I cooked it or someone from Ch'in cooked it. And it's like this for many things. So does that mean the enjoyment of roast meat is external?"

5   Adept Meng Chi asked Adept Kung-tu: "Why do you say Duty is internal?"

"I call it internal," replied Kung-tu, "because it's our reverence put into action."

"If someone in your village is a year older than your eldest brother, which do you revere?"

"My brother."

"In pouring wine, which do you serve first?"

"The village elder."

"First you treat this one with reverence, then you treat that one with the honor due an elder. So Duty derives from the external, not the internal."

Adept Kung-tu had no answer to this. Later, when he told Mencius what had happened, Mencius said: "Ask him which he reveres most, an uncle or a younger brother, and he'll say *An uncle*. Ask him which he reveres most, an uncle or a younger brother who's posing as the ancestral dead at a sacrifice, and he'll say *A younger brother*. Then ask what happened to his reverence for the uncle, and he'll say *It's because of the younger brother's position*. Then you can say: *If reverence is a matter of position, lasting reverence belongs to my elder brother, while fleeting reverence belongs to the village elder*."

When Adept Meng Chi heard this, he said: "I treat an uncle with reverence as reverence is due him, and I treat a younger brother with reverence as reverence is due him. So Duty derives from the external, not the internal."

"In winter we drink broth," commented Adept Kung-tu, "and in summer we drink water. Does that mean drinking and eating derive from the external?"

6   Adept Kung-tu said: "Master Kao says: *Human nature isn't good, and it isn't evil*. There are others who say: *Human nature can be made good, and it can be made evil*. That's why the people loved goodness

when Wen and Wu ruled, and they loved cruelty when Yu and Li ruled. And there are still others who say: *Human nature is inborn: some people are good and some evil. That's why a Hsiang could have Yao as his ruler, a Shun could have Blind Purblind as his father, a Lord Ch'i of Wei and Prince Pi Kan could have the tyrant Chou as their nephew and sovereign.*

"But you say: *Human nature is good.* Does that mean all the others are wrong?"

"We are, by constitution, capable of being good," replied Mencius. "That's what I mean by good. If someone's evil, it can't be blamed on inborn capacities. We all have a heart of compassion and a heart of conscience, a heart of reverence and a heart of right and wrong. In a heart of compassion is Humanity, and in a heart of conscience is Duty. In a heart of reverence is Ritual, and in a heart of right and wrong is wisdom. Humanity, Duty, Ritual, wisdom – these are not external things we meld into us. They're part of us from the beginning, though we may not realize it. Hence the saying: *What you seek you will find, and what you ignore you will lose.* Some make more of themselves than others, maybe two or five or countless times more. But that's only because some people fail to realize their inborn capacities.

"The *Songs* say:

> Heaven gave birth to humankind,
> and whatever is has its own laws:
> cleaving to what makes us human,
> people delight in stately Integrity.

Of this, Confucius said: *Whoever wrote this song knew the Way well.* So whatever is must have its own laws, and whenever they cleave to what makes us human, the people must delight in stately Integrity."

7   Mencius said: "In good years, young men are mostly fine. In bad years, they're mostly cruel and violent. It isn't that Heaven

endows them with such different capacities, only that their hearts are mired in such different situations. Think about barley: if you plant the seeds carefully at the same time and in same place, they'll all sprout and grow ripe by summer solstice. If they don't grow the same – it's because of inequities in richness of soil, amounts of rainfall, or the care given them by farmers. And so, all members belonging to a given species of thing are the same. Why should humans be the lone exception? The sage and I – surely we belong to the same species of thing.

"That's why Master Lung said: *Even if a cobbler makes a pair of sandals for feet he's never seen, he certainly won't make a pair of baskets.* Sandals are all alike because feet are the same throughout all beneath Heaven. And all tongues savor the same flavors. Yi Ya was just the first to discover what our tongues savor. If taste differed by nature from person to person, the way horses and dogs differ by species from me, then how is it people throughout all beneath Heaven savor the tastes Yi Ya savored? People throughout all beneath Heaven share Yi Ya's tastes, therefore people's tongues are alike throughout all beneath Heaven.

"It's true for the ear too: people throughout all beneath Heaven share Maestro K'uang's sense of music, therefore people's ears are alike thoughout all beneath Heaven. And it's no less true for the eye: no one throughout all beneath Heaven could fail to see the beauty of Lord Tu. If you can't see his beauty, you simply haven't eyes.

"Hence it is said: *All tongues savor the same flavors, all ears hear the same music, and all eyes see the same beauty.* Why should the heart alone not be alike in us all? But what is it about our hearts that is alike? Isn't it what we call reason and Duty? The sage is just the first to discover what is common to our hearts. Hence, reason and Duty please our hearts just like meat pleases our tongues."

8   Mencius said: "The forests were once lovely on Ox Mountain. But as they were near a great city, axes cleared them little by little. Now there's nothing left of their beauty. They rest day and night,

rain and dew falling in plenty, and there's no lack of fresh sprouts. But people graze oxen and sheep there, so the mountain's stripped bare. When people see how bare it is, they think that's all the potential it has. But does that mean this is the nature of Ox Mountain?

"Without the heart of Humanity and Duty alive in us, how can we be human? When we abandon this noble heart, it's like cutting those forests: a few axe blows each day, and pretty soon there's nothing left. Then you can rest day and night, take in the clarity of morning's healing *ch'i* – but the values that make you human keep thinning away. All day long, you're tangled in your life. If these tangles keep up day after day, even the clarity of night's healing *ch'i* isn't enough to preserve you. And if the clarity of night's healing *ch'i* isn't enough to preserve you, you aren't much different from an animal. When people see you're like an animal, they think that's all the potential you have. But does that mean this is the human constitution?

"With proper sustenance, anything will grow; and without proper sustenance, anything will fade away. Confucius said: *Embrace it and it endures. Forsake it and it dies. It comes and goes without warning, and no one knows its route.* He was speaking of the heart."

9   Mencius said: "Don't make the mistake of thinking the emperor lacks intelligence. Even the most vigorous plant in all beneath Heaven cannot grow if given sun for a day then left to freeze for ten. I very rarely see the emperor, and as soon as I leave, a crowd shows up to freeze him some more. So even if a new sprout appeared, what could I do?

"*Go* is surely a minor art, but if you don't give it your single-minded devotion you'll never master it. GoAutumnal is the finest player in all the land. But suppose he tries to teach the game to two people. One listens intently, studying with single-minded devotion. The other listens, but he's dreaming of swans in flight, the heft of bow and tethered arrow, the shot. Although he studies beside the first, he'll never be anywhere near as good. Is that because he's less intelligent? Not at all."

10   Mencius said: "I want fish, and I also want bear paws. If I can't have both, I'll give up fish and take bear paws. I want life, and I also want Duty. If I can't have both, I'll give up life and take Duty. I want life – but there's something I want more than life, so I won't do something wrong just to stay alive. I loathe death – but there's something I loathe more than death, so there are disasters I won't avoid.

"If you want nothing more than life, you'll do anything to stay alive. If you loathe nothing more than death, then you'll do anything to avoid disasters. But there are things people won't do to stay alive, and there are things people won't do to avoid disasters. So there must be something we want more than life, and something we loathe more than death. And it isn't something that only a sage's heart possesses: everyone has it. It's just that a sage never loses it.

"A basket of rice, a bowl of soup: to take them means life, to leave them means death. If they're offered with threats and abuse, a wayfarer won't accept them. If they're trampled on, even a beggar won't bother with them. But people accept ten thousand measures of grain as salary without even asking if they're violating Ritual or Duty. What could ten thousand measures of grain mean to me? A beautiful house? The esteem of wife and mistress? The gratitude of friends in need? If I refused to accept something even to save my life, am I now to accept it for a beautiful house, for the esteem of wife and mistress, for the gratitude of friends in need? Can't these people stop themselves? They're throwing away their original heart. There's no other way to describe it."

11   Mencius said: "Humanity is the heart, and Duty the road. To stop following the road and abandon it, to let the heart wander away and not know enough to search for it – what a sad sad thing. When chickens or dogs wander away, people know enough to search for them, but when their heart wanders away they don't. The Way of learning is nothing other than this: searching for the heart that's wandered away."

12   Mencius said: "Suppose your fourth finger were gnarled and crooked, though not lame or painful. If there was someone who could straighten it, you'd think nothing of traveling all the way from Ch'in to Ch'u. That's because your finger isn't as good as other people's fingers.

"When your finger isn't as good as other people's fingers, you know enough to resent it. But when your heart isn't as good, you don't know enough to resent it. That's what I call *not knowing what is what.*"

13   Mencius said: "Consider a young tree, an *wu-t'ung* or *tzu:* anyone who wants to keep it alive knows how to nurture it. Meanwhile they don't know how to nurture themselves. How can they love a tree more than themselves? This is thoughtlessness at its worst."

14   Mencius said: "People love all aspects of themselves equally. Loving them all equally, people nurture them all equally. When there isn't an inch of their flesh that they don't love, there isn't an inch they don't nurture. There's only one way to know if people are good or evil: look at the choices they make. We each contain precious and worthless, great and small. Never injure the great for the sake of the small, or the precious for the sake of the worthless. Small people nurture what is small in them; great people nurture what is great in them.

"Consider a gardener who nurtures the scraggly sour-plum and date-bramble, but neglects the magnificent *wu-t'ung* and *chia* – that's a worthless gardener indeed. If you neglect shoulder and back to nurture a finger, and don't even realize what you're doing, you're nothing but a reckless wolf. And if you're obsessed with food and drink, you'll be scorned as worthless because you're nurturing the small and neglecting the great. Even if you neglect nothing else in your obsession with food and drink, you've let your mouth and belly become so much more than just another inch of flesh."

15   Adept Kung-tu asked: "If we're all equally human, how is it some are great and some small?"

"Great people abide by what is great in them;" replied Mencius, "small people abide by what is small in them."

"If we're all equally human, how is it some abide by what is great in them and some abide by what is small in them?"

"The senses cannot think, and so ear and eye are easily deceived by things. And things interact together, which only makes it worse. It is the heart which thinks, and so understands. Without thought there is no understanding. Heaven has given us these two things: heart and senses. If you insist from the beginning on what is great in you, what is small cannot steal it away. This is what makes a person great without fail."

16   Mencius said: "There is the nobility of Heaven on the one hand, and human nobility on the other. Humanity, Duty, loyalty, sincerity, tireless delight in the virtuous – such is the nobility of Heaven. Duke, counselor, minister – such is human nobility.

"The ancients cultivated the nobility of Heaven, and human nobility followed naturally. Today people cultivate the nobility of Heaven only out of desire for human nobility. And once they win human nobility, they abandon the nobility of Heaven. This is delusion at its worst, and such people come to nothing but ruin in the end. "

17   Mencius said: "The heart we all share longs to be exalted. But the exalted is already there in us, though we may not realize it. What people exalt is not the truly exalted. What some mighty lord exalts today, he may scorn as worthless tomorrow.

"The *Songs* say

> *we've drunk deep your wine*
> *and feasted on your Integrity,*

meaning that if you feast on Humanity and Duty, you don't long for the lavish flavors of sumptuous meat and millet. And if you're renowned far and wide, you don't long for robes of elegant embroidery."

18   Mencius said: "Humanity overcomes Inhumanity the way water overcomes fire. But when people wield Humanity these days, it's like they're throwing a cup of water on a cartload of burning firewood. When the fire keeps burning, they claim water can't overcome fire. This is the promotion of Inhumanity at its worst, and such people come to nothing but ruin in the end."

19   Mencius said: "The five grains are the finest of all plants. But if they don't ripen, they aren't even as good as wild rice-grass. For Humanity too – the essential thing is that it ripens well."

20   Mencius said: "Yi always shot from a full draw when teaching archery, and his students also shot from a full draw. A master carpenter always uses a compass and square when he teaches, and his students also use a compass and square."

XII

1   Someone from Jen asked Adept Wu-lu: "Which is most important, Ritual or food?"

"Ritual," replied Wu-lu.

"Which is most important, Ritual or sex?

"Ritual"

"What if using food for the Ritual sacrifice meant starving to death, and not using it meant having something to eat – would you insist on using it for the sacrifice? And what if observing the Ritual of claiming the bride in her home meant not marrying, and not observing it meant marrying – would you insist on claiming your bride?"

Adept Wu-lu had no answer. The next day he went to Chou and told Mencius what had happened. Mencius said: "It's easy. If you compare the tops without checking the bottoms, you can make an inch-long twig taller than a lofty tower. And if you say gold is heavier than feathers, you certainly aren't comparing a wisp of gold to a cartload of feathers. It's pointless to compare food and Ritual at a moment when food is vital and Ritual isn't: you can make lots of things seem more important that way, not just food. And it's pointless to compare sex and Ritual at a moment when sex is vital and Ritual isn't: you can make lots of things seem more important that way, not just sex.

"Go say this to him: *Suppose the only way you could get food was by twisting your brother's arm behind his back and stealing his food. Would you do it? And suppose the only way you could get a wife was by climbing over your east wall and dragging off the neighbor's daughter. Would you do that?*"

2   Lord Chiao of Ts'ao asked: "Is it true anyone can be a Yao or Shun?"

"Yes," replied Mencius.

"I've heard that Emperor Wen was ten feet tall," said Chiao, "and T'ang was nine feet tall. I'm nine feet four inches, but I have nothing but grain to eat. What shall I do?"

"Isn't it easy?" said Mencius. "Just act like Yao and Shun. If you can't lift a baby chicken, you are weak indeed. If you can lift three thousand pounds, you are strong indeed. And if you can lift as much as Wu Huo,[1] you're an Wu Huo. Why do people agonize over what they cannot do? They simply aren't trying.

"If you follow your elders, walking with dignity and respect, you can be called a younger brother. If you hurry ahead of your elders, you cannot be called a younger brother. How can anyone say they haven't the capacity to walk slowly behind? They just aren't trying. The Way of Yao and Shun is simple: act with the respect proper to a son and younger brother. If you dress the way Yao dressed, speak the way Yao spoke, and act the way Yao acted – then you're a Yao. And if you dress the way Shun dressed, speak the way Shun spoke, and act the way Shun acted – then you're a Shun. It's that simple."

"The Chou sovereign would listen to me and give me a place to live," said Chiao, "but I want to stay here, receiving your beautiful teachings with the other disciples."

"The Way is like a great highway," replied Mencius. "It's easy to find. People just don't bother to look. Go back to your home. Look for it there, and you'll find teachers aplenty."

3   Kung-sun Ch'ou said: "Master Kao claims 'Tiny Wingbeats' is the poem of a little person."

"Why did he say that?" asked Mencius.

"Because it's so full of resentment."

"Old Kao was awfully dogmatic about the *Songs*," said Mencius. "Suppose a man from Yüeh drew his bow and shot someone: I might tell the story with a smile because the man's a stranger to me. But suppose my brother drew his bow and shot someone: then I'd be in tears when I told the story because he's my own flesh and blood. The resentment of 'Tiny Wingbeats' comes from the close bonds of family, for those bonds are themselves Humanity. Old Kao was impossibly dogmatic about the *Songs*."

"Why is there no resentment in 'Gentle Wind'?"

"In 'Gentle Wind' the parent's fault is slight, but in 'Tiny Wingbeats' the parent's fault is great. If you don't resent a parent's fault when it's serious, you're treating parents like strangers. And if you resent a parent's fault when it's slight, you're treating parents with abandon. Treating them like strangers, treating them with abandon – either is no way for a child to honor parents. Confucius said:

> *Shun was masterful in honoring his parents: at fifty, he was still longing for them."*

4   **S**ung K'eng was traveling to Ch'u. Meeting him at Chih Ch'iu, Mencius said: "Where are you going?"

"I've heard that war has broken out between Ch'u and Ch'in," replied Sung K'eng, "so I'm going to see the Ch'u emperor. I'll try to convince him to end the fighting. If I can't convince him, I'll go see the Ch'in emperor. I hope one of them will listen."

"I won't ask about the details, if you don't mind," said Mencius, "but I would like to ask about the essence of your plan, and how you intend to convince these emperors to act on it."

"I'll show them how there's no profit in it."

"Your intent is noble, but your appeal misguided. If you talk to these emperors about profit, and in their love of profit they stop their armies – their armies will rejoice in peace and delight in profit. Soon ministers will embrace profit in serving their sovereign, sons will embrace profit in serving their fathers, younger brothers will embrace profit in serving their elder brothers – and all of them will have abandoned Humanity and Duty. When these relationships become a matter of profit, the nation is doomed to ruin.

"But if you talk to these emperors about Humanity and Duty, and in their love of Humanity and Duty they stop their armies – their armies will rejoice in peace and delight in Humanity and Duty. Soon ministers will embrace Humanity and Duty in serving their sovereign, sons will embrace Humanity and Duty in serving their fathers, younger brothers will embrace Humanity and Duty in serving their elder brothers – and all of them will have abandoned profit. When these relationships become a matter of Humanity and Duty, then the sovereign is sure to be a true emperor. So why mention profit?"

5   When Mencius was living in Chou, Chi Jen was the governor of Jen. As a token of friendship and respect, he sent Mencius a gift. Mencius accepted it, but without any show of gratitude. When Mencius was living in P'ing Lu, Lord Ch'u was the prime minister in Ch'i. As a token of friendship and respect, he too sent Mencius a gift. Mencius accepted it, but again without any show of gratitude.

Later, when he traveled from Chou to Jen, Mencius went to visit Lord Chi Jen. But when he traveled from P'ing Lu to Ch'i, he didn't visit Lord Ch'u. Adept Wu-lu was overjoyed at this, and said: "Now I see!"

"You visited Lord Chi Jen when you went to Jen," he said to Mencius, "but you didn't visit Lord Ch'u when you went to Ch'i. Is this because Lord Ch'u is a prime minister?"

"No," replied Mencius. *"The Book of History* says:

> *The gift is in the giving. If the giving isn't equal to the gift, it's like no gift at all, for the gift isn't invested with your good will.*

That is, it isn't a true gift at all."

Adept Wu-lu was delighted at this. When someone asked why, he said: "Lord Chi Jen couldn't leave his responsibilities and go to Chou, but Lord Ch'u could have gone to P'ing Lu."

6   Ch'un-yü K'un said: "If you consider fame and achievement primary, you serve the people. If you consider fame and achievement secondary, you serve yourself. You were one of the three high ministers, but you left before your fame and achievement had spread to sovereign and people. Is that really how the Humane act?"

"Po Yi lived in a humble position," said Mencius, "and refused to put his wisdom in the service of an unworthy ruler. Yi Yin approached both the noble T'ang and the tyrant Chieh five times. And Liu Hsia-hui didn't despise defiled rulers and didn't reject common positions. Each of these masters had his own Way, but they all shared the same goal."

"What was it?"

"Humanity. The noble-minded are Humane, so why must they share anything else?"

"Lord Kung-yi was prime minister in Duke Mu's time, Master Liu and Master Szu were counselors – but Lu lost territory faster than ever. Does this mean the wise and worthy can do nothing for a country?"

"When the nation of Yü ignored Po-li Hsi," replied Mencius, "it perished. When Duke Mu employed him well in Ch'in, the duke became the finest of august lords. Whenever countries ignore the wise and worthy, they don't just lose a little territory: they perish entirely."

"In ancient times," said Ch'un-yü K'un, "when Wang Pao settled at the Ch'i River, people west of the Yellow River became eloquent carolers. When Mien Chü settled in Kao T'ang, people in Ch'i's right-hand regions became eloquent singers. And the wives of Hua Chou and Ch'i Liang wept so eloquently for their husbands that they transformed the country's mourning traditions.

"What lies within reveals itself without. No one's ever been devoted to a purpose and had no achievements for the world to see. So there cannot be anyone wise and worthy among us: if there were, I would know of them."

"When Confucius was justice minister in Lu," said Mencius, "he was ignored. He took part in the sacrifices, but received no sacrificial meat, so he left Lu without even taking off his ceremonial cap. Those who didn't understand him thought he left because of the meat. But those who did understand him knew it was because Lu was violating Ritual. Confucius preferred to leave over a slight offense rather than wait for a grievous wrong. Commoners never understand the ways of the noble-minded."

7   Mencius said: "The five chiefs of the august lords were offenders against the three emperors. The august lords of today are offenders against the five chiefs. And the high ministers of today are offenders against our august lords.

"When the Son of Heaven visited the august lords, it was called an Inspection Tour. And when the august lords went to the Son of Heaven's court, it was called a Duty Report. In spring, the purpose was to inspect the planting and provide whatever the farmers lacked. And in autumn, it was to inspect the harvest and help whoever didn't bring in enough. An august lord was rewarded with more territory if the Son of Heaven came to his domain and found the land opened up and the fields culti-vated well, the old nurtured, the wise and worthy honored, and the dis-tinguished serving in office. An august lord was reprimanded if the Son of Heaven came and found the land overgrown, the old abandoned, the wise and worthy neglected, and oppressors serving in office. The first time an august lord failed to appear at court, his rank was reduced. The second time, his territory was reduced. And if he failed to appear a third time, the Son of Heaven's armies removed him from power. Hence the Son of Heaven disciplined but never attacked. The august lords, on the other hand, attacked but never disciplined. Indeed, the five chiefs of the august lords often coerced august lords into attacking other august lords. That's why I say: *The five chiefs of the august lords were offenders against the three emperors.*

Duke Huan was the most illustrious of the five chiefs. When he called the august lords together at K'uei Ch'iu, they bound a sacrificial animal and recorded their covenant, but they didn't trace their mouths with blood to consummate the covenant. Their first article stated: *Children who don't honor their parents shall be punished. Descendants shall not be set aside. Mistresses shall not be given the status of wives.* The second article stated: *Let Integrity shine forth by honoring the wise and nurturing the talented.* The third article stated: *Show reverence for elders, gentleness for children, and never forget the traveler and guest.* The fourth article stated: *Let no one hold office by hereditary privilege, and let no one hold more than one office at a time. In selecting officials, select only the most qualified. No ruler shall have sole authority to execute a high minister.* The fifth article stated: *Let no one build threatening earthworks. Let no one ban the sale of grain. And let no one confer land and title without the proper announcements.* The agreement also stated: *All who are united in this covenant shall hereafter live in harmony.* The august lords of today all violate these five precepts. That's why I say: *The august lords of today are offenders against the five chiefs.*

"Encouraging a sovereign's evil is nothing compared to the high crime of collusion in a sovereign's evil. The high ministers of today are all colluding in their sovereign's evil. That's why I say: *The high ministers of today are offenders against our august lords.*"

8   When the Lu sovereign wanted to make Lord Shen commander of his armies, Mencius said: "Sending the people to war without training – that is called ravaging the people. In the time of Yao and Shun, there was no toleration for a person who ravaged the people. It would be wrong even if Ch'i could be defeated and Nan-yang reclaimed, all in a single battle."

Lord Shen's face darkened, and he said: "I don't understand this at all."

"Let me explain it to you clearly," responded Mencius. "The Son of Heaven's territory covers a thousand square miles. If it's any less than a thousand square miles, he doesn't have enough to provide hospitality for the august lords. An august lord's territory covers a hundred square miles. If it's any less than a hundred square miles, he doesn't have enough to keep the canons of the ancestral temple.

"When Duke Chou was given Lu to rule, he had a hundred square miles. Still, it was plenty because he used it wisely. When Duke T'ai was given Ch'i to rule, he too had a hundred square miles. Again, it was plenty because he used it wisely. Today, Lu is five times a hundred square miles. If a true emperor arose, do you think Lu is one of those states he would pare down or one he would enlarge? A Humane person wouldn't even take what belongs to one state and give it to another, let alone kill people in his pursuit of land. The noble-minded address fundamentals when they serve a sovereign: they make the Way his guide and Humanity his resolve."

9   Mencius said: "In serving their sovereign, people these days all say: *I'm expanding his territory and filling his treasury.* But what the world now calls a distinguished minister, the ancients called a plunderer of the people. To enrich a sovereign when he doesn't make the Way his purpose and Humanity his resolve – that is to enrich another tyrant Chieh.

"They say: *I'm forming alliances and winning wars for him.* But what the world now calls a distinguished minister, the ancients called a plunderer of the people. To strengthen a sovereign for war when he doesn't make the Way his purpose and Humanity his resolve – that is to empower another tyrant Chieh.

"When you abide by the Way of our times, leaving the practices of this world unchanged, then even if you're given all beneath Heaven, you won't keep it for a single morning."

10   Po Kuei said: "I'd like to see people taxed one part in twenty. What would you think of that?"

"Your Way is the Way of northern barbarians," replied Mencius. "In a nation of ten thousand families, would a single potter be sufficient?"

"No, there wouldn't be enough pottery."

"Northern barbarians don't grow the five grains, only millet. They

have no city walls or buildings, no ancestral temples, no sacrificial ritu-
als. They have no august lords, no diplomatic hospitality or gifts. And
they don't have the hundred government offices and officials. That's
why one part in twenty is enough tax for them. But here in the Middle
Kingdom, how can we do without noble-minded leaders and the bonds
of human community? If a country is crippled without potters, what
happens without noble-minded leaders? If our rulers levy tax rates
below that prescribed by the Way of Yao and Shun, they'll be nothing
but barbarians great and small. And if our rulers levy tax rates above
that prescribed by the Way of Yao and Shun, they'll be nothing but
tyrant Chiehs great and small."

11   P o Kuei said: "I can manage high waters better even than
Yü."[2]

   "You're wrong," replied Mencius. "Yü's management of water is the
very Way of water. And so he used the four seas as valleys to drain the
floodwaters away. But you use neighboring countries. When you force
water out of its natural course, it becomes a flood. And a flood is noth-
ing less than a deluge, which is something the Humane despise. No,
you're quite wrong."

12   M encius said: "If the noble-minded are not faithful and
sincere, how can they take command of a situation?"

13   T he Lu sovereign wanted Adept Yüeh-cheng to preside over
his government.

   "When I heard this," said Mencius, "I was so happy I couldn't sleep."

   "Is Yüeh-cheng a man of great strength?" asked Kung-sun Ch'ou.

   "No."

   "Is he a man of wisdom and foresight?"

"No."

"Is he a man of broad learning?"

"No."

"Then why were you so happy you couldn't sleep?"

"Because he's one of those men who loves virtue and benevolence."

"Is loving virtue and benevolence sufficient?"

"Loving virtue and benevolence is enough to govern all beneath Heaven," replied Mencius, "and what is Lu compared to that? If you love virtue and benevolence, people everywhere within the four seas will think nothing of a thousand miles: they'll come share their thoughts about virtue and benevolence. If you don't love virtue and benevolence, people will think your smug and arrogant manner says *I understand all things.* The tone and bearing of such smug arrogance – that alone will keep people a thousand miles away. And when worthy scholars stay a thousand miles away, people with flattering smiles and pleasing tongues come crowding around. Once that happens, how could anyone govern a country well?"

14   Adept Ch'en said: "In ancient times, when would a noble-minded man take office?"

"There were three situations where a noble-minded man would take office," replied Mencius, "and three where he would renounce office. First – he would take office when invited with reverence, according to Ritual, and told that his counsels would be put into practice. Then he would renounce office if his counsels were not put into practice, even if the Ritual courtesies hadn't been violated. Second – he would take office when invited with reverence, according to Ritual, even if his counsels weren't put into practice. Then he would renounce office if the Ritual courtesies were neglected. Third – if he had no food morning or night, and so lived in such hunger that he couldn't walk out his gate, he would accept office if the sovereign heard about his plight and offered assistance, saying: *I've failed in the great work of putting his Way into practice, and I've failed to follow his counsels. Now if I let him starve to death in my domain, how could I live with the shame? But in such a case, he accepts only to escape starvation."*

15 Mencius said: "Shun issued forth from farmlands. Fu Yüeh rose from builders, Chiao Ko from salt and fish, Kuan Chung from jails, Sun Shu-ao from the sea, and Po-li Hsi from markets. So it is that whenever Heaven invests a person with great responsibilities, it first tries his resolve, exhausts his muscles and bones, starves his body, leaves him destitute, and confounds his every endeavor. In this way his patience and endurance are developed, and his weaknesses are overcome.

"We change and grow only when we make mistakes. We realize what to do only when we work through worry and confusion. And we gain people's trust and understanding only when our inner thoughts are revealed clearly in our faces and words. When it has no lawful families or wise officials within and no enemy threats without, a nation will surely come to ruin. Then its people will understand that through calamity and grief we flourish, and through peace and joy we perish."

16 Mencius said: "There are many ways to teach. I don't bother with teaching and instructing, but that's just another way of teaching and instructing."

XIII

To Fathom the Mind   Book One

1   Mencius said: "To fathom the mind is to understand your nature. And when you understand your nature, you understand Heaven. Foster your mind, nurture your nature – then you are serving Heaven.

"Don't worry about dying young or living long. What will come will come. Cultivate yourself well – and patient in that perfection, let it come. Then you will stand firm in your fate."

2   Mencius said: "Whatever happens is destiny, but we should accept only what is truly fated. Hence, one who understands destiny won't stand beneath a wall teetering on the verge of collapse.

"To fathom the Way in life, and then die – that is our true fate. To live tangled in fetters, and then die – that is no one's true fate."

3   Mencius said: *"What you seek you will find, and what you ignore you will lose.* Where this saying is right, and to seek means to find, we're seeking something within ourselves.

"To seek is a question of the Way, and to find is a question of destiny. Where this is right, and to seek doesn't necessarily mean to find, we're seeking something outside ourselves."

4   Mencius said: "The ten thousand things are all there in me. And there's no joy greater than looking within and finding myself faithful to them. Treat others as you would be treated. Devote yourself to that, for there's no more direct approach to Humanity."

5   Mencius said: "To enact it without making it clear, to enact it over and over without inquiring into it, to enact it for a lifetime without ever understanding its Way – that's how it is for nearly everyone."

6   Mencius said: "It's impossible to be shameless. The shame of being shameless – that is shameless indeed."

7   Mencius said: "Shame is a great thing for people. Crafty schemers have no use for shame. And if you aren't ashamed of being inhuman, what will ever make you human?"

8   Mencius said: "In their love of virtue and benevolence, sage emperors of ancient times forgot about their exalted position. How could sage scholars of ancient times be any different? Delighting in the Way, they too forgot about exalted positions. So unless emperors and dukes came in reverence and according to Ritual, they were rarely admitted to see such scholars. And if it was nearly impossible to see them, how could those rulers ever convince them to take office?"

9   Mencius said to Sung Kou-chien: "You love to travel, offering your counsel to leaders, so I'll tell you something about such things: Know contentment when your counsel is valued, and contentment when it's ignored."

"What must a person be to know such contentment?" asked Sung Kou-chien.

"If you honor Integrity and delight in Duty you can know such contentment," replied Mencius. "The worthy never forget Duty when destitute, and never abandon the Way when they succeed. Not forgetting Duty when destitute, the worthy realize themselves. And when they succeed without abandoning the Way, the people's faith in them never falters.

"When the ancients fulfilled their ambitions, bounty rained down on the people. When they failed, they were still worthy exemplars for all the world to see. Cultivate virtue and benevolence in yourself when destitute and alone. And when you succeed, share that virtue and benevolence with all beneath Heaven."

10   *M*encius said: "A commoner only feels called to great work when an Emperor Wen appears. But a great man sets to work even when there's no sign of an Emperor Wen."

11   *M*encius said: "To live humble and dissatisfied with yourself, even if all the wealth of Han and Wei were added to your own – that is the mark of a person beyond compare."

12   *M*encius said: "If your Way is making life easier for them, the people won't resent hard work. And if your Way is helping them live, the people won't resent being led to their death."

13   *M*encius said: "Under the finest of august lords, the people seem peaceful and happy. Under a true emperor, they seem utterly content. They neither resent him when put to death, nor praise him when richly rewarded. They grow more virtuous and benevolent every day, without ever realizing who makes this happen.

"So it is that when the noble-minded pass through a place, they leave transformations behind. And when they dwell in a place, they work miracles. They grace the same stream as Heaven above and earth below: who can doubt their healing power?"

14   Mencius said: "It's Humane music that goes deep inside people, not Humane words. And it's virtuous teaching that wins people over, not virtuous government. The people fear virtuous government, but they love virtuous teaching. Virtuous government can win people's wealth, but virtuous teaching can win their hearts."

15   Mencius said: "To have an ability without being taught – that is true ability. To know without struggling to know – that is true knowing.

   "Young children all know love for their parents. And when they grow up, they all know respect for their elders. Loving parents is Humanity, and respecting elders is Duty. That's the secret. Just extend it throughout all beneath Heaven."

16   Mencius said: "When Shun dwelled deep in the mountains, he dwelled among trees and stones, roamed with boar and deer. The difference between him and the other mountain people was slight indeed. But then he heard a single word of virtue, saw a single act of virtue, and it was like a great river breaking through its banks: nothing could stop it."

17   Mencius said: "Don't do what should not be done, and don't desire what should not be desired. Abide by this one precept, and everything else will follow."

18   Mencius said: "Integrity, wisdom, skill, intelligence – such things are forged in adversity. Like the son of a common mistress, a forsaken minister is ever cautious, ever watchful. That's how he avoids danger and succeeds."

19   Mencius said: "There are people who find satisfaction in serving a sovereign. There are ministers who find satisfaction in keeping the gods of grain content. There are the denizens of Heaven who learn what will benefit all beneath Heaven and put it into practice. And then there are the truly great: they can rectify all things by rectifying themselves."

20   Mencius said: "The noble-minded have three great joys, and ruling all beneath Heaven is not one of them. To have parents alive and brothers well – that is the first joy. To face Heaven above and people below without any shame – that is the second joy. To attract the finest students in all beneath Heaven, and to teach and nurture them – that is the third joy. The noble-minded have three great joys, and ruling all beneath Heaven is not one of them."

21   Mencius said: "The noble-minded may want a large country and vast population, but that isn't what fills them with joy. To stand at the center of all beneath Heaven and bring contentment to people everywhere within the four seas – that's what fills the noble-minded with joy. But it isn't what answers to their nature. Their nature gains nothing if they manage the great affairs of state, and it loses nothing if they live in destitute obscurity. This is because the noble-minded know their given nature to be complete in itself.

"Humanity, Duty, Ritual, wisdom – such aspects of their nature take root in mind, flourish in appearance. There's a calmness in the face of the noble-minded, a calmness that also graces their back, radiates through their four limbs. And so the body of someone noble-minded speaks a parable without words."

22   Mencius said: "Po Yi fled the tyrant Chou and settled on the shores of the North Sea. On hearing Emperor Wen had come to power, he said *I hear Wen takes good care of the old, so why not go back and serve him?* Duke T'ai fled the tyrant Chou and settled on the shores of the West Sea. On hearing Emperor Wen had come to power, he said *I hear Wen takes good care of the old, so why not go back and serve him?* When there's a ruler somewhere in all beneath Heaven who takes good care of the old, the Humane flock to serve him.

"When every five-acre farm has mulberry trees along the walls and a woman to raise silkworms, the old can wear silk. And when there are five hens and two sows, and their proper seasons aren't neglected, the old need not go without meat. When every hundred-acre farm has a man to till the fields, even large families don't go hungry.

"This is what they meant by *Wen takes good care of the old.* He organized farmlands and villages, taught people to plant mulberries and raise livestock, showed the women how to care for the aged. Without silk at fifty, people can't keep warm. And without meat at seventy, they can't get full. Not warm and not full – that is called freezing and starving. Among Emperor Wen's people, the old never froze or starved. That's what Po Yi and Duke T'ai were saying."

23   Mencius said: "If you expand their fields and reduce their taxes, you'll make the people rich. And if they use food according to season and wares according to Ritual, they'll never exhaust their wealth.

"People can't live without fire and water. But if you go knocking on gates at nightfall, asking for fire and water, no one will refuse you. That's because fire and water are so plentiful. In ruling all beneath Heaven, the sage makes beans and millet as plentiful as fire and water. When beans and millet are as plentiful as fire and water, how can any of the people be Inhumane?"

24   Mencius said: "When Confucius climbed Tung Mountain, he realized how tiny Lu is. And when he climbed T'ai Mountain, he realized how tiny all beneath Heaven is. So it is that once you've seen oceans, water seems petty. And once you've entered the gate of a sage, words seem petty.

"But there's an art to seeing water: look at its ripples, for the brilliance of sun and moon ignite anything that will hold light. And when water flows, it fills every hollow before moving on. It's like this for the noble-minded in the Way: they succeed only if the pattern they make is beautiful."

25   Mencius said: "To rise at the cock's cry and practice virtue and benevolence with untiring diligence – that is to be a follower of Shun. To rise at the cock's cry and chase profits with untiring diligence – that is to be a follower of Chih the bandit. There's nothing more to the difference between Shun and Chih than this: the distinction between virtue and profit."

26   Mencius said: "Yang Chu valued self above all: even if it would bring great profit to all beneath Heaven, he wouldn't pluck a single hair from his head. Mo Tzu proposed universal love: if it would bring any profit to all beneath Heaven, he would toil long and hard, wearing every hair from his body.

"Now we have Master Mo who clings to the middle ground. The middle ground is closer to the mark, but unless he allows for the complexity of circumstance he's still clinging to a single doctrine. The problem with clinging to a single doctrine is that it plunders the Way: to glorify the one, you cast out a hundred."

27   Mencius said: "The hungry savor any food. The thirsty savor any drink. They have no discrimination in food and drink: hunger and thirst has ruined it. And hunger and thirst can ruin more than people's tongues: it can also ruin their minds. Once you free your mind from the ruin of hunger and thirst, you no longer worry about failing to equal the great sages."

28   Mencius said: "All the wealth of three dukes couldn't make Liu-hsia Hui waver in his resolve."

29   Mencius said: "Getting something done is like digging a well. You can dig a well seventy feet deep, but if you don't hit water it's just an abandoned well."

30   Mencius said: "Yao and Shun possessed it by nature. T'ang and Wu embodied it. And the five chiefs of the august lords borrowed it. But if you borrow something long enough, who would know it isn't yours?"

31   Kung-sun Ch'ou said: "Yi Yin banished T'ai Chia to T'ung,[1] saying: *I can't be so intimately involved with someone who is so contrary.* The people were greatly pleased. And when T'ai Chia returned to Yi Yin a sage, the people were again greatly pleased. When a sage serves as minister under a sovereign who is not a sage, can he banish the sovereign?"

"He can if his motives are like Yi Yin's," replied Mencius. "But if his motives aren't like Yi Yin's, it's usurping the throne."

       MENCIUS

32   Kung-sun Ch'ou said: "The *Songs* say the noble-minded *never eat the food of idleness.* What do you think of the noble-minded living on food they haven't grown themselves?"

"When a noble-minded man lives in a country and the sovereign values him," replied Mencius, "the sovereign gains peace and wealth, honor and glory. When disciples follow him, they learn to honor parents and elders, to earn trust and stand by their words. If there's anyone who *never eats the food of idleness,* surely it's him."

33   Prince T'ien asked: "What is the task of a worthy official?"

"To cultivate the highest of purposes," replied Mencius.

"What do you mean by *the highest of purposes?*"

"It's simple: Humanity and Duty. You defy Humanity if you cause the death of a single innocent person, and you defy Duty if you take what is not yours. What is our dwelling-place if not Humanity? And what is our road if not Duty? To dwell in Humanity and follow Duty – that is the perfection of a great person's task."

34   Mencius said: "If he were offered the state of Ch'i in violation of Duty, everyone believes Master Chung would refuse. But this is only the Duty that refuses a basket of rice and a bowl of soup.

"There's nothing great about abandoning your place in the bonds of parent and family, sovereign and minister, leader and citizen. How is it people see something so small and believe it to be great?"

35   T'ao Ying asked: "When Shun was the Son of Heaven and Kao Yao was the justice minister, what would have happened if Blind Purblind killed someone?"

"Kao Yao would have arrested him," replied Mencius.

"But wouldn't Shun have forbidden it?"

"How could he forbid it? Kao Yao had been given authority."

"Then what would Shun have done?"

"Casting all beneath Heaven aside meant no more to Shun than casting aside an old sandal," said Mencius. "He would have stolen away with his father on his back, and gone to live beside the sea. He would have lived out his life happily there, forgetting all beneath Heaven entirely."

36 When Mencius was traveling from Fan to Ch'i, he saw the Ch'i prince and said with a sigh: "A dwelling-place transforms the *ch'i*, just as food transforms the body. Great indeed is the influence of a dwelling-place – for aren't we all alike born of humankind?"

Then he continued: "This prince's house, carriage, and clothes aren't much different from other people's. And yet he's so different. If his dwelling-place can do that, imagine dwelling in the most boundless dwelling-place of all beneath Heaven.

"The sovereign of Lu once went to Sung and called out at Tieh-tse Gate. Hearing him, the gatekeeper said: *This isn't my sovereign. How is it he sounds so much like my sovereign?* The reason is simple: their dwelling-places were so much alike."

37 Mencius said: "To feed people without showing them love – that is to treat them like pigs. To love people without showing them reverence – that is to keep them like pets. But honor and reverence are gifts not yet given. Honor and reverence without substance – you can't lure the noble-minded with such empty gestures."

38 Mencius said: "Our appearance belongs to the nature of Heaven. Only as a true sage can you abide by your appearance."

39   When Emperor Hsüan of Ch'i wanted to shorten his mourning period, Kung-sun Ch'ou said: "A year of mourning is better than none at all, isn't it?"

"That's like watching someone twist an elder's arm and saying: *Gently. Do it gently,*" replied Mencius. "What you should do is teach him how to honor parents and elders."

At the same time, there was a prince whose mother had died. On the prince's behalf, his teacher asked that he be allowed a mourning period of several months. "What do you think of that?" asked Kung-sun Ch'ou.

"The prince wants to observe the full mourning period," replied Mencius, "but he cannot. In this case, even a single day is better than nothing. There was nothing preventing Emperor Hsüan from mourning: he just wanted to avoid it."

40   Mencius said: "The noble-minded teach in five ways. They transform like rain coming in its season. They realize Integrity. They perfect talents. They answer questions. They cultivate themselves and so stand apart as examples. These five ways are how the noble-minded teach."

41   Kung-sun Ch'ou said: "The Way is lofty and beautiful indeed, but it's like climbing to Heaven: it seems impossible to reach. Why not offer something people can hope to reach, something they can work at day after day with untiring diligence?"

"A great carpenter doesn't abandon the measuring string to make woodwork easy for inept apprentices," replied Mencius. "And Yi didn't give up a strong full draw to make archery easy for inept students. The noble-minded draw the bow and hold it. Then it seems they've leapt into the center of the Way, letting whoever is able follow them there."

42   Mencius said: "When all beneath Heaven abides in the Way, people use the Way to find themselves. When all beneath Heaven ignores the Way, people use themselves to find the Way. I never hear of using the Way to find the human anymore."

43   Adept Kung-tu said: "When T'eng Keng was your disciple, he seemed a man deserving of the Ritual respect, but you refused to answer his questions. Why?"

"When people wield such privileged positions as renown or wisdom, age or merit or friendship," replied Mencius, "I never answer them. And T'eng Keng wielded two of them."

44   Mencius said: "If someone stops where they should not, they'll stop anywhere. If someone slights a person they should treat generously, they'll slight anyone. And if someone races ahead, they retreat in a hurry."

45   Mencius said: "The noble-minded love things, but don't treat them with Humanity. They treat the people with Humanity, but don't treat them as kindred. Once you treat kindred as kindred, you treat the people with Humanity. And once you treat the people with Humanity, you love things."

46   Mencius said: "The wise understand all things, and so devote themselves to the essentials. The Humane love all things, and so consider kindred devotion to the sages essential. The wisdom of Yao and Shun was that they didn't treat all things alike: they devoted themselves to essentials first. And the Humanity of Yao and Shun was that

they didn't love all people alike: they devoted themselves to kindred affection for the sages.

"To be meticulous about mourning for a few months while declining to mourn the full three years, to ask about the etiquette of dining while swilling soup and wolfing down food – such things are called not understanding the essentials."

XIV

To Fathom the Mind   Book Two

1   **M**encius said: "Emperor Hui of Liang was utterly Inhumane. The Humane extend their love to those they hate. The Inhumane inflict their hatred on those they love."

"What do you mean by that?" asked Kung-sun Ch'ou.

"In his passion for more territory, Emperor Hui sent his people to war, tearing them asunder and suffering disastrous defeats. Soon he wanted to return to the battlefield, but was afraid he couldn't win. So he sent his beloved son to the grave too.[1] This is what I mean by *inflicting their hatred on those they love.*"

2   **M**encius said: "There were no just wars in *The Spring and Autumn Annals*. Some were better than others, but that's all. A sovereign may discipline his august lords by attacking them. But one country should never discipline another in such a way."

3   **M**encius said: "If people believe everything in *The Book of History*, it's worse than having no *Book of History* at all. In the entire 'War Successfully Completed' chapter, I accept no more than two or three strips.[2]

"The Humane have no match in all beneath Heaven. If a Humane ruler attacks an Inhumane one, how could *blood flow so deep fulling sticks3 begin floating away?*"

4   **M**encius said: "There are people who say: *I am an expert in war and tactics.* But they're just common criminals. If the ruler of a country loves Humanity, he will have no match in all beneath Heaven. When he marches south, the northern tribes will complain: *Why does he*

leave us for last? And when he marches east, the western tribes will complain: *Why does he leave us for last?*

"When Emperor Wu marched against Shang with three hundred war-chariots and three thousand illustrious warriors, he said: *Have no fear: I bring you peace. The Shang people are not my enemy.* At this, the Shang people bowed to the ground like animals shaking their horns loose. Hence, to invade was to rectify. People all want to rectify themselves, so what's the use of war?"

5   Mencius said: "A master carpenter or carriage-maker can hand down compass and square to his followers, but he cannot make them skillful."

6   Mencius said: "When Shun was eating cracked rice and wild greens, he lived as if he would spend his whole life like that. And when he was the Son of Heaven, wearing embroidered robes and playing his *ch'in* in the company of Yao's two daughters, he lived as if he'd always enjoyed such things."

7   Mencius said: "Only now have I realized the true gravity of killing a man's family members. If you kill his father, he'll kill your father. If you kill his brother, he'll kill your brother. There's precious little difference between that and killing your father or brother with your own hands."

8   Mencius said: "In ancient times, border stations were set up to resist attacks. Now they're set up to launch attacks."

9   Mencius said: "If you don't practice the Way yourself, how will you ever get your wife and child to practice it? And if you don't employ people according to the Way, how can you ever get your wife and child to practice it?"

10   Mencius said: "If you're always cultivating profit, you'll avoid death in bad years. If you're always cultivating Integrity, you'll avoid confusion in evil times."

11   Mencius said: "If you love renown, you can give away a nation of a thousand war-chariots. If you don't, you can't give away a basket of rice or bowl of soup without looking pained."

12   Mencius said: "If the worthy and Humane are not trusted, the country is an empty shell. If Ritual and Duty are ignored, leaders and citizens are confounded. And if the work of government is ignored, no amount of wealth will satisfy a country's needs."

13   Mencius said: "It has happened that Inhumane tyrants have gained control of a country. But such men have never ruled all beneath Heaven."

14   Mencius said: "The people are the most precious of all things. Next come the gods of soil and grain. The sovereign matters least.

"That's why a person must win over the people to become the Son of Heaven, win over the Son of Heaven to become an august lord, and win over an august lord to become a high minister.

"When an august lord neglects the gods of soil and grain, he should be replaced. When the sacrificial animals are perfect, the vessels of grain pure, the sacrifices observed in their proper seasons, and still drought and flood plague the land, then the gods of soil and grain should be replaced."

15   Mencius said: "A sage is teacher to the hundred genera-tions. Po Yi and Liu-hsia Hui are such men. That's why the greedy are cured of greed when they hear the legend of Po Yi, and the timid grow resolute; why the niggardly grow generous when they hear the legend of Liu-hsia Hui, and small minds grow broad. They arose a hundred generations ago, but a hundred generations from now they'll still inspire all who hear of them. If they weren't sages, how could this happen? And imagine what they meant to the people who knew them!"

16   Mencius said: "Humanity is the human. Put them togeth-er and you have the Way."

17   Mencius said: "When Confucius left Lu, he said: *There's no hurry, no hurry at all*. That's the Way to leave your parents' coun-try. When he left Ch'i, he simply emptied his rice steamer and set out. That's the Way to leave a foreign land."

18   Mencius said: "When Confucius suffered such hardship in Ch'en and Ts'ai,[4] it was because he had no friends among rulers and ministers."

19   Mo Chi said: "I've never been much good at talk."

"There's no harm in that," replied Mencius. "Thoughtful people despise those who talk too much. The *Songs* say:

> *My troubled heart is grief-stricken*
> *at this small-minded world's hatred.*

Confucius was like that. And Emperor Wen was like this:

> *Though he couldn't ease their hatred,*
> *his renown never faltered among them."*

20   Mencius said: "The wise and worthy used their bright insight to open bright insight in people. Now pundits use blind ignorance to open bright insight in people."

21   Mencius said to Adept Kao: "If a footpath in the mountains suddenly gets a lot of use, it becomes a road. And if it's never used, it's soon choked with underbrush. That's how it is with your heart: choked with underbrush."

22   Adept Kao said: "Yü's music was much finer than Emperor Wen's."

"Why do you say that?" asked Mencius.

"Because the bell-pivots in his orchestra were nearly worn through."

"That's hardly proof. Do the deep ruts passing through a city gate come from the power of a single team of horses?"

23   When there was famine in Ch'i, Adept Ch'en said: "The Ch'i people are hoping you can get T'ang to open its granaries for them again. But you can't do that, can you?"

"If I did," replied Mencius, "I'd be another Feng Fu. Feng Fu was a man in Chin who was good at seizing tigers, but eventually became a good official. Many years later he went out into the country and found a crowd of people chasing a tiger. They cornered the tiger against some cliffs, but no one dared tangle with it. When they saw Feng Fu, they ran to greet him. And seeing him boldly roll up his sleeves and climb out of his carriage, they were delighted. But the other scholars there only laughed."

24   Mencius said: "The mouth's relation to flavor, the eye's to color, the ear's to sound, the nose's to fragrance, the four limbs' to ease – these are human nature. But they're also the Mandate of Heaven, so the noble-minded never call them human nature.

"Humanity's relation to father and son, Duty's to sovereign and minister, Ritual's to guest and host, understanding's to the wise and worthy, the sage's to Heaven's Way – these are the Mandate of Heaven. But they're also human nature, so the noble-minded never call them the Mandate of Heaven."

25   Hao-sheng Pu-hai asked: "What kind of man is Adept Yüeh-cheng?"

"A man of virtue and sincerity," replied Mencius.

"What do you mean by *virtue* and *sincerity*?"

"What we aspire to is called *virtue*, and to possess it within us is called *sincerity*," began Mencius. "To possess it in rich abundance is called *beauty*, and to be ablaze with that rich abundance is called *great*. Someone transformed by that greatness is a *sage*, and to be a sage beyond all knowing – that is called *divinity*. Yüeh-cheng has mastered the first two, but the last four are still beyond him."

26   Mencius said: "When people abandon the school of Mo Tzu, they turn to Yang Chu. And when they abandon the school of Yang Chu, they turn to Confucius. When they turn to our Confucian school, we should take them in. That's all.

"But these days, people debate the followers of Mo Tzu and Yang Chu, and it's like they're chasing stray pigs. First they herd them back into the pen, then they tie up their legs."

27   Mencius said: "There are three forms of taxation: cloth, grain, and labor. The noble-minded levy one, and relax the other two. If you levy two at once, the people starve and die. If you levy all three at once, father and son are torn asunder."

28   Mencius said: "An august lord has three treasures: land, people, and government. If they treasure pearls and jade, they're destined for ruin."

29   When P'en-ch'eng K'uo took office in Ch'i, Mencius said: "He's as good as dead."

Eventually P'en-ch'eng K'uo was put to death, and the disciples asked: "How did you know he'd be put to death?"

"He was a man of little talent," replied Mencius, "and he'd never learned the great noble-minded Way. That's all it took to kill him."

30   When Mencius went to T'eng and stayed in the Upper Palace, there was a half-finished pair of sandals on the windowsill. At some point, the palace servants came looking for them but couldn't find them. So someone asked: "Can your followers really be so shameless?"

"Do you think we came all this way just to steal sandals?" replied Mencius.

"I wouldn't think so. But as a teacher, you don't chase after students who leave and you don't refuse students who come. If they come to you with an earnest mind, you accept them without any question."

31   Mencius said: "There are things people find unbearable. To see that and use it to understand what makes life bearable – that is Humanity. There are things people will not do. To see that and use it to understand what people should do – that is Duty.

"The heart detests harming others. If you apply that everywhere, you'll never exhaust Humanity. The heart detests peeking through holes and stealing over walls. If you apply that everywhere, you'll never exhaust Duty. People resent condescension. If you apply that everywhere, you can practice Duty wherever you go.

"To say what you should not say – that is to use words as a ploy. Not to say what you should say – that is to use silence as a ploy. Either way, it's no different from peeking through holes and stealing over walls."

32   Mencius said: "Words that speak of things close at hand and carry far-reaching implications – those are the good words. Guarding the essentials and applying them broadly – that is the good Way.

"The noble-minded always use forthright words, so the Way endures in them. And they cultivate themselves tenaciously, so all beneath Heaven is at peace.

"People keep leaving their own fields to weed the fields of others. It's a sickness. They demand everything of others, and nothing of themselves."

33   Mencius said: "For Yao and Shun, it was their very nature. And T'ang and Wu – they returned to it.

"When every movement of mind and body is in accord with Ritual – that is the fullest form of Integrity. When you mourn the dead utterly, it isn't to impress the living. When you abide by Integrity without swerving, it isn't to earn a fat salary. And when you speak with true sincerity, always standing by your word, it isn't to justify your actions. The noble-minded simply put the law into action, then await their fate."

34   Mencius said: "When you counsel great figures, do it with disdain. Don't let their majesty impress you. Ceilings thirty feet high and rafter-beams a yard across – if I realized my every dream, I wouldn't have such things. Serving girls by the hundred and tables ten feet wide spread with food – if I realized my every dream, I wouldn't have such things. Great fun drinking, riding, and hunting, always a retinue of a thousand carriages following behind – if I realized my every dream, I wouldn't have such things.

"The things they do are all things I would never do. And the things I do are all in accordance with the ancient precepts. So why should I cower before them?"

35   Mencius said: "For nurturing the mind, there's nothing like paring your desires away to a very few. If you have few desires, there may still be some capricious whims in your mind, but they'll be few. If you have many desires, there may still be some enduring principles in your mind, but they'll be few indeed."

36   Tseng Hsi loved sheep-dates. But his son, Master Tseng, couldn't bear to eat them.

"Which tastes better – roast mincemeat or sheep-dates?" asked Kung-sun Ch'ou.

"Roast mincemeat, of course," replied Mencius.

"Then why did Master Tseng eat roast mincemeat and not sheep-dates?"

"Roast mincemeat is a taste shared by many, but a taste for sheep-dates is unique. It's forbidden to use someone's personal name, but not their family name. This is because a family name is shared by many, while a personal name is unique."

37   Adept Wan Chang asked: "When he was in Ch'en, Confucius said: *Let's go back home. The young in our villages are full of impetuous ambition. They forge ahead but cannot forget their childish ways.*[5] But he was in Ch'en, so what made him think of the impetuous young scholars in Lu?"

Mencius replied: "Confucius said: *I can't find students who steer the middle Way, so I turn to the impetuous and the timid. The impetuous forge ahead, and the timid know what to avoid.*[6] Obviously, Confucius wanted to find students who steer the middle Way. But since he couldn't find such people, he started thinking about the best alternatives."

"What sort of person did he mean by *impetuous*?" asked Wan Chang.

"People like Ch'in Chang, Tseng Hsi, and Mu P'i."

"Why did he call them impetuous?"

"They were full of ambition," said Mencius, "and grand boasting about *The ancients! The ancients!* But if you examine their actions, you see they often violated the ancient precepts.

"And when he couldn't find the impetuous for students, all Confucius could do is look for arrogant scholars who wouldn't condescend to anything the least bit impure. These are the timid, and they are the next best alternative."

Wan Chang continued: "Confucius said: *I regret all those who pass by my gate without entering to become students – all but the righteous villager. A righteous villager is the thief of Integrity.*[7] What sort of person did he mean by *righteous villager?"*

"All that grand boasting of the impetuous is senseless," replied Mencius. "Their words ignore their actions; their actions ignore their words. And still they bluster about *The ancients! The ancients!* And how can the timid walk around so cold and self-contained? They live in this world, so they should act like they're a part of it. But if these two only act with virtue and benevolence, they're alright.

"As for those righteous villagers: they enfeeble themselves fawning all over this world."

"If a whole village praises someone as righteous," said Adept Wan, "then they'd be called righteous wherever they went. So why did Confucius call such a person *the thief of Integrity?"*

"If you want to accuse such a person, there's no place to begin," replied Mencius. "If you want to criticize, there's nothing to criticize. They do what everyone else does, in perfect harmony with this sordid world. They live that way, and yet seem loyal and sincere. They act that way, and yet seem pure and honest. They please everyone and believe they're always right. But it's impossible to enter the Way of Yao and Shun with them. That's why Confucius called such a person *the thief of Integrity.*

"Confucius said:

> *I hate things that are not what they appear. I hate weeds for fear they'll be confused with young rice. I hate sweet talk for fear it will be confused with eloquence. I hate calculating tongues for fear they'll be confused with sincerity. I hate the dissolute songs of Cheng for fear they'll be confused with music. I hate purple for fear it will be confused with the purity of vermilion. And I hate righteous villagers for fear they'll be confused with people of Integrity.*

"The noble-minded simply return to the changeless principle. When the changeless principle is established, the people flourish. And when the people flourish, the twisty ways of evil are unknown."

38   Mencius said: "It was over five hundred years from Yao and Shun to T'ang. People like Yü and Kao Yao understood because they knew Yao and Shun, and people like T'ang understood through learning. It was over five hundred years from T'ang to Emperor Wen. People like Yi Yin and Lai Chu understood because they knew T'ang, and people like Emperor Wen understood through learning. It was over five hundred years from Emperor Wen to Confucius. People like Duke T'ai and San-yi Sheng understood because they knew Wen, and people like Confucius understood through learning.

"Now it's hardly been a hundred years from Confucius to our own age. We aren't far from his time, and we're so near his home. But if no one here's gleaned anything from that great sage, then no one here's gleaned anything."

Notes

I. Emperor Hui of Liang, Book One

1 **miles:** The Chinese mile *(li)* is much shorter than our own, the ratio being 3 *li* per mile.

2 **Humanity:** See Key Terms: *Jen.*

3 **Duty:** See Key Terms: *Yi.*

4 **Emperor Wen:** Father of Wu, the founder of the Chou Dynasty, Wen was considered responsible for the resplendent culture of the Chou Dynasty, hence his name, which means "culture." See Historical Table.

5 **Way:** See Key Terms: *Tao.*

6 **acre:** The Chinese acre *(mu)* is much smaller than our own, the ratio being 6.6 *mu* per acre or less.

7 **square miles:** In ancient China this form of measurement seems to have meant something different than it does for us. Seven hundred square miles apparently means an area of land seven hundred miles on each side. Still, such measurements don't seem consistent, and seem more figurative than literal.

8 **Emperor Hsiang:** Emperor Hui died, and Hsiang was the son who became his successor.

9 **Duke Huan:** Most illustrious of the noble lords in the earlier years of the Chou Dynasty (reigned 685–643). See note III.2.

10 **Integrity:** See Key Terms: *Te.*

11 **Middle Kingdom:** Ancient heartland in the north inhabited by fully civilized Chinese, as opposed to the southern and other outlying regions, which were "barbarian" or only partially civilized. As those regions became fully Chinese, this term *(Chung Kuo)* extended to mean all of China.

12 **Ritual:** See Key Terms: *Li.*

II. Emperor Hui of Liang, Book Two

1 **Way:** See Key Terms: *Tao.*

2 **Emperor T'ai:** Chou sovereign who preceded King Wen. See Historical Table.

3 **Celestial Lord:** Shang Ti, the Shang Dynasty's supreme deity: see Introduction p. 386 f.

4 **Emperor Wu:** Chou Emperor who conquered the last Shang emperor and replaced the Shang Dynasty with the Chou Dynasty. Hence his name, which means "martial." See Historical Table.

5 **Ch'i:** Different from the Ch'i ruled by King Hsüan.

6 **Emperor Kung Liu:** Chou sovereign in a time well before the Chou state conquered the Shang Dynasty, when the semi-barbarian Chou was being forced east toward Shang by western tribes.

7 **Tyrant Chieh . . . Tyrant Chou:** Chieh and Chou were the last, debased rulers of the Hsia and Shang dynasties respectively. In overthrowing them, T'ang and Wu founded new and noble dynasties: the Shang and Chou, respectively.

8 **Ch'i invaded the nation of Yen:** Trying to make himself look like the sage-emperor Yao, who passed over his own son and bequeathed the throne to the most worthy successor, Emperor K'uai of Yen abdicated in favor of his prime minister, Lord Chih, in 315 B.C.E. The prime minister was expected to decline, but instead accepted. This sparked a very destructive civil war led by the rightful heir, and King Hsüan of Ch'i finally intervened. See also IV.8–9.

9 **Master Tseng:** Disciple of Confucius who became an influential teacher.

10 **Ch'i Mountain:** See next section for the entire story.

III. Kung-Sun Ch'ou, Book One

1 **Kung-sun Chou:** Disciple of Mencius.

2 **successes of Kuan Chung:** Duke Huan became sovereign in Ch'i by killing his brother Chiu. Kuan Chung was initially Chiu's advisor, but afterwards became a sage prime minister under Duke Huan. His talents turned Ch'i into a powerful and rich state, and made Huan first among the august lords.

3 **Duke Chou:** A cultural hero much admired by Confucius and Mencius, Duke Chou helped his brother, Wu, found the Chou Dynasty. He was also a major intellectual figure, another in legend at least of a good share of The Book of Songs (*Shih Ching*) and The Book of Change (*I Ching*). As the primary architect of the Chou political system, he set up the institutions of sagely government and is traditionally credited with developing the doctrine of the Mandate of Heaven, which introduced ethics into government (see Historical Table and Introduction, pp. 387 f).

4 **Mind:** The word *hsin*, which recurs throughout this section, means both "heart" and "mind." The Chinese made no fundamental distinction between the two.

5 **Meng Pin:** Courageous warrior of antiquity.

6   **Master Kao:** Philosopher contemporary with Mencius. See XI.1–6 for their dialogues on human nature.

7   **ch'i:** See Key Terms: *Ch'i*.

8   **Tsai Yü, Adept Kung . . . Jan Po-niu, Min Tzu-ch'ien, and Yen Hui:** These five were disciples of Confucius.

9   **Po Yi:** Po Yi and his brother Shu Ch'i (twelfth century B.C.E.) were heir to the throne, but they felt it would be wrong to accept it, so they refused. As a result, they lived in great poverty, finally dying of cold and hunger in the mountains.

10 **Yi Yin:** The great minister who helped T'ang found the Shang Dynasty. See Historical Table.

11 **Yao . . . Shun:** Two mythic sage-emperors from legendary prehistory. See Historical Table.

12 **disparage me:** *Songs* 155. A bird is speaking.

13 **"T'ai Chia":** The *Analects* IV.1.

14 **Liu-hsia Hui:** Sage governor in Lu (7th–6th century).

IV. Kung-Sun Ch'ou, Book Two

1   **Shen T'ung:** For an explanation of the events referred to in this and the following section, see note II.7.

2   **Ch'en Chia:** One of the Ch'i emperor's counselors.

3   **Master Szu:** The celebrated grandson of Confucius and reputed author of *The Doctrine of the Mean,* one of the Confucian classics. Mencius is said to have studied under one of Master Szu's disciples.

V. Duke Wen of T'eng, Book One

1   **Yen Hui:** Perhaps the most able of Confucius' disciples. Confucius admired his wisdom and ability above all others and grieved deeply when he died young.

2   **mutual assistance:** In the personal system *(kung),* each family cultivated its own land and paid ten percent of the produce as a tax. In the mutual system *(chu),* each family cultivated its own land, and also cultivated public land jointly with other families. The produce of the public land was paid as a tax. This is essentially the well-field system described below. In the communal system *(ch'e),* families cultivated land communally, dividing the produce between them and paying ten percent to the government.

3   **well-field system:** Under this system, each parcel of land is divided into nine plots and so looks like the character *(ching)* meaning *well:* 井. The

eight outer plots in this configuration are each cultivated by one family. In addition to cultivating their own plot, the eight families cultivate the center plot jointly. This is public land, and its produce is given to the government as a tax.

4   **Shen Nung:** literally: "Divine Farmer," a mythic emperor believed to have reigned from 2838 to 2698 B.C.E., is credited with the invention of the plow and the agricultural arts. He also discovered the medicinal uses of plants, and began the practice of trading in markets.

5   **Kao Yao:** Shun's sage justice minister.

6   **Mo Tzu:** Mo Tzu (5th c. B.C.E.), who lived in the century between Confucius and Mencius, was the founder of a major school of social philosophy that competed with the Confucian school. He is most famously associated with the idea that social ills can be resolved if we each love all others equally, rather than loving some (family, e.g.) more than others.

VI. Duke Wen of T'eng, Book Two

1   **Ch'en Tai:** Disciple of Mencius.

2   **summons:** See X.7 for a fuller version of this story.

3   **Ching Ch'un:** Politician in the time of Mencius.

4   **Kung-sun Yen and Chang Yi:** Itinerant scholars who were very influential as advisors of rulers.

5   **boundless dwelling-place:** That is: Humanity. See XIII.33 and 36.

6   **token of credentials:** Each government rank had its own prescribed token. Itinerant scholars wanting a position would present this token to a sovereign as a way of proving their qualifications.

7   **P'eng Keng:** Disciple of Mencius.

8   **Wan Chang:** Disciple of Mencius.

9   **K'uang Chang:** High official in Ch'i.

VII. Li Lou, Book One

1   **Three Dynasties:** Hsia, Shang, Chou.

2   **I rinse my feet clean:** This song also appears in "The Fisherman," part of the ancient *Ch'u Tz'u* anthology *(The Songs of the South)*.

3   **Duke T'ai:** Duke T'ai became a great counselor to Emperors Wen and Wu, helping them to overcome the Shang tyrant and found the Chou Dynasty.

4   **Jan Ch'iu:** Disciple of Confucius.

5   **Chun-yü K'un:** Scholar who rose to high position from humble origins.

VIII. Li Lou, Book Two

1   **Lord Ch'an:** Wise and worthy prime minister of Cheng much admired by Confucius.

2   **from the people:** The poems in the *Book of Songs* were folk songs gathered by emperors wanting to know how the people felt about their rule.

3   **without entering:** See V.4.

4   **wise and worthy:** See the *Analects* VI.10.

IX. Wan Chang, Book One

1   **ch'in:** An ancient stringed instrument played by all intellectuals in ancient China, ancestor to the more familiar Japanese koto.

2   **Hsien-chiu Meng:** Disciple of Mencius.

3   **half a person left:** There is nothing in the language itself to show that this is describing a future possibility, so it could literally be read in the present: "there *isn't* half a person left."

4   **T'ai Chia:** Son who suceeded T'ang after his death.

XII. Master Kao, Book Two

1   **Wu Huo:** A legendary strongman.

2   **better even than Yü:** For Yü managing floodwaters, see V.4 and VI.9.

XIII. To Fathom the Mind, Book One

1   **Yi Yin banished T'ai Chia:** See IX.6.

XIV. To Fathom the Mind, Book Two

1   **beloved son to the grave:** See also I.5.

2   **two or three strips:** Books were written on bamboo strips, which were tied together with leather string.

3   **fulling sticks:** Used by women as they prepared heavy winter clothes. In literary use, it usually implies the men have been conscripted and are far away at war.

4   **hardship in Ch'en and Ts'ai:** See the *Analects* XI.2 and XV.2.

5   **childish ways:** Cf. the *Analects* V.21.

6   **what to avoid:** The *Analects* XIII.21.

7   **thief of Integrity:** This sentence is the *Analects* XVII.11.

Historical Table

Emperors

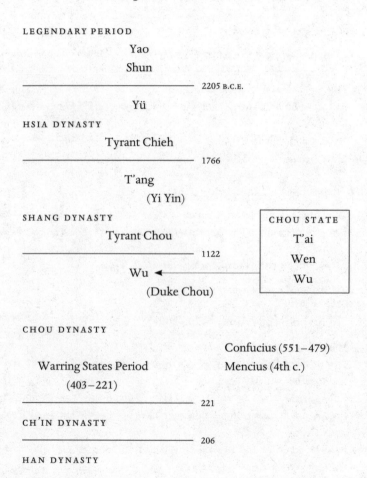

LEGENDARY PERIOD

Yao

Shun

————————————————————— 2205 B.C.E.

Yü

HSIA DYNASTY

Tyrant Chieh

————————————————————— 1766

T'ang

(Yi Yin)

SHANG DYNASTY

| CHOU STATE |
| T'ai |
| Wen |
| Wu |

Tyrant Chou

————————————————————— 1122

Wu ◄————————————

(Duke Chou)

CHOU DYNASTY

Confucius (551–479)

Warring States Period   Mencius (4th c.)

(403–221)

————————————————————— 221

CH'IN DYNASTY

————————————————————— 206

HAN DYNASTY

Key Terms
An Outline of Mencius' Thought

Li: 禮 Ritual

A religious concept associated with the worship of gods and spirits prior to Confucius, Ritual was reconfigured by Confucius to mean the web of social responsibilities that bind a society together. These include the proprieties in virtually all social interactions, and are determined by the individual's position within the structure of society. By calling these secular acts "Ritual," Confucius makes everyday experience itself a sacred realm. This Ritual structure of society is part of a vast cosmological weave: the Ritual structure of natural process as the ten thousand things emerge from the primal emptiness.

Jen: 仁 Humanity (Humane)

The character for *jen* is formed by a combination of the characters for "human being" and "two," and it means all of the moral qualities expressed in the behavior of ideal human beings toward one another. *Jen* is the internalization of *li*, and *li* is the codified external expression of *jen*. So, to be Humane means to master a kind of selflessness by which we dwell as an integral part of the Ritual weave. Or, more simply: to act with a selfless and reverent concern for the well-being of others. Jen is the touchstone of Confucian sagehood, a kind of *enlightenment* which Confucius claimed was beyond even him.

Yi: 義 Duty

The prescriptions of Ritual are general in nature. The ability to apply them in specific situations is Duty, and so Duty is the particular ethical expression of Humanity.

Tao: 道 Way

The effortless process of human society functioning according to its natural Ritual structure. It can be expanded to cover Ritual's cosmological dimensions, making it comparable to the more familiar Taoist

573

Tao. Hence: the effortless process of the cosmos functioning accord-
ing to its natural Ritual structure. The cosmos always abides by the
Tao, with the frequent exception of human societies.

Te: 德 Integrity

The ability to act according to the Tao (Way). Or more precisely,
the embodiment of the Tao in the sage, where it becomes a kind of
power through which the sage can transform others "by example."
This concept is deepened by *Te*'s etymological meaning at the level of
pictographic imagery: "heart-sight clarity."

T'ien: 天 Heaven

Natural process. Or, more descriptively, the inevitable unfolding of
things in the cosmological process. Hence, Heaven appears as a kind
of immanent fate in the human realm – and as Ritual is its organizing
principle, it becomes a kind of moral force encouraging societies to
abide by Ritual and the Tao.

Ch'i: 氣 Ch'i

The universal breath, vital energy, or cosmic life-force. It is the
breath-force that pulses through the Cosmos as both matter and en-
ergy simultaneously, giving form and life to the ten thousand things
and driving their perpetual transformations. And so it is the tissue
of which the Cosmos is made. In its originary form, it is primal-*ch'i*
(*yüan-ch'i*), which is present in Absence and is perhaps the aspect that
gives the primordial emptiness of Absence pregnant with possibility.
Primal-*ch'i* is made up of *yin* and *yang* completely intermingled and
indistinguishable. Once primal-*ch'i* separates out into *yin* and *yang*,
yang rose up to become sky and *yin* sunk down to form earth. As the
universal breath, *ch'i* is in constant motion, animating all things, and
so is a kind of tissue that connects us always to the empty source.

Further Reading

Chan Wing-tsit. *A Source Book of Chinese Philosophy*. New York: Columbia University Press, 1969.

DeBary, William T., Wing-tsit Chan, and Burton Watson, eds. *Sources of Chinese Tradition*. 2 vols. New York: Columbia University Press, 1960.

Eno, Robert. *The Confucian Creation of Heaven*. Buffalo: SUNY Press, 1990.

Fingarette, Herbert. *Confucius: The Secular As Sacred*. New York: Harper & Row, 1972.

Fung Yu-lan. *A History of Chinese Philosophy*. Translated by Derk Bodde. Princeton: Princeton University Press, 1952–53.

Graham, A. C. *Disputers of the Tao*. LaSalle, Ill.: Open Court, 1989.

Hughes, E.R. *The Great Learning and the Mean in Action*. London: Dent, 1942.

Mencius. *Mencius*. Translated by D. C. Lau. London: Penguin, 1970.

———. *Mencius, Vol. 1, The Chinese Classics*. Translated by James Legge. 1861–73. Reprint Hong Kong: University of Hong Kong Press, 1960.

Mote, Frederick. *Intellectual Foundations of China*. New York: Alfred A. Knopf, 1971.

Ropp, Paul, ed. *Heritage of China*. Berkeley: University of California Press, 1990.

Schwartz, Benjamin. *The World of Thought in Ancient China*. Cambridge: Harvard University Press, 1985.

Shun Kwong-Loi. *Mencius and Early Chinese Thought*. Palo Alto, Calif.: Stanford University Press, 1997.

Tu Wei-ming. *Humanity and Self-Cultivation: Essays in Confucian Thought*. Berkeley: Asian Humanities Press, 1979.